D0930228

MANSFIELD
and
VIETNAM

MICHAEL J. MANSFIELD

MANSFIELD and VIETNAM

A STUDY IN RHETORICAL ADAPTATION

GREGORY ALLEN OLSON

Michigan State University Press
East Lansing
1995

All Michigan State University Press books are produced on paper which meets the
requirements of American National Standard of Information Sciences—Permanence of
paper for printed materials ANSI Z23.48-1984.

Printed in the United States of America

Michigan State University Press
East Lansing, Michigan 48823-5202

03 02 01 00 99 98 97 96 95 1 2 3 4 5 6 7 8 9 10

Library of Congress Cataloging-in-Publication Data

Olson, Gregory Allen.
Mansfield and Vietnam : a study in rhetorical adaptation / Gregory Allen Olson.
　　　　p.　　　cm. — (Rhetoric and public affairs series)
　Includes bibliographical references and index.
　ISBN 0-87013-386-1 (hard cover : alk. paper)
　1. United States—Foreign relations—Vietnam. 2. Vietnam—Foreign relations—United
States. 3. Vietnamese Conflict, 1961-1975—United States. 4. Mansfield, Mike, 1903-　　．
5. United States—Foreign relations—1945-1989. I. Title. II. Series.
E183.8.V5045　1995
327.730597—dc20　　　　　　　　　　　　　　　　　　　　　　　　　95-12880
　　　　　　　　　　　　　　　　　　　　　　　　　　　　　　　　　　　CIP

Michigan State University Press Rhetoric and Public Affairs Series
Senior Editor: Martin J. Medhurst, Texas A & M University
Editorial Advisory Board:
G. Thomas Goodnight, Northwestern University
Richard B. Gregg, Pennsylvania State University
Robert Hariman, Drake University
Robert L. Ivie, Indiana University
Jay Mechling, University of California, Davis
Michael Osborn, Memphis State University
Kathleen J. Turner, Tulane University

For Jane, Jackie, Mara, Lars, and Snickers

CONTENTS

PART IV
1969-1975: CAMBODIA AND THE END OF MANSFIELD'S "QUIET" CRITICISM

ACKNOWLEDGMENTS

M any contributed to this project. J. Vernon Jensen guided the work through the dissertation stage and beyond. Martin J. Medhurst was not the first editor who saw potential in the project, but he was the first who was willing to take the time to extract the diamond from the rough. Kathleen J. Turner thoroughly edited the work on two different occasions. I greatly appreciate the expertise and professionalism of the staff at Michigan State University Press and am especially indebted to Kristine M. Blakeslee.

Marquette University supported this undertaking in a number of ways, including the provision of a number of talented and diligent research assistants. Over the years, Karen Schumi-Couture, Susan Tauscher, Jennifer Kwasny, Jill Tracy, and Jennifer Smith tracked down numerous clues and contributed to the final product in diverse but meaningful ways. Bob Worman and Marquette's computer center provided valuable support, as did Memorial Library's interlibrary loan department. Marquette's Graduate School and College of Communication awarded grants that helped fund my travel to Missoula, Montana; Washington, D.C.; Abilene, Kansas; Ann Arbor, Michigan; and Austin, Texas for archival research.

Without exception, the archivists I encountered at the various libraries I visited proved helpful and encouraging. Dale Johnson and Claire Rhein made my four trips to Missoula both fruitful and enjoyable. Herbert L. Pankratz and Thomas W. Branigar of the Eisenhower Library, Jennifer Warner and Regina Greenwell from the Johnson Library, Byron Parham of the Nixon Project, Jennifer A. Sternaman from the Ford Library staff, and James A. Yancey Jr. at the Carter Library all helped me locate valuable material.

ABBREVIATIONS

DDE Library	Dwight D. Eisenhower Library, Abilene, Kansas.
JFK Library	John F. Kennedy Library, Boston, Massachusetts.
LBJ Library	Lyndon B. Johnson Library, Austin, Texas.
Nixon Project	Richard M. Nixon Project, Washington, D.C.
Ford Library	Gerald R. Ford Library, Ann Arbor, Michigan.
Carter Library	Jimmy Carter Library, Atlanta, Georgia.
WHCF	White House Central File.
ESSFRC	Executive Sessions of the Senate Foreign Relations Committee.
FRUS	Foreign Relations of the United States.
PPP	Public Papers of the Presidents of the United States.
MP	Mansfield Papers, Mansfield Library, Missoula, Montana.

INTRODUCTION

The embers of anti-war sentiment burst into flame on May 1, 1970, as President Richard Nixon ordered the invasion of North Vietnamese military sanctuaries in Cambodia. Chaos erupted throughout the nation: four student protesters were killed by National Guardsmen at Kent State University, more than 400 university campuses shut down, and nearly 100,000 demonstrators marched on Capitol Hill.[1]

Nixon's decision not only had a severe impact on the American public, but it sparked profound change within the United States Senate. One of the most dramatic changes was the way in which Majority Leader Michael J. Mansfield viewed presidential power. Until that time, Mansfield had been a "quiet critic," privately criticizing the conduct of the war to three presidents, while publicly supporting the commander in chief. The Cambodian incursion pushed Mansfield to alter his long-held deference to executive decisions on matters of foreign policy. Mansfield noted in his files shortly after the invasion:

> I have reached the point in my thinking where, for the first time, I am giving the most serious consideration to a *termination date after which no more funds will be appropriated* for military operations in Indochina. The American people feel let down, disappointed, concerned. They have appealed to the White House. They have appealed to the Congress. *Their only hope, I think, is the Senate.*[2] [Emphasis added.]

Mansfield's decision to fight for the termination of funds did not come easily. He had always believed that the war must be ended by the president. Shortly after his 1952 election to the Senate, Mansfield had voiced his belief in executive supremacy over foreign policy:

> Inasmuch as the whole of the national experience thus far shows conclusively that there can be no substitute for the Presidential power to stake out foreign policy and to take all preliminary steps for implementing it in the form of international

engagements, the constitutional checks placed in the hands of the Senate too often prove to be obstructions rather than safeguards.

Yet the newly elected Senator added prophetically: "the only check on the will of the Executive lies in the congressional power of the purse."[3]

Throughout his thirty-four year congressional career, Mansfield had a consuming interest in foreign policy—particularly U.S. policy toward the Far East. From 1953 to 1975, through five administrations, Mansfield waged a private rhetorical battle to influence U.S. policy in Vietnam. No other public official shared Mansfield's continuous twenty-two year involvement with Indochina, which included six fact-finding trips to the region. Mansfield had always been constrained by his belief in executive primacy in foreign affairs, and his change of heart in 1970 was his ultimate rhetorical adaptation, for it freed him to begin a public campaign of persuasion to end the war through congressional action. *Newsweek* concluded that Mansfield was instrumental in building congressional opposition to the war.[4]

There are a wealth of insights available when research is based on archival material. This study utilizes primary sources to examine Mike Mansfield's role in the Vietnam conflict. Mansfield's papers proved to be the most important source, but the papers of presidents Eisenhower, Kennedy, Johnson, Nixon, Ford, and Carter were also used. Because Mansfield was more comfortable developing his arguments in writing, most of his persuasive efforts are preserved in speeches and memoranda.

This work is subtitled "a study in rhetorical adaptation" because Mansfield was, above all else, adaptable. His actions epitomized Aristotle's definition of rhetoric as "the faculty of discovering all the possible means of persuasion."[5] Mansfield was able to adapt to changing world conditions, changes in administrations, and changes in his own party position. All the while, Mansfield was trying to influence the sitting administration.

In 1940 Mansfield first ran for the House of Representatives by opposing American entry into World War II, a necessary position for one wanting to be elected in Montana and a position he shared with his three Democratic opponents and Republican Jeanette Rankin, the ultimate winner of the House seat. In his ten years of service in the House of Representatives, however, Mansfield adapted to the changes brought by a world war and established the reputation as an internationalist with an abiding interest in the Far East.

When Mansfield ran for the Senate in 1952, that reputation was used against the representative, as he was held personally responsible by Montana Republicans and Senator Joseph McCarthy (R-Wis.) for the "loss" of China. Even so, Mansfield won the closest election of his career. He then adapted to the viciousness of the 1952 campaign by becoming a staunch cold warrior. Mansfield resolved to make himself *the* Senate expert on Indochina and to avoid being accused of losing Indochina to communism. Once the perception of Mansfield's expertise was established in the minds of the media and government officials, he was able to influence the Eisenhower administration into first supporting Vietnamese nationalist Ngo Dinh Diem, and then to continue its support for the Vietnamese leader when the administration was ready to pull the rug out from under Diem's reign. Townsend Hoopes argued that Mansfield caused a "national self-imprisonment" with Diem because the senator had the influence to terminate aid to Vietnam if Diem was replaced. Thus, Secretary of State John Foster Dulles was forced to back Diem to maintain Mansfield's support.[6]

With the election of his friend, John Kennedy, Mansfield rose to the post of majority leader, perhaps the most powerful position in government after the president and Speaker of the House. Mansfield's new position of leadership started him down a long and arduous path of attempting to balance his party role and his institutional role as Senate leader with his personal conscience. Mansfield rhetorically adapted to balancing these competing pressures through quiet criticism, arguing against Kennedy's increased commitment to Vietnam only in private, while generally supporting the president with his public statements. Surprisingly, Mansfield's influence over Indochina policy decreased with his ascension to power. Mansfield's friendship with Kennedy and party position compromised his opposition to American involvement in Vietnam. When Kennedy and his advisors decided to purge Diem, they did not fear, as Dulles had, that Mansfield would cut off military aid.

Mansfield retained his role as quiet critic when his political mentor, Lyndon Johnson, became president. Journalist John Finney suggested that Mansfield became Johnson's "most troublesome critic on the Vietnam war."[7] Mansfield recalled that in 1964-65 meetings on Vietnam with the cabinet and joint chiefs of staff, "on at least three occasions I was the only one who differed from all the rest. He [Johnson] took it but I don't think he liked it."[8] While Mansfield's relations with Johnson became strained, they never broke. After Johnson committed ground forces to Vietnam in July 1965, Mansfield spent the rest of Johnson's term proposing numerous ways to get the United States to the negotiating table.

Beginning in 1969, with Republican Richard Nixon in the White House, Mansfield was unchained from the constraints of party leadership. Yet he gave the new president the necessary time to fulfill his promise of extracting the nation from the Vietnam quagmire. With the invasion of Cambodia, Mansfield's patience ran out. He adapted by deserting his quiet criticism and joining fellow war critics in the Senate to wage a rhetorical battle with Nixon for the hearts and minds of the American public.

The story of Mansfield and Indochina ended in Washington, but it began in New York City and was shaped by stops in Montana and China. This book is an account of how U.S. involvement in Vietnam happened, as seen through the life and words of Senator Mike Mansfield. Foreign policy is essentially a rhetorical process, one in which words compete with other words for supremacy. Once accepted as facts or definitions or controlling theses, these words guide actions and constrain options. As rhetoric changes, so too does policy. In no instance was this linkage between language and action more clearly articulated than in the deliberations of Mike Mansfield and his colleagues over the question of American involvement in Indochina. By understanding Mansfield's use of language to propose, guide, modify, constrain, and finally, to limit policy options, one is better able to appreciate the rhetorical forces that sustained American involvement in Southeast Asia for thirty years and that eventually served to undermine that involvement.

Part I

1903-1955

A Freshman Senator Helps Commit America to South Vietnam

CHAPTER 1

MANSFIELD BECOMES AN ASIA EXPERT

MANSFIELD'S PRE-CONGRESSIONAL BACKGROUND

Michael Joseph Mansfield's start in life did not portend his future interest in the Far East. Born in Greenwich Village, New York, on March 16, 1903, he was the first of three children born to Irish immigrant parents. Soon after Mansfield's sixth birthday, his mother died of pneumonia. His father asked Mansfield's great-uncle Richard Mansfield and his wife Margaret to care for his young children until he could assume their care. In the summer of 1909 the three Mansfield children took the train from New York to their new home in Great Falls, Montana.[1]

Young Mansfield was a marginal student who did not get along with his great aunt. After several unsuccessful attempts at running away, he succeeded in June 1917, at the age of fourteen. That fall, Mansfield forged his father's signature, lied about his age, and joined the Navy, becoming the youngest Montanan to serve in World War I.

This was the beginning of a remarkable military career that included tours of duty in all three branches of the armed services. The future senator was nearly seventeen years old when he was discharged from the Navy. He decided he was too old to return to the eighth grade, and in fewer than three months he joined the Army. When his one-year Army enlistment ended in November of 1920, Mansfield signed up for a two-year stint in the Marine Corps. Still only seventeen years old, he was serving in a third branch of the military.

Beginning in April 1921 Mansfield was stationed at Subic Bay in the Philippines. One year later he was part of a group of Marines sent to Tientsin, China, with forces representing Britain, France, Italy, Germany, and Japan assigned to protect the rail link to Beijing and to prevent looting. Two War Lords were fighting in the area, threatening the international community in Tientsin. Mansfield and the other Marines patrolled five days before the crisis ended without any shots fired.[2]

Years later Mansfield said, "I loved the sights, sounds, smells and the people of China," and he credited the visit with the start of his life-long interest in Asia. The experience clearly made an impact on Mansfield; he would later claim that he had spent four or five months in China when, in reality, his time there lasted about twelve days.[3]

Discharged in November 1922, Mansfield returned to Butte, Montana, where work in the copper mines was plentiful and the pay for this was considered quite good. He spent most of the next nine years there working in a number of different mining jobs.[4] He also tried to combine work with classes at the Montana School of Mines in Butte, seeking to become an engineer. One instructor remembered Mansfield as a "likable boy" who was "very poorly prepared for college."[5]

The direction not only of Mansfield's education but also of his life would be changed in 1928, when he met his wife, Maureen Hayes. A Butte native, Hayes had a degree from St. Mary's College in Indiana and taught English at Butte High School. Mansfield recalled the meeting by saying, "suddenly, I had a new friend—perhaps the only genuinely close friend in my life." Mansfield always credited Maureen with being the greatest influence on his life.[6] At Maureen's urging, Mansfield decided to become a history teacher. Completing high school equivalency courses, Mansfield quit the mines in December 1931 to attend the University of Montana.[7]

In the fall of 1932, when Maureen joined him in Missoula, they were married. At age thirty, Mansfield graduated in 1933 with a degree in history and political science. He later admitted his grades were "nothing to brag about except in history." Mansfield failed to get the two high school teaching positions for which he applied in rural Montana, and he thought it might have been because he was Catholic.[8]

Mansfield was offered a graduate assistantship at the University of Montana, where he pursued his master's degree. Even though the school lacked a specialist in the Far East, he chose the thesis topic "American Diplomatic Relations With Korea, 1866-1910." Mansfield concluded in his thesis that the United States had no business in Korea. He opposed "entangling ventures," and had already developed a cautious attitude about U.S. involvement in the affairs of nations in the Far East. Mansfield was critical of European "power grabs," including those in French Indochina.[9]

Both Mansfields received their master's degrees in June 1934. Mike accepted a makeshift job at the University of Montana as assistant registrar and instructor for the history department. In 1936 he was hired full-time in the history department with the provision that he begin work on his Ph.D. He studied Far Eastern and Latin American history at U.C.L.A. for two summers and returned to Missoula to teach Far Eastern history. This became Mansfield's favorite and most-frequently taught course. The text he used was critical of the French in Indochina, as he would be in the future. Mansfield enjoyed teaching and he soon developed a reputation as one of the University's most popular teachers. Students described Mansfield as "shy, reticent, modest, quiet," but also as "compelling."[10]

Mansfield's colleagues agreed with his students; his evaluations were excellent. A former colleague said that Mansfield "was not fiery as a lecturer" but students liked him and helped him when he ran for public office.[11] Mansfield had already developed the cautious approach that made him a "quiet critic" of the Vietnam War in the 1960s. One former student said that Mansfield was skillful at "fence straddling," that he could sound like he agreed with both sides in a controversy. When Mansfield chaired a report on whether to discontinue ROTC on campus, one university official said that he turned in a "weaseling report" that avoided the main question. Whether construed as fence straddling or balance, Mansfield's natural inclination seemed to be to present both sides.[12]

MANSFIELD'S ELECTION TO CONGRESS

Mansfield began considering a political career by 1936. Because of his Irish-American heritage and amiable character, he and Maureen believed that politics was his true vocation. Mansfield's experiences as a laborer in Butte and as secretary-treasurer of the faculty union in Missoula gave him a certain edge as a Democratic candidate. In addition, Montana had a propensity for sending Democrats to Washington. In his dissertation, Charles Hood put Mansfield's advantage this way: "here was no smooth-talking, briefcase-toting university egghead, but a straight-talking young former working man who pulled off his suitcoat, rolled up his sleeves, and talked comfortably with the men in the hard hats."[13]

In 1939 Mansfield prepared his run for Congress by delivering both live and radio speeches in western Montana. Edmund Freeman, the president of the Missoula teacher's union, spoke highly of Mansfield in a letter to Senator James Murray (D-Mont.):

> Everybody who knows him likes him. . . . He is patient and persistent. I have not seen him slight or avoid any hard or unpopular job. As a member and officer of our union he has been invaluable—for his zeal, his tact, and his faithfulness. He makes friends and has many connections. He is keenly interested in politics and is a very thoughtful person. I simply do not know how well he would do in the public-speaking phase of the job. He does fine classroom work and would do excellent work on the radio—and he might do well on the public platform.[14]

Murray was noncommittal at the time, but he later became Mansfield's ally. The four Democratic primary candidates held similar positions favoring avoiding the European war. Mansfield finished third in the four-person race, losing to Democrat Jerry O'Connell, who lost to Republican Jeanette Rankin.

Montana's senior Democratic senator, Burton K. Wheeler, was an enemy of O'Connell and his supporters worked for Rankin in 1940, aiding her victory. Wheeler was a major player in the America First Committee, which worked to avoid U.S. entry into the European war. To Wheeler, Rankin seemed the best candidate. She became the only member of Congress to vote against American entry into World War II.[15] The split in Montana's Democratic Party between Wheeler Democrats and the regular Democrats who supported President Franklin Roosevelt and Montana's junior Senator Murray, aided Mansfield in his early political career.

After his loss, Mansfield immediately began his campaign for 1942. Rankin's vote against entry into World War II meant that she was not a viable candidate in this race. Mansfield learned from his only loss and changed his campaign style, emphasizing face-to-face campaigning that employed former students. He emerged from a primary field of five and defeated his Republican opponent by more than 14,000 votes, carrying all seventeen counties in the district. A prominent Montana Democrat wrote to Mansfield: "Your energy and industry were marvelous to behold. You never again will have to make a real campaign as you did a lifetime job during the last two and a half years." Shortly thereafter, Mike, Maureen, and their only child, Ann, left for Washington.[16]

MANSFIELD GAINS FAR EASTERN EXPERTISE

Despite his lack of seniority, Mansfield's academic background helped him land a seat on the House Foreign Affairs Committee. J. William Fulbright (D-Ark.) was also selected for Foreign Affairs as a first-term member in 1943. Mansfield recalled, "I spoke up right from the start" when the Far East was discussed, because "I felt I knew what I was talking about. If not, I remained silent." One writer concluded that "in an astonishingly short time, he had established himself as the committee's spokesman on the progress of the war in the Far East."[17]

Mansfield cemented his perceived expertise on the Far East in 1943 and 1944 when he made three live national radio addresses on the war in the Pacific. One key theme was the importance of the Pacific war. In his first address, Mansfield claimed: "the conflict in the Pacific will settle our future for generations to come. It is time we stop laboring under the delusion that the European war is our major struggle and that the Pacific front is only a sideshow." He added, "we might just as well face the fact now that the Japanese are our most dangerous and particular enemy and that our civilization is at stake."[18]

A second theme dealt with colonialism. In his second radio address, Mansfield credited some of the Japanese success in the Far East to hatred of whites caused by imperialism. In his final radio address, Mansfield asserted, "we are not fighting this war to bring about the return of the status quo ante in the Far East. To do so would only mean another war in the future."[19] Given America's later backing of the French in Indochina, this seems prophetic.

A third theme involved racism against the Japanese, mainly due to the war itself. Mansfield often referred to the Japanese as "Japs" and also talked of "exterminating its fanatical war clique." In his first radio address Mansfield called the Japanese "these small, myopic, buck-toothed sons of Nippon."[20] When examining Mansfield's career, this rhetoric seems uncharacteristic, particularly coming from a future ambassador to Japan. In the 1930s, American historians of Asia tended to favor either Japan or China and Mansfield was squarely in the Chinese camp. Mansfield's attitude was also revealed in his class notes, which suggested: "the Chinese smile and mean it; the Japanese smile and do not mean it. The Chinese are reasonable, the Japanese fanatical."[21]

Mansfield worked diligently to increase his credibility as an expert on Asia. Beginning in 1943, he made several unsuccessful attempts to visit the Pacific theater. In October 1944 he was called to the White House, where he remembered President Roosevelt saying: "Mike, I have asked you to come here to request that you undertake a confidential mission for me to China. I've had economic and military reports but what I want is an overall picture and I think you are the man to get it for me."[22] This trip and the report that it generated were important events in Mansfield's career, contributing to his becoming known as *the* Asian expert in Congress.

On November 14, 1944, Mansfield left for a five-week fact-finding trip to India, Burma, and China. His China Mission Report, and the speech he delivered on it in the House on January 16, 1945, received considerable attention. Mansfield argued: "from a combat point of view we have no interests in Burma, Malaya, Thailand, or French Indo-China." He cautioned against involvement "in political squabbles in that part of the world," because "we have no direct interests in that area."

While Mansfield saw Chiang Kaishek as the future of a unified China, he also was critical of Chiang's government and emphasized the need for reform. He was balanced in his view of the communists. While he talked of their sanctimoniousness, and their being totalitarian, he praised them as fighters. One specific aspect of the young representative's characterization of the Chinese communists would come back to haunt him: "they are not Communists in the sense that Russians are as their interests seem to focus on primarily agrarian reforms. They are more reformers than revolutionaries and they have attacked the problems most deepseated in agricultural China."[23] Although this statement did not create a stir at the time, it was used against Mansfield for the remainder of his congressional career. As late as 1970, a right-wing critic of Mansfield charged: "the fall of mainland China to the Communists was . . . inevitable once the American public became accustomed to that defusing phrase," that phrase being "agrarian reformers."[24]

Surprisingly, Roosevelt seemed to have little interest in the report. The president's appointment secretary was in no hurry to schedule for Mansfield a meeting with the president. Mansfield's appeal to Eleanor Roosevelt finally got him a 15-minute appointment with the president on January 9, hardly enough time to discuss his findings in depth. Roosevelt apparently never discussed Mansfield's trip or report; all publicity for it came from Mansfield himself. Mansfield worked hard to enhance his reputation based on this report. For example, he invited John Carter Vincent, a State Department expert on China, to discuss his trip.[25]

Why did Roosevelt send an obscure representative to China and subsequently show no real interest in his report? One possibility is that Roosevelt wanted someone in Montana to challenge Wheeler in 1946. Wheeler was a maverick Democrat who often opposed New Deal programs, beginning with Roosevelt's 1937 effort to pack the Supreme Court. The publicity generated from the trip would likely help Mansfield in such an effort, giving him credentials as an internationalist, contrasted to the isolationist label pinned on Wheeler. Mansfield considered challenging Wheeler, but ultimately decided against the inter-party squabble.[26]

In the short run, the China Mission Report did help Mansfield's political career. It established him as a Far Eastern expert in the eyes of the public, the press, his peers, and even American servicemen in the Far East. Roosevelt's invitation and the report were also an asset to Mansfield in the 1944 election, and he defeated his Republican opponent 57,008 to 26,141.[27] With the fall of China, however, the report became a political liability.

In 1946, after the Japanese surrender, Mansfield made his second congressional visit to Asia, which included stops in China and Japan. Mansfield wanted the troops sent home to help ensure that the United States would not become involved in the Chinese civil war. The senator was so disturbed by the situation in China during this visit that he avoided a press conference "for fear of being asked about the Chinese situation." He believed that "no matter what we do we stand to lose," and prophetically recorded in his trip diary: "I would not care to live anywhere in the Far East as all I can see is trouble ahead for years to come."[28]

While Mansfield became noted for his expertise on the Far East during his years in the House, his initial credentials were exaggerated. One University of Montana official said that Mansfield "simply made himself an authority on the Far East by proclaiming himself one."[29] Both Mansfield and the press contributed to these exaggerations. In a 1947 letter to President Harry Truman, Mansfield claimed to have completed "three-quarters of post-graduate work on my Ph.D.," even though he spent only two summers at U.C.L.A., completing six courses without starting work on a dissertation. In that letter, Mansfield asserted that he "served overseas in the Philippines, Japan, and China," although his stay in China was only twelve days, and his time in Japan consisted of a one-day fueling stop.[30]

Mansfield tended not to correct errors made about him concerning his academic background and time spent in the Far East. Drew Pearson started the inflated reports before Mansfield's 1944 trip, suggesting that Mansfield spoke Chinese.[31] These errors were repeated as journalists merely checked their clip files. In 1958 the *New York Times* called Mansfield "one of the few Chinese speaking members of Congress."[32] A 1983 book suggested that Mansfield had "long been familiar with Asia as a resident."[33] As late as 1993, a book asserted that Mansfield "was an intelligence officer in World War II"![34]

President Truman further contributed to Mansfield's internationalist reputation when he appointed him to be a delegate to the United Nations General Assembly sessions in Paris in 1951. There, news photographs of Mansfield and Soviet foreign minister Andrei Vishinsky in a sharp exchange gained wide publicity, and many delegates praised Mansfield for his defense of the American position. This incident proved helpful to Mansfield when he ran for the Senate in 1952.[35]

Truman offered Mansfield the important government posts of under secretary of the Interior and assistant secretary of state for public affairs, which would have put Mansfield in charge of *Voice of America*. Mansfield declined both, saying he preferred to represent Montana in Congress.[36] In reality, Mansfield had his sights set on the Senate. To obtain that goal, Representative Mansfield diligently built his reputation as an internationalist and expert on Asia.

"CHINA MIKE" MOVES TO THE SENATE

In 1946, shortly before his second congressional visit to Asia, Mansfield handily won reelection to his House seat. By that time, the "China Mike" label was being used in a derogatory sense by Mansfield's opponents, implying that he did not pay attention to issues affecting Montana. Two years later, with his strong support for the United Nations and the Marshall Plan, Mansfield won reelection by a landslide—suggesting that the "China Mike" label did not stick.

The 1950 race became a precursor of Mansfield's 1952 Senate race, as Mansfield's opponent, Ralph McGinnis, employed negative tactics based on Mao Tsetung's victory in China. For example, McGinnis suggested that Russian and Chinese troops might slaughter citizens in Butte because of Mansfield's China Mission Report. McGinnis quoted liberally from the China Mission Report in charging Mansfield with appeasement that led to the fall of China and caused the Korean War. Mansfield refused to debate his opponent, who was the debate coach at the University of Montana, but chose to answer McGinnis' charges on the radio.

Mansfield's Irish-Catholic background became an issue in 1950. Montana Republicans distributed literature in the eastern congressional race that attacked the Democratic candidate as "a product of Southern Ireland [who] has never had any experience in public affairs, a yes man, if he gets up early enough in the morning to say yes. And DON'T let the Catholics have another voice in Washington." Mansfield easily defeated McGinnis, but the tone was set for a nasty 1952 race.[37]

The split in Montana's Democratic party helped Mansfield earn the Senate seat he coveted. In 1942 Wheeler had supported Republican Wellington Rankin over Senator Murray, the Democratic incumbent, and in 1944 Wheeler had supported the Republican candidate for governor over the Democrat, Leif Erickson. The regular Democrats sought revenge. When Mansfield decided not to challenge Wheeler in the 1946 Democratic primary, Erickson challenged and defeated Wheeler. Many of Wheeler's traditional supporters refused to support Erickson in the general election, which contributed to Zales Ecton becoming the first Republican senator elected in Montana since direct election of senators began in 1913. Erickson's 1946 bid created an opening for Mansfield six years later.

Wheeler considered running for his old seat in 1952 but decided against it. With no serious Democratic opposition and Montana's tradition for electing Democratic senators, election seemed certain for Mansfield. Ecton had not distinguished himself in his six years in Washington. He was best known as an unabashed supporter of the private utility industry. One of Mansfield's political ads cited Redbook, which listed Ecton among the two dozen of "Our Worst Congressmen." The article quoted Ecton: "if I thought it took extraordinary intelligence to represent the people of Montana I wouldn't be a candidate." Further, Ecton had a speech impediment that hurt him by reminding voters of his alleged alcohol problem.[38]

Yet this campaign was the most difficult of Mansfield's long career. Eisenhower's coattails proved a potent weapon for Republicans across the nation in 1952. The attacks used against Mansfield were an escalation from the 1950 campaign. The "agrarian reformer" line resurfaced, Mansfield was accused of losing China, and his religion was questioned. Dirty tricks included random telephone calls where the caller would say, "Mike Mansfield is a communist" and then hang up. Montana Republicans used the wife of an American pilot captured in Korea to denounce Mansfield. In a radio broadcast, Mrs. John Brockus suggested that Mansfield was one of the State Department experts who slandered Chiang, that his position equaled the communist line, that Korea was caused by "bad guessing on China," and that Mansfield was yet more gullible than a communist. Her message was broadcast over two-hundred times in Montana and nationwide the day before the election. Mansfield devoted much time in his speeches refuting Brockus' charges. Some Republicans later admitted the tape was unfair.[39]

Moreover, Joseph McCarthy (R-Wis.) made the Montana election a test for his cause. McCarthy himself traveled to Montana to speak against Mansfield. At one campaign stop, McCarthy said that Mansfield was "either stupid or a dupe."[40] More importantly, McCarthy sent Harvey Matusow, a supposed former communist, to smear Mansfield. Matusow was sponsored by a Republican front organization—the Montana Citizens for Americanism—and often spoke under the auspices of the American Legion.

The Senate Judiciary Committee investigated the campaign and printed a Matusow speech in which he challenged Mansfield:

> I am just bringing the facts to the voters of Montana. I don't play partisan politics; I go out after communism and I go out after the way communism has duped innocent people such as Mansfield. . . .
>
> But I think it should be asked of him why, in 1945, after the Attorney General in 1942 listed New Masses as a Communist Party publication, the official cultural publication of the Communist Party, . . . Mr. Mansfield, wrote an article in New Masses.[41]

Mansfield's China Mission Report was quoted in *New Masses;* he did not write an article for the publication.

Matusow later said that he was paid to campaign in Montana, and admitted:

> McCarthy had a violent hatred for Mansfield and told me that if he was elected "you might just as well have an admitted Communist in the Senate; it's the same difference. . . ." Throughout the campaign I used the McCarthy tactics of foul play and hitting below the belt. My charges were literally and morally unjustified.[42]

While not referring to Matusow by name, Mansfield talked with emphasis during the campaign about his opposition bringing a *"paid* carpet-bagger, an admitted communist, to spread more slander." He referred to McCarthy in describing *"These Desperate Men* who will do anything, tell any lie, for a vote" and the "slick and ugly way they are trying to blacken the record of every honest man who dares to oppose them." Mansfield was not kind to Ecton, either, suggesting that Ecton had accomplished nothing, had "struck out—every time," Ecton "tinkers with the truth too easily." Yet Mansfield tried to keep the campaign on a higher plane; in two drafts of his campaign speeches he called Ecton a demagogue, but he deleted the sentence before delivery. Mansfield emphasized his anti-communist sentiments in his final campaign speech and won the closest election of this career, 133,109 to 127,360 votes.[43]

As closely contested as the election was, Mansfield kept his legendary loyalty to friends. When his advisors suggested that his aide, Jimmy Sullivan, should be kept out of eastern Montana because his Irish brogue was hurting Mansfield in that heavily Protestant area, he replied that "hurting Sullivan's feelings isn't worth a Senate seat."[44]

The vicious attacks during the campaign caused Mansfield to consider giving up his political career. Mansfield told Marquis Childs, "if I had known what I was getting into, I would not have run for office."[45] When Matusow later attempted to apologize to Mansfield, the Montanan would not allow him admittance to his office and did not return his calls. Mansfield said, "some things you can't apologize for."[46]

Mansfield's campaign propelled him to the Senate where his background and interest positioned him at center stage in the unfolding drama in Indochina. After being held personally responsible for the loss of China by McCarthy and Montana Republicans in the 1952 campaign, he soon faced the danger of being accused of losing Indochina.

CHAPTER 2

MANSFIELD BECOMES AN INDOCHINA EXPERT

Mansfield would come to be viewed as *the* congressional expert on Indochina, but he had little knowledge of the region when he was elected to the Senate. While his lecture notes as a Professor of Far Eastern History are comprehensive when dealing with Japan and China, only one and one-half pages of lecture material on Indochina are extant. In 1949 he said, "unfortunately, I do not know too much about the Indochinese situation. I do not think that anyone does." Two foreign policy speeches Mansfield delivered in his last House term talked of the Far East without mentioning Indochina.[1]

This relative absence is not surprising considering that in 1941 the government files on Southeast Asia contained only one folder with four magazine articles. In 1954 there were no U.S. books on Indochina, and one estimate put the number of American scholars who were experts on the area at fewer than five. Before the 1954 Geneva Conference, there was no public interest in Indochina and thus, no demand for expert academics or journalists. After Geneva and the vastly expanded American role in Indochina, there was a great demand for knowledge about the region.[2]

Mansfield stepped into that vacuum and quickly came to be perceived as one of this nation's experts on Vietnam. His involvement between 1953 and 1955 led one writer to claim: "Mansfield was able to influence American policy at decisive moments, and perhaps change the course of Southeast Asia history."[3]

JOHNSON, KENNEDY, AND A SEAT ON FOREIGN RELATIONS

The Montanan's rise to power in the Senate was aided by his relationships with Lyndon Johnson (D-Texas) and John Kennedy (D-Mass.). Even though he served in the House with Johnson and Kennedy, Mansfield did not get to know either man well until the three of them moved to the Senate.

Mansfield supported Johnson when he sought minority leadership after Mansfield's 1952 Senate election. Johnson's only competition came from Senate liberals who supported James Murray (D-Mont.). Mansfield supported his new mentor [Johnson] over his former one [Murray]. It is likely that Mansfield's support for LBJ was pragmatic once the rookie senator realized that Johnson had the necessary votes to prevail in the race.[4] Mansfield was the first Northern liberal to publicly support Johnson, and the Montanan's decision proved beneficial for both.[5]

Both Kennedy and Mansfield became indebted to Johnson as first term senators. Mansfield did not expect to be appointed to the Senate Foreign Relations Committee in 1952 because of his lack of seniority. As the new minority leader, Johnson changed the system to guarantee each new senator one important committee assignment, collecting "political IOUs" from them in return. Thus, Mansfield and Hubert Humphrey (D-Minn.) found themselves on Foreign Relations and Kennedy on Labor and Public Welfare. Humphrey wrote that "both Johnson and [Speaker of the House Sam] Rayburn thought well of Mansfield."[6] Johnson aide Bobby Baker thought Mansfield was flattered by this assignment and that Johnson awarded the Montanan this plum partially because "Mansfield was not a compulsive seeker of power, nor was he wildly ambitious."[7] The seat on Foreign Relations helped Mansfield build his reputation as a Far Eastern expert, and he used that position as a springboard for his three trips to Indochina between 1953 and 1955.

While adjusting to the Senate and to the Foreign Relations Committee, Mansfield delivered two tributes to colleagues in his first year there—one to Kennedy and one to Johnson. Either Mansfield was incredibly lucky with the men to whom he tied his Senate future, or he was prophetic in choosing men who would help elevate him to heights never achieved by a politician from Montana. Of Kennedy, Mansfield said that he was "one of the hardest working and most respected Members of the Senate. While young in years, he is wise in experience, and he has given freely of his advice and counsel to many of his colleagues." In his 1953 tribute to Johnson, the Montanan said:

> I have been . . . flattered by the attention he has shown to those of us who have come to the Senate for the first time. He certainly has indicated to us a great wisdom, a wide field of knowledge, and a good deal of understanding. He has treated us as equals and he has asked us for our opinions, upon occasion.[8]

Both tributes smack of pandering. Kennedy did not have a reputation as a hard-working senator. In a 1964 interview, for example, Mansfield admitted that Kennedy "wasn't the most conscientious of senators. He would miss a lot of sessions."[9] Modifying the statement about Johnson asking for first-term senators' opinions "upon occasion" seems a Freudian slip. Johnson was legendary as someone who used his leadership position for control rather than fostering equality among senators.[10] Mansfield curried favor with the Democratic colleagues whom he admired, but who also seemed likely to become prominent in the party's future. His choices paid off later.

Mansfield may have pandered to Johnson and Kennedy, but he was assertive in his Foreign Relations assignment. As he had as a rookie on the Foreign Affairs Committee, Mansfield spoke up right from the start when the Far East was discussed. In a February 1953 meeting, Mansfield did not feel knowledgeable enough to ask questions about Indochina, but had questions pertaining to China. By April, Mansfield had done his homework and played an active role when Rene Pleven, French Minister of Defense, appeared. He asked Pleven what would happen to the free world should it lose Indochina. Pleven's response indicated a belief in the domino theory, but Mansfield's paraphrase of Pleven's response was even stronger, showing the first-term senator to be a staunch cold warrior:

> There would be a chain reaction to the countries in the East which eventually would go beyond the Suez into Africa, and in addition to that the wealth of the Indies would be open, that is, the rubber and oil and the tin in Malaya, all those things which are so important, plus the rice granary in Indochina, Thailand, and Burma.

Pleven accepted Mansfield's paraphrase, and the two men agreed that Indochina was strategically more important than Korea.[11]

The senator's paraphrase of Pleven was not spontaneous; in February the senator typed a memorandum for his files expressing the same thought in almost identical language. In the memo Mansfield added in pen: "because of the importance of Indochina in the common struggle against Soviet encroachments, I believe that military shipments should be stepped up considerably to that area."[12] He would later regret and ultimately reject these views.

Ngo Dinh Diem

Mansfield's interest in Indochina was sparked on May 7, 1953, when Supreme Court Justice William O. Douglas hosted a luncheon at the Supreme Court Building. Here Douglas introduced Mansfield and Kennedy to Vietnamese nationalist Ngo Dinh Diem. John Cooney concluded that Diem's "two most strongly held positions were readily apparent: he believed in the power of the Catholic Church and he was virulently anti-Communist." Both positions appealed to Mansfield, Kennedy, Douglas, and many Americans.[13]

Diem was born to a prominent mandarin family in central Vietnam. He was a Catholic who considered becoming a priest and who never married. The future leader of South Vietnam served in the French colonial administration as a district chief in 1921, at age twenty, and as the governor of a small province in 1929.

In 1933 Diem briefly became minister to the interior under Emperor Bao Dai, but resigned that position because under French rule, he lacked the power to introduce reform. Diem did not hold a government post for the next two decades. His strongest nationalist credential was that he did not collaborate with the French. This credential was offset by his willingness to work with the Japanese occupation forces during World War II. Diem's nationalist credentials were further weakened because he spent most of the first Indochina war in exile. Diem's exile became both a blessing and a curse. It was a blessing because nationalists who stayed and refused to join Ho Chi Minh's Vietminh (national-ist/communist forces who fought the Japanese and then the French) were forced to collaborate with the French. Thus, Diem was competing for power with nationalists who were tainted by their colonial connection. Diem's exile was a curse when competing with Ho and the Vietminh. They had fought both the Japanese and French. Diem had not.

Bao Dai asked Diem to become prime minister in 1949. Diem turned the emperor down because the position had little power under French governance. Instead, Diem left Vietnam and spent time in Catholic monasteries in Japan and Belgium before spending several years in Maryknoll seminaries in New Jersey and New York. There he spoke out on the need for an independent Vietnam. In October 1950, Diem met Francis Cardinal Spellman of New York, who became his most important American benefactor. Ellen Hammer concluded that "Diem's fervent Catholicism opened many doors," including those of Spellman and Douglas.[14] They viewed Diem as a "third force," a true nationalist because he opposed both communism and French colonialism. In the midst of the McCarthy era, Diem appeared to be concerned with social and political reform, which pleased liberals. Yet he was dogmatically anti-communist, which pleased both liberals and conservatives. Both the conservative Cardinal Spellman and the liberal Mansfield developed a passion for Diem.[15]

Douglas had visited Vietnam before the luncheon meeting with Mansfield, and wrote a book, *North from Malaya,* that heavily praised the Vietnamese nationalist, claiming he was "a hero in Central and North Vietnam, with a con-siderable following in the south." Douglas hyperbolically claimed that Diem was revered by the Vietnamese people "because he is honest and independent and stood firm against the French influence."[16]

Douglas recalled the May 1953 luncheon with Mansfield:

> I had been out to Vietnam. . . . I had met the under-ground, most of whom were not Communists but rabid nationalists. The one man who had survived the corruption of the French, and had preserved his integrity, was Ngo Dinh Diem. And I got him to come to Washington. . . . I wanted some important people to meet Ngo Dinh Diem. So I gave a luncheon. I invited Mike Mansfield and Jack (Kennedy) from the Senate.[17]

Diem told the gathering that French concessions were "too little and too late" and explained the dilemma in his native country: more French troops were needed to avoid a communist victory but the French could not win the war; only the Vietnamese could win and they would not fight unless the French granted "more freedom." The nationalist leader expressed little confidence in Bao Dai. Like Douglas, Kennedy had visited Vietnam and the two of them asked most of the questions at the luncheon.[18] It was not Mansfield's nature to speak about issues with which he was unfamiliar. The meeting impressed Kennedy enough to write a letter to John Foster Dulles later that day, parroting Diem's arguments, even using the "too little and too late" phrase.[19] Mansfield was impressed, too, and began studying Vietnam in earnest.

Douglas' book had made it clear that Diem's brother was a Catholic bishop; the Justice emphasized the plight of Vietnam's Catholics.[20] Mansfield later claimed: "it wasn't a question of religion—the fact that we were all Catholics was just coincidental."[21] The senator undoubtedly believed that, but religion made Diem stand out from his competitors. Thomas Boettcher argued that "Diem's Catholic faith was his most positive political attribute in this country, for it was the only thing about him that did not seem irredeemably foreign to America's parochial leaders."[22]

A letter to Mansfield during this period suggests the centrality of religion in Mansfield's initial commitment to Diem. Augustine Nguyen-Thai was a Vietnamese citizen attending Cornell University who wrote to Mansfield, including an article which he had published in the Catholic magazine *The Shield*. Nguyen-Thai argued that as one of the few minorities with a definite philosophy, "Catholicism is Vietnam's only firm opponent to Communism." Further, the young nationalist argued that the Catholic Church needed to be extended in Vietnam, and expressed support for the best known Catholic/nationalist, Ngo Dinh Diem. Mansfield's response contradicts his assertion that religion was mere coincidence, for he wrote that he was "in full accord" with Nguyen-Thai's views, and he agreed to meet with the student.[23] Nguyen-Thai's letter hints at the problems America would create by aligning with a Catholic nationalist in a Buddhist country.

Francis Valeo, Mansfield's long-time aide and Asian specialist, claimed that Diem was "a name [Mansfield] carried" after the Douglas introduction.[24] Mansfield's narrow election still haunted him. He did not intend to be blamed for losing Indochina. Diem seemed a way to avoid that.

MANSFIELD SUPPORTS THE ADMINISTRATION'S INDOCHINA POLICY

Mansfield appeared on *Meet the Press* in early July 1953. While asked no questions about Indochina, Mansfield expressed such strong pro-administration foreign policy positions that Jack Bell was prompted to inquire: "you are a Democrat, aren't you?" The senator replied defensively: "yes. . . . I hope I am enough of an American to give credit to people in the opposition party who I think are doing the right thing."[25]

The administration's policies in Indochina were precisely what Mansfield favored in 1953. His first Senate speech on Indochina was delivered later in July when Mansfield argued against a proposed cut in the administration aid request for the French effort in Indochina. That position must have surprised some Senate colleagues, because several weeks earlier Mansfield had called for the termination of the U.S. foreign aid program in Europe. While praising the European aid program's results, Mansfield argued that it had accomplished its purpose and it was time to end it. The program was beginning to cause resentment and division. *Newsweek* was shocked at Mansfield's position on European aid, suggesting that he sounded more like a "Mid-west Republican" than the "stalwart internationalist" he had been in the House.[26] Mansfield's position on aid was one he continued to follow; aid should be given a reasonable amount of time to succeed, and then be suspended.

Clearly Mansfield believed that the U.S. aid program for Indochina had not yet had a reasonable amount of time to work. In his July speech, Mansfield argued against a 25 percent cut from President Dwight Eisenhower's request for $400 million in Indochinese aid. He believed that the war could be won with U.S. aid in two years. He added, "I do not want American boys sent to Indo-China but I am afraid that a possible consequence we face is a possible withdrawal from Indo-China by the French." Mansfield praised France but encouraged more independence for the Associated States (Vietnam, Cambodia, and Laos).[27] His fear of French withdrawal and encouragement for the French to grant more freedom to Indochina were undoubtedly influenced by the May meeting with Diem.

This debate on aid for Indochina was precipitated by a Barry Goldwater (R-Ariz.) amendment and a Kennedy substitute amendment, tying the aid package to a French announcement of a date for granting independence to the Indochinese states. Kennedy's amendment was friendly; it softened Goldwater's language to gain votes. The Arizonan predicted that if France did not grant freedom, "as surely as day follows night our boys will follow this $400 million." Dulles was sufficiently concerned about the amendments to have Eisenhower intervene personally with members of Congress. Goldwater and Kennedy received considerable support in Senate debate, but their amendment was defeated 64-17 and the full amount of Eisenhower's request was reinstated.[28] For the only time during the American involvement in Vietnam, Mansfield was squarely on the side of the sitting administration. His support was short lived.

MANSFIELD'S FIRST VISIT TO INDOCHINA

Mansfield used his position on the Senate Foreign Relations Committee to take three trips to Indochina during the 1950s, with the first in fall 1953. The *New York Times* considered this an important visit since "Mansfield was the earliest and most persistent backer" for aid to France short of the use of U.S. troops.[29] He was trying to learn about this new prize in the cold war, but he was also positioning himself to become the Senate expert on the region. Although the September visit included stops in France and other countries, Indochina was the focus. Prior to departure, Mansfield had a list prepared of press representatives stationed in the cities that he visited.[30] Mansfield met with a number of journalists on this trip and continued to correspond with them after his return. He used these contacts to gain information, and these reporters helped to build Mansfield's reputation as the Senate's resident Indochina expert.

At the time of this trip, however, Mansfield was not yet an expert. He later admitted that on this first visit to Indochina, "I had to check a map to be certain of the capital cities of the more remote nations. And the maps often did not agree, so little interest was there in that part of the world at the time." Mansfield added that "when I visited Laos with [Valeo], the two of us doubled the American population there" and that there were only about four U.S. officials in Cambodia.[31] Mansfield received the first visa ever issued by the Laotian Legation in the United States, and Valeo received the second. Valeo tells of getting lost when trying to find the royal capitol of Laos [Luang Prabang] from the administrative capitol [Vientiane]. They were using a Navy plane but there were no American navigation charts. The pilot overshot Luang Prabang by 400 miles and finally found it by flying low and following the Mekong River.[32]

Mansfield received briefings from French and Indochinese military and civilian leaders, including General Henri-Eugene Navarre, commander of the French military, Laotian Prime Minister Souvanna Phouma, and Cambodian Prime Minister Penn Nouth. Ambassador Donald Heath cabled the State Department with a summary of Mansfield's meeting with Penn Nouth. Mansfield acted as a conveyer of administration opposition to any Cambodian shift toward neutralism or negotiation with communists. When Penn Nouth argued that Cambodia could do nothing without its independence, Mansfield claimed that "independence was meaningless if it was won only to be lost to Communist attack." The Prime Minister also sought direct U.S. aid, instead of its being funneled through France, but Heath reported that Mansfield "dodged" that issue. When the senator stopped in France on his way home, he suggested that his discussion with Penn Nouth was unsatisfactory and that the French should "get tough" with Cambodia. Mansfield was following the administration line on Cambodia in 1953. Cambodian-U.S. relations remained troubled throughout Mansfield's

Senate career, but Mansfield became one of the few Americans to support Cambodia's neutrality.

While in France, Mansfield met separately with Vice-Premier Paul Reynaud and Marc Jacquet, secretary of state for Relations with the Associated States. When Mansfield was critical of Emperor Bao Dai, Jacquet reminded him that the emperor was "the most intelligent Vietnamese" and that Mansfield "must not judge his qualities on occidental standards. The wine-woman-song aspects of his life are part of the picture expected of an oriental potentate by his people."[33] Mansfield, of course, preferred Diem's austere life style.

In his written report, Mansfield concluded that the communist military situation was becoming weaker in the south but remained strong in the north. Three factors had improved France's position as the senator saw it: the expansion of native forces, U.S. aid, and the new military approach of General Navarre which included the use of "mooring points," like Dien Bien Phu, to wage a more aggressive war. Politically, Mansfield saw nationalism as the key, but he believed Ho Chi Minh was the beneficiary of "mis-directed nationalism." Mansfield felt that the United States and France needed to use nationalism to help the allied cause, needed to improve the lot of the citizens, and needed to raise the "ethical standards of government." The senator also considered it important that France grant independence to the Associated States to improve nationalism as a force. Mansfield viewed U.S. aid as "justified and essential," repeating that "American aid . . . does not and should not involve the commitment of combat forces" as the United States was bearing its burden in Korea. The senator concluded that the Vietminh would face defeat without military intervention by China.[34] On January 19, 1954, when Mansfield delivered an oral report on his trip to the Foreign Relations Committee, he was even more forceful about the need to defend Indochina, short of committing U.S. troops.[35]

The Montanan's report received favorable attention in the United States. Douglas MacArthur II from the State Department sent Mansfield a letter praising the report's clarity in stating the problems and estimating future possibilities. Assistant Secretary of State Livingston Merchant called the report "a remarkably clear and concise statement of the problem in that area of the world." Frederick Nolting Jr., then special assistant to the secretary of state and later President Kennedy's ambassador to South Vietnam, viewed the report as "heartening because of its general endorsement of U.S. policy toward Indo-China" and because it concluded that "the probability of success warrants the very large contribution that the United States is making."[36] This support from the administration is not surprising, given that Mansfield's report "strongly supported the position of the executive branch."[37]

Mansfield promoted his report by sending copies to prominent businessmen, military officers, educators, and members of the press. He continued to correspond with the journalists he met on this trip. Clearly the senator sought answers, but he took steps apparently designed to promote himself as a Far East expert as well. Two media contacts are noteworthy. First, while in Paris, Mansfield took Volney Hurd of the *Christian Science Monitor* to lunch. In his letter of thanks, Hurd praised the report as excellent and useful. The journalist idealistically predicted that time was on the U.S. side "for history shows that only truth finally survives and all lies lapse into their native nothingness, if we can but keep cool and see the things through."[38]

A second important contact was Arnaud de Borchgrave of *Newsweek,* who covered Vietnam from Paris. Finding Mansfield's report "immensely interesting," de Borchgrave was optimistic about the outcome in Vietnam, thinking that with increased U.S. aid, the "Vietminh movement will probably peter out as it did in Greece." In Mansfield's responses to both correspondents, he courted their support by asking that they continue to share their thoughts with him, "because it will help me greatly in trying to put across my views on this perhaps most critical area in the world today." Mansfield requested de Borchgrave's original reports, before *Newsweek* "condensed" them, of which the journalist sent at least one. Both men continued to correspond with Mansfield, as did other contacts that Mansfield made on this visit.[39]

Yet Mansfield was wrong in 1953. The French suffered their major defeat at Dien Bien Phu seven months after his report was issued, less than four months after the optimistic oral report Mansfield delivered to the Foreign Relations Committee. While he was in Vietnam, a member of the press expressed pessimism about France's chances for victory and Mansfield replied, "I'm sure you can't be right." That writer later concluded that Mansfield's 1953 report "ought to be framed and kept as an international treasure. For here was Mansfield, the cooing dove of the 1960s and 1970s, wearing all the feathers of the hawk."[40]

MANSFIELD BREAKS WITH THE ADMINISTRATION

Although subsequent events would prove him wrong, Mansfield's 1953 report had moved him into the center of the nation's discussion on Indochina, and he used it as the basis for a number of speeches on Indochina early in 1954, to carve an even deeper niche for himself as the congressional expert on Indochina. Congressional debate on Indochina began after Eisenhower dispatched Air Force technicians to Vietnam on January 29, 1954. Many in Congress objected to sending American personnel.

Mansfield approved of Eisenhower's action and called it "a logical extension of a practice already underway." He built his credibility in an February 8 speech, based on traveling "several thousand miles in the three states of Indo-China" the previous September. The problem, he claimed, was manpower, but it could not come from France or the United States; it had to come from the three

Indochinese states. Mansfield correctly assessed that the will of the Indochinese non-communist nationalists was the major stumbling block to defeating the Vietminh. He approved of Eisenhower's decision to ship B-26 bombers to Indochina, which would be serviced by the U.S. technicians. But he feared that Eisenhower and Dulles were drifting toward involvement, including the possible use of nuclear weapons, without a coherent policy and without consulting Congress. In the debate that followed his speech, Mansfield borrowed a phrase from Majority Leader William Knowland (Calif.), saying that he hoped "Democrats at this time will be 'in' on the 'take-off,' as well as on the 'crash landing'—although of course we hope there will not be a 'crash landing.'"[41]

At a February 16 executive session of the Foreign Relations Committee with Under Secretary of State Walter Bedell Smith, Mansfield was more militant than many of the other senators. He praised the sending of B-26s and technicians, proclaiming: "I want to say that I am very glad that this Government is spending $1,200 million this year in Indochina, and as far as I am concerned, I will vote for another billion or more next year." It was clear at this meeting that there was little concern by the Committee about manipulation of Vietnamese politics. Smith reacted to a question by J. William Fulbright (D-Ark.) about Bao Dai's leadership by declaring: "if you handle it properly you can make a *synthetic* strong man out of almost anyone who is not a coward." Fulbright, who later became a leading opponent of the war, talked of the need for a strong native leader for Vietnam, and added: "but if [Bao Dai] is not any good, *we* ought to get another one." Smith suggested that a change in leadership had been considered and alluded to "providing certain religious leadership," which was probably a code phrase for Diem.[42]

When John Foster Dulles met with the Foreign Relations Committee on February 24, Mansfield sided with the administration. Guy Gillette (D-Iowa) called the U.S. position "unsound, illogical and untenable," while Humphrey talked of the "conflicting testimony, the nebulous quality of this testimony, the conflicting statements as to the military situation, and the political situation." When the discussion got hot, Mansfield tried to defuse the situation, telling Dulles: "but it is good to see you with your Scotch-Irish up once in a while; it relieves the tension." MacArthur reported that Mansfield "chimed in to the effect that our policy with respect to Indochina was thus far sound."[43]

Mansfield had sent a copy of his February 8 speech to Volney Hurd and the two men continued to share their ideas through a series of letters. Hurd called Mansfield's speech "right on the line." The journalist attacked the myth of monolithic communism, saying that China "is absolutely no satellite and in fact *much* to the *contrary*. If I were in the Kremlin I would indeed have bad dreams." There is no indication at this early date that Mansfield shared Hurd's belief that China was independent of Moscow. When Mansfield disagreed with a Hurd position, the journalist proclaimed: "I bow before the keen thought which produced the exceptional memorandum you enclosed in your letter. . . . It was a first-class and brilliant weighing of the pros and cons and you have become my favorite candidate for Secretary of State." In one letter, Hurd indicated that the Bao Dai government had no support and "the way for the Chinese and Russians to win Indo-China would be to *insist* on immediate free elections in our best western manner—and Ho Chi Minh would win hands down." Mansfield agreed with that assessment. In another letter, Hurd quoted his wife:

> We believe in majority rule and people having the government they want, don't we? What right have we then to help bombard (with napalm) people who represent the majority in their country? Have we any right to stop a country from even going Communistic if that is the wish of the majority?

Mansfield did not respond to the question posed by Mrs. Hurd.[44]

Another contact that Mansfield made on his 1953 trip was William vanden Heuvel, assistant to U.S. ambassador to Thailand, William Donovan. Vanden Heuvel sent Mansfield a letter on March 8 that included a non-classified paper that he mailed with Donovan's permission. Donovan's assistant chose Mansfield to receive the paper because "I have long admired your judgment and recently known your friendship." Mansfield "incorporated some of the material" from vanden Heuvel's paper in a speech he wrote. The rough draft was dated March 18, and Mansfield delivered it in the Senate four days later.

Once again, Mansfield alluded to his September trip to establish credibility. He had moved away from the administration's position and was highly critical of the Eisenhower/Dulles policy. "Drifting" and "appeasement" were terms used frequently by Mansfield: the administration was "drifting in Indo-China and drifting towards appeasement at Geneva." Mansfield thought that it had been a mistake to agree to sit down with Communist China because that equaled "de facto" recognition. That decision, too, was made without consulting Congress.

Mansfield was also critical of France for the "obscureness" of its position on linking independence with joining of the French Union. Yet Mansfield complimented France for its sacrifices in men. The factor that Mansfield found lacking was nationalist leaders, especially in Vietnam where potential leaders were failing to rally their people to defend freedom.[45] Mansfield desperately sought a nationalist leader for Vietnam and even though he did not mention Diem by name, Diem was still the "name he carried."

Once again, Mansfield sent copies of his speech to establish his credentials with members of the press and others; he wrote vanden Heuvel that he would appreciate "yours and the Ambassador's comments or criticisms. I value your giving me the benefit of your thoughts because you are so much closer to the scene than I am and evidently you are seeking a solution." Jack Dowling of Time-Life referred to his meeting with Mansfield in Saigon and talked of the clarity of the Montanan's views on Indochina, adding: "I am deeply honoured that you should keep me informed on your progress in this growing debate and that you should find my opinion is worth noticing."[46]

De Borchgrave called the speech "first rate" and provided Mansfield with some information on the situation in Vietnam. Larry Allen of the Associated Press was another correspondent with whom Mansfield took the time to meet while in Indochina. Allen called Mansfield his "favorite Senator" and agreed with Paul Douglas's (D-Ill.) comment after the March 22 speech that Mansfield was performing a "public service of great magnitude." The AP correspondent offered Mansfield access to the incoming file at the Washington bureau of AP and volunteered to answer any of Mansfield's questions as long as Mansfield did not quote the source. Mansfield already had praised Allen in the *Congressional Record,* and Allen asked him to write a letter to his boss sharing that praise. Of course Mansfield did, and in May he enclosed another Allen article in the *Record* with the Montanan's praise.[47]

On April 6, Kennedy delivered a Senate speech containing views similar to Mansfield's. The future president agreed that the lack of nationalist support was the crucial element. In 1954 Kennedy understood that without such support, the United States could no more succeed in Indochina than had the French. At the end of the speech, Mansfield praised Kennedy's "scholarly and statesmanlike address."[48]

Kennedy became one of Mansfield's closest friends in the Senate. The shared Irish-Catholic background[49] and a common interest in Indochina were important parts of that friendship. They consulted each other and were in basic agreement on what the U.S. policy should be in that part of the world. The day after his speech, Kennedy sent Mansfield a note saying: "I appreciate very much your attendance on the floor of the Senate yesterday during my speech on Indo-China. It was of great assistance in presenting the subject." Mansfield recalled that "we both had an intense interest in Indo-China as it was at that time," but modestly suggested that the belief that Kennedy sought Mansfield's advice and counsel on Vietnam was "overdone a little bit."[50]

On April 14, Mansfield followed up on Kennedy's speech. Mansfield wanted the message from this speech to be heard. For the first time, his office issued a formal press release summarizing his major points and conclusions. One continued theme was that of the administration's failure to consult Congress. Mansfield said, "our advice is not asked; our consent not required," adding, "the only information I get is what I read in the newspapers."

Mansfield said that he feared that Eisenhower already had made a military commitment. If not, the administration was still in a dilemma that would result in either U.S. military commitment or appeasement, leading to a communist Indochina. World War III could result from the crisis in Indochina.

Eisenhower needed to spell out U.S. objectives, and the main objective must be freedom for the nations of Indochina. Yet Dulles and Eisenhower "must bear the responsibility for dealing with the situation." Mansfield promised bipartisan support even though the administration had not allowed for bipartisan consultation.

As Mansfield defined it, the problem was political and not military. French military forces, including Indochinese, numbered 500,000, and the United States provided considerably more aid than the Vietminh were receiving. Mansfield feared that many expected the battle to be fought by the French and Americans while the Indochinese "remain on the sidelines." The problem, he said, was that nationalist leaders were interested only in "their own welfare, profit and pleasure." The Vietminh had "wrapped themselves in the cloak of nationalism and social reform and so developed considerable popular support." Mansfield understood it would be difficult for many nationalist leaders to win over the population as many had been officials in the French colonial system. This made Diem even more appealing to Mansfield and others.

Two ideas that Mansfield crossed out of his rough draft showed that he was struggling with a more militant position. They involved sending "training technicians from Korea, Formosa and the Philippines to speed the expansion of nationalist armies of Indochina," and a conference of France, the United States, other interested nations, and Indochinese leaders "with a view of broadening the base of military resistance."[51] During the entire U.S. involvement in Indochina, Mansfield never endorsed committing U.S. forces to Vietnam, but in April and May of 1954, he at least flirted with that position.

Once again, Mansfield sent copies of his speech to a number of people. Chester Bowles called it an "excellent statement," and vanden Heuvel said: "I would have jumped to my feet and cheered until hoarse at the conclusion of your speech of April 14. It was a superb job and done in the best tradition of American bipartisanship." Vanden Heuvel added a comment that would be true for the Americans after they replaced the French: "what has been the source of the greatest harassment to the French has been the hostility of the people whom they are supposedly defending." Hurd wrote it was "pretty hard to criticize a speech of yours because you are so thorough, so clear thinking and so objective."[52]

Mansfield's contact with Hurd proved useful when the journalist wrote him about a communist massacre of civilians in Cambodia, suggesting, "who better than you could launch [publicity about the incident] with a strong Senate speech for your speeches are all getting excellent coverage here [Paris] these days—and deservedly so." Mansfield followed Hurd's suggestion, blaming the incident on "Ho Chi Minh and his Communist masters in Red China."[53]

THE FRENCH DEFEAT, DIEM, AND GENEVA

France was defeated at Dien Bien Phu on May 7, 1954. Mansfield continued to struggle with the question of committing U.S. troops. When he invited Paul Sturm of the State Department to lunch on May 12, Sturm noted:

> On each previous occasion on which I have talked with Senator Mansfield, and as recently as April 21, he has been vehemently opposed to the use of American ground troops in Indochina. Today, however, he did not react adversely when I mentioned this possibility.[54]

As the shock of the French loss at Dien Bien Phu started to wane, Diem arrived in Vietnam on June 26 as prime minister under Bao Dai.[55] The origins of Diem's appointment are unclear. It is often argued that a Vietnam lobby composed of prominent Catholics, including Mansfield, Spellman, and Joseph Kennedy, worked through John Foster Dulles and the CIA to bring Diem to power in order to squeeze France out. One writer asserted: "Diem was being groomed by Senator Mike Mansfield and Cardinal Spellman for his job" as prime minister.[56] This position overstates Mansfield's role. Mansfield undoubtedly favored Diem. Yet he lacked the clout to be influential with the administration in the summer of 1954. The likely scenario is that the French selected Diem because he was the most probable candidate to attract Vietnamese nationalists and receive U.S. support. As Mansfield put it in 1977, "if [the French] took him they only took him because they had no other choice." Dulles admitted that "Diem was picked not by us but by the French." Other Americans with first-hand knowledge of Vietnam share that view.[57] The appointment backfired as Diem's hatred for Vietnam's colonial masters caused the French much consternation in the future. France quickly decided that a new candidate was needed.

Vanden Huevel reinforced Mansfield's thoughts of Diem in a letter on June 17, 1954:

> At least, in this dark and demoralized hour [Diem] appears to be the last hope to capitalize the nation's spirit. I have heard criticisms of Diem which describe him as "too religious" and "too much the fanatic." My reply is that at this late hour perhaps only a fanatic zeal can galvanize the forces necessary for victory.[58]

The news of Diem's assumption of power was overshadowed by fear of the agreement being negotiated in Geneva. On July 8, Mansfield reacted to the Geneva talks with a 39-page Senate speech that was highly critical of administration policy. Referring to that policy as one of "bluster and retreat," and objecting to the "massive" words coming from Dulles, Mansfield expressed concern that too many administration figures were articulating conflicting statements. Democrats were being used as scapegoats, with the loss of Indochina being blamed on decisions made after World War II. Mansfield again pointed out that the Senate had not been consulted about Geneva and was critical of the agreements being reached, saying that he viewed the conference as occurring "under a threatening cloud of appeasement." In his view, "Geneva was a mistake; and the result is a failure of American policy. It is a profoundly humiliating result."

The Montanan warned against unilateral U.S. military involvement in Indochina because "the terrain of the Indochinese conflict—the flooded deltas, the thousands of scattered villages, the jungles—is made to order for the 'nibbling' of mechanized forces." Mansfield then asked a rhetorical question that should have been repeated in 1965: "should the Senate have sat in silence while the administration stumbled into the war in Indochina? Into a war without preparation, without popular support, without any concept of where it would take us or where it would end?"[59]

After his speech, Republicans suggested a contradiction in Mansfield's position: he criticized the administration for not defending Indochina, yet opposed direct U.S. intervention. Senator John Sherman Cooper (R-Ky.) said that Mansfield "cannot have it both ways."[60] In a phone conversation between Vice President Richard Nixon and Dulles, Nixon predicted that "after Mansfield's speech, the line will be that Geneva is a sell-out—a failure of diplomacy." Dulles prepared a response to Mansfield that said the fundamental mistake occurred in 1945 when the United States allowed France and Britain to persuade it to become involved in Indochina; it was a disservice for Mansfield to assume that America should be a "Mr. Fixit" around the world. Dulles never made his response public.[61]

Eisenhower and Dulles were also disturbed by the agreement being reached in Geneva. They had decided that the United States would not be an active participant at Geneva and that American representatives would attend only at French insistence. Eisenhower made a strong rhetorical statement by recalling Dulles after the Korean phase of the conference in early May. There Dulles refused to shake hands with Chinese Foreign Minister Zhou Enlai. Bedell Smith returned to the United States in June, leaving the U.S. delegation with the third in command, U. Alexis Johnson.[62]

Johnson remained in charge of the American delegation from June 20 until July 17, when Smith briefly returned. The diplomat called his instructions a "holding pattern," trying to walk the fine line between observer and participant, while agreeing to nothing. These instructions were frustrating to U.S. allies, and Johnson found them difficult to follow. The settlement was reached on July 21, and Eisenhower issued a separate statement pointing out that the United States did not sign and was not "bound by the decisions taken by the conference." Eisenhower threatened that "any renewal of Communist aggression would be viewed by us as a matter of grave concern," but he also promised that "the United States will not use force to disturb the settlement."[63]

Future administration actions showed Eisenhower was insincere about the pledge not to disturb the settlement. Diem, too, refused to sign the Geneva agreement. Mansfield's assessment of the results of the negotiation were incorrect. The Vietminh believed that the Soviet Union and China forced them to make concessions that were not justified. Ho had opposed a divided Vietnam; the French and Chinese proposed it after secret negotiations. China was anxious to avoid the installation of American bases in Indochina, and a continued French presence seemed the best way to achieve that. Based on political control and the military situation, the 13th parallel would have been a more realistic demarcation line than the agreed upon 17th. The Vietminh were forced at Geneva to cede about one-quarter of the land they controlled. Against Ho's wishes, the agreement delayed unification elections until 1956. The promised elections were the reason Hanoi accepted the final agreement. The Vietminh fully expected the elections to be held and had good reason to be confident of winning.[64]

CHAPTER 3

MANSFIELD'S REPORT BECOMES THE "CORNERSTONE" OF U.S. SUPPORT FOR DIEM

MANSFIELD AND THE SEATO ALLIANCE

The idea for a defensive alliance that included Asia had been discussed as early as 1948. President Dwight D. Eisenhower originally called for such a treaty in Southeast Asia in 1953. In order to compensate for the potential loss of Indochina, the president made the decision to seek an alliance on March 21, 1954. "United Action" was delayed because the British were unwilling to begin discussions until after a settlement for the Indochina crisis was found at Geneva.[1]

Before the beginning of the Manila conference in September 1954, Secretary of State John Foster Dulles called Alexander Wiley (R-Wis.), chairman of the Senate Foreign Relations Committee, to discuss Senate appointments to the conference. Wiley recommended Mansfield as a second member since the Montanan would be in the Far East anyway, on his second trip to Indochina. Dulles checked with Walter George (Ga.), the ranking Democrat on the Foreign Relations Committee. George said of Mansfield: "he would be good, he is developing and will be a great fellow in the Senate."[2]

The appointment was based on more than availability, though. Even after Mansfield's attacks on the administration during the summer of 1954, Dulles seemed to trust Mansfield not to play partisan politics with foreign policy.[3] Mansfield's selection may have also been an attempt to coopt him as a potential critic of SEATO. He had been a thorn in the administration's side during the Geneva Conference. Mansfield had spoken against such a pact in the past, because it involved largely white nations defending Asians and excluded India from membership.[4] His direct involvement in SEATO would keep him from criticizing the administration for not consulting Congress. In fact, Mansfield established credibility with Dulles on this trip, and the two men developed some closeness and "mutual respect."[5]

By including members of the Foreign Relations Committee, the administration increased the likelihood of quick ratification in the Senate. Both Mansfield and H. Alexander Smith (R-N.J.) signed the Manila Pact, creating the Southeast Asian Treaty Organization. With the exception of the United Nations Treaty, this was the first and only time that members of Congress have been treaty signatories.[6] Not surprisingly, Dulles worked with Mansfield, Smith, and William Knowland (R-Calif.) to obtain rapid ratification of the treaty in February of 1955.

Mansfield and Smith had protected Senate prerogatives in Manila and insisted on the inclusion of language declaring that "constitutional processes" would be followed. At a Foreign Relations Committee meeting, Mansfield was asked, "In other words, there is no possibility then for the President under this treaty to go to war on the scale, let us say, of the Korean war, without getting a declaration of war by Congress?" Mansfield replied, "That is my understanding."[7]

Dulles and Smith both accepted Mansfield's language. Indeed, during Dulles's testimony, Smith asked him, "you used the words 'constitutional processes,' having in mind that the president undoubtedly would come to Congress in case of any threat of danger in the area, unless we had some sudden emergency." Dulles replied, "unless the emergency were so great that there had to be some prompt action to save a vital interest of the United States, then the normal process would of course be to act through Congress if it is in session, and if not in session, to call Congress."[8]

Dean Rusk, secretary of state for presidents Kennedy and Johnson, wrote of the irony in Mansfield's being a signatory of SEATO and then an opponent of its use in Vietnam during the Johnson administration. When pressed, Mansfield told Rusk that he signed SEATO "reluctantly." Rusk checked the *Congressional Record* and correctly reported that Mansfield's arguments in favor of SEATO ratification did not indicate any reluctance on his part. Rusk, who would be at the center of Vietnam escalation decisions in the 1960s, considered the SEATO Treaty a mistake because it "became the law of the land" linking South Vietnam to the U.S. structure of collective security. When asked why the United States fought the second Indochina war, Rusk replied: "there was the pledge [SEATO]. We had given our word." Rusk and the Johnson administration chose to interpret SEATO in that manner. William Conrad Gibbons pointed out that Mansfield and the delegates to Manila "were given 'four uncompromisable pre-conditions'" ignored by Johnson: "the U.S. would refuse to commit any U.S. forces unilaterally"; "were military action to be required, one or more of the European signatories would have to participate"; "the U.S. intended to contribute only sea and air power, expecting that other signatories would provide ground forces"; and "the U.S. would act only against communist aggression."[9]

Even though Mansfield had serious doubts about the efficacy of SEATO, he went along with the administration. Mansfield would come to regret his active role in this effort to protect Indochina and Asia from communist encroachment. Before the Senate ratified SEATO, though, Mansfield returned to Vietnam.

MANSFIELD'S SECOND VISIT TO INDOCHINA

Mansfield visited Indochina for the second time on his way to and from the Manila conference. As in 1953, Mansfield borrowed Francis Valeo from the Library of Congress to accompany him.[10]

On his way to the Far East, Mansfield stopped in Paris and talked with Guy La Chambre, the French Minister for Relations with the Associated States, and U.S. Ambassador C. Douglas Dillon. La Chambre assured Mansfield that France was moving as quickly as possible to grant independence to Vietnam, but painted a dark picture of the situation there. The French Minister viewed Diem as "honest but not very efficient" and hinted at a coup d'etat that would lead to a coalition government. Dillon agreed that the situation in Vietnam was bleak, and while finding the situation in Cambodia "pretty good," thought the one in Laos was "less favorable."[11]

The senator spent one day in Cambodia meeting separately with the Cambodian Prime Minister and Foreign Minister. Cambodia had turned to the United States for protection after gaining independence from France, but sought Chinese help after the United States embraced Cambodia's traditional enemy, South Vietnam. Prime Minister Penn Nouth thanked Mansfield for his speeches which made the Cambodian situation known. As in 1953, Cambodia wanted direct military assistance instead of aid funneled through France. Penn Nouth assured Mansfield that as a monarchy, Cambodia was anti-communist. He asked for U.S. understanding that Cambodia might be forced to act in a way that did not seem consistent with anti-communism in order to coexist in Indochina.[12] Cambodia tried to walk that fine line into the Nixon administration.

Mansfield's position on Cambodia had changed drastically since his 1953 visit. In his report submitted after his 1954 trip, Mansfield was optimistic, saying: "the Cambodian Government under the young and energetic King Norodom Sihanouk Varman was both leading and being led by the powerful nationalist surge."[13] Sihanouk was a nationalist leader whom Mansfield befriended and would support into the 1990s.

In Vietnam, Mansfield found that many shared the views of La Chambre and Dillon.[14] The difficulties Diem faced in creating a government in Saigon seemed insurmountable. Diem disliked the French, and the French quickly concluded that the new Prime Minister was not capable of leading. The American position became one of supporting Diem until a better candidate emerged.

One problem Diem faced was the lack of experienced officials, since the French had held all responsible positions in previous governments. The few Vietnamese trained to be administrators by the French were suspect because of perceived pro-French leanings. Diem's government was dominated by people from the north and central parts of Vietnam, many of whom were Catholic, which created animosity among southerners and Buddhists. The new Prime

Minister relied too heavily on family members in key positions, leading to charges of a family oligarchy. The Diem government also faced the problem of settling more than 800,000 northerners who were in the process of migrating south. Rumors and plots of coups were rampant in Saigon.

The most likely coup leader was General Nguyen Van Hinh, Chief of Staff of the Army. Like many southern leaders, Hinh held dual French citizenship, including a commission in the French military. French elements opposed to Diem prodded the Chief of Staff to lead a coup. Diem lacked a strong enough mandate from Emperor Bao Dai to remove Hinh. When Diem ultimately tried to fire him, Hinh refused to leave.

Diem also faced continuing coup threats from the sects that controlled their own "quasi-autonomous religious, economic, political and military 'kingdoms.'" These sects stepped into the power vacuum at the end of World War II and effectively opposed the Vietminh in the Saigon area, allowing the French to concentrate on the war in the north. One sect was the Cao Dai, an exotic mixture of Confucianism, Buddhism, spiritualism, and Catholicism, with its own Pope, female cardinals, and saints, including Victor Hugo, Christ, Buddha, Joan of Arc, Sun-Yat-Sen, Shakespeare, and Clemenceau. The other two sects were the Hoa Hao, a fundamentalist Buddhist group, and Binh Xuyen, which was not religious, but originally comprised of river pirates who dominated gambling, prostitution, and opium trade in the Saigon area and ran the police through payments to Bao Dai. The three sects controlled a significant portion of the population. Each group had a private army, totaling 40,000 to 50,000. The sects could not be ignored. The Cao Dai controlled the region north and northwest of Saigon, the Hoa Hao controlled the area to the southwest, and the Binh Xuyen was a powerful force in and near the city of Saigon.[15]

Lacking real control over the military, police, the judiciary, and finances, Diem held his government together through sheer will and stubbornness. A CIA intelligence estimate of September 15, 1954, said: "trends in South Vietnam since the end of the Geneva Conference have enhanced the prospects of an eventual extension of Communist control over the area by means short of large-scale military attacks."[16]

On September 2, Mansfield met with Donald Heath, U.S. ambassador to South Vietnam and Cambodia. Following the meeting, he and Heath met with Diem, with the French Acting Commissioner General, and finally with the Vietnamese Minister for Foreign Affairs. The ambassador said that Diem had been concentrating on dealing with the refugee crisis rather than consolidating his power. Diem was "utterly honest but tended to operate in a cloister." The cabinet was loyal to Diem but unknown to the people. Diem was stubborn and refused to deal with the sects, whereas Heath considered such dealings essential. Heath said that Diem was "bitterly anti-French," which created French "coolness" toward Diem. The ambassador indicated that he had personally averted a coup the past weekend by interceding with the sects. If Diem should fall, Heath did not think there was a suitable replacement. Mansfield's notes on the meeting with the French Acting Commissioner General bore out Heath's opinion on French coolness toward Diem.

Mansfield recorded that "Diem is in a very difficult political situation and he is aware of it." The sects were his principal concern and in order to deal with them, he needed to gain the confidence of the army. Diem believed that General Hinh was "coming around" and that the government would be able to deal effectively with the sects with Hinh's support. Ambassador Heath cabled Washington stating that he was perplexed that Diem "glossed over" his political problems in the meeting with Mansfield to hide the bleakness of the situation.

Heath described Foreign Minister Tran Van Do as "much less optimistic." Tran believed that a conspiracy was afoot to depose Diem, but that U.S. intercession had prevented it so far. He blamed Hinh and possibly the French, who were expected to pressure Bao Dai to ask for Diem's resignation. If that happened, there was little the United States could do, since Bao Dai had appointed Diem. Tran considered the sects short-sighted for not seeing that the Vietminh were their real enemy. He was urging Diem to be conciliatory with the sects, at least in the short run.[17]

While Mansfield was meeting with South Vietnam's leaders, Valeo visited two American observers, Paul Everett and Wesley Fishel.[18] Everett was convinced that Diem was the answer for Vietnam: "he can make it; he hasn't made it yet. If he is solid, if in fact he survives, then it is worth going all out to support him. If he fails, only the old discredited hacks are available, and we should begin figuring our losses in preparation for getting out." Everett also believed that the United States had transported too many refugees; the south was overwhelmed by the numbers, and it caused the United States a deep and unnecessary commitment.

Fishel was not optimistic about the situation in 1954. He said that Bao Dai had told several people that he appointed Diem president "to finish him more quickly." Fishel indicated that Diem took the job "with his eyes opened and closed at the same time," meaning that he knew how difficult the task would be, but believed that his "unimpeachable honesty and integrity, his moral rectitude would triumph."

According to Fishel, the French undercut Diem. For the first two months of his presidency, Diem had been unable to accomplish anything. Fishel thought Diem was underrated and that he could survive if "he gains confidence in himself," acts constructively, and is "assured of American support." Diem only had about two weeks to produce or he would be replaced. If Diem fell from power, Fishel predicted a series of "French-sponsored puppets" followed by Vietminh control. Fishel thought that Diem needed to "unbend a bit" and work with the sects. He also needed to fire Hinh, whose loyalty was to the French. Fishel said, "we do not have a good chance here, we have a 'chance.'" Fishel did not believe that Diem's Catholic background contributed to his lack of popularity, but he did point out one problem in the situation: Diem was forced to turn to Catholic refugees from the North to form a military unit that would be loyal to him.[19]

On September 8, Mansfield and a counselor from the U.S. Embassy visited with La Chambre in Saigon. La Chambre had met with Dulles in Manila two days earlier, where the Minister of State had pushed for the replacement of Diem. Dulles had said to La Chambre: "Senator Mansfield had recently been in Indochina and had expressed the view that Diem might possibly be the last chance of a Prime Minister who could be effective." In the meeting with Mansfield, the Minister of State agreed with Fishel that Diem had only "two or three weeks" to produce. La Chambre agreed with Fishel on little else. In the view of the French minister, "although a man of good will, Diem is not a man of will." He quoted the French ambassador as calling Diem "totally ineffectual." La Chambre believed that Diem's being a northerner diminished his influence in the south. His unwillingness to work with the sects was a major weakness. As in Mansfield's other meetings with French officials, La Chambre emphasized that French and U.S. aid in Vietnam must be "closely coordinated"—an attempt to keep U.S. aid controlled by France.

Mansfield reacted strongly, concluding the meeting by commenting "that a change in Government every few weeks in Viet Nam would be disastrous. In the absence of a good alternative to Diem, we believe that his Government must be supported and encouraged to broaden its base so as to make it truly effective."[20]

On September 11, Mansfield met with Colonel Edward Lansdale and Frank Meloy. Lansdale had successfully coordinated the war against the Philippine communist Hukbalahap rebels before being sent to Indochina as a CIA operative. He became America's most colorful character in Indochina.[21] On their meeting on the 11th, Lansdale, Meloy, and Mansfield discussed Diem's inadequacies, especially his failure to utilize people because of their alleged shortcomings. Fishel joined the meeting late.[22] Lansdale, Fishel, and Mansfield would each play prominent roles in Diem's survival in the spring of 1955.

While in Europe on his return from Indochina, Mansfield received the following message from the State Department: "the Secretary of State requests you to advise him what you think about the Vietnamese situation and especially your judgment of the ability of Diems [sic] to form a government worthy of our support."[23] Dulles was using Mansfield's strong belief in Diem in conversations with the French and within the administration to justify continued U.S. support for Diem. Kenneth Young, assistant secretary of state for the Far East, said, "Mansfield was an old friend of Diem's and we knew what the answer would be in advance, of course, but it stunned the French."[24] Mansfield's cable from Berlin shows that his recent trip had not lessened his confidence in Diem:

If Diem fails, the alternative is a government composed of his present opponents, no combination of which is likely to base itself strongly in the populace.
Such a government would be indefinitely dependent on support of the French and
could survive only so long as the latter are able to obtain Viet Minh acquiescence in
its survival.

The fundamental question, therefore, may well be not can Diem form a worthy
government but do the French really want Diem and what he stands for to
succeed?[25]

In a Washington meeting with La Chambre and the French the day after
receiving this telegram, Under Secretary of State W. Bedell Smith read
Mansfield's telegram and added that Mansfield was "a powerful Democratic
Senator in opposition who believes that Diem is the best hope there is." In an
administration meeting the next day, Dulles referred to Mansfield's appraisal
and noted "that the Senator's views would carry a lot of weight in the Foreign
Relations Committee, especially with the Democrats." That became the standard
administration line. For example, in talking with the French in October, Young
said: "Senator Mansfield is particularly well informed on Indochina and . . . his
views may be expected to be influential when the subject comes up in Congress."
The administration's use of Mansfield's expertise and forceful support of Diem
temporarily ended French opposition to Diem, until after the American elections
in November.[26]

In writing of Mansfield's trip, Ellen Hammer stated that the senator could not
understand why "the population did not close ranks behind Diem," how nationalists in the south could "speak with so many voices" and be "so chaotic and negative." Hammer questioned Mansfield's cultural sensitivity and pointed out: "it
did not seem to occur to Senator Mansfield that there could be many people in
South Vietnam who had no wish to live under a regime like that in the North,
and yet did not want any part of an American military alliance directed against
the Communists."[27]

In these heady days of nation-building in South Vietnam, all things seemed
possible. Mansfield, like most Americans, was unable to view the situation by
any standard except his own. The weaknesses inherent in the artificially created
leader were shrouded from America's ethnocentric view because Diem possessed
traits deemed admirable by the vast majority of Americans.

MANSFIELD'S 1954 REPORT INFLUENCES THE ADMINISTRATION

The senator issued his second Indochina report on October 15, 1954; it was
his most important one. It has been seen by many as forming the basis for U.S.
support of Diem. Eisenhower appears to have been leaning toward supporting

Diem at that time, and Mansfield's report helped cement that position. Mansfield's most far-reaching conclusion was that there were no "promising" alternatives to Diem: *"in the event that the Diem government falls, therefore, I believe that the United States should consider an immediate suspension of all aid to Vietnam and the French Union forces there, except that of a humanitarian nature."*[28] (Emphasis added.)

David Anderson claimed that Mansfield's report "immediately became the cornerstone of the pro-Diem position."[29] Chester Cooper argued:

> Mansfield's report had an important influence on the Administration's decision to move forward with an aid program for the struggling Saigon Government. On October 23, 1954 President Eisenhower sent a letter to Premier Diem, and it was that letter that was cited by the members of the Kennedy Administration and even more often by officials in the Johnson Administration to relate the origin and continuity of U.S. policy in support of Diem.[30]

Eisenhower's letter to Diem was planned in August and drafted in early September. The interval between the drafting of the letter and decision to send it indicates Eisenhower's hesitancy. On October 22, Under Secretary of State Herbert Hoover Jr., indicated to Dulles and Heath that Eisenhower's letter was being released and that the "conclusions of Senator Mansfield are relevant" as to aid. Hoover's cable was remarkably similar to Mansfield's of September 24. The *New York Times* suggested that the release of the letter so soon after Mansfield's report was more than coincidence.[31]

Valeo agreed with Cooper's conclusion, writing that prior to Mansfield's report, the Eisenhower administration had been "inclined to support whatever the French wanted." Mansfield's aide thinks the senator was influential, particularly with Dulles. Dulles and French Premier Pierre Mendes-France had agreed in September to support a successor government if Diem should fall from power. Mansfield's report undercut that agreement since he likely had the influence in Congress to cut off aid if Diem were purged.[32]

While Mansfield often criticized the administration for failure to consult with Congress, no such criticism was forthcoming when Eisenhower committed U.S. support to Diem without direct congressional input. Victor Bator wrote that by November 1954 U.S. Vietnam policy

> was no longer determined in the State Department. It followed the direction of Congress, more particularly that of Senator Mike Mansfield, head of a special subcommittee on Indochina who associated the unconditional support of Diem with resolute policy to eliminate "colonialist" France.[33]

On October 25, Pierre Millet of the French Embassy in Washington asked Young if he thought Mansfield's report went "too far." Young reiterated that Mansfield had influence in Congress where Diem was concerned and that congressional reaction would be "adverse" if Diem was replaced. On November 5, Young drafted a memo for Dulles, instructing Dillon to tell Bao Dai that Mansfield's conclusions about cutting aid if Diem were deposed were "relevant." Dillon, too, "reminded Mendes of Senator Mansfield's report and the importance it would have on congressional opinion and decisions regarding further aid to Indochina." However, Dillon was concerned with the "rigidity" of Mansfield's position. The idea that if Diem "goes down all is lost," would "increase conviction [in] certain quarters here that South Vietnam [is] finished," since Diem was expected to fail. Clearly, the administration was suggesting to the French that it was forced to support Diem because of Mansfield's power in Congress.

When Mendes-France visited Washington in mid-November, Dulles urged the French Premier to find time to meet with Mansfield, emphasizing the senator's knowledge of the area, influence in the Senate, and strong conviction that Diem was the best hope for Vietnam. Mansfield was unaware that Dulles attempted to arrange a meeting with the French Premier and the meeting never took place.[34] But, Mansfield's stature with Dulles had grown since his August trip to Paris when the secretary of state wrote him: "I am telling Paris not to press Mendes-France for an appointment in view of his very heavily burdened schedule."[35]

All of this attention and influence had to be flattering for a first-term senator from Montana. Gibbons refers to "the *pas de deux* between the State Department and Senator Mansfield."[36] Mansfield's dance with the State Department continued through April 1955. The senator described his relationship with Dulles during this period:

> [We had] very close and fairly intimate dealings. He called on me many times for advice and counsel as to what should be done in Diem's early days. For a while I was quite free with my information and advice.
>
> I think it was a new area for Dulles—and for Mr. Young, too. I suppose they were looking around for advice from people who may have been there in order to get some guidance until they got their feet firmly on the ground and made up their minds definitely.
>
> I think he leaned a little bit too heavily on me in the matter of Diem . . . to such an extent that I felt it had to be broken off, because it was outside the ken of my responsibility and entirely within the purview of the Executive branch under the Constitution.[37]

Besides influencing the administration, Mansfield's report gave a boost to Diem. As the *Pentagon Papers* put it: "the Mansfield Report elated Diem, subdued the French, and annoyed Paris." Heath claimed that the report made

Diem's supporter's "jubilant" and anti-Diem groups "angry." Indeed, Diem distributed 100,000 copies of the report.[38]

MANSFIELD HELPS TO STRENGTHEN DIEM'S "CATHOLIC SECT"

The greatest weakness of Mansfield's report is that it accepted the premise that the United States could create a nationalist leader in the south to rival Ho in the north, a premise that led to our disastrous involvement in the 1960s and 1970s. Like most Americans, Mansfield continued to consider communism and nationalism mutually exclusive, once describing Ho's supporters as "Communists masquerading as nationalists" and considered the Vietminh part of international communism. Mansfield's cold war view prevented him from seeing what his report made obvious, that Diem lacked the support to succeed. In the report, Mansfield conceded that Diem's strength rested on the recently arrived refugees from the North, 80 percent of whom were Catholic—admitting the lack of native southern support for the American regime.[39] Eight years later, during Mansfield's fourth visit to Vietnam, the senator was forced to concede that Diem still was not well known in the countryside. Valeo, too, wrote: "Diem was an authentic nationalist of good reputation with a semblance of a political base in the strong catholic community, particularly after the U.S. Navy evacuated thousands of catholics from the north."[40]

While in Hanoi in the fall of 1954, Mansfield visited one of the American ships transporting refugees and said they "were mostly Catholics, led by their priests" and that they had chosen to move "south with nothing but the rags on their backs rather than to live under the Communists."[41] The religious issue was real in 1954. The senator wrote a constituent that the leaders of the refugees "were the Catholic priests who stayed as close to their parishioners as possible and they were the ones to whom the refugees looked for guidance."[42]

This rejection of communism by Vietnam's Catholic community inspired Mansfield and America. Many in the United States came to believe that Vietnam was predominantly a Catholic nation. Dr. Thomas A. Dooley Jr., who took part in the evacuation, contributed to that perception. His emotional and one-sided lectures and writings about Vietnam's Catholic refugees made Dooley an American folk hero and helped to gain public support for Diem. Numerous Americans formed their opinions about Indochina solely on Dooley's exaggerated accounts. One writer pointed out that Dooley helped to "blur the distinction" between the Vietnamese Catholics who shared Dooley's faith and the more than 90 percent of the Vietnamese population who did not.[43]

The Geneva settlement allowed for free movement north or south from August 1954 until May 1955. During that period, the CIA helped persuade Catholics in the north to move south to increase Diem's constituency and balance the populations of the two regions in the event of nationwide elections (the north had 12 million people and the south 10 million at the time of Geneva). Slogans like "the Virgin Mary has departed from the North" and "Christ has gone to the South" were broadcast by the CIA in a campaign spearheaded by Lansdale. Catholic charities in the United States raised considerable money to aid in the resettlement, leading one writer to conclude that the movement was "primarily a Catholic operation."[44]

The 860,000 refugees who moved south far exceeded U.S. estimates. Many fled the north because they had worked for the French and feared reprisals. Catholic peasants likely thought that they would have more religious freedom in the south. America's well-coordinated propaganda effort made it clear that the south's government was headed by a Catholic supported by American aid. "A water buffalo and five acres" was one promise made to the refugees.[45]

More than one-half of the Catholic population in the north moved south. More would have migrated but were prevented from doing so by the Vietminh.[46] Even after this population shift, the south had fewer than 1 million Catholics, still less than 10 percent of the south's total population. In contrast, estimates on the numbers of Cao Dai ranged from 1.5 to 2.5 million, and the Hoa Hao counted between 1 and 1.5 million adherents. Indeed, Bernard Fall, Graham Greene, Ellen Hammer and others writing in this period categorized Vietnamese Catholics as a "sect." Before their evacuation south, the north Vietnamese Catholic "bishoprics" of Phat-Diem and Bui-Chu and the south Vietnamese province of Ben Tre operated independently, much as the sects did, and they were considered sect areas by the French. During the first Indochina war, some of these Catholic districts fought both the French and Vietminh. Fearing retribution, their leaders felt compelled to flee south under the terms of the Geneva settlement. While Greene called Diem's "Catholic cadres" a "fourth sect," the difference for Diem was that the Catholic areas supported him, while the other sect areas were considered a threat to his fledgling government. When Diem's opponents referred to his "Catholic sect," they were mindful that 75 to 80 percent of the south's population could have been classified as Buddhist.[47]

Many Vietnamese Buddhists viewed the Catholic Church as an alien religion, and Catholics traditionally suffered persecution. The French favored the Catholic Church because it was their own, and many Vietnamese Catholics supported the French in the first Indochinese war. French law discriminated by declaring the Catholic Church a religion, while Buddhists were defined as members of an "association." This law continued during the Diem regime. All of these factors weakened the nationalist credentials of Catholics in the eyes of non-Catholic Vietnamese, and many viewed the Americans as merely replacing the French as the protectors of Vietnamese Catholics. While some American liberals worried about the effectiveness of a Catholic leader in Asia, there was no hint that Mansfield was among them.[48]

The Catholic refugees became Diem's staunchest followers and provided him with the first reliable troops used to protect his Saigon palace. Upon his return from Vietnam in October, Mansfield admitted that "Diem's strength rests on the recently arrived refugees and on a tenuous alignment" with the Cao Dai and Hoa Hao. As late as 1962, U.S. Ambassador Frederick Nolting Jr. told Mansfield that the northern refugees "provided some of the strongest anti-Communist elements in the country"[49]—which translated to support for Diem. Yet General J. Lawton Collins argued that the Catholic refugees never assimilated with the native southern population and were viewed by the Buddhist majority as intruders favored by Diem's "Catholic government."[50]

American responsibility in moving the refugees south made it difficult for the United States to later abandon Vietnam. When the Diem government verged on collapse in April 1955, for example, Dulles cabled the Paris and Saigon embassies: "mockery will be made of sacrifice and heroism of anti-communist Vietnamese including refugees."[51]

THE COLLINS MISSION

Diem's government faced a continuing crisis at the end of 1954. When Diem dismissed General Hinh as head of the Vietnamese armed services in September, Hinh refused to leave. As Eisenhower was prone to do, he turned to a military man to solve the problem between Hinh and Diem, as well as the numerous other problems the Diem government faced. In early November, General Collins came to Saigon as Eisenhower's personal emissary and a temporary replacement for Ambassador Heath. The president borrowed Collins from NATO and gave him the power to coordinate the activities of all U.S. agencies in Vietnam. Collins's instructions were to help support the fledgling Diem government. Eisenhower named Collins ambassador and downplayed his military background. Collins's two-to-three week assignment stretched to over six months, and the temporary ambassador spent most of that time battling Mansfield and others for influence over the administration's Vietnam policy.

In meetings preceding his departure, Dulles predicted Collins's chances of success at one in ten. Dulles told the General he did not want Eisenhower's prestige too closely tied to the Collins mission. The secretary of state talked of the Mansfield report, which "deserves serious consideration." Dulles said that Mendes-France was "aghast" when Dulles told him that aid would likely be cut off if Diem fell from power, and he emphasized to Collins that the French must be reminded of Mansfield's position.[52]

Collins's briefing book contained a copy of Mansfield's 1954 Indochina report for the ambassador's consideration. It also included an example of American/Christian ethnocentrism toward Buddhism. The briefing book asserted that the Vietminh possessed what the French called "mystique," that is, they were "dedicated men imbued either by the spirit of nationalism or of Communism or a combination of both." That quality was "almost completely lacking in Free Vietnam with the exception of the Catholic Church and such confessional groups as the Cao Daists."[53] Since most members of the Vietminh were Buddhist, why would the State Department believe that only non-Buddhist South Vietnamese had the potential to be militant nationalists with "mystique"? Such a lack of understanding of the culture helped to doom the U.S. effort.

In November, French and American authorities persuaded Bao Dai to recall Hinh to France, and the French offered Hinh the restitution of his commission in the French military. Mansfield's threat to cut off aid proved crucial in ending the crisis. Hinh called Mansfield's October report "pure slander" and told a reporter: "I had only to lift my telephone and the *coup d' etat* would have been over. But the Americans let me know that if that happened, dollar help would be cut off."[54]

Yet Collins quickly came to agree with the French and Hinh that Diem was not capable of leading. In his memoirs, Collins wrote that his first impression of Diem "was of a pleasant, pudgy little man, self-conscious and not quite sure of himself." On November 15, Collins sent his "first general impressions and recommendations" back to Washington: "I am by no means certain [Diem] has inherent capacity to manage country during this critical period. My clear impression, moreover, is that each passing day of indecisiveness is bound to lessen any confidence that people may have in his Govt."[55]

Collins's greatest frustration with Diem was his failure to appoint talented men to the cabinet, particularly Dr. Phan Huy Quat as Minister of Defense. Collins thought Quat was "one of the ablest Vietnamese leaders." In mid-November, Collins was so certain Quat would prevail that he prepared a memorandum for his files, under the heading "accomplishments." In it, he announced the appointment of Quat to the defense post, leaving the date blank. The date was never filled in.[56]

On December 6, Collins cabled the State Department that Diem must be replaced if he did not improve in the next two weeks.[57] Mansfield's 1954 trip had strengthened the Montanan's credentials as the congressional expert on Vietnam. Young and Assistant Secretaries of State Walter Robertson and Thruston Morton visited Mansfield on December 7 to ask his advice on Collins's telegram. For the next five months, Mansfield lobbied intensely with the State Department to retain his friend, Diem. Mansfield's reply to Collins's telegram admitted that Diem's chances of survival were dim and Ho would likely win the 1956 elections. Yet Mansfield argued that the United States must support Vietnam as long as possible, even if the cost were high, in order to protect Cambodia and Laos. Diem should be encouraged to share power with Quat and others, but Collins's time limit of several weeks was not enough time for the Prime Minister to get results. It was important for Bao Dai to give Diem the power to run the government effectively and that Fishel work with Diem on "the problem of delegation and political adjustments." While admitting Diem's "weaknesses as an administrator and manager," Mansfield believed "that the remarkable aspect of Diem was unlike most of the Vietnamese, he really was honest, incorruptible and a devoutly dedicated nationalist as well."[58]

Young and Robertson sought out Mansfield because they shared his support for Diem, and the three men became allies on the issue. In a conversation with Robertson on December 15, Mansfield repeated his support for Diem, but emphasized the need for Diem to cooperate with the United States as well, which meant broadening his government and not ruling through his family. If Diem failed to make those changes, he recommended that the United States terminate support.

This message was cabled to the U.S. Embassy in Saigon for possible use with Diem. Robertson reported that "Mansfield thought his views might carry some weight with Diem" because he was a "good friend" and was considered impartial and objective by the South Vietnamese leader.[59] Young wrote to Collins: "of course Senator Mansfield believes that there isn't much else besides Diem and the process of replacement would create far more chaos and confusion than is even present today in Free Viet-Nam."[60]

Remarkably, on December 17, Robertson once again shared a Collins telegram with Mansfield and sent Collins Mansfield's dictated views. Rarely, if ever, has the State Department been so solicitous of a senator's views. Mansfield suggested the debate on Vietnam boiled down to two questions: "will the return of Bao Dai act materially and in a manner consistent with our policy to break political impasse in Saigon?" and "what are implications of recommendation of General Collins that we go along with Diem for few weeks and if it still seems that situation is insoluble to consider possibility of withdrawing from Viet-Nam entirely?" Mansfield opposed the return of Bao Dai and a U.S. withdrawal from Vietnam. If other nationalists were necessary to South Vietnam's government and if Diem was adamant in his refusal to accept them, then Collins's recommendation was "extremely pertinent." However, Mansfield cautioned that if Collins's recommendation was implemented, the French would choose a successor government that could very well reach an accommodation with Ho and the Vietminh. That would not be in the U.S. national interest.[61]

The U.S. policy became one of supporting Diem until a more suitable candidate could be identified. Dulles made this point at a meeting with French General Paul Ely and Mendes-France on December 19, adding: "Congressional committees, particularly the two foreign affairs committees, led by Mansfield and [James] Richards (D-S.C.), were intensely interested in [the] problem and would have to be consulted. They both have strong feelings. Mansfield believes in Diem."[62]

Dulles cabled Collins on December 24: "Under present circumstances and unless situation in Free Viet-Nam clearly appears hopeless and rapidly disintegrating, we have no choice but [to] continue our aid [to] Viet-Nam and support of Diem. There [is] no other suitable leader known to us." So, at the end of 1954, Dulles reaffirmed U.S. support for Diem—support that was tenuous and influenced by Mansfield.[63]

CHAPTER 4

MANSFIELD BECOMES "THE DECIDING FACTOR" IN SAVING DIEM

The end of 1954 and the first part of 1955 were the busiest periods for Mansfield in defining America's effort at nation-building in South Vietnam. President Dwight Eisenhower called the situation "strange and inexplicable"; the *New York Times* described it as "weird."[1] J. Lawton Collins wrote a military friend in the early days of 1955 about how bizarre the situation was in South Vietnam:

> We have five separate armies . . . gambling houses and worse, all operated with the tacit approval of the Chief of State; two religious sects with their own private domains; a pope; an active underground Viet Minh; a Foreign Expeditionary Force; and an absent emperor who still remains the only legal source of power.[2]

Yet Collins was briefly won over by the pro-Diem arguments, writing Secretary of State John Foster Dulles on January 20: "on balance I believe that Diem's integrity, strong nationalism, tenacity, and spiritual qualities render him the best available Prime Minister to lead Vietnam in its struggle against Communism." Collins felt that Diem had improved in the last three months, and he admitted the lack of a better candidate. The ambassador continued to be aware of Diem's weaknesses, including his reliance on members of his family, and Collins bemoaned the Prime Minister's failure to appoint Phan Huy Quat to his cabinet. On balance, Collins gave South Vietnam an "even chance" of surviving free of communism. Dulles summoned Collins to Washington on January 22 and Collins recommended continued assistance to Diem's government.[3]

Dulles was even more optimistic, telling the Foreign Relations Committee that "the odds that were looked on at the beginning as being almost desperate odds today are reasonable odds."[4] Yet Mansfield was less hopeful than Collins or Dulles. He wrote Larry Allen in January 1955: "I realize that under the very best of circumstances, the odds will be against Ngo Dinh Diem but at least he seems to be holding fairly well with his ideals and seems at last to be taking hold among free Vietnam."[5]

Mansfield sounded more supportive in his first extant letter to Diem, sent the same month. In it, Mansfield referred to Diem's "outstanding leadership, adherence to principles and sound moral grounds, integrity, patriotism," and "great courage." Mansfield ended the letter by saying: "may God continue to guide you in the great task you have undertaken and may He continue to give you courage and understanding in the difficult days ahead."[6]

The Montanan's Indochinese involvement may have made him consider a career change. An unsigned note located in Eisenhower's papers and dated January 20, 1955, states: "<u>Montana</u> <u>Senator Mansfield</u> (D) very interested in <u>Far East Post</u>. Truman sent on special mission to China" (the writer must have been referring to the China Mission Report for Roosevelt). The author of the note considered the appointment of Mansfield feasible, jotting down specific precedents of people who had made similar moves. The precedents indicated that the author hoped to move Mansfield to a diplomatic post to open the Montana Senate seat for a possible Republican replacement.[7] If Mansfield orally had indicated that he desired a diplomatic appointment, his ambition would not be achieved for over two decades. In 1991 Mansfield wrote that he would not have accepted a Far Eastern post in 1955, as "the Senate was the achievement of my highest ambition."[8] It is possible that the tortuous 1952 campaign was fresh in Mansfield's mind, and he was exploring options to seeking reelection in 1958. Frank Valeo was surprised to hear of this note and said: "you know he wasn't an ordinary politician, Mansfield, by any means. He was more a scholarly type, somebody you would normally look for in the bureaucracy and not politics. There were a lot of things about politics he didn't like, but down deep it was in his blood, enough to keep him in office for a long time."[9]

THE VIETNAM LOBBY

Collins's transformation as a supporter of Diem was short-lived. In spring 1955, Mansfield and Collins renewed their struggle to influence the Eisenhower administration over retaining Diem. Events in January proved pivotal when the battle resumed and Diem's earlier lobbying efforts in the United States bore fruit. Mansfield was aided by a powerful group of men known as the "Vietnam Lobby."[10]

William Conrad Gibbons credited Joseph Kennedy and Cardinal Spellman with helping to persuade the administration to continue supporting Diem in 1955. Joseph Buttinger's January 1955 visit to Washington appeared central to getting the Vietnam Lobby rolling, but much of the evidence comes from Buttinger himself. *Ramparts* recounted a story from Buttinger that hints at the influence the men in the Vietnam Lobby exerted:

The telephone operator in the Chancery was used to such things, but even she blinked a little when Cardinal Spellman picked up the telephone and said: "Get me Joe Kennedy." When these two powerful men got on the line together, one winter afternoon in 1955, they settled quickly, as men of decision do, the steps that had to be taken to swing the wavering Eisenhower Administration solidly behind the young regime of Ngo Dinh Diem.[11]

Buttinger apparently met Colonel Edward Lansdale when he was sent to Vietnam by Leo Cherne to set up an office for the International Rescue Committee [IRC] that aided northern refugees in their migration south. There, Lansdale brought Buttinger into Diem's inner circle, and Buttinger became devoted to the Vietnamese leader. Harold Oram did public relations for the IRC and introduced Buttinger to Spellman in New York. Spellman, in turn, introduced Buttinger to Joseph Kennedy in the telephone call Buttinger recounted for *Ramparts*. Representative Walter Judd (R-Minn.) first told Mansfield about Buttinger, and Joseph Kennedy has been credited with arranging the January 1955 meeting between Mansfield and Buttinger. Oram called Mansfield on January 10, mentioned a recent meeting with Judd, and successfully encouraged the senator to meet with Buttinger. The Buttinger/Mansfield meeting likely took place on January 11. On his Washington visit, Buttinger also was introduced to Kenneth Young and both Young and Mansfield became crucial players to Diem's survival in April. John Kennedy was in California during Buttinger's visit, so Buttinger talked to Kennedy's administrative assistant, Ted Sorenson.[12]

Buttinger later recounted:

> Since I was unknown in Washington and by the American press, I looked for support in order to get access to people whom I wanted to convert to my views. This support I received largely from Cardinal Spellman and Joseph Kennedy. They arranged for me not only to get access to the State Department and many senators and other personalities in Washington, but also to meet editors of the *New York Times*, the *Herald Tribune, Newsweek, Time & Life*, the *New York Post* and others. On my first trip to Washington, where you [Mansfield] were the first person I met, I took along a paper I had written, explaining my views about the Diem regime, and the policy that has to be pursued if South Vietnam should be saved. This statement I sent to quite a few members of Congress and American newspapers and magazines. Without exaggeration I can say that this campaign was successful beyond my expectations. The *Times, Tribune, Newsweek* etc., after the meetings I had mentioned, all came out strongly in support of Diem.[13]

Buttinger's claim does not seem exaggerated. The *New York Times* wrote a pro-Diem editorial reflecting the views contained in Buttinger's paper two days after talking to him. On the very next day, the *New York Times* printed a guest editorial from Buttinger that heavily praised Diem and condemned the French. By February 1955 Buttinger wrote Mansfield that the press had changed its attitude and was writing more favorably about Diem. Buttinger contributed to the favorable reporting with pro-Diem articles for both the *Reporter* and the *New Republic*. Cherne penned a January piece for *Look*.[14]

Favorable reporting of Diem was not limited to the Buttinger visit. While one-sidedness became the norm in the American media, it was the most pronounced at Time-Life. Henry Luce, the founder, editor and publisher of *Time*, later served on the National Committee of American Friends of Vietnam (the formal organization that replaced the Vietnam Lobby in late 1955). *Time's* coverage of the Indochina situation featured Diem more and displayed a stronger partiality toward him than other media sources. Luce did not stop with *Time*; in early 1955, *Life* twice featured positive pictorials on Diem.[15]

The pro-Diem stance of secular publications was magnified in the Catholic press. When the Jesuit magazine *America* praised Buttinger's January visit, it suggested that the trip countered the negativism of Joseph Alsop's reporting in the *New York Herald Tribune* and that Buttinger and Cherne were "better serving the cause of freedom" than Alsop. *America* editorialized in March: "it is no secret that Ngo Dinh Diem is our man. If he fails it can only mean another setback for American prestige." In May the Jesuit magazine refuted British novelist Graham Greene's attacks on Diem, remarking that "oddly enough" this criticism of Diem was coming from an "English Catholic." Evidently Catholics were expected to support one of their own.[16]

Others encouraged this support of Diem. William Douglas, Cardinal Spellman and other Catholic leaders visited Vietnam in 1955. Spellman used his visit to deliver in person the first check from the Catholic Relief Agency. By 1958 Catholic charities contributed more than $38 million to Diem's government. The Vietnamese press made much of Spellman's influence on Diem. In March 1955, Collins found it necessary to caution Diem's brother, Bishop Thuc, not to have any further visits by Catholic dignitaries for at least six months. The perception of Diem's "Catholic government" hurt him with Vietnam's Buddhist majority.[17]

It was clear that America's ethnocentrism mandated support of a devout Catholic over any Buddhist alternative. Critics of Diem had no such advocates in the United States. Since the small amount of information available to Congress and the public favored Diem, pressure on the Eisenhower administration to continue its support for the Catholic Premier increased during the coming spring crisis. At the end of January, Mansfield and his powerful allies seemed to be in the driver's seat.

THE BATTLE OF THE SECTS

Dulles met with the Foreign Relations Committee on March 8, 1955, to report on a trip to Vietnam. The secretary of state considered Mansfield to be expert on Vietnam, seeking factual corroboration by saying, "you know the situation," and once asking Mansfield if he had questions because "Southeast Asia is your part of the world." Dulles also described the problem Diem faced with the sects, which had: "exercised virtual sovereign rights in the areas of the country which they occupy. They have their own armed forces, their own police. They collect the taxes, and operate quite independently of the central government."[18]

In January Diem had closed down the gambling casinos in Cholon, which deprived the Binh Xuyen of their major source of income. With the aid of Lansdale and the CIA, Diem managed to keep the sects under control and even appointed members of the Cao Dai and Hoa Hao to his cabinet. Gibbons speculated that the United States spent as much as $12 million in sect payments during March and April 1955. At the same time, Diem cut subsidies to the sect armies which forced many troops to desert in order to support their families. Alarmed by the defections, the three sects united. In the third week of March, when Diem refused a sect demand that he reorganize his government, the Cao Dai and Hoa Hao ministers left Diem's cabinet.[19] The three sects then formed the United Front of Nationalist Forces. On March 29, fighting broke out between Diem's forces and the Binh Xuyen. Collins cabled Washington that he did not think Diem could survive the crisis.[20]

When Diem ordered his chief of staff to occupy the Binh Xuyen-controlled police headquarters, French General Paul Ely countermanded the order and French tanks blocked any government action. The French wanted to avoid bloodshed because of the number of its citizens in Saigon, but some Americans suspected France did not want Diem to defeat the Binh Xuyen. Lansdale was among the suspicious; he believed that Collins sided with the French. Many in the U.S. government considered the Binh Xuyen gangsters who were the aggressors in this case. The French claimed to be unsure about who initiated hostilities. Further, the French grouped the Binh Xuyen with the Cao Dai and Hoa Hao, while Americans recognized the need to deal with the religious sects, but not the Binh Xuyen.[21]

On April 1, Dulles called Eisenhower and suggested that they meet to talk about Diem's crisis in Vietnam. The president saw no reason for a meeting since they were in agreement on the situation. Then, the conversation turned to Mansfield:

> The Sec. said Mansfield is devoted to Diem. He thinks we ought to talk with him about it to see what line he will take. The Pres. said he does not know that we

should. The Sec. might tell Collins that he is on the spot and will have to play it by ear. His telegram comes as a surprise because we bet pretty heavily on . . . [Diem]. The Sec. said he still thinks we should talk with Mansfield, and the Pres. indicated assent. The Sec. said though we should not be controlled by [Mansfield's] judgment.

Dulles requested an immediate meeting with Mansfield, saying that Vietnam was "getting progressively worse."[22] The Montanan recorded his recollections of that meeting: "I . . . read certain cables relative to the situation in Vietnam. In these cables, Collins seemed to imply that Diem was too rigid; his authority too personal; and that team-work in the cabinet was lacking." Collins recommended that Tran Van Do or Quat replace Diem. Baring that, Bao Dai needed to "exert some sort of pressure on Diem to broaden his government," or the Emperor should "return to Vietnam as President with the retention of Diem as Premier." Mansfield believed that Collins's "alternatives were worse than keeping Diem in office; that we did not have too much time; that if Diem quit or was overthrown, there would very likely be civil war; and that as a result that Ho Chi Minh could walk in and take the country without any difficulty."[23]

The secretary of state cabled Collins on April 4, expressing his confidence in the ambassador but indicating that Dulles and Eisenhower believed it was time to see if Diem could survive with French and U.S. logistical and moral support. Dulles complained: "I thought we felt when I was in Saigon that the decision to back Diem had gone to the point of no return and that either he had to succeed or else the whole business would be a failure." He once again reminded Collins of congressional opposition to a shift in leadership.[24]

On that same day, Henry Luce dealt a blow to Collins's and Diem's opponents. *Time* featured Diem on its cover and wrote a strongly pro-Diem piece. Diem was described as "a resilient, deeply religious Vietnamese nationalist." The three sects were portrayed as "an exotic consortium of religious fanatics, feudal warlords, uniformed hoodlums and racket bosses." Time-Life followed with a *Life* pictorial on Diem. Diem's Catholicism was emphasized, while one caption referred to the Hoa Hao as practicing "crude Buddhism," whatever that meant. If the cliché about a picture equaling 1,000 words has any validity, the feature in *Life* surely benefited the Diem public relations effort.[25]

Ely decided that he could not support Diem any longer, which caused Collins to cable Washington on April 7 that Diem would have to be replaced. Young once again shared Collins's cable with Mansfield, and he recorded the senator's reaction:

Ngo Dinh Diem and Ho Chi Minh are the only two national leaders in Viet-Nam. To eliminate Diem will leave the field to Ho. Diem has a lot of support in Central Viet-Nam and even in the southern part. We cannot ignore over a half million refugees who probably know of and support Diem.

Dropping Diem now would probably lead to chaos and disintegration. The Binh Xuyen would clearly be on top if we drop Diem. . . . The Cao Dai and the Hoa Hao are self-interested. The issue with them has to be met head on sooner or later. Diem has demonstrated that he understands this problem and will meet it. The French have stopped him. Even the second truce is probably undesirable. The government should be free to take care of the Binh Xuyen challenge or go down.

Mansfield saw no new evidence to prove him wrong. The administration needed to make clear the extent to which it was supporting Diem.[26]

On April 9, Collins sent a number of telegrams to Dulles pushing for Diem's removal. He believed that Diem's support came from the United States and France and that he had little support within Vietnam. The ambassador claimed that most nationalists felt that a Ngo family dictatorship was being formed. While Diem had support in the Catholic community, Catholics were not yet politically organized and represented less than 10 percent of the population. Thus, Diem could be forced out with little or no bloodshed.

Dulles replied to Collins on April 9 that he and Eisenhower were "disposed to back" Collins's decision, but the secretary of state was still cautious, questioning why nationalist leaders who were unacceptable several months ago now looked like better alternatives than Diem. Since Diem was perceived to be the American candidate reluctantly accepted by France, Dulles feared a loss of U.S. prestige: "we will be merely paying the bill and the French will be calling the tune." Dulles believed that Diem had not been given a fair chance by the French, who always referred to him as the "Diem experiment" or "American-backed Diem." Finally, Dulles warned Collins of congressional opposition, adding: "Mansfield, who is looked upon with great respect by his colleagues with reference to this matter, is adamantly opposed to abandonment of Diem under present circumstances." Collins responded on April 10:

I have no way of judging Mansfield's position *under present conditions.* These conditions are rather different than those existing when he visited Vietnam in September, 1954 when he feared military dictatorship as only alternative to Diem. As practical politicians, I would think that Mansfield and his colleagues on Senate committees would give considerable weight to the arguments I have advanced.

Clearly, the perception of Mansfield's clout continued to influence the administration's position and frustrate Collins.

The next day, Dulles spoke to his brother, Allen:

The Sec. said it looks like the rug is coming out from under . . . [Diem]. The Sec. said he talked with the boss on Saturday and he said you can't send [Collins] down here and have him work on it if his judgment is the way it is. We have to go along with it. The Sec. said he has sent 2-3 strong messages urging the other view-point but these have not shaken [Collins].

Both of the brothers wanted to retain Diem. Clearly, Eisenhower was leaning toward supporting the judgment of his commander in the field.[27]

Dulles became equivocal in his support for Diem, but continued to fear Mansfield's ability to cut U.S. aid. On the same day he talked with his brother, Dulles cabled Collins and agreed with the need to replace Diem. Yet on that same day, the secretary of state met with the French ambassador to advise that the administration would have difficulty obtaining appropriations from Congress if Diem were replaced. He added: "Senator Mansfield, who was very influential in these matters, felt strongly that Diem should be backed to the limit and that there was no adequate substitute for him."[28] Dulles expressed concern about Mansfield's position in a conversation with Walter George (D-Ga.), and the secretary of state had his assistant, Walter Robertson, talking to Mansfield about replacing Diem. On April 20, Dulles cabled Collins, concerned with the amount of financial support a replacement government could expect to receive:

> This is a matter not just for the Executive but for the Congress and those who have leadership in this matter, such as Mansfield in the Senate and Walter Judd in the House, are very strongly opposed to any shift. As things now stand, they would, I think, throw their influence, perhaps decisively, against backing any substitute that now seems in sight.[29]

Collins was recalled to Washington on April 17 and arrived four days later. Before departing Vietnam, Collins met with nationalist leaders Do, Quat, and others to discuss their opinions of a new government. All believed that Diem must be replaced. Collins also met with Diem, who agreed on the need for a coalition government, but rejected the names the French and Americans were suggesting, calling them "men from small opposition parties who actually repre-sent only a handful of people." In reality, Diem wanted a coalition government only if he were free to choose its members.[30]

On April 22, Pierre Millet, Minister of the French Embassy in Washington, visited Mansfield to discuss the possibility of replacing Diem. Millet pointed out that both Collins and Ely had arrived at the conclusion that Diem must be deposed. Mansfield recalled:

> Evidently, he was here to pressure me into changing my position on Diem but I still feel he is the only man who stands a chance and it is a long chance of keeping South Vietnam free. It appears to me that the Administration in discussing the Indo-China situation with the French Ambassador here *is in effect putting the major responsibility on me.* As to what our future decision will be vis-a-vis the retention or

overthrow of Diem I pointed out to Mr. Millet that the responsibility lay with the president and secretary of state and that it was up to them to assume that responsibility. All I could do was to make my views known.[31] [Emphasis added.]

Mansfield had successfully worked to obtain influence over decision making in South Vietnam, but once he obtained that leverage, he seemed uncomfortable with the power. Part of his discomfort came from his belief in executive responsibility in foreign affairs. Mansfield also was uneasy with the realization that in conversations with the French, the administration was holding him responsible for American support of Diem.

Collins spent Friday, April 22, with the Vietnam Working Group, headed by Young. The group was comprised of members of the State Department, Defense Department, and CIA. Collins left this meeting at midday to go to the White House for lunch with Eisenhower. Collins wanted Diem replaced with Quat and surprised Eisenhower when he claimed that Diem's weaknesses were personal, not caused by the French undercutting him. No decision was made at the luncheon except to continue studying the matter and "that Mansfield would be asked in." Young and the members of the Working Group proposed a number of alternatives, but Collins was adamant: Diem must be replaced. Young recalled, "we seemed to be confronted with a *fait accompli;* it appeared to be a Presidential decision that Diem had to go."[32]

On Monday morning, April 25, the Working Group reluctantly accepted the need for a change in government and decided on a provisional government with Quat as president, Do as vice president, and Diem as chairman of a consultative council until a national assembly could create a permanent government structure. Dulles and Collins conferred over lunch and the secretary of state accepted the compromise.[33]

A number of histories of this period conclude that Mansfield was eventually persuaded to accept this compromise, but there is little proof to support that claim. Robert Shaplen was the first to assert this idea in 1966. Shaplen did not cite any hard evidence, but based his book on personal experience and interviews. He interviewed Young extensively and Young may have given the impression that Mansfield came to accept the need to replace Diem. William Conrad Gibbons repeated the claim that Mansfield agreed on the need to replace Diem, but it is not clear from his footnote where he drew his conclusion. Gibbons cited Shaplen and it is likely that he accepted Shaplen's interpretation. A book by David Anderson also accepted Shaplen's view. Anderson cited Shaplen, but also suggested that Mansfield worked with the Dulles brothers, Collins, Young and Paul Sturm on several complicated telegrams to Paris and Saigon to carefully initiate the change in government. The telegrams themselves did not indicate that Mansfield was consulted. Lansdale's biographer, Cecil Currey, credited Mansfield and Robertson with persuading Dulles to accept a new government.

Curry cited that claim to the *Pentagon Papers*, but the *Pentagon Papers* did not mention Mansfield's involvement.[34]

If Mansfield accepted the need to replace Diem, it was not mentioned in the official record. Moreover, Mansfield's sense of executive prerogatives would have made him uncomfortable with the kind of direct intervention in executive decision making suggested by Anderson and others. Finally, Mansfield claimed he never favored deposing Diem, neither in 1955 nor 1963. When asked about Shaplen's claim in 1993, Mansfield responded: "I did not accept a compromise suggested to me by General Collins acting, I presume, with Secretary Dulles's support to replace Ngo Dinh Diem as Premier of South Vietnam." The senator emphatically added that "at no time, to anyone, did I or ever would [I] have accepted such a proposal."[35]

Members of the Vietnam Lobby remained active during this period. Returning to Washington in April to lobby for Diem, Buttinger met with Mansfield. Buttinger believed his April visit "contributed to a change of mood in Washington in favor of Diem." On April 25, Valeo and Wesley Fishel talked and Valeo wrote a memorandum to Mansfield summarizing the conversation.[36] Fishel had received a cable from Diem, who was so optimistic that he was proclaiming a general election in three months. This optimism stemmed from defections in the armies of the Binh Xuyen and Hoa Hao. Diem described "fanatical" morale in his army and expected a victory. Fishel believed that Diem's problems came from the French, and that Collins was "half-way on their side at the moment." Professor Fishel thought Diem would survive with continued American support and called Mansfield's recent remarks "timely and good."[37]

Collins met with the Senate Foreign Relations Far East Subcommittee and had a private meeting with Mansfield. These meetings confirmed that there would be great difficulty with Congress if Diem were forced out of office. Mansfield recorded Collins saying:

> after months of attempting to work with Ngo Dinh Diem he had reached the conclusion that the Premier did not have the executive ability to handle "strong-willed men," that he concerns himself with minor matter[s] and has not originated a single constructive idea since he came to power. Able men in the cabinet had been alienated by Diem's habit of going over their heads, preferring instead to rely on two brothers and a number of "yes men."
>
> There was no question of Diem's honesty, anti-communism and anti-colonialism, but he is so completely uncompromising, acetic [sic] and monastic that he cannot deal with realities like the Binh Xuyen and the Cao Dai.
>
> . . . Collins believes there are able modern-minded men like Quat who could sit around the table and talk with any of us, talk our language, or Tran Van Do who could handle the job of premier.[38]

Valeo remained in the hall when the senator met with Collins and remembered Mansfield telling him that "Collins really doesn't know much and he just bought what . . . [the French] handed to him."[39] Since Mansfield was not persuaded by Collins, it is hard to believe that he ever accepted the decision to phase Diem out.

While the decision to replace Diem was being made in Washington, Diem dismissed the Binh Xuyen head of police and fighting broke out on April 27. Collins met with the National Security Council the next day and told them that "Diem's number was up." Dulles said that Saigon had been instructed to "hold up action on our plan for replacing Diem." The battle "could either lead to Diem's utter overthrow or to his emergence from the disorder as a major hero." Eisenhower sided with his secretary of state, saying "that it was an absolute sine qua non of success that the Vietnamese National Army destroy the power of the Binh Xuyen."[40]

Diem knew of the decisions being made in Washington, which might have prompted him to act decisively. Lansdale and General John O'Daniel aided Diem in ways they would not have been able to had Collins been in Vietnam. Collins recalled that Lansdale was Allen Dulles's "own representative out there" and Lansdale was in a position to undercut Collins. Later, Collins called Lansdale's actions "mutiny."[41] Diem's forces were victorious. While Americans believed that the Binh Xuyen first attacked Diem's palace, the French and Bao Dai thought Diem the aggressor. Clearly, Diem had the most to gain from the confrontation.

Mansfield had prepared a pro-Diem speech for delivery on May 2, but he felt compelled to issue it as a long statement on Friday, April 29, before delivering it in the Senate that Monday. In the statement Mansfield charged a French-Bao Dai conspiracy and once again urged the cessation of all non-humanitarian aid if Diem were overthrown. He denounced Diem's opponents as "the black hand, the pirate, the mercenary, the racketeer and the witch doctor."[42] Mansfield's language and arguments provide further evidence that he had no intention of deserting Diem.

Others joined the pro-Diem chorus. On April 30, Young wrote Robertson:

> If Diem is forced out, Mansfield would have us stop all aid to Viet-Nam except of a humanitarian nature. Senators [William] Knowland and [Hubert] Humphrey have also backed Diem. A large number of members of the House Foreign Affairs Committee after hearing Collins have informed the Department that they would not favor the State Department withdrawing support from Diem. Collins met with the Far East Subcommittee of the Senate Foreign Relations Committee, separately with Senator Mansfield and with about a dozen of the House Committee. In fact there are going to be real difficulties on the Hill if Diem is forced out by what appears to be French-Bao Dai action.[43]

Columnist Joseph Alsop believed that Dulles was confronted with the joint demand that Diem be replaced from Collins and Ely. All he had to weigh against it was a cable from Lansdale urging the secretary of state to retain Diem. Then, Mansfield entered the fray and became the "deciding factor." In 1966, Alsop posited, everyone had "forgotten that Mansfield was a great friend of Diem's on account of the church." James Arnold concluded that Lansdale's role was "decisive" in Saigon. With Collins in Washington, Lansdale was able to wire Dulles selective information designed to convince the Eisenhower administration of the need to reaffirm its earlier support for Diem.[44] In reality, Diem needed both of these key members of the Vietnam Lobby, Mansfield in Washington and Lansdale in Saigon, plus a lot of luck to retain power.

Collins wrote that after Diem's bold action and success, "whatever influence I might have had either with the congressional committees I had briefed, or the State Department was quickly dissipated. Senator Mansfield announced that if Diem were replaced he would oppose any further military aid to Vietnam." On April 30, Dulles sent instructions for the Paris Embassy to inform Bao Dai of the likely termination of aid if Diem were replaced: "Senator Mansfield's statement is clear evidence [of] this position." The following day, the administration reversed itself and returned to its earlier support for Diem. Dulles wrote Collins on May 1: "it is no longer simply a question of whether and under what conditions Diem government should be altered. In the United States and the world at large Diem rightly or wrongly is a living symbol of Vietnamese nationalism struggling against French colonialism and corrupt backward elements." He added: "there is increasing congressional support for Senator Mansfield's views with which you are already familiar."[45] Mansfield won his battle with Collins to keep Diem, but Collins's predictions about Diem's limitations proved accurate.

Diem's victory over the sects led the American press and government to celebrate this "miracle." Mansfield's role in the miracle led to his being labeled the "Godfather" of Diem.[46]

Ely and the French were bitter about Mansfield's influence. France's clout in Vietnam weakened as the French were perceived to have supported the Binh Xuyen in the battle with Diem's troops. Ely's strong anti-Diem position in late April made it impossible for him to continue effectively in his position. The animosity of the Vietnamese toward the French increased. The underlying enmity between the French and U.S. personnel came to the surface after Diem's victory.[47]

The American elation over Diem's so-called miracle and the weakening of the French position gave Diem the power to defy the sects. The sects had always been fiercely anti-communist and might have been incorporated into Diem's government. Instead, the remnants of the sects later emerged as Vietcong. One Vietnamese nationalist wrote Mansfield that, like Diem, the sects were "staunchly anti-Communist," but unlike Diem, the sects had actually fought the

Vietminh: "while . . . [Diem] was for years wrapping around himself the mantle of splendid isolation . . . [the sects] were out there in the ricefields organizing and training peasants."[48]

Diem understood Mansfield's role in continued U.S. support, writing a warm letter to Mansfield on May 4: "if I am permitted to quote Confucius, the sage said: 'Only in winter do we know which trees are evergreen.' Figuratively speaking, you are the evergreen, as luxuriant as always; not only have you been the stark fighter for democracy and human rights but also the true friend of the Vietnamese people." Mansfield responded, "the present situation in Vietnam has brought comfort to me." The senator closed with "my prayers are with you on the long road ahead." In a commencement address to a Catholic college later in May, Mansfield said that with Diem, "a Vietnamese patriot of deep religious conviction, there is at least a glimmer of hope that communist totalitarianism in Viet Nam may be stopped and turned back."[49]

A number of people writing about the period credit Mansfield with saving Diem in late 1954 and 1955. Townsend Hoopes claimed that since Mansfield had the influence in the Senate to terminate aid if Diem were replaced, Dulles was forced to back Diem to keep Mansfield's support.[50] Fishel credits Mansfield's speeches and his reports from Indochina with persuading Congress and the administration to support Diem's government in 1954-1955.[51] Thomas Boettcher considered Mansfield's support for Diem the most crucial because "his views on Vietnam were accorded greater weight" due to his academic background.[52]

Certainly the State Department telegrams between Washington, Paris, and Saigon in the spring of 1955 confirm those opinions. There may never have been another time in the nation's history when the opinion of one member of Congress was given so much credence. This is all the more remarkable because as a first-term senator from a state with little political clout, Mansfield should not have been a powerful figure in the Senate. He became influential on this issue because of the perception that he was the resident expert on Indochina. This was possible only because he had little competition, even in the State Department.

One hint that Mansfield might have worried about his influence during this period came in a letter to Heath, when Mansfield wrote: "I certainly feel lots better with your encouragement and backing on my position relative to the situation in Vietnam."[53] Indeed, Mansfield's future comments showed pride in his accomplishment. In 1966, Mansfield recalled this incident for the Dulles Oral History Project: "it was because of the impetus given by some of us—I hope I'm being modest enough when I make this statement—in behalf of Diem that gave . . . [Diem] the initiative to wipe out the Binh Xuyen and to put down the Cao Dai and the Hoa Hao."[54] In 1990 Mansfield modestly claimed: "I hope I had some part in preventing the Eisenhower Administration from ending its support for Diem in 1955 but I do not know."[55]

Diem quickly consolidated his power after his victory over the sects. Before the confrontation with the Binh Xuyen, Bao Dai had ordered Diem to report to France and to change the army chief of staff. Diem refused. With the success of the national army against the Binh Xuyen, Bao Dai sent General Hinh to South Vietnam as his personal mediator. Diem would not allow Hinh in the country.[56] With U.S. approval, Diem announced that he would not abide by the Geneva Conference, which called for unification elections with the North in 1956. That decision made a second war inevitable.

Next, Diem scheduled October elections in the South where voters could choose between Bao Dai's monarchy or a Republic that Diem would head, again, with U.S. concurrence. In its coverage, *Time* contrasted Bao Dai, a "playboy Chief of State," to Diem, an "austere Premier," leaving little doubt which candidate they endorsed. Lansdale had Diem's ballot printed in red, the Asian color for happiness and good luck, and Bao Dai's in green, the color of misfortune and cuckolds. In an election filled with fraud, Diem was proclaimed the winner in October with 98.2 percent of the vote, winning 605,000 votes in Saigon where there were only 405,000 registered voters. The dishonesty in the election was largely ignored by the American press.[57]

On July 25, 1955 Mansfield endorsed Diem's repudiation of the 1956 elections, justifying his position because of "the repeated violations of the Geneva Agreement by the Viet Minh in refusing to allow refugees to go South, in aiding . . . the Pathet Lao, and the fact that South Viet Nam was not a signatory to the Geneva Agreements of 1954." Mansfield was supported by other voices from the Vietnam Lobby. *Time* scoffed at North Vietnam Premier Pham Van Dong's call for reunification as required in the Geneva agreement. Spellman had told the American Legion Convention that elections would mean "taps" for freedom in Vietnam.[58]

MANSFIELD'S THIRD VISIT TO INDOCHINA

The senator's third trip to Indochina in three years received less coverage than the previous two. After the excitement of the rebellion of the sects, the issue of Vietnam drew scant public attention in the United States during the remainder of the Eisenhower administration.

Valeo accompanied Mansfield and the two men again kept notes on their various conversations. Before arriving in Vietnam, Mansfield talked with Tillman and Peggy Durdin of the *New York Times* in Singapore. The Durdins thought that Diem was not acting quickly enough to base his rule on a broader popular base, that his land reform program was not satisfactory, and that Diem's family was involved in graft and corruption. Diem thought as a mandarin, feeling that "if the leader of the government is honest and correct in his behavior and dealings, then everything will be satisfactory beneath him." President Diem's authority came mainly from U.S. support and the Catholic refugees. The Durdins believed Diem's popularity was gradually improving, but he needed to develop support in the countryside.[59]

On August 18, 1955, Mansfield and Valeo had separate interviews with Diem and Ambassador G. Frederick Reinhardt that covered parallel subjects. Reinhardt was less optimistic than Diem. Diem talked of the current census both to prepare for future elections and to help with military conscription. Reinhardt indicated that the population feared the census because the Diem government seemed to be delaying elections and people thought the census would be used for conscription. Diem said that "for all practical purposes," the sects had been defeated, while Reinhardt thought the problem of the sects "was still a considerable way from being solved." Diem believed that communist strength in the country had been reduced 50 percent. "For the past year," Diem claimed, "he has had to deal essentially in negatives. The problem was one of consolidating his authority in rooting out the dissidents and of making the government a going concern. Now he felt Viet Nam was entering a new and a constructive phase."[60]

Colonel William Tudor shared Diem's optimism, telling Mansfield that Diem was "growing in strength and self-confidence." Tudor believed Diem's intolerance of strong leaders was understandable given his background with military leaders seeking power. Once Diem gained confidence in someone, Tudor claimed, the confidence was complete. The Colonel thought that "barring an invasion from the North, there is a good possibility that Diem can consolidate in the South." Tudor was less positive about the other Indochina states. He believed that the United States should avoid a deep commitment in Laos because it was militarily untenable. In Cambodia, the United States may have been "pushing too hard," causing "an anti-American reaction" and forcing Cambodia to "all-out neutralism."[61]

Mansfield and Valeo met with Prince Norodom Sihanouk for the first time on this trip, at Sihanouk's invitation. Sihanouk had been made king by the French in 1941, at age eighteen. He had resigned as king on March 2, 1955, and he was succeeded by his father, Norodom Suramarit. Suramarit had never been king. In Cambodia, the king was selected from a large group of royalty rather than passing from father to son. On September 11, in another fraud-filled election, Sihanouk led his followers to victory at the polls and became premier.[62]

Sihanouk was in the countryside during Mansfield's 1953 visit, but Mansfield visited with Suramarit in 1954. Penn Nouth was Sihanouk's "confidante and chief minister," and Valeo and Mansfield met with him in both 1953 and 1954. Mansfield had changed his tune about Cambodian neutrality since his 1953 report. Valeo recalled:

Sihanouk was favorably disposed towards the Mansfield Reports of 1953-55. He felt that the Senator, unlike most Americans with whom he was dealing in those years understood his situation, appreciated his concept of a genuinely independent Cambodia which as an oasis of peace in Indochina could remain outside the conflict in Vietnam. You will recall that this was the period in which the idea of neutrality by any country in the struggle with communism in Asia was treated with disdain by most proponents of U.S. foreign policy. In Sihanouk's ears, Mansfield sounded a different drum.[63]

French propaganda had painted a negative picture of Sihanouk as a "playboy king" who played the saxophone, chased women, and made and starred in his own motion pictures. While most Americans accepted the French view, Mansfield rejected it, seeing Sihanouk as a patriot and "astute nationalist leader." While admitting that Sihanouk might be "a little crazy," Valeo praised Sihanouk for gaining independence from France and protecting Cambodian sovereignty until 1970.[64] The 1955 meeting of Sihanouk and Mansfield was the beginning of a remarkable friendship that lasted into the 1980s.

In his report to the Foreign Relations Committee, Mansfield praised Diem and Sihanouk, sounding mildly optimistic: "There is today a reasonable chance of the survival and development of a free Viet Nam. It should be emphasized, however, that what has been gained during the past year is a chance not a guaranty. It has been gained largely through the dedication and courage of Ngo Dinh Diem." Mansfield advised continued U.S. financial support to Vietnam and showed a continued belief in the domino theory: "it should be forthcoming promptly for if totalitarian communism envelops the rest of Viet Nam, there is little likelihood that it will stop at the borders of that country." The plebiscite between Diem and Bao Dai occurred after Mansfield's trip, but the Montanan emphasized the need to elect a constituent assembly, quoting Diem's self-description as an "optimistic democrat." Yet Mansfield continued to justify the decision to defy the Geneva agreement's mandate for 1956 Vietnam unification elections. Mansfield was in the mainstream of congressional opinion; two other congressional study missions went to Vietnam that fall and also praised Diem's leadership.[65]

AMERICAN FRIENDS OF VIETNAM

After Mansfield's return from his third Indochina trip, members of the Vietnam Lobby formed a lobbying group—American Friends of Vietnam (AFV)—to support Diem and Vietnam. AFV was a more public organization than Fishel's informal Vietnam Lobby in which Mansfield had been active during spring 1955. AFV also was successful in getting American media to focus on Diem's virtues while ignoring his regime's considerable shortcomings.

AFV's origins are hazy, but Cherne and Buttinger, both leaders in the IRC, were among the founders, and the two groups were interrelated. AFV portrayed itself as "a non-partisan group organized in support of a free and democratic Republic of Vietnam." Gibbons speculates that AFV was directly or indirectly supported by the U.S. government. Mansfield and John Kennedy have been listed as "charter members" and even organizers of the lobbying group. The organization was attractive to liberals and conservatives alike. Listed in various sources as members of AFV are John Foster Dulles; Judd; Justice Douglas; Dr. Fishel; Senators Lyndon Johnson (D-Texas), Knowland (R-Calif.), Humphrey (D-Minn.), Karl Mundt (R-S.D.); House Majority Leader John McCormack (D-Mass.); Representative Eugene McCarthy (D-Minn.); Luce; historian Arthur Schlesinger Jr.; and Governor Christian Herter (R-Mass.), who would later replace Dulles as secretary of state. In 1956 AFV claimed five senators and thirty-two representatives in its membership. AFV's members were so prominent that they were often called upon by journalists writing about Vietnam, which contributed to the one-sided reporting throughout the 1950s.[66]

Mansfield denies formally belonging to AFV, but there is much evidence linking him to the organization. The strongest evidence is that Mansfield was listed on AFV letterhead as a member of the National Committee several times in the late 1950s and early 1960s. In 1961 Mansfield wrote an introduction to a book edited by Fishel and published by AFV which blatantly exaggerated the accomplishments of Diem and South Vietnam.[67]

AFV's efforts on behalf of Diem were pervasive and, apparently, highly effective. Just before the formation of AFV, the Newcomb-Oram agency signed a contract to represent the Diem government, and the public relations firm actively represented the Diem government in the United States from 1955-1961. Elliot Newcomb served on AFV's Executive Committee and Harold Oram on the National Committee. One Vietnamese dissident wrote Mansfield that Diem's "high-handed methods" were ignored in the United States because Diem "has at his disposal a public relations apparatus financed with American aid money and wholly devoted to his cause, whereas the opposition is virtually without resources, financial or otherwise."[68]

One example of AFV's efforts can be found in Graham Greene's 1955 novel about Vietnam, *The Quiet American*. Joseph Mankiewicz, a member of AFV's National Committee, purchased the film rights, wrote the screen play, directed the movie in Saigon, and released it in 1958. The movie became a propaganda piece for AFV. Where the novel had warned of tragic consequences if the United States replaced France in Vietnam, the film argued that only America could save Vietnam from colonialism and communism. The *New York Times* described the American character from Greene's novel as "a rather officious diplomatic type, meddling much more than was healthy in Vietnamese politics" and wrote that Mankiewicz removed "the anti-American venom" from the story. In its place,

Mankiewicz had World War II hero Audie Murphy playing an idealistic young American who was killed by the communists he was opposing. Greene was reported to be incensed with the changes to his novel. While Diem was not mentioned by name in the movie, he was discussed in the abstract, in almost mystical terms, and was praised in the film's credits.[69]

AFV's membership included influential members of the media besides Luce, making it unlikely that Diem's shortcomings would be explored by the American press. Malcolm Muir Jr., whose father published *Newsweek,* was a member of AFV's National Committee, as was Walter Annenberg who headed the *Philadelphia Inquirer.* Other important media people serving on AFV's National Committee included Herbert Bayard Swope, Max Lerner, William Randolph Hearst Jr., Sol Sanders, and Norbert Muhlen. With that kind of support in the fourth estate, it is easy to see why Diem was treated so well by the U.S. media. Members of AFV and the U.S. government-funded Michigan State University project, hired by the U.S. government to aid the Diem government, had little difficulty getting pro-Diem propaganda published during the 1950s.

The media's infatuation with Diem even bolstered the support of former critics. Ambassador Heath joined *America* in attacking Joseph Alsop for not jumping on the Diem bandwagon, writing Mansfield: "I am utterly unimpressed by Joe Alsop's criticism of Diem." Mansfield responded prophetically: "I hope that on the basis of the strength and political savvy shown by Diem to date that . . . [Joseph and Stewart Alsop] and other American correspondents will be able to see the picture in a more even light." Joe Alsop did see the light. In an article for the *New Yorker* in June 1955, he was not as effusive about Diem as the majority of the U.S. media but, nonetheless, for the first time he was not critical. James Aronson reported that Buttinger, Spellman, and Lansdale all helped to persuade Alsop to become a proponent of Diem and the American commitment. It did not hurt Alsop's conversion that his boss, Whitelaw Reid, the editor and publisher of the *New York Herald Tribune,* became a member of AFV's National Committee. Few in the U.S. media failed to jump on the bandwagon after Diem's "miracle."[70]

Many of Mansfield's friends shared the nation's enthusiasm for Diem. John Kennedy was the principal speaker at an AFV symposium in 1956 and Chester Bowles was a keynote speaker for AFV in 1959. Kennedy gave a speech containing cold war views similar to those of Mansfield, including belief in the domino theory and opposition to Vietnamese unification elections. The future president's rhetoric would have made disengagement difficult after his 1960 election; he hyperbolically claimed: "Vietnam represents the cornerstone of the Free World in Southeast Asia, the keystone to the arch, the finger in the dike," and "if we are not the parents of little Vietnam, then surely we are the godparents." In his AFV address, Kennedy referred to Mansfield as "a great friend of Vietnam" and quoted Diem's letter to Mansfield that compared the Montanan to the evergreen. Kennedy again quoted the evergreen metaphor in the Vietnam portion of the book he wrote to explain his views prior to his 1960 presidential bid.[71]

By the early 1960s, AFV ceased to be influential and lost many important members due to disenchantment with Diem. Buttinger, for example, began to think he had misjudged Diem after a 1958 visit to South Vietnam. Even so, AFV would reemerge after Diem's assassination with Fishel as its chairman, and it became a proponent of U.S. escalation.[72]

CONCLUSION TO THE EARLY YEARS

The major accomplishment of Mansfield's three 1950s missions to Vietnam was ongoing U.S. support for Diem. While Mansfield's interest in Vietnam continued, he would never again exert the influence on administration policy that he had from October 1954 through April 1955. John Montgomery concluded that it is "unquestionable that the Senator's intervention was an essential element" in keeping Diem in power.[73] Mansfield found the Vietnamese nationalist he sought, and he helped gain and keep Eisenhower administration support for Diem. It is easy to criticize that accomplishment with hindsight, but even with the predictable problems caused by his minority religion, Diem may have been the best option in 1955 *if the U.S. had to make a choice.*[74]

Mansfield justified his position in a May 1955 response to Heath: "I feel that if Diem goes down, the way will be open to civil war and chaos and the road paved for Ho Chi Minh to walk right into all of Vietnam and perhaps eventually elsewhere." Heath had written Mansfield that "at the time I left Saigon there was no alternative to Diem in sight; he has very sizable defects, but his assets outweigh them."[75] When asked if Diem was the best alternative, Valeo responded: "given the Administration's determination to oppose Ho Chi Minh, yes. Certainly, I knew of no other realistic possibility nor was anyone offering greater promise brought to Mansfield's attention in the course of those early missions."[76]

Dulles was never able to find an alternative to Diem; he told French Premier Pierre Mendes-France in December 1954: "the ideal Vietnamese prime minister is either dead or not yet born." In truth, the United States never found a better candidate. As early as the Truman administration, Secretary of State Dean Acheson called Vietnamese leaders "inefficient and unwilling to assume the responsibilities of government."[77]

In April 1962 Averill Harriman said to President Kennedy that "while he thought that Diem was a losing horse in the long run, he did not think we should actively work against him, because there was nobody to replace him." On the eve of the coup to replace Diem, Secretary of Defense Robert McNamara believed the coup "was not viable" because of the lack of an alternative. John McCone, director of the CIA, doubted that "alternative leadership existed in Vietnam." That sentiment was shared by former U.S. ambassador to South Vietnam, Eldridge Durbrow. U. Alexis Johnson thought the 1963 coup a poor idea "because I could see no one better equipped to lead the country." William Trueheart, deputy chief to the U.S. Embassy in Saigon at the time of the Diem coup, favored the coup but admitted that no better leader was available.[78] The men who followed Diem failed.

Buttinger believed that Diem "could have been replaced only by a regime of former collaborators with Colonialism" and such a regime would have forced more people into the communist camp. Based on a "close personal relationship," Buttinger thought "that contrary to the picture painted of [Diem] in most of the American and international press, he was not a weak, undecided and politically inexperienced man, but rather the opposite." Lansdale agreed that Diem was effective in 1954-55. Years later, Young and Robertson continued to believe that the decision to stick with Diem was the correct one in 1955. U. Alexis Johnson suggested that no one expected South Vietnam to survive after Geneva, but because of Diem, a "nationalist zealot of considerable political skill," South Vietnam was able to survive during the 1950s.[79] Journalist Robert Shaplen believed Diem was "the right man in the right place at the right time" in 1954-55. Dean Rusk estimated that Diem had "only 1 chance in 100 of making a go of it" in 1954-55, and yet Diem did succeed in the early period.[80]

Thus, a more fundamental question is, should the United States have made the choice at all? A Swiss journalist concluded in 1955: "the Nationalists can never rid themselves of a secret inferiority complex, the feeling that at bottom the Vietminh has a more legitimate claim to the prestige of liberator." In justifying his decision to replace Diem in early April, Collins cabled Dulles: "there is no proper grass roots support of any leader in Viet Nam, leaving aside Ho Chi Minh." Walter Judd, Mansfield's House ally, wrote to David Anderson many years later: "our choice was between a 'bad' government that was friendly, and a worse government that was *hostile* to us."[81]

Had Mansfield and others not felt compelled to create an artificial nationalist, the second Indochina war could have been avoided. Yet the cold war assumptions of Mansfield and America's political leaders found a communist government in South Vietnam unacceptable. The decision to commit to Diem and deny the promised 1956 elections made the second Indochina war inevitable. What Mansfield failed to anticipate was that once the United States committed to preserve a non-communist South Vietnam, the momentum of that commitment would prove difficult to curb. Mansfield played a vital role in that initial commitment, and he spent the next twenty years fighting to reign in the consequences of that commitment.

Part II

1956-1963

Senate Leadership Brings Decreased Indochina Influence

CHAPTER 5

THE WARMING OF A
COLD WARRIOR

M ansfield never again achieved the influence over Indochina policy that he wielded in the spring of 1955. During the remainder of the Eisenhower administration, the senator started to moderate his cold war vision. By the end of the decade, Mansfield had developed serious doubts about Ngo Dinh Diem, but his sense of loyalty kept him from ever publicly expressing his skepticism. However, Mansfield did turn against the U.S. aid program to Diem's government.

MANSFIELD'S HARPER'S ARTICLE

In January of 1956 Mansfield was still solidly behind Diem and the American commitment to him. The senator wrote Diem in January, thanking him for an "exquisite table cloth and napkins" that President Diem had sent the Mansfields for Christmas. Mansfield added: "when grace is said over it, it will be with a special prayer that your country will continue to advance toward complete freedom and that you will continue in good health so that you may contribute of your abilities to that end."[1]

Mansfield joined others in American Friends of Vietnam (AFV) and wrote a pro-Diem article for *Harper's Magazine* on the progress that was being made in Vietnam. In the issue that carried Mansfield's article, *Harper's* claimed:

> Few Americans realize that Senator Mike Mansfield of Montana is widely regarded abroad as the chief architect of U.S. foreign policy for Southeast Asia. The French, especially, blame him for putting Diem at the head of the Viet Nam government in Indochina—and keeping him there, in the teeth of French intrigue, propaganda, and slander.[2]

For the first time, Mansfield discussed the plebiscite between Diem and Bao Dai. Even though Mansfield must have known of the dishonesty in the election, he merely wrote that Diem received "almost all" of the votes.[3] Mansfield's comparison of Diem's power in the South with Ho's in the North showed his ethnocentrism: "Diem's star is likely to remain in the ascendancy and that of Ho Chi Minh to fade—because Diem is following a course which more closely meets the needs and aspirations of the Vietnamese people." The senator was considerably more optimistic in this more public forum than he had been in his report to the Foreign Relations Committee three months earlier. He admitted many difficulties were ahead, but concluded that while United States involvement in the area had decreased, "the prospects for success" had increased.

The Montanan justified the lack of reunification elections:

> The all-important questions are: What kind, and when? Elections tend to degenerate into mere ritual when the conditions for a free choice are lacking or when preparations are inadequate.
>
> He [Diem] favors and will in all probability advocate them—if and when the ironclad Communist dictatorship in north Viet Nam has been modified. Meanwhile he does not regard the date set by the 1954 Geneva Conference as binding on his government. He was not consulted on the agreement, and he denounced it as soon as its terms were revealed. Diem can afford to wait; Ho cannot.[4]

Mansfield's precondition that the North's government be "modified" precluded elections. Modifying his government was not part of the deal Ho had struck at Geneva.

The New Republic later called Mansfield's writing for Harper's "totally uncritical" and linked the piece with the propaganda that AFV put out in the late 1950s.[5] Yet at the time it generated a warm letter from Chester Bowles who called it "excellent and encouraging." Bowles's letter illustrated the hypocrisy of the American position on elections insofar as most in the United States were not concerned with self-determination, but rather with preserving an anti-communist South Vietnam.

> But could Diem hope to win a really free nation-wide election? How could the terms of the election be legitimately arranged to at least provide a free Vietnam south of the 17th parallel?
>
> If they [Moscow and Beijing] are smart enough to appear to favor *really free elections* wouldn't we be faced with the following choices: Send in the Marines, drop a few tactical A bombs, or retreat?[6]

Mansfield's reply showed his vision for Diem and Vietnam—a vision perceptive of Ho's response, but in hindsight, too optimistic about Diem.

> If they do go to war, it is more likely that Ho Chi Minh will say something like this: "Our brethren in the south are oppressed and must arise against their oppressors and overthrow them." It may be expected, then, that there will be insurrections in the

south by Viet Minh underground groups, probably in concert with the remnants of the sects but without overt northern intervention. These should be controllable by the National Army. All the while, *Diem's position should be growing stronger, always provided of course his leadership continues to be effective.* At some point Diem should be in a position of sufficient strength to demand negotiations for free elections. It remains to be seen, then, what the Viet Minh reaction will be.[7] [Emphasis added.]

The senator expected Diem to remain "effective," but his letter indicates that he knew the American experiment in Vietnam would fail if Diem was not successful.

Bowles, Mansfield, and the Eisenhower administration knew that Ho and the communists were sure to win the elections called for in the Geneva Accords. Denial of the elections was essential to preserve South Vietnam as an American ally. Even though South Vietnam and the United States did not sign the Geneva agreement, the elections were legally binding. The Eisenhower administration had pledged not to use force to disturb the agreement.[8]

Mansfield played a role in the denial of the 1956 elections, but like many of his cold war positions of the 1950s, he later regretted that role. In 1967 Mansfield admitted:

> I knew that under that Agreement there was supposed to be an election two years later and I urged that the election not be held. The State Department at that time felt the same way and gave encouragement to Ngo Dinh Diem to oppose putting that part of the Geneva Agreements into effect.[9]

MANSFIELD RECEIVES CONFLICTING REPORTS ON DIEM

Mansfield's *Harper's* article generated a letter from Hilaire du Berrier, a native North Dakotan. Du Berrier spent ten years in China and Indochina and was employed for a time by the Office of Strategic Services. He wrote several articles and a book about Vietnam. He met Mansfield on a lobbying trip for Diem in April 1955, when he worked for Diem's brother, Luyen. William Langer (R-N.D.) reintroduced du Berrier to Mansfield in a 1956 letter, saying, "Mr. du Berrier has been a friend of mine for years and is unusually reliable."[10] Du Berrier's response to Mansfield's *Harpers'* article was quite different from Bowles' reply:

> Due to your position as the recognized American senator interested in South Viet Nam, your article had a singular effect abroad. Coming as it did at a time when the edifice was crumbling, when everyone else was beginning to face the fact that Diem had no popular support and his elections were rigged, it was regarded as a declaration of policy. Anti-Diem nationalists . . . figured, if America was not

going to permit them to have a man of their own choosing,—if America was determined to force Diem on them at all costs and sink with him if necessary, there was
no other way of getting rid of him than by following into the Red-sponsored "neutralist camp."

But now, isn't there something we can do about Diem? You have no idea to
what extent Europe and the world look to you as the author of our policy vis-a-vis
Diem and count on you to get all of us out of it.[11]

Du Berrier wrote an anti-Diem letter to Hubert Humphrey (D-Minn.), too,
and Humphrey passed it on to Mansfield, asking: "I thought you might be interested in the attached letter. After you have read it, would you mind giving me
your impressions and observations. Is this something that we ought to talk to the
State Department about?"[12] No response to Humphrey was located, but
Mansfield's response to du Berrier showed his continuing optimism.

> There are tremendous difficulties still inherent in the Viet Namese situation,
> but when I think . . . of the strides which have been made . . . I cannot help but be
> impressed by the progress made by this remarkable man. It is true that he may be
> stubborn and obdurate, that he may not listen to counsel; but it is a fact that a free
> Viet Nam exists at the present time and that in large part this free entity is the
> result of the efforts by Mr. Diem.[13]

Mansfield received other negative reports on Diem by 1956. The senator and
Frank Valeo found a French article attacking Diem's rule and had it translated. A
critical article from the *Economist* remains in Mansfield's papers, and Mansfield
continued to receive correspondence from South Vietnamese dissidents.[14] In
1956 Mansfield clearly was not persuaded by the negative reports he was hearing
about his friend.

Part of that reason may have been that Mansfield was also hearing positive
things about Diem. Dr. Thomas Dooley, who opened a medical mission in Laos
in 1956, wrote good reports about Diem to Mansfield. Diem helped Dooley and
his staff get their equipment to Laos so they could begin their work. Mansfield
and Dooley corresponded until 1958, but they never met.[15]

Dulles, too, praised Diem, telling the Senate Foreign Relations Committee on
March 23, 1956 that Diem had done a "wonderful job" with U.S. help. The secretary of state continued to credit Mansfield with helping the administration make
the right decision in South Vietnam during the Battle of the Sects.[16]

When Diem survived an unsuccessful assassination attempt in early 1957,
Mansfield conveyed his personal relief and support for the leader: "I am thankful
that God in his wisdom spared you. You have made a magnificent record in weld-
ing together the various elements and sections of your country. It is to be
devoutly hoped that you will have many long years ahead." Diem responded: "I

have appreciated for a long time the heart-warming and effective manner in which you have supported my efforts to make of my country a sturdy, democratic state. Vietnam has had no more far-sighted and understanding friend than you."[17]

DIEM'S 1957 VISIT TO THE UNITED STATES

Ngo Dinh Nhu, Diem's brother, visited the United States in April 1957, to lay the groundwork for a visit by Diem. Nhu talked to the Eisenhower administration about a secret plan to get 2,000,000 North Vietnamese to move south. Nhu justified an increase in the South's armed forces for an eventual invasion of the North and admitted that it would not be desirable "to send American troops into Vietnam since this would be, after all, a civil war." Diem had requested that Nhu meet with Mansfield, but no record of such a meeting was located. In 1993, Mansfield did not recall meeting with either Nhu or Diem in 1957.[18]

In May Diem was enthusiastically received in the United States. Diem was greeted at the airport by President Eisenhower, who loaned him his personal airplane for his American visit. Eisenhower called Diem the "miracle man" of Asia. Diem's reception was considered royal. He spoke to a joint session of Congress and the National Press Club, was honored by American Friends of Vietnam, had a reception with the Council on Foreign Relations, had breakfast and a private mass with Cardinal Spellman, had a private luncheon with John D. Rockefeller, attended a banquet in his honor hosted by Time-Life's Henry Luce, received an honorary degree from Michigan State University, and was feted with a parade up Broadway to City Hall in New York.[19]

In addition to these social occasions, President Diem met with Eisenhower and members of the State Department. Diem planned to introduce universal conscription to increase the size of his military, and he sought additional American aid to help achieve that aim. The South Vietnamese leader asserted that his 150,000-member military had been the principle deterrent to an armed attack from the North. Several times during the meeting Diem indicated the likelihood of an invasion from the North, although he also talked of a potential guerrilla war. Diem said that he was willing to consider the use of tactical nuclear weapons in his country if the North invaded. He also claimed that he would need to increase the size of his military if the North chose a guerrilla war. Of course, American money was necessary for such a build-up.

Diem also sought American help to build a highway system in the plateau area to protect against an invasion from Laos. Although Eisenhower jokingly reminded Diem of the old adage that roads were a "golden bridge for your enemies," U.S. aid did help build Diem's project.[20]

The American press was effusive in its praise of South Vietnam's leader during his American visit. The *New York Herald Tribune* used the headline, "Miracle

Maker From Asia" to define Diem, and the *New York Times* said that Thomas Jefferson "would have no quarrel" with Diem's comments to Congress. *Life* went even further, justifying Diem's refusal to hold the unification elections because of the likelihood of a Ho victory: "Diem saved his people from this agonizing prospect simply by refusing to permit the plebiscite and thereby he avoided national suicide." American ethnocentrism was apparent as most press reports and the administration press release referred to Diem as being a "deeply religious man."[21] It is doubtful that a devout Buddhist could have captured the American imagination in the same way this Catholic Christian did. Mansfield joined in the praise: "Diem is not only the savior of his own country, but in my opinion he is the savior of all Southeast Asia." The Senator gave "the chief credit" in defeating communism in Southeast Asia to "the determination, the courage, the incorruptibility, and the integrity of President Diem."[22]

Diem's 1957 visit marked the pinnacle of his popularity in the United States. While there was still little American criticism of Diem, Mansfield began to receive more negative reports. Huynh Sanh Thong, a South Vietnamese dissident that Mansfield had met in 1956, wrote of the long arm of the Diem government, which had managed to get Huynh fired from two jobs in the United States, a story later confirmed by the *New Republic*. Huynh bitterly complained that Diem's opponents were not being heard in the United States because of the influence of AFV. Valeo attached a note to the letter, advising: "I don't think this should be answered," and apparently it was not.[23]

At the time of Diem's visit, Mansfield also received a letter from Norman Thomas, the well-known American Socialist who had been a member of AFV, but had resigned. Thomas was critical of the Diem regime and suggested that Mansfield was "in a position perhaps to do something about it." As Thomas wrote Mansfield: "I know that your position is one of positive support of democracy against fascist as well as communist forms of oppression. I should not expect Viet Nam to be a perfect democracy. We have hardly got that far ourselves under far more favorable conditions." Mansfield apparently did not respond to Thomas's 1957 letter and Thomas's defection from Diem's camp did not cause Mansfield to try to "do something" about Diem's failures[24]

MANSFIELD'S 1958 REELECTION

Mansfield was not seriously challenged for reelection in 1958.[25] Since the 1940s, when the "China Mike" label was pinned on Mansfield, he had been sensitive to charges that he spent too much time on foreign affairs. In 1956 he turned down a request from Eisenhower and Dulles to attend the London Conference to discuss the Suez crisis. Mansfield wrote Dulles that he would have to attend the Chicago convention as a Montana delegate: "it is important that I look after my state's interests at the Convention. I have in the past been subjected to criticism within my own state that I spend too much time on foreign affairs and not enough on the affairs of Montana. This happens to be an inaccurate and unjust criticism."[26]

With some assistance from Hilaire du Berrier, Mansfield's Republican opponent tried to make the senator's support for Diem an issue in the campaign. In 1958 du Berrier published a rare anti-Diem piece in *American Mercury*. Du Berrier called South Vietnam a police state and called AFV a "paid propaganda agency" that misled the American public. Before the article was published, du Berrier requested a meeting with Mansfield, but the senator declined. Du Berrier then wrote to a number of Montana newspapers trying to influence the Montana election: "You will understand my very great fear indeed that you Republicans out there wont [sic] find a way to get Mike Mansfield back to teaching school where, aside from doing the sort of deformation job on the minds of his pupils that Mangbetu Africans do to their skulls, he will be comparatively harmless." He claimed that Mansfield's "stubborn insistence on forcing Ngo dinh (sic) Diem down the throats of a nation that does not and never did want him is costing us all of Southeast Asia."

Mansfield was defensive about the Diem issue in 1958, once responding to a Montana editor, "frankly, I do not know what is behind the attack on me, but I certainly have no apologies to make whatsoever for my part in keeping South Vietnam away from the communists." The Diem issue was not persuasive in the 1958 election; Mansfield won in a landslide, carrying all fifty-six counties and breaking Burton K. Wheeler's 1940 record for margin of victory in Montana by defeating his Republican opponent by more than 117,000 votes.[27]

THE END OF THE MYTH OF DIEM'S "MIRACLE"

Diem not so modestly credited his so-called "miracle" to God, "of whose invisible hand [Diem] was but an instrument."[28] The myth in the United States was that Diem had created a miracle in Vietnam. While there was progress for several years, many of the advances were due to massive U.S. aid rather than Diem's leadership. After Diem refused to hold the reunification elections, virtually no one in the United States thought that a communist insurgency could succeed in the South. Americans like Mansfield, who understood the situation in Vietnam, chose to emphasize Diem's accomplishments and downplay his shortcomings. Diem's greatest asset was the perception of his integrity, and Mansfield contributed greatly to establishing that reputation.

The American press and government continued to deny the evidence of South Vietnam's failures and told the public that Diem was creating a miracle. Wilfred Burchett was one of the few critically reporting on Diem in his writings for the

National Guardian. When Burchett's editor, James Aronson, sent the proofs of these stories to the wire services and major dailies, "they were ignored." One of the true "miracles" of Diem was his successful propaganda effort spearheaded in the United States by AFV. The foreign press was much less generous in its appraisal of Diem's accomplishments. Journalist Ellen Hammer claimed that Diem "had never been popular, except in the United States."[29]

Mansfield and other members of Congress, the administration, and most of the American press ignored signs of Diem's failure. Most American press reports praised Diem's agrarian reform, but South Vietnam's land reform effort was minimal, and largely focused on legalizing the changes made by the Vietminh in areas they had controlled. Diem's officials returned land to landlords who had lost it during the first war and rarely sided with peasants in landlord-tenant disputes. The land reform made through 1956 was considered a beginning by American officials, but was never expanded by the Diem regime. Reform largely favored the northern Catholics, further exacerbating religious tensions. American ethnocentrism combined with the compulsion to keep South Vietnam as an anti-communist bastion in the cold war blinded Americans to the anger festering among South Vietnamese Buddhists. Forced resettlement was also practiced by Saigon and was predictably unpopular with the peasants. Resentment of the government in the South was building, and Diem made little effort to win over his compatriots. Industrial growth in the South was also slower than that in the North.

Diem spoke of democracy, but his actions were antithetical to its implementation. In many ways, the Ngos were a family oligarchy that copied the communists they denounced. One American who spent six months in South Vietnam commented on how regimented life was under Diem: "if the Communists ever take over this country, there will be very little that they will have to change."[30] South Vietnam became a one-party (Can Lao) state that did not tolerate dissent, had secret police, and used concentration or reeducation camps. When eighteen leading non-communist opposition leaders, including Phan Huy Quat, Tran Van Do, and elements of the Cao Dai and Hoa Hao, issued the Caravelle Manifesto in April 1960, no newspaper in South Vietnam printed it for fear of reprisal.[31] The signers of the Caravelle Manifesto were eventually jailed, and some remained there without trial until the overthrow of Diem in 1963. The U.S. press ignored the Manifesto. Wesley Fishel wrote to Mansfield about the Manifesto, but Mansfield, too, chose to ignore it.[32] People sympathetic to the Manifesto were likely involved in an unsuccessful 1960 coup against Diem. Many Vietnamese who were denied political participation in the South, even as the loyal opposition, eventually joined the Vietcong.

South Vietnamese elections continued to be a mockery. Village autonomy had been a political tradition since the fifteenth century through the election of village councils. The Diem regime changed that, appointing officials in their place to maximize personal control. Diem often appointed northern Catholics to these posts—outsiders who were viewed as carpetbaggers and who were often involved with graft.

The U.S. State Department was well aware of corruption in South Vietnam's national elections. The Diem government deleted the names of opponents from ballots and used threats and intimidation to control the opposition.[33] In the 1959 election, for example, Dr. Phan Quang Dan, Diem's best known critic, was easily elected to the national assembly. The Diem regime trumped up charges of electoral fraud to keep Phan and the one other non-Can Lao candidate from taking their seats. By 1960 Diem's support came from his own bureaucracy and the refugees from the North.[34] The only surprising aspect is that the Vietminh waited so long after the thwarted reunification elections to resume the conflict.

Life in the North also was hard. Vital industry and transportation were destroyed in the war with France and the loss of trade with the South deprived the North of much of its traditional source of rice. Communist land reform led to atrocities and thousands of deaths. There was also repression of intellectuals. Hanoi's considerable problems delayed the beginning of the second Indochina war. Unlike Diem, however, Ho learned from his mistakes and made necessary adjustments.

Diem had been quite successful in purging former Vietminh who had stayed behind legally after the division of the country. In doing so, however, many innocent peasants were killed or imprisoned and the population was further antagonized by the Saigon government. The initiative to begin the second phase of the war thus came from the cadres in the South, and Hanoi was reluctantly forced to accept the decision. Beginning in 1957 the Vietminh had been concentrating on political goals and the assassination of selected officials, killing effective government officials but leaving the ineffective in place. In the spring of 1959, the armed rebellion resumed with America as the foreign presence. Diem became known as "My Diem," "My" meaning United States in Vietnamese.

Diem's policies had pushed enough peasants into the Vietminh camp that they controlled most of the countryside by the end of the year, and 85 percent of the population was rural. The level of the insurgency not only caught U.S. and South Vietnamese officials by surprise, it exceeded the degree of combat desired by Hanoi. Most Americans stubbornly clung to the belief that the rebel activity was a desperate communist attempt to overcome the successes of the Diem government.[35]

THE AID PROGRAM AND A COOLING TOWARD DIEM

Mansfield became a critic of U.S. aid programs in Southeast Asia during his 1955 visit to that area. He started corresponding with Under Secretary of State

Herbert Hoover Jr. shortly after his return, and he continued to seek ways to improve U.S. aid for the remainder of his Senate career. He argued that huge amounts of U.S. aid to many countries often "outweigh by far their capacity to absorb and use them effectively."[36] Mansfield thought the bureaucracy was excessive and that aid was often based entirely on competition with the Russians. Moreover, the senator believed that U.S. aid led to dependency, arguing that loans were better than grants. Mansfield concluded that aid programs should be ended after they had spent a reasonable period of time trying to achieve their aims.

The Montanan also became a critic of military aid, contending, "we have got to face the fact that military aid is a two-edged sword. We have been told many times of its virtues. We have not been sufficiently alerted to its dangers." One of the dangers, according to Mansfield, was that the Vietminh obtained U.S. weapons through defections and defeats and used the weapons against U.S. allies.[37]

Mansfield's perceived expertise on the region gave him credibility with the administration when he recommended an on-site audit of the aid program. Assistant Secretary of State for Far Eastern Affairs Walter Robertson, wrote Hoover: "aside from the fact that this is a recommendation of one of the most influential and knowledgeable senators with respect to Viet-Nam, I believe there would be considerable merit in sending such a mission to Viet-Nam."[38]

By 1958, J. William Fulbright (D-Ark.), John Kennedy (D-Mass.), Wayne Morse (D-Ore.), and other Democrats joined Mansfield's criticism of the aid program. In 1958 Diem sent Wolf Ladejinsky, an American who served as Diem's agricultural advisor, to America to lobby for increased aid for South Vietnam. Ladejinsky reported that Congress in general, and Mansfield in particular, were in the mood to reduce foreign aid everywhere, and that the perception of Diem's authoritarianism was becoming a real problem.[39]

The administration was sensitive to the Democratic attack of its aid program and debated the advantages of military versus economic aid for developing nations. This became a chicken-and-egg debate. In order to survive, was it more important for South Vietnam to improve the economic lot of its citizens or to achieve military security? The Ngo family preferred military aid, but Mansfield was among those favoring economic aid.

The 1958 best-selling novel *The Ugly American* attacked the U.S. aid program in Asia and contributed to a questioning of the Eisenhower administration's program. The novel claimed to be factually based and was publicly endorsed by Kennedy, Humphrey, and other prominent Americans. Mansfield and many in Congress read the book.

Because of the publicity generated from *The Ugly American* and Democratic attacks, Eisenhower appointed William Draper Jr., an investment banker and former general, to head a committee to visit South Vietnam to study the issue and make recommendations on military assistance programs. Draper met with

Fulbright and Mansfield before his departure and reported to Eisenhower that both senators were impressed with the committee's membership. Yet Diem refused to meet with the committee because of his earlier differences with committee member J. Lawton Collins. Lansdale, another member, eventually persuaded Diem to meet with the entire committee by allowing the Nhus to observe the meeting unseen from behind a silk screen![40]

The committee provided one last chance for the Eisenhower administration to reverse the growing commitment to Diem. Mansfield battled the administration to gain access to the report's conclusions on Vietnam. In a letter to Mansfield, Eisenhower argued that "under the historic doctrine of the separation of powers" and executive privilege, it would be a bad precedent to share the report. Mansfield was forced to wait until the Draper Committee report was finally published in August 1959 to read its conclusions. The report was generally supportive of U.S. military aid to South Vietnam. This endorsement contributed to expansion of the military aid program to the Diem government.[41]

In July 1959, shortly before Mansfield read the Draper report, the Foreign Relations Committee investigated charges of waste and mismanagement in the U.S. aid program to Vietnam brought on by the investigative reporting of Albert Colegrove for the Scripps-Howard newspapers. One of Colegrove's charges involved a pet peeve of Mansfield: "lush living" by Americans living overseas. Combined with charges from *The Ugly American,* Colegrove's indictment led to public outrage.

As Chairman of the Far Eastern Affairs Subcommittee, Mansfield pushed to have the Foreign Relations Committee investigate Colegrove's charges, at least partially because he hoped to reform the U.S. aid program in Vietnam.[42] Mansfield was aided by Morse and Frank Lausche (D-Ohio). During both the Senate and the House hearings, chaired by Clement Zablocki (D-Wis.), a number of administration witnesses claimed that Colegrove's charges aided the communist cause in Vietnam. Zablocki himself called the series "irresponsible journalism," although he admitted to reading only one of Colegrove's six articles and announced that he "didn't intend to read the rest." Zablocki asked: "shouldn't we let the public know how Scripps-Howard organization has aided the Communists?" The State Department considered Zablocki's House subcommittee "markedly friendly." That proved not to be true of Mansfield's subcommittee.[43]

Yet Colegrove was vilified by just about everyone else. Republicans, Democrats, AFV, and members of the Michigan State project attacked Colegrove. The nation was not ready to challenge its commitment to Vietnam. The *New Republic* argued that Colegrove was "literally 'roasted over the coals'" because AFV's influence made it unacceptable to be critical of Diem's government.[44]

After the July committee hearings, and before Mansfield's subcommittee held additional hearings, Fulbright wanted to issue a mild interim report to protect the program in Vietnam and U.S. relations with the Diem government.

Mansfield and Valeo disagreed with Fulbright and Carl Marcy, Foreign Relations Committee chief of staff, on the need for an interim report. Valeo wrote Mansfield a memo that likely influenced Mansfield's thinking.[45] Mansfield's aide said the interim report revealed "a marked predisposition to accept the arguments of the Executive Branch at face value and to dismiss those of Colegrove very lightly." Valeo argued that the interim report "puts Colegrove on trial and convicts him, as an inaccurate reporter and a bad journalist." In legislative hearings, "the Executive Branch can pick and choose from the total documentation to sustain its position. A newsman is limited to what he can dig out and the few people who are willing to put their heads on the block to substantiate his contentions." If Fulbright insisted on issuing the interim report, Valeo recommended that Mansfield "abstain from endorsing it or file an exception." Mansfield did balk at Fulbright's recommendation and called for a thorough study.

One of Valeo's recommendations was for "several weeks of intensive examination on the spot by competent staff not just a casual look in Saigon."[46] Before a compromise could be reached between Fulbright and Mansfield, the committee dispatched Valeo and Marcy to South Vietnam to investigate the U.S. aid program. Diem was angry that Colegrove's charges had been given credence in the United States. He said he "would fail in my responsibility as a human being towards our American friends who have been attacked wrongly for carelessness, if I did not say that, in my opinion, American aid has been extremely effective." Mansfield gave Valeo a message to convey to Diem. Valeo remembered it as expressing Mansfield's confidence in Diem, but concern for the aid program: "I can almost see Diem's face now when I spoke with him at that time; he was a little perturbed by what I said, but not anything extraordinary."[47]

Marcy concluded that "most of the Colegrove specifics were way off base."[48] Friction continued between Mansfield/Valeo and Fulbright/Marcy. While Mansfield's subcommittee was preparing its report, Valeo edited the draft report prepared by Marcy and John Newhouse to "substantially harden" its conclusions. Marcy charged that while Valeo was writing only for Mansfield, Marcy and Newhouse had to draft the report in a way to gain the approval of the ranking Republican, Bourke Hickenlooper (Iowa). The differences were reconciled and the subcommittee issued a unanimous report.[49]

Valeo thought Marcy might have felt some minor irritation because Valeo left the committee to work for Mansfield. If Marcy or Fulbright felt friction toward Mansfield, Valeo said it was because "Mansfield had this consuming interest in foreign relations," sometimes "acting almost as his own Foreign Relations Committee."[50]

Gibbons called the 1960 Mansfield subcommittee report "thoughtful and constructive." While praising Diem, the report called for a reshaping of U.S. aid to Vietnam in order to become more "efficient and effective," leading to its eventual termination. In April 1960, Under Secretary of State C. Douglas Dillon told Nguyen dinh Thuan, secretary of state for the Presidency of Vietnam, that the current amount of U.S. aid could not continue indefinitely, and that while Mansfield "was very sympathetic to Viet-Nam," he "insisted on an eventual cessation of grant aid."[51] Mansfield was beginning to challenge aspects of the U.S. commitment to Vietnam by the end of the Eisenhower administration.

The first hint of Mansfield's disillusionment with Diem came in 1959 during the Colegrove hearings. Ambassador Elbridge Durbrow suggested that Mansfield was beginning to have serious doubts.

> Whether it was the Colegrove articles or something else, or an accumulation of things, he was as cold as ice. To me personally [Mansfield] was polite, nothing rude, but he was cold, and he had been fairly warm before, particularly about Diem. He talked to me personally about Diem's lack of democracy and alleged corruption and all of that. As far as I was concerned, he was turned off to Diem by that time.[52]

Mansfield was never able to admit his break from supporting Diem. When asked about Durbrow's claim, Mansfield replied: "I was not so much disillusioned by Diem's leadership as I was deeply concerned about the influence his brother, Nhu, and his wife had on him and the part they played, in effect taking over the government from Diem."[53]

The Caravelle Manifesto of April 1960 offered a strong indication to Mansfield and America that Diem's rule was failing. In November, a coup attempt further emphasized Diem's weakness. Three battalions of paratroopers surrounded Diem's palace. The coup leaders did not want to depose Diem; they only wanted Diem to reform his government. Diem stalled until reinforcements arrived and defeated the rebels. After the 1960 coup attempt on his old friend, Mansfield cabled Diem: "deeply concerned by difficulties in Viet Nam but relieved to learn that you are safe and well and in a position to deal with wisdom and compassion with the difficulties in a way which will preserve Viet Nam's integrity and contribute to your country's continuing growth in freedom."[54] This is the last extant correspondence between Mansfield and Diem.

On the day that Mansfield sent the telegram to Diem, Dr. Fishel, at Valeo's suggestion, sent the senator his reactions to the coup attempt. Fishel had left Vietnam in 1958 but remained in close contact with Diem. The letter to Mansfield talked of the excessive political power of members of the Ngo family and the hostility that this created which helped lead to the coup. Fishel added:

> this revolt should serve as a signal to Ngo that there is serious unrest in the country; one hopes that he will react by making reforms in his administration, rather than accepting advice which he is certain to be offered by certain of his aides, to the effect that the solution to the problem is increased repression.

Fishel suggested that one of the "unpleasant truths" was the influence of Diem's family and talked of the rumored profiteering by the Nhus and their friends. He then addressed the honesty of Diem himself and rationalized:

> I would hazard an educated guess that the Ngo administration is considerably less corrupt than most Asian governments today; or to put it another way, it is relatively honest. It is interesting also that *no one* accuses Ngo Dinh Diem himself of being in any way involved in anything shady or devious.[55]

The failure of the Caravelle Manifesto and the 1960 coup attempt to bring change to the Diem regime left non-communist nationalists with limited choices. In December 1960, the communists established their political arm in the National Liberation Front, welcoming all "nationalists" who opposed the Diem government. Many non-communists joined.[56]

Other issues dominated the attention of the Eisenhower administration, and the belief continued to be that Vietnam was progressing reasonably well. In August 1960, Secretary of State Christian Herter reported the situation as "relatively quiet" in South Vietnam. When Kennedy became president, there were about the same number of American personnel in Vietnam as in 1956.[57]

Indochina returned to the headlines at the end of the Eisenhower administration, this time in Laos. Communist rebels had renewed the conflict in northern Laos. The rebellion was a response to an American-supported anti-communist coalition taking control of the government in 1958. Mansfield feared that Eisenhower and Herter were not making the decisions in Laos, but were instead allowing executive agencies, including the CIA and Defense Department, to set policy. The Montanan spoke to Dillon late in 1959 about his fear that the State Department was acquiescing to Defense. In a September 1959 Senate speech, Mansfield called for United Nations action and a SEATO meeting over the crisis, but he cautioned against direct U.S. military involvement. With the renewed fighting, U.S. aid to Laos was increased sharply. By December 1960 Mansfield charged that excessive administration aid totaling $300 million had led to "chaos, discontent, and armies on the loose" and could lead to a "blood bath" and the loss of Laotian neutrality.[58]

Mansfield's December assault was questioned by Eisenhower at a National Security Council meeting. Deputy Assistant Secretary of State for Far Eastern Affairs Livingston Merchant told the president that the State Department was shocked by Mansfield's statement, that the Montanan "was generally helpful and well-informed on foreign policy but three times recently he had made rather damaging statements." Eisenhower believed that Mansfield and Fulbright "together seemed to be endeavoring to exert steady pressure on the State Department."[59]

Managing Laos would become the most troublesome issue in the early months of the Kennedy administration. Before Kennedy assumed office, though, Mansfield faced pressures from Johnson and Kennedy to become Senate majority leader. Mansfield bowed to the pressure and reluctantly accepted the most powerful position in the Senate at a time when America faced difficult choices in Indochina. His failure to influence the choices made in the next two administrations remained his greatest disappointment.

CHAPTER 6

THE BEGINNING OF MANSFIELD'S PRIVATE DISSENT

MANSFIELD RELUCTANTLY BECOMES MAJORITY LEADER

When the position of majority whip had opened up in 1956 Mansfield had been the compromise choice to assist Majority Leader Lyndon Johnson. Mansfield initially declined, maintaining that he preferred to concentrate on his Foreign Relations Committee assignment, but he accepted after much urging. Mansfield admitted: "Lyndon insisted I had to take it because I was the least objectionable to most of the Democratic senators. It was not a flattering argument, but after several meetings I finally lost my resolve against becoming whip."[1]

Mansfield had little power as Johnson's Whip. Rowland Evans and Robert Novak referred to Mansfield's "loose guidance" as whip and concluded that "he helped Johnson with all the routine chores, but stayed at arm's length from the center of Johnson operations."[2] George Reedy added that the Johnson/Mansfield relationship in this period was "terribly difficult to describe. It was a good working relationship but there certainly was no warmth to it, which was unusual because Johnson could be a very warm man."[3] Francis Valeo agreed with Reedy's assessment of the relationship, adding: "Nobody ever got warm with Mansfield."[4]

Despite these assessments, Johnson's correspondence with Mansfield during the period that the Montanan served as whip was warm. Johnson often praised Mansfield in his correspondence, frequently calling him "my right arm."[5]

As Johnson's assistant, Mansfield supported LBJ over Kennedy for the Democratic nomination in 1960, but his support was passive. Johnson received only two of Montana's fourteen votes. Yet there was no evidence that Johnson perceived Mansfield's support to be lukewarm. The majority leader wrote his whip a letter after the Montana Democratic Convention thanking him for his remarks there, his friendship and "devotion through a difficult time for me."[6] Both President-elect John Kennedy and Vice President-elect Johnson wanted Mansfield to be majority leader. When Kennedy called Mansfield with the offer on November 11, 1960, Mansfield told the president-elect that he had "put me into a very delicate situation—that I didn't want the job but I would consider it."[7] Later that day Johnson called Mansfield to keep the pressure on: "listen, now, I want you to take this Leadership. Everybody wants you to. Have you talked with Jack this morning? Did he tell you the same thing?" Mansfield replied: "I don't want to do it, Lyndon, but I will think it over."[8] Mansfield recalled that "both asked me. I declined Johnson's request & accepted Kennedy's."[9]

Mansfield's start as majority leader was inauspicious, because he was reluctant to take the reins from his old boss. Vice President Johnson seemed reluctant to give up the prerogatives gained as leader, and many speculated that he hoped to remain as de facto leader while serving as vice president.

First, Johnson attempted to retain his spacious and ornate quarters off the Senate floor and in the Senate Office Building—quarters dubbed the "Taj Mahal" by the Washington press corps, which Johnson had originally justified taking over because of the needs of the majority leader. Second, Mansfield retained Johnson's aides. At Johnson's urging, the new leader kept Bobby Baker as secretary to the majority. Johnson told Baker that "Mike's a good man but unless somebody's spurrin' him on he'll just let things drift. He needs somebody who knows the ropes." Mansfield persuaded Baker by saying, "you know the operation here better than anyone I might train for the job. I'd certainly hate to lose you and I'll consider it a personal favor if you'll reconsider."[10] In addition, Harry McPherson was retained as general counsel to the Policy Committee.

Most importantly, Johnson had Mansfield propose that the new vice president continue to preside over the Democratic caucus. This final perceived power grab by Johnson caused strong opposition. Senators argued separation of power, stating that they would look ridiculous being presided over by a non-senator. While Mansfield's motion passed 46-17, the strong opposition sent a message to Johnson, who afterward rarely showed up at the caucus.[11]

Mansfield defended his motion by claiming that "in my view this would only constitute an honorary position, and I had no objection." The new majority leader was embarrassed, though, and threatened to resign if his motion did not pass. Evans and Novak speculate that Mansfield deferred to Johnson in this instance because Mansfield was uncomfortable with power.[12] Clearly, Mansfield was uneasy moving from his old role as Johnson's lieutenant to his new one as leader.

This incident may have been the beginning of the deterioration in the Johnson/Mansfield relationship. Rumors were circulating that Johnson considered Mansfield a weakling for letting Johnson stay in the Taj Mahal and for his willingness to let Johnson preside over the Democratic caucus. Bobby Baker allegedly called Mansfield "the nothing majority leader," and Johnson reportedly said that Mansfield was the only "Minnow who served as majority leader and yet remained a Minnow."[13]

In the first few years of his leadership, Mansfield struggled to earn the leadership position he had been elected to serve. While Mansfield was liked throughout the Senate, likability was considered a weakness in a leader. Many wanted a leader who could knock heads together and twist arms in the Johnson manner. Evans and Novak referred to Mansfield's leadership as "a tragic mistake," while columnist Doris Fleeson quoted a senator and former Johnson detractor as saying Johnson was "imperious, unfair and played favorites," and "I wish I had him back." Thomas Dodd (D-Conn.) yearned for Johnson's leadership, comparing Johnson to an orchestra leader who "stood up and blended into a wonderful production all the discordant notes of the Senate."[14]

In 1963 Mansfield felt compelled to defend his leadership:

> I confess freely to a lack of glamour. As for being a "tragic mistake," if that means, Mr. President, that I am neither a circus ring-master, the master of ceremonies of a Senate night club, a tamer of Senate lions, or a wheeler and dealer, then I must accept, too, that title. I am what I am and no title, political face-lifter, or image-maker can alter it.[15]

Mansfield's remarks were considered an attack on Johnson's leadership style and he took it as a "slap."[16] Yet Mansfield's limited philosophy of leadership later would serve President Johnson well, for it kept Mansfield from organizing opposition to LBJ's Vietnam policy.

The criticism of Mansfield's leadership that was prevalent in 1962 and 1963 ended after the civil rights battle of 1964. The Senate felt good about itself after passing that legislation, and this feeling was increased after passage of Great Society legislation in 1965. Mansfield's colleagues credited him with shepherding this legislation through Congress, and these successes created the perception that Mansfield was an effective majority leader. Mansfield did earn his elected position.[17]

By mid 1964 Mansfield had passed the period of testing that must be faced by all new leaders.[18] He was in a potentially powerful position to deal with the issue that was weighing the heaviest on his mind: America's involvement in Vietnam. Yet Mansfield's philosophy would not allow him to utilize the potential power of the leadership position.

Mansfield's leadership position also impinged on his role in the Foreign Relations Committee. As majority leader, Mansfield often missed important Foreign Relations Committee meetings that dealt with Indochina, where he had rarely missed such meetings during the Eisenhower administration. Carl Marcy, chief of staff to the Foreign Relations Committee, recalled: "Mansfield was majority leader and we left him alone. He was so busy."[19]

The new majority leader was excited with the spirit of adventure and hope that Kennedy brought to the nation. With his close friend and same-party president in the White House, Mansfield became less critical of administration policy.

MANSFIELD'S PRIVATE ARGUMENTS TO KENNEDY OVER LAOS

In a conversation with Dean Rusk, President-elect Kennedy called Laos "the worst mess the Eisenhower Administration left me." President Eisenhower had successfully resisted direct military involvement in Indochina, but he warned his young successor at a transitional meeting that Laos was "the key to the entire area of Southeast Asia" and the "cork in the bottle" of the Far East, suggesting the need for SEATO intervention or unilateral intervention by the United States to save that country. Clark Clifford observed that the warning "had a powerful effect on Kennedy, Rusk, [Robert] McNamara, and me," because none of them were aware of the seriousness with which the outgoing administration viewed the Laotian situation. It was Laos, bordering South Vietnam, Cambodia, Thailand, and Burma, that had been central to the Eisenhower administration's creation of the domino theory.[20]

The situation in Laos was so pressing by early 1961 that Kennedy spent more time on this issue in February and March than on any other. The tiny country seemed an improbable place for the focus of the world's attention. American military advisors working with the Royal Laotian Army and native Hmong forces called Laos the "Land of Oz" because the nation seemed so alien to Americans. Laos had a King living in Luang Prabang, two royal brothers residing in their own capitals, the neutralist Prince Souvanna, and communist Prince Souphanouvong. Kennedy himself never mastered the pronunciation of Laos, rhyming it with "chaos" when it should rhyme with "mouse."[21]

William Bundy noted that the "store of experts on Laos and Vietnam was, indeed, thin and centered in the Pentagon and the CIA," and that Kennedy had no "personal oracle" on Southeast Asia.[22] Although Mansfield tried to be that oracle, he was unsuccessful. The earliest extant communication between the president-elect and majority leader is a transcript of a January 2, 1961 telephone call from Kennedy to Mansfield. Kennedy seemed unsure about what his policy would be in Laos, referring to the Laotian situation as "pretty lousy." The president-elect was concerned that "they" [the press?] were going to call him, Mansfield, and Vice President Johnson, and he wanted Mansfield "to be thinking of what we should say."[23]

As a result of the telephone conversation Mansfield sent Kennedy a memorandum on Laos. In it, Mansfield argued that the United States had helped prevent Laos from moving toward neutralism and contributed to making it a military pawn in the cold war. He added that America's mistakes had been the "gross over-commitment" of all types of aid, the vast increase in the presence of U.S. officials, the allowance of the dissolution of the International Control Commission, America's "eager replacement of the French military training mission," and American support for the military opposition to Prince Souvanna

Phouma. Mansfield believed Souvanna was, next to the king, the key political figure able to steer Laos on a neutral course.

Mansfield suggested two solutions to avoid another Lebanon—and possibly another Korea. First, Mansfield wanted to back British, French, Cambodian, and Indian attempts to place Souvanna in power. His second suggestion was to select India as the major enforcer of a truce in Laos. Mansfield predicted a "bloodbath" with Thai, northern and southern Vietnamese, and Cambodians fighting in the country if his suggestions were not followed, and that the United States would supply weapons to one side and the Russians and Chinese to the other. Mansfield even warned of the possibility of Chinese and Americans fighting in Laos with Russia remaining on the sidelines, a scenario that haunted the majority leader throughout the Vietnam conflict.[24]

On January 7, 1961, Prince Souvanna Phouma sent Mansfield a letter through State Department channels. Souvanna explained:

> I should like . . . to bring an action against the policy of your country regarding mine, a policy which is outmoded and which is not, I believe, that of your Party.
>
> America wishes to preserve us from Communization, but those responsible for its policy have, ironically, done everything to the contrary and pushed the Kingdom back into an impasse which, in the long run, is going to thrust it into the abyss of Communism. The Lao people are tired of insecurity, of fratricidal strife. You understand that, under these conditions, pacification by arms is an impossible solution in view of the topography and configuration of the country which lends itself to battles without end.

The Prince went on to indict U.S. policy for backing only prominent families in Laos and making anti-communism its principal weapon, even though there were fewer than 100 communists in the Neo-Lao-Haksat. Souvanna ended with a plea for strict neutrality represented by the Cambodian proposal of Prince Norodom Sihanouk.[25]

Mansfield wrote to Kennedy on January 21 agreeing with the points raised by Souvanna. The majority leader suggested another shortcoming: "the corrupting and disrupting effect of our high level of aid on an unsophisticated nation such as Laos."

The senator made three recommendations to Kennedy. The first was for a new approach to neutralize Laos, using Burmese or Cambodian neutrality as a model. Second, to achieve neutralization, the United States should work with India, Britain, France, and Cambodia. Finally, Mansfield called for a neutralization commission composed of Asian nations, and he wanted to bring back the French military training mission to replace the U.S. one.[26]

Mansfield was seeking a prominent role in decision making over Indochina. Two days later, he sent Kennedy a supplemental memo. In this he provided a rationale for putting India, Pakistan, and Afghanistan on the neutrality commission that he had proposed. The essence of the rationale was the need to put the burden for an Asian problem on Asians. Mansfield thought that such a solution would likely be accepted by Russia and China and it might allow the United States to extricate itself from an "untenable over commitment in a fashion which at least holds some promise of preserving an independent Laos without war."[27] It is likely that Mansfield and Kennedy discussed the majority leader's Indochina memos, but the president never responded in writing.

The senator remained silent on the Laotian situation for several months, but he continued to give it much thought. On March 22, Mansfield sent a memorandum on the subject to Secretary of State Rusk. He was motivated to write because Rusk was about to attend a SEATO meeting where he would have the opportunity to meet with Prime Minister Jawaharial Nehru of India, and Mansfield hoped that Nehru could play a positive role in resolving the Laotian conflict.

The majority leader argued that Nehru would take a "dim view of military intervention of SEATO neighbors in Laos and an even dimmer view of direct U.S. intervention, even if the only alternative was Pathet Lao domination of the entire country." Second, he admitted that a Pathet Lao victory was not desirable, but noted that it did have "some compensations." It would shift the financial drain from the United States to the communist countries; it would extend communist lines into difficult terrain; and it would "stiffen the resolve of neighboring countries, notably India, towards communism in general." The senator also claimed that the loss would be mitigated somewhat by knowledge that Kennedy had inherited the problem from Eisenhower, portraying the cost of status quo policy in American dollars and casualties as worse for the administration than the loss of influence over Laos.

The senator then argued that SEATO intervention with American material assistance was unlikely to be decisive. Even with U.S. air support, the Vietminh and Chinese were likely to intervene. Mansfield predicted the "decimation of the Laotian people for which we may well be held primarily responsible in Asian opinion." He warned against U.S. military intervention, drawing the analogy to Korea. Mansfield then put the domino theory to rest: "to put it another way the domino-theory, of the communist advance in Southeast Asia, so popular a few years ago has not proven accurate."

Mansfield ended his memo to Rusk by claiming that a "last-ditch effort at a peaceful solution" was essential and by recommending acceptance of Sihanouk's neutrality proposal as well as a temporary government composed of the King, Souvanna, and Boun Oum. He wanted Rusk to hold a "*personal*" meeting with Nehru to persuade him to accept Sihanouk's neutrality suggestion and the temporary government. Mansfield asserted that his proposals would cost the United States little and could lead to a major achievement. He sent a copy to President Kennedy with another warning against attempts at forcing a military solution.[28]

The week after sending this memo to Rusk, Mansfield publicly talked about the need for a coalition government, which may have been a trial balloon on Kennedy's behalf.[29] At a April 27 meeting of Kennedy and the Foreign Relations Committee, only Senator Styles Bridges (R-N.H.) expressed support for the use of U.S. forces in Laos. Mansfield felt "the whole thing would be rather fruitless." Minority Leader Everett Dirksen (R-Ill.) and Richard Russell (D-Ga.) agreed with Mansfield.[30]

Laos became a secondary issue in April, for the Bay of Pigs disaster occurred on April 17. Caution instilled by the Bay of Pigs experience, as well as the lack of a strategic reserve force, may have convinced Kennedy to pursue the Cambodian suggestion for neutralization in order to avoid direct involvement in Laos. These negotiations started in May 1961 and lasted for thirteen months.[31]

Mansfield wrote a memorandum to Kennedy on May 1, 1961, two days before the negotiations on Laos were to begin. The senator was likely trying to counter the recommendation from most of Kennedy's advisors to intervene in Laos. Mansfield began the memorandum by suggesting four options short of armed intervention: ask the other thirteen nations involved in the conference to urge a cease-fire; ask India, as chair of the cease-fire commission, to call for the sealing of the Laotian borders; request that India quickly send the cease-fire group to Laos; and keep the United Nations out of the question unless it was clear that the 14-member conference would not work.

The senator told Kennedy that the United States should not intervene because Russia would look like the peaceful power and score a public relations coup. Further, while intervention could begin with Pakistani, Thai, and Filipino forces on the ground and U.S. forces in the air and sea, American troops were likely to become involved. Mansfield suggested the following scenario: U.S. ground troops would be needed in Laos; covert attacks would increase in South Vietnam, with the possibility of open invasion from the North; China would pressure Formosa with a possible invasion; North Korea would increase its pressure on the South and the Soviets would create trouble in Berlin. Mansfield was prescient in predicting initial public approval if the U.S. intervened, which would end with increased costs and casualties. He said that eventually critics would call the intervention "Kennedy's war." Mansfield forecast initial criticism at home if Kennedy did not intervene, but claimed it would be mild compared to the criticism if troops were committed.

Mansfield suggested a better scenario if the United States did not intervene: Souvanna Phouma and Kong Le would emerge as leaders in Laos. Souvanna was a nationalist and Kong probably was as well. Mansfield viewed Souvanna as "extremely astute, skilled in eastern court politics," with "considerable knowledge of the West." The Eisenhower administration had alienated Souvanna through "poor policies, excessive aid and pressure to conform to our concepts of how to handle his internal politics and foreign relations." While Souvanna would be heavily dependent on Russia, it might prove too costly for the Soviets and could become a "bone of contention" between Russia and China. Mansfield projected that the United States could get out with "dignity." While admitting some negative impact on neighboring countries, Mansfield predicted: "in my opinion, to station a regular contingent of our ground forces in Viet Nam and Thailand at this time would probably cost more in adverse propaganda among the peoples of these countries than it would be worth in terms of reassuring the governments."[32]

On the day Kennedy received Mansfield's memo he met with his advisors on the situation in Laos. William Conrad Gibbons reports:

> Facing a difficult choice, and feeling the effects of the Bay of Pigs, Kennedy struggled with the possibility of "losing" Laos to the Communists, apparently feeling that the domestic political consequences of such an outcome would be more serious than Mansfield estimated. He is said to have told [Walt] Rostow that whereas Eisenhower was able to withstand the political fall-out from the loss of Dien Bien Phu because it was the French, rather than the Americans, who were defeated, "I can't take a 1954 defeat today."[33]

At the time of the May 1 meeting, John Newman reports "overwhelming sentiment among Kennedy's advisors for intervention there." They reached no consensus on committing troops to Laos, but it was decided to threaten military action if a cease-fire were not agreed upon.[34]

After the Bay of Pigs disaster, Kennedy was wary of his military advice. He told Arthur Schlesinger: "'if it hadn't been for Cuba, we might be about to intervene in Laos.' Waving a sheaf of cables from [General Lyman Lemnitzer, Chairman of the Joint Chiefs of Staff], he added, 'I might have taken this advice seriously.'"[35] Mansfield was one of the few making the argument against intervention.

Yet the negotiated settlement in Laos may have tied Kennedy's hands in Vietnam. After being charged with two retreats against communism in Cuba and Laos, Kennedy was unwilling to allow a third charge for Vietnam. Republican criticism had questioned Kennedy's courage and competence, and Richard Nixon suggested that Kennedy must be willing to risk small-scale war to avoid a large-scale one. Even if Hanoi would have settled for a neutral South Vietnam at this time, Kennedy would not. Mansfield's old friend Under Secretary of State Chester Bowles was the only administration official to argue for South Vietnamese neutrality, and he was soon moved to a different position in the administration, partially because of his differences over Vietnam policy. After Kennedy had made the decision not to commit U.S. troops in Laos, he told his advisors: "if we have to fight for Southeast Asia, we'll fight in South Vietnam."[36]

When Mansfield appeared on ABC's *Issues and Answers* on May 7, 1961, he took a more noncommittal tone than in his private communication with the president. When asked, "do you think it is worth risking a global war to keep the communists from getting, say, Vietnam, Thailand, and Cambodia?" Mansfield responded, "I would again have to refer you to the responsibility of the President of the United States as far as this country is concerned."[37]

On May 10, Mansfield sent a confidential memorandum to Kennedy concerning his impressions gleaned at a luncheon with Soviet Ambassador Mikhail Menshikov. Mansfield and Menshikov talked about a number of issues, including Laos. Menshikov indicated that Laos "was *not* of great importance or significance" and that Laotian neutrality should be guaranteed by its neighbors. The ambassador saw no danger from a neutral Laos, Cambodia, Thailand, or South Vietnam. Mansfield agreed with Menshikov except with regard to South Vietnam.[38] Apparently Mansfield continued to view South Vietnam as a potential anti-communist bastion in Southeast Asia.

Sixteen days later Mansfield sent Kennedy his observations on the upcoming talks in Vienna and continued to push his view on the situation in Indochina. Mansfield wanted the president to prod Soviet Premier Nikita Khrushchev to see if the Soviets were willing to undertake a general guarantee of Laotian neutrality. Concerning Vietnam, Mansfield wanted Kennedy to press for a reaffirmation of the 17th parallel until the Vietnamese themselves could reconcile their differences. Then, Mansfield criticized the administration's foreign policy record as leaving

> much to be desired. Your statements in this field have been, for the most part, outstanding. The Vice-President's recent trip to Southeast Asia has been helpful.
>
> But the fact remains that, apart from these expressions at the top, the performance of the bureaucracy is still little improved over the Eisenhower days. . . . Our remedies have been those of our predecessors, only more of the same. I know that we have not had much time. I know the problems are still very intractable. Nevertheless, I am concerned by the trend and I feel that I owe it to you to express this concern.

Mansfield ended the memo by suggesting that if Khrushchev took the hard line in Vienna that he was rumored to be planning, Kennedy should consider walking out of the conference.[39]

Khrushchev took a hard line on most matters, but he agreed to attempt to settle the Laotian crisis. Bowles suggested that Kennedy's later policy in Vietnam was the result of Khrushchev's attack at Vienna and the young president's "desire to be tough and resolute, to prove we couldn't be pushed around."[40]

Civil war continued in Laos, but Mansfield remained consistent in his opposition to U.S. military involvement. He recalled a meeting on February 21, 1962:

> Many people in the Administration were advocating that we ought to move into Laos. I said that I thought it was the worst possible move we could make. The President and the others listened respectfully. . . . I think that the congressional

leadership . . . [was] in full accord with my views, and I have an idea that the President was too although he didn't say anything.[41]

In May 1962 the Kennedy administration rebuked Boun Oum and General Phoumi Nosavan for failure to live up to their pledges to form a coalition government with the Pathet Lao. When talks resumed, an agreement was reached on June 7. Boun Oum retired from government, Souvanna returned as premier, with Phoumi and Souphanouvong as deputy premiers. The government assumed power on June 22 and quickly renounced SEATO protection.

Yet the settlement in Laos was doomed to failure without resolution in South Vietnam. North Vietnam's refusal to live up to the agreements made in the Laotian accords of 1962 made Rusk and the administration leery of future negotiations. A neutral Laos also made it easier for North Vietnam to infiltrate troops and equipment into South Vietnam through the long border with Laos. The 1962 settlement in Laos shifted American attention back to Vietnam where communist guerrilla activity was increasing. American equipment and personnel were soon pouring into South Vietnam.[42]

Mansfield was cognizant of his party role. He wrote Kennedy that he expected Republicans to attempt to use the Laotian settlement against Democrats in the coming elections. The majority leader suggested that Democrats emphasize their achievements in Laos, but showed his caution about the developing situation in Vietnam:

> It is not without . . . significance to have prevented the loss of American lives and an endless expenditure of vast foreign aid resources in the Laotian trap which we inherited from the previous administration. The Laotian settlement may yet be an asset to us rather than a liability provided we are bold enough to make the most of it and provided we do not neutralize the gain by growing casualties in Viet Nam.[43]

MANSFIELD'S PRIVATE ARGUMENTS TO KENNEDY ON VIETNAM

During the 1960 election campaign, Vietnam had barely been mentioned. Candidate Kennedy had attacked Vice President Nixon's desire to aid the French at Dien Bien Phu, calling the first Indochina conflict "a war where we would have been engaged in a hopeless struggle without allies, for an unpopular colonialist cause." After Kennedy's transitional meeting with Eisenhower, the focus temporarily turned to Laos. The Kennedy administration assumed office believing that the situation in South Vietnam was stable.[44]

As Kennedy was being inaugurated, Edward Lansdale, now a Brigadier General, returned from a twelve-day visit to South Vietnam and issued a disturbing but accurate report. Lansdale concluded that Vietnam was in "critical condition" and in need of "emergency treatment." Diem's old friend and confidante was "shocked" at the amount of Vietcong infiltration and thought Diem's regime was in trouble. Lansdale argued that a communist victory "would be a major blow to U.S. prestige and influence, not only in Asia but throughout the world" and recommended "a changed U.S. attitude, plenty of hard work and patience, and a new spirit by the Vietnamese."

On January 28, 1961 Lansdale discussed his report and the administration's developing counterinsurgency plan with Kennedy, Johnson, Rusk, Secretary of Defense McNamara, and others. Kennedy was stunned by Lansdale's report and said to Rostow: "this is the worst one we've got, isn't it? You know, Eisenhower never uttered the word Vietnam." The president asked his aides, "how do we get moving?" So while focusing on Laos in the early days of his administration, Kennedy could not forget Vietnam. In March 1961 McGeorge Bundy wrote of "repeated questioning which we get here on Vietnam from the President. He is really very eager indeed that it should have the highest priority for rapid and energetic action."[45]

As he had since 1953, Mansfield shared his opinions on Vietnam with Kennedy. In a September 20, 1961 memo to the president, Mansfield argued that U.S. aid was "distorted" toward military assistance, causing the "deterioration" occurring in Vietnam. The majority leader blamed the worsening situation, too, on the "absorptive capacity" of South Vietnam for North Vietnamese infiltration and in worsening relations between the Soviet Union and the United States. He thought that increased Soviet-U.S. tensions caused the Soviets to prod North Vietnam to increase Vietminh activity.

Mansfield believed that U.S. policy must seek to remedy the absorptive quality of South Vietnam, and that military aid had not proven effective in doing that. Specifically, the senator proposed a program of propaganda that emphasized peaceful unification of Viet Nam; an expansive, coordinated effort of economic development that looked Vietnamese no matter how much the United States contributed to it; a rapid introduction of democracy in the villages and provinces; the utilization of Vietnamese intellectuals which meant the acceptance of opposition by Diem; and getting Diem and his officials to use "continuous Johnson-like shirt-sleeve campaigns from one end of the country to the other."[46] Gibbons questioned Mansfield's cultural sensitivity for this last statement:

> Here, once again, is an example of the tendency to apply American values and practices to Vietnam. Although Mansfield had more training and experience in Asian culture and political traditions than most Members of Congress and many U.S. officials dealing with Vietnam, his basic frame of reference was his own cultural and political training and experience. Thus, he apparently assumed that an American-style political campaign technique would produce similar results in Vietnam.[47]

Yet Mansfield had a frame of reference that Gibbons lacked. He recalled Diem's Western-style presidential campaign in 1955, which was stage-managed by Lansdale.[48] The senator likely believed that Diem had lost his closeness to the peasants and thought that such a campaign might help to restore the so-called "miracle" of 1955.

Mansfield also wanted Kennedy to change the U.S. mission in Saigon. He suggested an ambassador with increased power "who is not a career-man but who is nevertheless knowledgeable in the affairs of the region." Kennedy's eventual selection of Henry Cabot Lodge Jr. fit this suggestion. Next, Mansfield proposed "new blood" among the U.S. establishment in Saigon, as well as cutting the number of people stationed there. Finally, Mansfield wanted an independent State Department unit under Kennedy's control to coordinate what various U.S. agencies were doing in Vietnam. The senator predicted that if his policy suggestions were not implemented or effective in stemming rebel activity, then there was the likelihood of a military coup and deepening U.S. involvement.[49]

The senator was concerned with the possibility of committing U.S. troops in Vietnam. In an effort to prevent that escalation, he submitted another Vietnam memorandum to Kennedy on November 2, 1961, the day after General Maxwell Taylor, Rostow, Lansdale, and others returned from Vietnam. Taylor had wired Kennedy from the Philippines, and the president told Mansfield that the Taylor mission would recommend U.S. military involvement to reverse the situation which was going badly for the South.

Once again Mansfield was among the few urging restraint. As with his arguments on Laos, Mansfield argued that the United States would lack "significant allies." The Chinese would make such a commitment "quicksand for us." Further, he feared that a U.S. presence would be considered a revival of colonialism. If SEATO forces were deployed, U.S. forces would need to follow and if they were not committed at that time, "we will suffer disastrous repercussions throughout all of Asia and we will indeed become the laughing stock of the world."

The senator found it hard to believe that Diem would even accept U.S. forces since he had fought the French presence so diligently. He implicitly criticized Diem by stating, "if the necessary reforms have not been forthcoming over the past seven years to stop communist subversion and rebellion, then I do not see how American combat troops can do it today." Yet the senator recommended direct talks between Kennedy and Diem in an apparent effort to force change on Diem.

Mansfield saw four possible adverse scenarios from U.S. involvement: "a fanfare and then a retreat, an indecisive and costly conflict, . . . a major war with China while Russia stands aside," or "a total world conflict." Mansfield conceded that there was the bare possibility U.S. combat forces [not S.E.A.T.O. allied forces] might provide that bare margin of effectiveness which would permit a solution of the guerrilla problem in South Viet Nam or prevent further encroachments southward—assuming of course that the Chinese . . . let alone the Russians, do not become involved. Even then, we will have achieved a "victory" whose fruits, if we would conserve them, will cost us billions of dollars in military and aid expenditures over the years into the future.[50]

MANSFIELD'S MICHIGAN STATE ADDRESS

In January 1962 J. William Fulbright (D-Ark.), chairman of the Senate Foreign Relations Committee, admitted he knew very little about Vietnam. Michael Forrestal, McGeorge Bundy's deputy for the Far East, viewed Mansfield as the only member of Congress with much interest in Southeast Asia in early 1962. One Fulbright biographer suggested that "Mansfield was the Senate's resident expert on the subject and only he, in private, and Wayne Morse, Ernest Gruening, and George McGovern, in public, dared to raise questions about John Kennedy's growing commitment to Saigon after 1961."[51]

In June 1962 Mansfield briefly shifted his arguments about Vietnam to a public forum in a commencement address at Michigan State University. Wesley Fishel indicated that he "worked a long time" to bring Mansfield to the MSU campus.[52] In the speech, Mansfield alluded to his friend from the Vietnam Lobby: "I cannot remember the number of times that I have run into your Professor Wesley Fishel in Saigon."[53] Certainly the East Lansing location with its Fishel connection suggested a Vietnam theme for this address.[54]

Mansfield's arguments were the same ones he had been using with Kennedy, but here he offered them more mildly. Early in the speech, Mansfield explained why he was going public:

> Support of the President, and I give him mine whole heartedly, does not preclude public discussion of the situation in Southeast Asia. On the contrary, it presupposes it. The President would be the last to expect a moratorium on public participation of this kind. It is politics that needs to stop at the water's edge, not serious consideration of the nation's course in its relations with the rest of the world. Rather than less, we need more public consideration of this matter.

His deference to the president on matters of foreign policy and his call for public discussion on Vietnam became frequent Mansfield themes. Mansfield's deference explains why Gibbons concluded that this speech demonstrated Mansfield's "acquiescence" to Kennedy and that Mansfield saw Congress's role merely as a forum in which to debate the issue.[55]

There was truth to what Gibbons said. Mansfield was limited both by his party position and by his philosophy of presidential prerogatives over foreign policy. Yet Mansfield deserved credit as one of the few voices in government warning of the dangers in Vietnam in the summer of 1962. Unfortunately, neither Kennedy nor the nation was ready to heed Mansfield's admonition.

Mansfield told the graduates that "extravagant" U.S. aid to Laos had failed and the aid program to South Vietnam went for "the wrong kind of forces." Vietnam was less secure than it had been five or six years before and it had become dependent on U.S. aid. Modest aid programs in Cambodia and Burma were more successful. SEATO had not succeeded, and U.S. allies were "either unwilling or unable to assume but the smallest fraction of the burdens of the alliance."

The senator remained publicly loyal to Diem. In what appeared to be an afterthought, since he inserted the argument after the original text was prepared, he praised Diem as "a man whose integrity and honesty are unquestioned, and without whom there would be no free Vietnam."

Mansfield argued that U.S. interests in Southeast Asia had traditionally been limited with "a policy of minimum involvement." He reasoned that the situation had not changed, but American policy had shifted 180 degrees to a point of deep involvement at enormous cost. Mansfield suggested that the United States was approaching the point of deciding whether the policy shift was to become permanent. If so, then the United States must spend several hundred millions of dollars annually and be prepared for a long conflict, dependent largely on American forces.

The majority leader then asked a series of rhetorical questions which suggested that "yes" answers to his questions were "doubtful."

> Is a permanent policy of that kind justified on the basis of any enduring interests of the people of the United States in Southeast Asia? Is it more valid now, than in the past, to involve ourselves in internal political situations in the countries of that region—to maintain any government in a state of quasi-dependency on us for the indefinite future? Is it more valid now, than in the past, to assume the primary burden for the political, economic and social future of these lands?

Mansfield suggested a number of solutions: avoiding unilateral U.S. activity in Southeast Asia; a reexamination of SEATO that could lead to its modification or alteration; an attempt to use the United Nations or other agencies to help Southeast Asian nations economically and socially; using traditional diplomacy as opposed to cold war devices to create stability; an adjustment of U.S. relations based on how governments in the region addressed the needs and aspirations of their people; and consideration of the relevance of the Burma and Cambodian experience to the rest of Southeast Asia.[56]

Gibbons called this a "major speech" and the MSU address found an audience beyond those assembled—as Mansfield no doubt hoped it would. On June 13, Bowles sent Kennedy a memorandum urging the administration to define political objectives in Southeast Asia, based partially on Mansfield's address "which has focused public and congressional attention on our ultimate aims in Southeast Asia." At a press conference on June 14, a reporter asked Kennedy whether he agreed with Mansfield that a review of U.S. policy in Indochina was necessary because the United States might be "on a collision course."

Kennedy agreed with Mansfield on several points, but expressed a continued belief in the domino theory by saying that withdrawal from Vietnam "might mean a collapse of the entire area."[57] While Mansfield had privately argued with Kennedy and Rusk as early as March 22, 1961 that the domino theory had "not proven accurate," he still claimed in public as late as 1964 that to deny financial assistance to South Vietnam would cause its fall "and the effect on its neighboring countries, Thailand, Malaya, Cambodia, and Laos, would be in my opinion devastating to the security of the free world in that part of the globe."[58] This speech showed that although Mansfield was willing to differ with aspects of administration policy, he was not ready to attack its central tenets.

Mansfield's speech received limited attention in the United States,[59] but it caused alarm in South Vietnam. John Mecklin, the public affairs advisor in the U.S. Embassy in Saigon, recalled:

> This one could not be shrugged off as "irresponsible reporting." Mansfield had been an early, invaluable supporter of the regime in the mid-fifties and now seemed to have turned against Diem. Because of Mansfield's position as Senate majority leader, Diem and Nhu assumed [erroneously] that the speech had been cleared with President Kennedy and thus reflected high-level American opinion.

Mansfield's address had the unintended result of causing the Diem regime to increase its harassment of members of the American press corps in Vietnam, whom they blamed for "misleading" Mansfield.[60]

Madame Tran Van Chuong also responded to the MSU speech. She was Diem's representative at the United Nations, wife of the Vietnamese ambassador to Washington, and mother of Madame Nhu. The thrust of Madame Tran's attack was Mansfield's suggested "correlation between less U.S. involvement and more stability." She argued: "the instability in Viet Nam is definitely not homegrown, it is master minded by the Communist world." Insufficient U. S. involvement rather than too much led to the growth of communist power in Southeast Asia. The Marshall Plan and NATO saved Europe after World War II, and a stronger SEATO and Southeast Asian Marshall Plan, not neutralization, was the answer in that part of the world. Cambodia was buffered geographically by Laos and South Vietnam and both Cambodia and Burma "are indirectly protected by the strong and valiant Vietnamese resistance against Communist encroachment." Further, Madame Tran attacked the senator's implicit argument for neutrality since both Burma and Cambodia were neutral. She requested a response to her concerns.[61]

Mansfield responded the next day, suggesting that most of their differences came from divergent perspectives caused by their citizenship in different nations. He stated that the rationale for the MSU speech was that the situation in Southeast Asia was not satisfactory and might be worsening despite a deep U.S. involvement and commitment of many billions of dollars. While the media had drawn an exact parallel to Burma and Cambodia, Mansfield quoted his speech to show that such a comparison had not been his intention. The senator conceded some relevance to Madame Tran's comparison to Europe. Mansfield ended the letter by assuring her of his concern for her nation's success, but wrote he must also consider his responsibilities to his own people.[62]

On the same day that his wife wrote to Mansfield, Ambassador Tran Van Chuong asked Valeo to visit him. Valeo received Mansfield's permission for the visit and described the conversation as covering "a great range of matters; much of it was confused and disjointed." Yet several principal ideas emerged that the ambassador wanted to convey to Mansfield. Tran suggested that "the Diem government is in deep trouble and has little prospects for survival" because Diem was oblivious "to the realities around him" and had "mandarin tendencies." He predicted that a coup was imminent and was likely to come from the military and dispossessed intellectuals who would be more militant in the pursuit of the war. Tran was concerned about the effect the MSU speech would have on foreign aid appropriations.

Valeo believed that the ambassador's real purpose for the meeting was to determine what "Mansfield's position would be in the event of such a coup." Ambassador Tran remembered Mansfield's position from 1954-55, and wanted to determine if the senator would attempt to cut off aid if Diem were purged.[63]

Mansfield made his fourth visit to Vietnam in late 1962. With his visit in mind, Madame Tran invited Valeo to dinner on October 30 regarding a "very important matter to be discussed." Valeo dined at the Vietnamese Embassy with the U.N. representative and the ambassador that evening. Madame Tran had just returned from a trip to Saigon where "respectable" people pleaded with her to do something about the situation with the Nhus. The couple attempted to persuade Valeo on the need for the United States to get their daughter and son-in-law out of Vietnam. They considered the Nhus to be "drunk with power" and felt that Diem would never remove them on his own. Madame Tran "seemed almost in deadly personal fear of her own daughter and the daughter's husband." The Tran Van Chuongs expected that a coup was imminent. Indeed in February of 1962, two South Vietnamese Air Force pilots bombed Diem's palace in an abortive coup. Madame Tran emphasized the "highest confidence" with the contents of their conversation and told Valeo that he was the only person with whom they had shared their concerns.[64]

By 1962 Mansfield had his doubts about Diem's ability to successfully lead South Vietnam. In one instance, Mansfield met with a South Vietnamese dissident and listened to his views. That was something Mansfield had been unwilling to do in the late 1950s.[65] Mansfield soon returned to Vietnam to see for himself if Diem's position was as grim as the Tran Van Chuongs had painted it.

CHAPTER 7

THE DEATHS OF TWO PRESIDENTS

MANSFIELD AND CAMBODIA

S oon after the disturbing report from the Tran Van Chuongs, at the request
of John Kennedy, Mansfield made his fourth visit to Vietnam along with
Senators J. Caleb Boggs (D-Del.), Claiborne Pell (D-R.I.), and Benjamin Smith
(D-Mass.). Once again Francis Valeo, Mansfield's assistant, accompanied the
group. The visit led to a "secret" report to Kennedy on December 18, 1962 and a
public report in February 1963.[1]

Before arriving in Vietnam, Mansfield stayed in Cambodia and talked to
Herbert Spivack, the Counselor of the U.S. Embassy in Phnom Penh. Spivack
chronicled the continuing problems between Cambodia and the United States.
Since Cambodia feared the Thais and Vietnamese more than the Chinese, they
were disturbed by border incidents with Thailand and South Vietnam, both of
which treated Cambodia with disdain. Prince Norodom Sihanouk believed that
America rejected the French and Cambodian calls for a neutralization conference because the United States would be embarrassed by its allies' violations of
Cambodian neutrality. Because of Sihanouk's difficulties with the United States,
he was turning toward China for aid.[2]

Mansfield was one of the few American admirers of Sihanouk. Valeo believed
that American officials despised Sihanouk, and the embassy staff in Phnom Penh
freely used his derogatory nickname, "Snooky." The Prince knew of the
embassy's use of the nickname and this infuriated him.[3]

In the public report Mansfield issued after the trip, he credited Sihanouk with
making Cambodia into "one of the most stable and progressive nations in
Souteast Asia." In his private report to Kennedy, Mansfield was more critical,
condemning U.S. policy toward Cambodia as "erratic" and "unnecessarily so."
Mansfield found it "essential" that the United States find solutions to Cambodia's
"desire for reassurance that it won't be overwhelmed" by either Thailand or
Vietnam. Cambodia was likely to seek a further reduction in American "one-
sided aid," and Mansfield wanted Kennedy to "welcome the opportunity."[4]

105

Mansfield was always held in high regard by Sihanouk and Cambodian officials were pleased with Mansfield's report because they perceived it to be critical of Thailand and South Vietnam. In March 1963, a Cambodian official praised Mansfield's understanding of the situation in Southeast Asia and concluded that if Kennedy followed Mansfield's advice, the burden on the United States would be reduced.[5]

MANSFIELD'S FOURTH VISIT TO VIETNAM

Ambassador Frederick Nolting Jr. wrote that Mansfield's visit started on a sour note when Nolting urged the Mansfield party to delay their arrival from Cambodia because of an expected monsoon. The ambassador said Mansfield seemed disgruntled when he arrived in Saigon, and Nolting believed that the Mansfield party may have thought that the embassy was trying to prevent their arrival. Nolting claimed the Mansfield group met only briefly with U.S. military and civilian leaders at the embassy, appearing disinterested and asking few questions.

Valeo had forgotten the monsoon warning but doubted that he or Mansfield interpreted it as a stall. Rather, several members of the party had become ill at Angkor Wat and were not feeling well when they arrived in Saigon. Valeo remembered the briefing as "exhausting in its length and that coupled with the carryover illnesses explains any irritations which Nolting may have noted. Mansfield was unhappy not with Nolting but with what he found in Saigon."

Nolting's recollections seem flawed. Mansfield's transcript from the meeting runs 52 pages on legal sized paper. The meeting ran more than four hours exclusive of a lunch break in excess of two hours. After Nolting's initial comments, the transcript indicates that Mansfield's questions were frequent and provided the direction for the meeting. The Mansfield party and Nolting adjourned at 4:05 P.M. in order to meet Diem at 5:00 P.M. at his palace.[6]

At the embassy meeting Mansfield heard reports that were unrealistically optimistic.[7] Nolting based his positive outlook on the "increased effectiveness" of South Vietnamese forces, the establishment of programs that would help to "hold the allegiance of the people," and the shift to the government by Montagnard tribesman in the plateau region. Nolting and General Paul Harkins, in charge of the military advisory mission to South Vietnam, shared the view that the United States had enough military presence to win the war. Mansfield commented that Harkins was the first military man he had ever heard admit that he had enough men and material to accomplish his task. Mansfield "was not impressed by General Harkins' estimate that the war can be won in one year—in fact, he was apparently annoyed by Harkins' 'undue optimism.'"[8]

Nolting said that "we can see the light at the end of the tunnel but we are not yet at the point of emerging into the sunlight."[9] Nolting, too, claimed that the

Vietcong insurgency could be controlled within a year if all the "various elements mesh together toward this end." The ambassador further asserted that Diem's government controlled 70-75 percent of the population and estimated that 80 percent of those Vietnamese supported the government of South Vietnam.

When Pell asked how Diem would "come out" in an election in the countryside, Nolting deferred to William Trueheart, Deputy Chief to the U.S. mission in Saigon. Trueheart remembered responding: "I honestly think that if you really went out in the boondocks of this country I'm not sure that half the people know who Diem is, if you really mean the peasants." Both Pell and Mansfield seemed irritated by the response,[10] but Mansfield tested Trueheart's claim for the remainder of his visit.

Part of the discussion at the embassy concerned the problems between the government of South Vietnam and the press. John Mecklin wrote that Ngo family bitterness toward the U.S. press became uncontainable by mid 1962.[11] Mansfield was told that the press was harassed, deceived, and treated with contempt. Madame Nhu had recently stated that "the U.S. press is intoxicated with communism." Mansfield was concerned that such statements "might well affect the degree to which the U.S. people would wish to support the U.S. program in Viet Nam." Nolting argued that while a public rebuttal of Madame Nhu would help with the press, it would make working with the Vietnam government more difficult. The embassy staff portrayed the Ngo family as "proud, unsophisticated about the press and incapable of forgetting past insults," and Madame Nhu as "apparently waging a personal vendetta with the press." The staff argued that for its part the press expected too much from an "underdeveloped country at war."

Mansfield expressed his continued loyalty to Diem at the embassy meeting, saying that "apparently Diem's ultimate aim is to provide the people with more freedom and a greater voice in their government. Diem has had a rough road to follow. He is a man of great integrity and honesty, which are decided assets, and he is obviously devoted to Viet-Nam."

In his own meetings with Diem, though, Mansfield was disturbed by the condition of his friend. The senator found the June warning from the Tran Van Chuongs to be accurate. Diem was "very withdrawn, very secluded. He was not the Diem I knew. So the only conclusion I could come to—it was at best a guess, an estimate—was that he had fallen under the influence of his brother and his wife and they were taking control. I think he was gradually being cut off from reality."[12] Mansfield's notes showed that this visit destroyed whatever optimism the senator retained about Diem's leadership:

> President Diem is a depressed man and I think he has a feeling of lack of accomplishment. I came away with a feeling of depression and with the belief that our chances may be a little better than 50-50. It is my belief, also, that the peasants

are extremely tired of war, that a [growing] number of them have no interests in either communism nor freedom but would just like to be left alone, go their own ways and live their own lives.[13]

Diem's capacity to talk incessantly was legendary, and Mansfield reported that in his first meeting with Diem, the president spoke at length about the strategic hamlet program without letting the Mansfield party question him on other matters. A state department employee reported:

> The Senator got the impression that Diem is a good deal older and more withdrawn from reality than when he last saw him. The Senator was a little miffed because Diem insisted upon recounting the whole history of his regime as though the Senator were a stranger to the Viet-Nam situation.[14]

Mansfield held two meetings with Nhu, including a dinner meeting at which Madam Nhu was present. He referred to Madame Nhu as "quite aggressive" in their conversations on Cuba and press relations. Madame Nhu attacked Mansfield over an erroneous press release that said he would "bring up with her the question of American press relations in Vietnam." The senator and Madame Nhu discussed her charge of communism in the U.S. press corps, but Mansfield was not persuaded by her arguments.

The senator asked Nhu if something could not be done about the press problem "because it is a serious problem, and really the only one between the two countries." Nhu responded that the American press "is not adapted to subversive war, and lags in the world evolutionary process. For example, American newspaper correspondents in Vietnam are very young and inexperienced." He added that while "it was difficult for the United States press to send high-level correspondents to Viet Nam, newsmen must meet minimum standards of intellect and of emotion in order to grasp the problems in Vietnam." Nhu also believed that the press was not "up to date" on progress made through the strategic hamlet program and thought that the American correspondents tended to stay in the cities and miss the "realities" of the conflict. Mansfield concluded that both of the Nhus were "whistling in the dark to keep up their hopes."[15]

The strategic hamlet program was a topic of concern in all of Mansfield's conversations. It was designed to separate the peasants from the Vietminh through large-scale agricultural resettlement. The French had tried a similar pacification program that the United States had helped fund. However, the French "agrovilles" ultimately failed. The strategic hamlet program was headed by Nhu and was initially considered to be successful by most observers, but it, too, ultimately failed. Views of the program varied. Harkins was a vocal advocate of the strategic hamlet concept. One U.S. official told Mansfield that the program had a "50-50 chance of success" but if it did not succeed there would be a "total collapse." A British official whom Mansfield consulted was impressed by the strategic hamlet program and thought the United States on the "right track."[16]

Nhu told Mansfield that the program would succeed in eighteen months and "would perfect an answer to the communist war of subversion." Hardly a democrat, Nhu saw the key to its effectiveness as paying "'attention to the little interests of the peasants' and stimulation of the peasants to participate in their own defense." Mansfield reported that Nhu "kept repeating the word 'organization' as being essential and seemed obsessed with technique almost as an end in itself or at least as the key to power." Nhu said: "the West pays too much attention to winning the sympathy of the population, and not enough to organizing. If the population is not organized, the Communists will be able to mobilize it against the government over night."[17]

Mansfield feared that arms provided through the program would fall into rebel hands. Nhu conceded the danger, but believed the weapons could be protected and eventually collected. Mansfield was correct in his concern. By mid 1963, the United States had stocked 250,000 weapons in the countryside, and many were captured by the communists, which enabled them to increase the number of armed men they could put in the field.[18]

At the end of Mansfield's trip, Nolting tried to get him to issue a statement provided by the embassy, but Mansfield refused. Nolting's version was that he called Mansfield on the day he was leaving, telling Valeo that he "hoped [Mansfield] would tell me generally what he intended to say in his parting statement at the airport." Valeo said that "he had no intention of discussing the statement, that Mansfield would 'say what he wants to.'"[19]

The statement prepared for Mansfield was located in his papers with the hand-written notation, "not used." It praised Diem and the strategic hamlet program and recommended a "more tolerant attitude towards the honest attempts of American journalists." The language that likely caused Mansfield to balk praised the Diem regime for "restor[ing] justice and respect for human liberties," complimented the relationship between the embassy and Diem, and implied continued U.S. support.[20]

The *New York Times* reported that Mansfield refused the embassy statement at the airport, becoming the "first high ranking official in a year who did not go out of his way to assert that considerable progress was being made against the guerrilla or Vietcong." David Halberstam later said that the embassy acted "with incredible arrogance and stupidity" in attempting to get Mansfield to issue their statement. Joseph Buttinger wrote that when Mansfield refused Nolting's statement, he was "one of the few not sucked in by official self-delusion."[21]

Mansfield sought out Trueheart at the airport and told him, "I think you're right" about Diem's lack of support in the country.[22] Then, instead of issuing Nolting's statement, Mansfield simply praised Diem's personal integrity. Nolting thought Mansfield's action "very negative," and that the majority leader had been influenced by journalists. He believed it was "a great mistake on the part of anyone who is as influential as Mansfield to come out there and sort of knock the legs from under U.S. policy, which ought to have been supported by the leader of the Senate." When Nolting visited Diem after Mansfield's departure, he apologized:

> "Mr. President, I'm awfully sorry. Something must have gone wrong here. I don't know what it was but those were rather discouraging remarks." And Diem said, "I have been a friend of Senator Mansfield and he has been so good to me for so many years that I'm not going to let that stand in the way of our friendship. . . ." But he was shocked. He couldn't believe it. What impelled Mansfield to do this I've never understood.

Nolting believed that press coverage of Mansfield's report on this trip made up "the first nails in Diem's coffin." Harkins considered Mansfield's visit the first "crucial turning point" against Diem. Hammer wrote that "of all Diem's visitors in these months, Mike Mansfield, who was supposed to be his friend, was the most pessimistic." She added that reports of what Mansfield had written after his trip "set off rumors of a pending coup d'etat."[23] Ironically, the senator called Diem's "Godfather" in the 1950s would be accused of causing his death in 1963.

Ambassador Nolting believed that Mansfield spent most of his time with journalists, and that he "submerged" the views of the other senators. Mecklin wrote that the problem between the embassy and the press "was the fact that much of what the newsmen took to be lies was exactly what the Mission believed and was reporting to Washington." George Kahin was even harsher in his judgment, suggesting that the embassy engaged in conscious deception that produced bitter disputes with the press. John Newman concluded that this attitude led the administration to sink "slowly but surely into a policy of deliberate deception known and approved of by the President himself."[24]

Ambassador Nolting was correct about the press's influence on Mansfield. In Trueheart's estimation: "what happened with Mansfield was that he had talked to a lot of people in the lower ranks of the mission probably, and above all I think he'd talked to a lot of the press. Of course, he was a very astute man and he had been following this situation a very long time."[25] Valeo commented on how Mansfield used the press to glean information not available in official channels:

> In traveling abroad, it was Mansfield's habit to pick the thoughts of newsmen, in reverse informal press conferences, if you will. This was especially so in places where he believed that the United States government was not reading the situation accurately, as was the case in Vietnam not only in 1962 but throughout the American involvement.[26]

Mansfield skipped some official briefings in order to have a meeting with the press in Vietnam. Halberstam recalled that session:

> [Mike] wanted to have lunch with a group of us reporters. . . . If you wanted to get a non-official, non-embassy briefing in Saigon in those days, there was only one place—American reporters. Mike already had his doubts, and, of course, by then we were all very, very discouraged and pessimistic and we had become the enemies of the mission and of the regime. . . . So, Mike had lunch with us and it lasted for five hours. I remember going on and on and on. What was clear was that Mike Mansfield was really listening. He wanted to know.[27]

After visiting Asia, Mansfield often stopped in Hong Kong to rest and write his reports. On this trip, he also met with correspondents. Mansfield recorded that "many doubts and irritations were expressed regarding the Diem government." Takashi Oka, a reporter for the *Christian Science Monitor*, criticized Nhu and the strategic hamlet program. About Diem, Oka asserted that "we cannot win unless we get a new leader and a new atmosphere—either an entirely different man, or a President Diem so radically different from what he is today that he would be in effect a new man."[28]

MANSFIELD'S PRIVATE AND PUBLIC REPORTS

A letter from Wesley Fishel was waiting for Mansfield when he returned from his journey in the middle of December. Fishel shared Mansfield's bleak reaction, writing that his impressions were "strikingly negative" based on three trips to Vietnam in 1962.[29] These comrades from the Vietnam Lobby helped to create Diem in 1954-55, but had independently decided that their experiment was failing.

Mansfield submitted his secret report to Kennedy on December 18 and met with the president in Palm Beach on December 26 to discuss his findings. The majority leader remembered the meeting:

> We spent about two hours going over my written report, which he read in detail and about which he questioned me minutely. He had a tremendous grasp of the situation. He didn't waste much time. He certainly never wasted any words. What effect the report had on him I don't know, but he did start to raise a few points which were in disagreement with what I had to say, but at least he got the truth as I saw it and it wasn't a pleasant picture that I had depicted.[30]

After reading the majority leader's "brutally frank" assessment, "Kennedy rebutted Mansfield's gloomy report. 'You asked me to go out there,' answered Mansfield, to which Kennedy replied frostily: 'Well, I'll read it again.'"[31] Kahin argued that the report "let in a blast of genuinely fresh air, but for Kennedy it was politically chilling"; had "Kennedy been disposed to change course in Vietnam, he could have used this well-publicized assessment as a foundation upon which to build a new policy."[32] Kenneth O'Donnell reported that Kennedy said to him later: "I got angry with Mike for disagreeing with our policy so completely, and I got angry with myself because I found myself agreeing with him."[33]

Although Mansfield's 1962 report on Vietnam initially met with the president's rejection, it did force Kennedy to reexamine his policies. At a spring 1963 follow-up meeting between Mansfield and Kennedy, Kahin reports:

> The president stated that he had been having serious second thoughts about the senator's argument and now agreed on the need for a complete military withdrawal from Vietnam. "But," Kennedy cautioned, "I can't do it until 1965—after I'm reelected." O'Donnell stated that "President Kennedy felt, and Mansfield agreed with him, that if he announced a total withdrawal of American military personnel from Vietnam before the 1964 election, there would be a wild conservative outcry against returning him to the Presidency for a second term. . . ."
>
> After Mansfield had left, the president said, "If I tried to pull out completely now from Vietnam we would have another Joe McCarthy red scare on our hands, but I can do it after I'm reelected. So we had better make damned sure that I *am* reelected."[34]

In his correspondence, Mansfield denied the ethical implications from O'Donnell's account:

> The only thing discussed at that meeting . . . was the President's desire to bring about a withdrawal but recognizing that it could not be done precipitantly but only over a period of months. The election was not even mentioned nor thought of and I must disassociate myself with any inference that the President and I agreed that "the party image" would or should be taken into consideration. What conversations Mr. O'Donnell and the President had after my meeting, I am not aware of.[35]

While we can never know whether the O'Donnell or the Mansfield account of that meeting is the more accurate, we do know that both Kennedy and Mansfield remembered the 1952 Republican question "Who lost China?" Neither man wanted Kennedy running for reelection against the question: "Who lost Indochina?"

Mansfield shared his secret report with Senators Pell, Boggs, and Smith, and they gave it their "general concurrence." The majority leader appeared to have been the primary author of the public report. Because of the different audiences of the two reports, their formats were not the same. Primarily, the public report included background material and history, information that Kennedy would not have needed. It also included much information on the role China was playing in the area. Yet there were also subtle differences in the two reports in order to disseminate different information for public consumption. Halberstam described the public report as one of "mild caution" and the private one as "blunt and pessimistic about the future of it all."[36]

Both reports suggested the need for improvement from the South Vietnamese. The private report suggested that the United States could succeed *"provided"* the South Vietnamese display "vigor and self-dedication." The public report also emphasized the likelihood of success if the South Vietnamese showed "leadership." More importantly, it emphasized that while U.S. support was important, it was not "controlling," for Saigon had ultimate responsibility. This was an effort to counter the belief that the United States was pulling the strings in the war.

Each report emphasized that the United States could not withdraw abruptly, but the public statement was more emphatic:

> if the attempt is made to alter aid to south Viet-nam via a congressional meat-ax cut of foreign aid to Southeast Asia it runs the risk of not merely removing the fat but of cleaving a gap which will lay open the region to massive chaos and, hence, jeopardize the present Pacific structure of our national security.

The public report also emphasized the need not to lessen the commitment in Southeast Asia as long as China remained hostile to the United States. Undoubtedly, Mansfield wanted to send a message to China to discourage any Chinese adventurism in the area.

The sharpest contrast between the two reports was one of tone, and involved the issue of increasing the numbers of American troops. Mansfield put it unequivocally in his private report: "in short going to war fully ourselves against the guerrillas" and establishing "some form of neocolonial rule in south Vietnam . . . is an alternative which I most emphatically do not recommend." While the group report also cautioned against making the war an American one—in three different places it added *"in present circumstances."* This seemed to be a clear signal to Hanoi not to assume that the United States would not increase its commitment.

Mansfield ended the private report by offering Kennedy a way out through negotiation rather than military escalation. The majority leader suggested that Vietnam was only "desirable" to our national interests, and that by rhetorically painting that interest as essential or vital, the United States was paving the way for an increased role: "we may well discover that it is in our interests to do less rather than more than we are now doing. If that is the case, we will do well to concentrate on a vigorous diplomacy which would be designed to lighten our commitments without bringing about sudden and catastrophic upheavals in Southeast Asia."[37]

The public report received little press coverage. The *New York Times* merely summarized the report and the weekly news magazines ignored it. The *New Republic*, however, called it explosive, especially coming from a man once known as "Diem's godfather." Yet the magazine was concerned that the Kennedy administration continued to escalate even after the criticism from a man in its inner circle.[38]

Kennedy frequently sent members of the administration to South Vietnam in order to justify escalation decisions already made.[39] Two such visits were made after Mansfield's visit to counter his report. Kennedy sent Roger Hilsman and Michael Forrestal at the end of 1962 to report on the situation. Both men were committed to the U.S. program in Vietnam and the visit strengthened that commitment. They, too, saw a long war even though the situation was improving and the government was "probably winning." The Joint Chiefs of Staff sent an investigation team in January 1963 that largely refuted Mansfield's findings.[40] So, while Mansfield's report disturbed Kennedy, the president made sure that a large body of evidence was created to deny Mansfield's position.

MANSFIELD AND THE PRESS

As Mansfield's contacts with the press on his 1962 Vietnam trip attest, the senator was sympathetic toward the fourth estate. Mansfield had cultivated a friendly relationship with the press beginning in his House years. As majority leader, the press came to appreciate his accessibility, candor, willingness to operate without a press secretary, and the fact that his press conversations were "on the record."[41]

Mansfield specifically demonstrated his support for members of the media in Vietnam. On February 21, 1963 the majority leader placed an article written by Richard Dudman for the *St. Louis Post-Dispatch* in the *Congressional Record.* The article discussed press criticism coming from Nolting and members of the state and defense departments. Mansfield mentioned that he had spent considerable time with the American press corps in Vietnam and that "they had the same objectivity, alertness, and appropriate skepticism of official handouts" as members of the press elsewhere. He added that the press reported the situation as they saw it, but that they were denied access to information by government officials— information that the public had a right to know. When Dudman was denied a visa to return to South Vietnam, Mansfield interceded with Rusk on the reporter's behalf, calling Dudman's earlier writing on Vietnam "exceptional pieces of reporting in the best tradition of American journalism."[42]

The U.S. press corps clearly viewed Mansfield as an ally. In March of 1962 Diem informed the embassy that he would expel Homer Bigart of the *New York Times* and Francois Sully of *Newsweek.* Nolting dissuaded Diem, but Bigart was transferred to New York. In August, Ben Bradlee of *Newsweek* called Mansfield because Sully was being threatened with expulsion from Vietnam for the third time. Sully's offense was interviewing historian Bernard Fall and an anonymous member of South Vietnam's military for the August 20th issue of the magazine. The interviews suggested that the war was going badly for Diem, that Harkins displayed undue "optimism," and that too many decisions were made for political and not military reasons. With hindsight, it is hard to dispute those conclusions, but after years of kid-glove treatment by a U.S. press influenced by American Friends of Vietnam, the Ngos were deeply offended. Earlier efforts through the administration to get Nolting to intervene with Diem had been successful, but the most recent one had failed. Bradlee wanted Mansfield to send a telegram on Sully's behalf, although it was not clear whether the telegram was to be sent to Nolting or Diem. Mansfield promised Bradlee that he would "issue a statement deploring it when he [Sully] gets kicked out." Nolting appealed on *Newsweek's* behalf but Diem expelled Sully anyway.[43] Kahin concluded that Sully's expulsion "was hardly displeasing to the embassy."[44]

In June 1963 Mansfield wrote to McNamara, calling Neil Sheehan and Malcolm Browne "extremely competent correspondents," urging the secretary of defense "to do everything possible" to help all reporters carry out their assignments in Vietnam. In July, Mansfield attempted to intervene when members of the press were roughed up by South Vietnamese authorities while covering a Buddhist protest. Sheehan, Halberstam, Browne, Peter Arnett and other journalists cabled Mansfield: "YOU MAKE US ALL WISH WE WERE VOTING RESIDENTS OF MONTANA." In his memoirs, Browne called Mansfield a "great senator and statesman of the era."[45]

One journalist concluded that few politicians have been "respected more— and criticized less" by the media than Mansfield.[46] This helps explain the press's lack of scrutiny on Mansfield's influence over the Eisenhower administration's Indochina policy making when the decisions of 1954-1955 began to look flawed.

Mansfield's 1963 Vietnam Discourse

Mansfield's final extant memorandum to Kennedy on Vietnam came in August 1963, after a lapse of eight months. This memo was written during the Buddhist crisis that contributed to the coup and the assassination of Diem. Nhu's forces viciously repressed Buddhist protests, which led to the self-immolation of several Buddhist monks. The suicides triggered negative American public opinion toward Diem, but Madame Nhu's ridicule of such self-immolations as "barbecues" was even more damaging.[47] Mansfield's eight-page memo demonstrated a strengthening of his private opposition to U.S. commitment in Vietnam.[48] Early in the memo, Mansfield complimented Kennedy on the selection of Henry Cabot

Lodge as ambassador and recommended that Lodge be given great power, even to the point of removing those U.S. officials in Vietnam who disagreed with him. Mansfield followed this memo with a speech in which he demanded the removal of bureaucrats who failed to cooperate with Lodge.[49]

In the memo, Mansfield warned that while "the die" of direct U.S. involvement "is not yet finally cast, we are very close to the point where it will have to be." The cost "in men and money could go at least as high as Korea." As in his Michigan State University speech, Mansfield chose several rhetorical questions to make his point:

> Have we, by our own repeated rhetorical flourishes on "corks in bottles" and "stopping Communism everywhere" and loose use of the phrase "vital interest of the nation" over the past few years given this situation a highly inflated importance and, hence, talked ourselves into the present bind? In short, have we, as in Laos, first over-extended ourselves in words and in agency-programs and, then, in search of a rationalization for the erroneous initial over-extension, moved what may be essentially a peripheral situation to the core of our policy-considerations?[50]

Mansfield answered his own rhetorical questions in the affirmative and then justified his answers, saying it was "almost inconceivable" that policy in the Western Pacific would include the deployment of hundreds of thousands or even millions of U.S. troops on the Asian mainland. He quoted Eisenhower's dictum, "let Asians fight Asians."

The Montanan offered an alternative premise: "the essential interests of the United States do not compel this nation to become unilaterally engaged in any nation in Southeast Asia. Indeed, it is doubtful that it is in the interests of the peoples of those nations themselves, for the United States to become so engaged." He reminded Kennedy that his predecessor never considered committing troops; "the most sanguine proposal" was a one-strike aerial attack at Dien Bien Phu and that was ultimately rejected by Eisenhower. Mansfield used the term "agencied" several times to describe how the original limited commitment had been expanded by the bureaucracy to be close to an "irrevocable total commitment." He opposed any commitment if it were to be unilateral without international sanction.

The memo did not mention Diem by name but alluded to the South Vietnamese president. Mansfield wrote that "whether to support the present government or not is the secondary or tactical question"; the real issue was to keep down the costs of American lives and money. He also asserted the right to "withdraw assistance in the absence of responsible and responsive indigenous leadership." While Mansfield did not directly apply that last statement to Diem, the implication seems clear. Mansfield did refer to Diem's brother, suggesting that Kennedy could justify a 10 percent reduction in U.S. advisors by using Nhu's comment that there were "too many Americans in South Viet Nam."[51]

Even though Mansfield and Kennedy were both having serious doubts about the effectiveness of Diem, Mansfield said surprisingly little on the subject in any of his memoranda. This seems especially odd since, as freshmen, the two senators had been among the handful of Americans who sponsored Diem, helping to bring him to power. Mansfield's loyalty was legendary, and explains his reluctance to directly attack his friend.[52]

Mansfield's Influence on Kennedy's Thinking on Indochina

Those who believe Kennedy would have withdrawn from Vietnam link the assertion to O'Donnell's account. Kennedy aide Theodore Sorensen does not accept that "the United States ever would have sent 500,000-plus men into Vietnam" if Kennedy had lived. Arthur Schlesinger Jr. stated: "I don't think he [Kennedy] would have ever Americanized the war. He told quite a number of people that after the '64 election, he had plans for the withdrawal of American forces." Columnist Jack Anderson reported that "shortly before his [Kennedy's] death, he indicated to me that he wanted to pull all American military people out of Vietnam."[53]

Mansfield was too modest to explicitly claim that he changed Kennedy's thinking on Vietnam. Yet the senator thought that Kennedy would have ended U.S. commitment after his expected reelection, and he has stated that his arguments were persuasive with Kennedy, while failing with Johnson.[54] In 1975 Mansfield told Jack Anderson that Kennedy "felt we had made an error. He was going to order a gradual withdrawal." Two years later, Mansfield repeated his version in more detail:

> [Kennedy] called me down and said he had changed his mind and that he wanted to begin withdrawing troops beginning the first of the following year, that would be in January 1964. He was very unhappy about the situation which had developed there and felt that even then with 16,000 troops we were in too deep.

When asked why Kennedy changed his mind, Mansfield became nostalgic: "Maybe he was listening to others besides the Pentagon. And maybe he was going back to his old thinking about Indo-China while he was a Senator and reviving some of the views he held then."[55]

Robert Kennedy was among those who believed that Mansfield's dissent over U.S. policy in Vietnam did not influence his brother, suggesting that JFK intended to "win" in Vietnam. Rusk agreed with Robert Kennedy and commented on the Mansfield/O'Donnell account:

Kennedy liked to bat the breeze and toss ideas around, and it is entirely possible that he left the impression with some that he planned on getting out of Vietnam in 1965. But that does not mean he made a decision in 1963 to withdraw in 1965. Had he done so, I think I would have known about it.

In his memoirs, Rusk hinted at why the president may have shared his doubts with O'Donnell and Mansfield but not with his secretary of state. Rusk wrote that his relationship with Kennedy "was always official, never personal," and that Kennedy always called him "Mr. Secretary, never Dean." Kahin described O'Donnell as "much more than Kennedy's appointments secretary," but one of the president's closest confidants, and he quoted Pierre Salinger as describing O'Donnell as the White House staffer with "the greatest responsibility, influence, and accessibility to the president."[56] Mansfield and Kennedy had been close since they became Senate seat mates in 1952.

It seems reasonable that Kennedy would share his doubts with close friends like O'Donnell and Mansfield while concealing those doubts from Rusk. Kennedy also expected a sympathetic audience from Mansfield when discussing withdrawal, while Rusk likely would have disapproved. The president tended to leave Rusk out of decision making, and Robert Kennedy claimed that his brother planned to replace Rusk in his second term, which offers an independent reason why Rusk would have been left in the dark on the president's feelings about Vietnam.[57]

What does seem strange is that the president never discussed his plans for Vietnam with his brother, Robert. A number of Kennedy's advisors suggested that the president relied on his brother's advice on foreign policy.[58] If Kennedy had really committed to withdrawal after reelection, it seems likely that Robert would have known.

Kennedy was likely confused and uncertain of what to do. Charles Bartlett, a journalist friend of Kennedy's, thought that the president was "totally out to sea about what to do in Vietnam."[59] Even though Kennedy was probably serious in thinking he could pull out after his reelection, the record in the last months of his life suggested he would have had difficulty in ending U.S. involvement. In 1963 Kennedy continued to escalate both militarily and politically. Militarily, Kennedy had increased the presence of U.S. advisors in Vietnam from 685 to 16,300, some of whom were engaged in combat. Kennedy's plan to bring 1,000 advisors home at the end of 1963 was more symbolic than substantial, and may have been an attempt to manipulate opponents like Mansfield. The president also told Jack Anderson that he was troubled by North Vietnamese infiltration into the South, branding it "a new form of aggression."[60] Kennedy would have had difficulty resisting the outcry from the military and congressional conservatives in abandoning South Vietnam to its certain fate.

The primary political escalation was the coup to depose Diem. The major reasons the administration worked with elements of South Vietnam's military to purge Diem on November 2, 1963, were his reluctance to accept U.S. combat troops and the American fear that his brother, Nhu, was negotiating with Hanoi. Tensions were so great that the administration feared that the Ngo regime might kick the United States out of South Vietnam if Diem were allowed to stay in power. Roger Lalouette, the French ambassador in Saigon, urged Diem to ask some American advisors to leave and to open talks with North Vietnam.[61]

Because Mansfield remained committed to Diem, he was not consulted by anyone in the administration when the decisions to purge the Vietnamese leader were made. He was one of the few to express sorrow at the death of Diem, saying he was "shocked and grieved at the death of an old and valued friend." Mansfield also said that he was sure the coup was a surprise to the administration.[62] It was not. The Kennedy administration was deeply involved in the coup plotting.[63]

Mansfield chose not to ask the right questions about U.S. involvement in the coup. When Rusk appeared before the Foreign Relations Committee immediately after Diem's death, he was not forthcoming about the role of the administration in the overthrow of Diem. Some committee members were harsh in their judgment. George Aiken (R-Vt.) said, "I am not exactly bursting with pride this morning over our operations in South Vietnam," and he questioned the administration decision to immediately recognize the new government. Frank Lausche (D-Ohio) claimed that the immediate recognition created the impression that the United States participated in the coup. Hubert Humphrey (D-Minn.) suggested that the United States was "mixed up with a bunch of bandits" in Vietnam. Frank Church (D-Idaho) and George Smathers (D-Fla.) were the only two committee members voicing approval for the coup. Throughout this discussion, Mansfield remained silent.[64]

For the remainder of his career, Mansfield continued his loyalty to Diem, once using the metaphor "we were getting off the right horse and getting on the wrong horses." He frequently made such comments as:

> the greatest tragedy was the assassination of Ngo Dinh Diem. No matter what you think of him—and I thought highly of him—he did give South Vietnam stability, a degree of permanence and an ability to look forward. With his passing, we have had nothing but coup and U.S.-supported client Governments, but in the last analysis we have become a sort of client of South Vietnam.[65]

Ironically, Mansfield's friendship with Kennedy made him powerless when the coup was planned, and the Montanan's leadership position kept him from attacking the administration after the coup. In 1954-55, Eisenhower and Dulles feared that Mansfield had the clout in the Senate to end U.S. aid if Diem were deposed, even though Mansfield was in his first term. The Tran Van Chuongs remembered the early years and found it necessary to "check out" the senator to see if he would assume a similar stance in 1963. Even with his position of majority leader, the

Kennedy administration decision makers did not have similar concerns. Mansfield's affection for Kennedy and his party affiliation constrained his independence on the issues of Vietnam and Diem.

The rebels took advantage of the chaos in South Vietnam caused by the coup and the new South Vietnamese government's military and political situation deteriorated rapidly, especially in the central highlands. Efforts to win over the peasants, such as the strategic hamlet program, were neglected by South Vietnam's leaders in the frequent changes of government that followed Diem's overthrow. Future South Vietnamese leaders shunned the idea of negotiation, and their American allies expected them to demonstrate a desire to pursue a military victory. Diem's death ended the last chance for a South Vietnam independent from American control.[66]

Many conclude that American involvement in the coup imprisoned the United States in the war. After Diem's death, U.S. officials felt even more responsible for South Vietnam's plight, making disengagement unlikely. General William Westmoreland claimed:

> the young president made a grievous mistake in assenting to the overthrow of Diem in 1963. In my view that action mortally locked us into Vietnam. If it had not been for our involvement in the overthrow of President Diem, we could perhaps have gracefully withdrawn our support when South Vietnam's lack of unity and leadership became apparent.[67]

In the wake of the coup in South Vietnam, Sihanouk became more suspicious of the United States, fearing that he would be next. Thus, Cambodia quit accepting U.S. economic aid. Mansfield was one of the few Americans to support Cambodia's position. *Realites Cambodgiennes* called Mansfield "a 'man alone,'" and noted that his views, "so penetrating on the Far East, are still shared only by a very small group." They predicted that if "some day Khmer-American amity again flourishes, it will be due above all to Mr. Mansfield and other men of his caliber."[68]

The administration's desire to place U.S. combat troops in Vietnam and to prevent negotiation between Saigon and Hanoi did not indicate Kennedy would have lessened the commitment after 1964. At the time of his death, though, Kennedy had only hinted to a few confidants that he was considering withdrawal. His public statements and his actions indicated the path of escalation.

While it seems likely that Kennedy would have continued to escalate in the short term, he did want to avoid the commitment of ground troops that Johnson ordered in July 1965. Johnson was interested primarily in domestic legislation and became dependent on the foreign policy advisors he inherited from Kennedy. Kennedy tended to act as his own secretary of state and might have weighed the opinion of Mansfield and others over that of Rusk and McNamara.

While we can never know, Kennedy might have reversed his policy of escalation before the ultimate commitment of troops in July 1965.

Kennedy died in the same month as Diem, and the shock of the death of the U.S. president caused America to forget Diem's murder. Yet the two deaths in November would haunt Lyndon Johnson. Rusk said that Johnson thought the coup a "great mistake." The new president showed Humphrey a picture of Diem hanging in his house and said, "we had a hand in killing him. Now it's happening here."

Johnson was determined to maintain continuity by retaining as many of Kennedy's advisors as possible.[69] The men who had advised Kennedy toward an increased commitment to South Vietnam would now be advising the new president. Mansfield, too, remained in his familiar role, wasting no time in shifting his persuasive efforts toward Lyndon Johnson.

Part III

1963-1968

Private Dissent Yet Public Compliance

CHAPTER 8

JOHNSON MOVES TOWARD WAR IN VIETNAM

Lyndon Johnson expressed little interest in Indochina during the Eisenhower administration, and his experience with the issue that would bring down his administration was limited. During the Kennedy years, Johnson was more cautious than Kennedy or his advisors regarding Laos. He thought that Laos was "one hell of a poor place to fight."[1]

Kennedy sent his vice president to South Vietnam in May 1961. Before embarking on the trip, Johnson discussed his mission with Mansfield and J. William Fulbright (D-Ark.). As majority leader, Johnson had always deferred to Fulbright on foreign policy issues, and Johnson respected Mansfield's expertise on Vietnam. Johnson took Francis Valeo, Mansfield's assistant, with him to Vietnam, a move that one writer saw as a desire for a "foil" against State Department advice on a trip that committed the vice president to Vietnam.[2] Valeo responded to the claim:

> Johnson did request that I give him a straight story when he asked for it and that I did. His principal advisors were drawn from his personal entourage and from the Department of State and the advice given him from those sources adhered very closely to the prevailing wisdom with regard to Indochina. Johnson reached the conclusion that some increased aid effort on our part at that point would resolve the problem of our involvement in Vietnam forthwith.[3]

Vice President Johnson made a controversial toast calling Ngo Dinh Diem the "Churchill of Southeast Asia," and he compared the South Vietnamese president favorably to George Washington and Franklin Roosevelt. In his report to President Kennedy, Johnson described Diem as complex, with many problems, possessing "admirable qualities but remote from the people [and] surrounded by persons less admirable and capable than he." Johnson seemed to genuinely like Diem, and he opposed early Kennedy administration discussions for a coup against the South Vietnamese leader.[4]

One day into his presidency, Johnson arrived in Washington from Dallas. He talked for hours to his assistants about his goals. Jack Valenti remembered that "Vietnam at the time was a cloud no bigger than a man's fist on the horizon. We hardly discussed it because it wasn't worth discussing." That changed the very next day. On November 24, 1963 Johnson spent the afternoon with his national security advisors being briefed by the U.S. ambassador to South Vietnam, Henry Cabot Lodge. Johnson reported that Lodge claimed South Vietnam could "go under—any day." The army would not fight and the people did not support the government. The president committed to more aid so the Soviets and Chinese would not think the United States "lost heart" after Kennedy's death. Johnson wanted Vietnam behind him so he could concentrate on his domestic agenda, but he felt like he had "just grabbed a big juicy worm with a right sharp hook in the middle of it."[5]

One week later at an Executive Committee meeting, Johnson wrote: "Day of Reckoning coming, we could have kept Diem." George Ball suggested that "President Johnson was anxious to avoid an irreversible embroilment [in Vietnam]. At every stage, he moved reluctantly—pushed by events and the well-meant prodding of the same men who counseled President Kennedy." Joseph Alsop believed that in the area of foreign policy, "Johnson lacked any kind of internal compass" and "relied on the leftovers from the Kennedy time. And when these men failed him, he was left, in the case of Vietnam, to pursue a policy that he neither believed in nor understood."[6] Just as he had with Kennedy, Mansfield would be one of the few and most vocal opponents to each escalation decision.

As he had with Kennedy, the Montanan adhered to a policy of criticizing his president's policies in private and backing him in public whenever possible. Early in 1964 Mansfield allowed that Johnson had a "terrible, awesome, lonely job," and that when criticizing any president, one should place oneself in that person's shoes and ask the question, "what would I do in his place?"[7] Even so, Mansfield did not give the new president much time to get acclimated to his new job after Kennedy's death before beginning his private campaign to influence administration policy in Indochina. He sent his first memo to Johnson on December 7, 1963.

MANSFIELD'S PURSUIT OF NEUTRALIZATION

In August 1963 French president Charles de Gaulle had launched a peace initiative calling for a unified and neutralist Vietnam, free from outside influences. After the Diem coup, there were signals from both the National Liberation Front, the political arm of the Vietcong, and Hanoi of interest in such a settlement. In September and November, Cambodian prince Norodom Sihanouk called for neutralization of Cambodia. Mansfield favored these neutralization proposals, which put him at odds with Johnson administration officials.[8]

Mansfield argued for neutralization in a December 7 memo. The memo was written as a result of an earlier conversation held with the new president. Included with the memo were copies of memoranda that Mansfield had sent to President Kennedy on Indochina, his Michigan State speech, and his February 1963 Senate report. One Johnson biographer believes that Mansfield's December argument "reads persuasively in *retrospect* as an alternative to the Vietnam policies that were actually pursued during this presidency."[9]

In the memo, Mansfield asserted that while some details had changed, "the basic observations and conclusions [from his communication to Kennedy] remain valid." Mansfield added the thought that U.S. policy was based on two assumptions that might be in error: that the war "can be won in south Viet Nam alone" and "that the war can be won at a limited expenditure of American lives and resources somewhere commensurate with our national interests in south Viet Nam."

Mansfield posed the rhetorical question: "what national interests in Asia would steel the American people for the massive costs of an ever-deepening involvement of that kind?" Specifically, Mansfield called for the Saigon government to strengthen its hold on the parts of the country that it controlled, even if it meant conceding areas to the Vietcong and using an "astute diplomatic offensive" that employed "France, Britain, India, and, perhaps, even Russia" to end the conflict. *"France is the key country,"* Mansfield emphasized. He appealed for "U.S. understanding, sympathy and sensible encouragement for the Cambodian desire to stand on its own feet without one-sided U.S. aid." In Mansfield's mind, a neutral Cambodia was the "prototype" of a peaceful Southeast Asia.[10]

Stanley Karnow argued that Johnson admired Mansfield, counted on his support for domestic legislation, and listened to Mansfield as an expert on Asia who had been involved in early U.S. commitments to that region. Yet Johnson feared the "soft on communism" charge as he prepared for the 1964 election.[11] At a Christmas Eve reception in 1963, Johnson reportedly told the Joint Chiefs of Staff: "just let me get elected, and then you can have your war."[12] Johnson was not yet ready to write Mansfield off, though. In that same Christmas week, the president called Valeo, which led to another Mansfield memorandum to the president on January 6.

Johnson had admitted to Valeo that he feared another "loss of China" charge over Vietnam. Mansfield's memo revisited a theme he had used with Kennedy. He suggested that administration rhetoric forced the United States into a position from which retreat was difficult:

> A key . . . factor in both situations was a tendency to bite off more than we were prepared in the end to chew. We tended to talk ourselves out on a limb with over-statements of our purpose and commitment only to discover in the end that there

were not sufficient American interests to support with blood and treasure a desperate final plunge. Then, the questions followed invariably: "Who got us into this
mess?" "Who lost China?" etc.

We are close to the point of no return in Viet Nam. . . . There ought to be less
official talk of our responsibility in Viet Nam and more emphasis on the responsibilities of the Vietnamese themselves and a great deal of thought on the possibilities
for a peaceful solution through the efforts of other nations as well as our own.[13]

George Kahin speculated that neutralization would deny the interventionist policy that Johnson's advisors had championed during the Kennedy administration,
thereby destroying their credibility. Thus, Mansfield's efforts were undercut by
nearly all of Johnson's senior advisors.[14] McGeorge Bundy, Secretary of State Dean
Rusk, and Secretary of Defense Robert McNamara saw neutralization as a "devil
term," and they all wrote memoranda refuting Mansfield's neutralization rationale.

Bundy argued that moving in Mansfield's direction of neutralization would
cause the collapse of anti-communist forces in South Vietnam, leading to communist unification, neutrality in Thailand, the defeat of anti-communist forces
in Laos, increased pressure in Malaysia, increased neutrality in Japan and the
Philippines, and damaged U.S. prestige in South Korea and Taiwan. This would
force an increase in U.S. commitment or retreat from those countries. Bundy
went on to call neutralization a "betrayal," suggesting that the anti-communist
Vietnamese could cost Johnson the 1964 election. He also opposed negotiations,
writing Johnson, "*when* we are stronger *then* we can face negotiation." Bundy
wanted a trade with Mansfield: the administration would support needed new
programs in Vietnam if Mansfield would support the war effort. Rusk believed
the South Vietnamese could still win the war and also opposed negotiation until
"after the North Vietnamese become convinced that they cannot succeed in
destroying the Republic of Vietnam by guerrilla warfare." He called neutralization "a phony." McNamara agreed that the war could still be won and wrote that
neutralization would lead to a communist-dominated government. He argued
against Mansfield's position on national interest, saying that to draw the line
against communist gains was indeed in the U.S. interest.[15]

More than thirty years later, McNamara admitted: "All three of us felt
Mansfield's path would lead to the loss of South Vietnam to communist control
with extremely serious consequences for the United States and the West. . . ."
McNamara conceded that the three advisors were "limited and shallow" in their
"analysis and discussion of the alternatives to our existing policy in Vietnam—
i.e., neutralization or withdrawal."[16]

In 1964, though, Walt Rostow and Theodore Sorensen followed up the
Bundy, Rusk, and McNamara memoranda with anti-neutralization memoranda
of their own.[17] In Johnson's mind, the big guns of his senior officials outweighed
Mansfield's argument for neutrality.

On January 30 a second coup occurred in Vietnam, replacing General Duong Van Minh with General Nguyen Khanh. Khanh justified the coup because members of Minh's government favored the French proposals for neutrality.[18] The governments of South Vietnam and the United States were now in lock step against neutrality.

The Khanh coup led Mansfield to write another memo to Johnson on February 1. Mansfield must have doubted that Johnson read or paid attention to his memos since he included copies of his December 7 and January 6 memos, calling them "valid." In the new memo, Mansfield correctly predicted that the recent coup would not improve the situation and that more coups would likely be forthcoming. He praised the de Gaulle approach as offering "a faint glimmer of hope." Mansfield foretold:

> A deeper military plunge is not a real alternative. Apart from the absence of sufficient national interest to justify it to our own people, there is no reason to assume that it will settle the question. More likely than not, it will simply enlarge the morass in which we are now already on the verge of indefinite entrapment.

Mansfield emphatically opposed military involvement and argued that the administration should not reward the new junta's violent shift to anti-communism and anti-neutralism. He argued that Johnson should denounce the junta's hostility toward France, and that the United States needed to encourage France to explore solutions in Laos and Vietnam and join her in supporting Cambodia.[19]

In public Mansfield remained supportive of Johnson's Vietnam policy. He wrote a constituent: "for at least the present . . . the United States has no choice but to continue to provide financial assistance to Vietnam and keep a sizable group of military advisors there."[20] Mansfield had a competing task with that of extracting the United States from Vietnam, which he expressed to the Democratic National Committee: "my job is to keep the Democratic Party together and that is just what I am going to do."[21]

MANSFIELD TAKES HIS PURSUIT OF NEUTRALIZATION PUBLIC

Mansfield met with Johnson on the evening of February 10. No record of the meeting exists, but a memo from McGeorge Bundy makes it clear that Vietnam was to be discussed. Bundy urged Johnson to argue that "any weakening of our support of anti-communist forces in South Vietnam would give the signal for a wholesale collapse of anti-communism all over Southeast Asia. Khanh's government may be our last best chance, and we simply cannot afford to be the ones who seem to pull the plug on him." Bundy suggested that Johnson "urge Mansfield himself not to express his own doubts in public, at least for a while."[22]

Assuming that Johnson followed Bundy's advice, Mansfield flaunted Johnson's request. He was concerned enough about the situation in Vietnam to choose a public forum to discuss it on February 19, 1964. This was his first major address on Vietnam since the summer of 1962, and his first in the Senate since the Eisenhower administration. Mansfield argued that the war was Vietnamese, that U.S. interests did not dictate a larger role, that the second coup made a third one likely, and that the United States should not dismiss de Gaulle's neutralization proposal. Mansfield's arguments were similar to the private arguments he had been making to both Kennedy and Johnson, but the speech gained attention because the arguments were new in the public forum.

Jacob Javits (R-N.Y.) engaged Mansfield in debate the following day. Javits feared that talk of neutralization could demoralize U.S. allies in Vietnam and that the public approved of U.S. involvement in Vietnam. Clement Zablocki (D-Wis.), Chairman of the Far East Subcommittee of the House Foreign Affairs Committee, refuted Mansfield's Senate speech in the House on the same day.[23]

Officially, there was no reaction to Mansfield's speech, but unofficially, Gibbons reported that the reaction ran from "shock to dismay to anger." One government official charged: "of course it wasn't the Senator's intention to give aid and comfort to the communists and undermine Vietnamese and American morale, but that's exactly what he did. And he couldn't have done a better job if his speech had been written in Hanoi." President Johnson cabled Lodge in Saigon about this issue: "I think that nothing is more important than to stop neutralist talk whenever we can by whatever means we can. I have made this point myself to Mansfield and [Walter] Lippmann and I expect to use every public opportunity to restate our position firmly." In Saigon, Mansfield's speech increased the belief that the United States was sick of the war and seeking a way out. [24]

Mansfield's speech also sparked reaction outside of government. James Reston took issue with Mansfield's position in the *New York Times,* while journalist Lippmann agreed with the Montanan. The most interesting reaction came from columnist William White, a close friend of Johnson and a fellow Texan. White was considered a mouthpiece for the president, someone who often "sailed a kite" for him.[25] He wrote a scathing editorial that likely reflected Johnson's thinking. White attacked Mansfield by accusing him of undercutting bipartisan foreign policy, embarrassing the president, forming a "quasi-alliance" with de Gaulle, and causing fear in South Vietnam. The journalist also refuted Mansfield's contention that he spoke as an individual, claiming: "there is no difference abroad between what Mansfield says as an individual and what he says as majority leader."[26]

Mansfield's February 19 speech generated large amounts of mail, most of which was positive. The Montanan replied to some of these letters, expressing his philosophy on dissent as well as his concern that Vietnam policy needed to be publicly debated. In one letter, Mansfield explained:

The primary responsibility in foreign policy rests with the President and I have tried, regardless of the party of the incumbent, to give the President such support from the Senate as I might. However, Senators also have a measure of responsibility in matters of policy. We do have a duty to bring up . . . alternatives which for one reason or another may not be receiving adequate consideration.[27]

While Mansfield's view of congressional and presidential power explains his February break from Johnson's policy, it proved maddening to the administration. They expected unquestioned support from a Democratic majority leader. Later, Mansfield's philosophy proved equally frustrating to war critics who wanted Mansfield to better utilize the potential power of his elected position.

The senator's quiet criticism also provided a public service in February 1964. For the first time during the Johnson presidency, there was public debate about alternatives to Johnson's inherited policy of gradual escalation. Mansfield lost the debate, but he was responsible for its occurrence.

Rusk testified in executive sessions of the Foreign Relations Committee four times in the first half of 1964. With the increased duties of leadership, Mansfield attended only the March meeting. He attended then in order to question Rusk about neutralization. When Mansfield asked Rusk if it would be necessary to increase U.S. forces and financial aid to South Vietnam, the secretary of state answered: "we believe that the forces and the materiel that are required to do this job are present in South Vietnam." The cross-examination that followed seemed to be an effort to expose the contradictions in administration policy:

MANSFIELD: It is my understanding that we are in South Vietnam to restore it to the position which was accorded to it under the Geneva agreement in 1954.

RUSK: That is correct, sir.

MANSFIELD: And . . . if that objective is attained, what is the status of South Vietnam then? Is it a neutral state?

RUSK: It is an unaligned state.

MANSFIELD: Is it a neutral state?

RUSK: I am a little worried about the word "neutral" because that carries psychological implications that are not necessarily there. It would certainly be unaligned.

MANSFIELD: Are you willing to consider it [neutrality]?

RUSK: Yes, but, Senator, there are overtones about the French attitude [over] there that are quite disturbing. [discussion off the record][28]

Rusk's testimony showed that Mansfield was destined to lose the neutralization battle because the administration did not want a neutral or an unaligned Vietnam—they wanted to maintain the status quo with an anti-communist state in place.

In a March news conference Johnson publicly separated the administration from the majority leader. The president admitted that Mansfield had "given me his counsel over the years in the general area of Southeast Asia." Yet he made it clear that Mansfield "spoke for himself" and there was "no division in the administration between Secretary Rusk and Secretary McNamara and myself." On the surface, at least, the relationship between Johnson and Mansfield remained close. In an April meeting with a group from Montana, Johnson joked that both he and Mansfield "outmarried ourselves."[29] Beneath the surface, however, Mansfield's dissent strained the relationship with his mentor.

Mansfield still tried to be supportive of Johnson, even in such private meetings with other members of Congress as a National Security Council Meeting on April 3. McNamara indicated that the situation in Vietnam was deteriorating: the Vietcong were increasing control in the countryside; an apathetic population led to increased South Vietnamese desertions; "many fortified hamlets had been overrun or disbanded"; frequent changes in the government in Saigon had contributed to a deteriorating political structure in the hamlets with the Vietcong moving into the vacuum; and the Vietcong were receiving better weapons.

McNamara rejected the options of withdrawal and neutralization, which he argued would both lead to a communist government, and the option of broadening the U.S. military involvement. The course McNamara asserted the administration had chosen was to "make the present program of assistance more effective." In response to a question, McNamara indicated that U.S. soldiers would remain in their role as advisors. Senator Wayne Morse (D-Ore.) stated that he disagreed "entirely with the program in South Vietnam" and wanted to utilize SEATO or the United Nations. Minority Leader Everett Dirksen (R-Ill.) questioned whether SEATO was viable, and Mansfield agreed that it was not, calling SEATO a "paper tiger." Mansfield then expressed support for Johnson: "the President's policy toward Vietnam was the only one we could follow."[30] This support of the president came even as Mansfield's private correspondence with Johnson clearly suggested different policies.

In May and June the situation in Laos heated up, and Mansfield publicly endorsed a de Gaulle proposal to reconvene the Geneva Conference, saying "it may be the last train out for peace in southeast Asia."[31] Mansfield kept most of his statements private, delivering a letter to Johnson over breakfast on May 26. In the letter he cautioned against a Barry Goldwater (R-Ariz.) diatribe that the United States burn "some foliage with atom bombs," because such an action "cannot be related in any rational way to our national concerns." Mansfield went on to argue for neutralism in Laos, "even if we abhor the term," to end the "*heavy dependence on United States dollars, not to speak of military support for years on end.*"[32]

A phone conversation between Johnson and Mansfield on June 9 led to another memo. Two U.S. reconnaissance planes were shot down over Laos, leading the Johnson administration to bomb anti-aircraft sites in Laos and announce that fighter planes would accompany future flights. The senator quoted Johnson as saying "that a deepening of the involvement is not desirable or necessary in terms of the nation's interest." Mansfield jumped on that statement to warn that the United States could be starting on a "process of action and reaction [that] can continue and grow deeper." He started and ended the memo by describing again his position on presidential prerogatives on this foreign policy matter:

> You alone have all the available facts and considerations. You alone can make the decisions. From the Senate, we can only give you, in the last analysis, our trust, our support and such independent thoughts as may occur to us from time to time.
>
> But if our interests justify, in the last analysis, becoming fully involved on the Southeast Asian mainland then there is no issue. What must be done will be done.[33]

Of course, Mansfield's disclaimer made it easy for Johnson to ignore the majority leader's warning.

THE GULF OF TONKIN RESOLUTION

During the Eisenhower administration, several congressional resolutions that foreshadowed the Gulf of Tonkin Resolution were considered. Mansfield was always skeptical of these resolutions, which could be viewed as predated declarations of war, since they tilted the balance of power dramatically toward the executive branch. Once such a resolution was made public, Mansfield believed that Congress had little choice but to accept it or weaken the president's hand in foreign policy. He had displayed more skepticism during a Republican administration, but had reluctantly supported the Formosa and Middle East resolutions.[34]

During the Kennedy administration, Congress passed both the Cuba and Berlin Resolutions, similar precedents to the Gulf of Tonkin Resolution. Partisanship played a role; Democrats like Mansfield, Fulbright, and Wayne Morse (D-Ore.), who had serious doubts about the Formosa and Middle East Resolutions during a Republican administration, expressed none of those misgivings with Kennedy in the White House. Mansfield even introduced the Cuba Resolution in the Senate.[35]

The idea of a similar resolution on Vietnam intrigued the Johnson administration. Walt Rostow suggested such a resolution in February 1964. William Bundy endorsed the concept in a March 1 memo to the president. By late May Bundy had completed a rough draft. He worried about Morse and Mansfield, who opposed an extension of the war. Bundy warned Johnson of "doubtful friends" in Congress. The administration finished the resolution early in June during a meeting in Honolulu.

McGeorge Bundy drafted a memorandum on June 12, 1964, indicating that such a resolution should be presented in such a way to avoid "extended and divisive debate." In order to do that, the resolution would need to stress peaceful objectives and negotiation "so that we might hope to have the full support of the school of thought headed by Senator Mansfield and Senator [George] Aiken (R-Vt.) and leave ourselves with die-hard opposition from Senator Morse and his very few cohorts." Ultimately, McGeorge Bundy's strategy would work exactly as he planned, but Johnson decided on June 15 to postpone the effort to obtain a congressional resolution. With elections in November, an effort to pass the resolution seemed an unnecessary risk.

The incident in the Gulf of Tonkin led the administration to remove their resolution from the table. On August 4, Johnson met with sixteen congressional leaders and reported on the North Vietnamese torpedo boat attacks on U.S. Naval vessels and the retaliation the president had already ordered. Mansfield was the only one of the sixteen to speak against Johnson's decision to retaliate, reading a prepared statement at that meeting.[36]

Mansfield had learned of the North Vietnamese attack and Johnson's decision to retaliate at a Democratic leadership breakfast at the White House that morning. He used the day to prepare his response. Mansfield expected the United States to bomb North Vietnamese torpedo boat bases, which might lead to North Vietnam's invasion of the South. He predicted that the communists would not be "faced down" and feared a "prolonged and massive military involvement by the United States throughout Viet Nam." Mansfield urged restraint, including "a moratorium on the militant words from General Khanh and all other sources including our own." He urged the administration to treat the incident as "isolated acts of terror" and confine retaliation to international waters. The senator wanted to take the matter to the United Nations or call on the chairmen of the 1954 Geneva Convention to consider the Tonkin incident with urgency.[37]

Walter Jenkins's notes indicate considerable congressional support for a resolution before Mansfield spoke. The president did not think a resolution was necessary, but argued that it was better than a situation like Korea, where President Truman committed U.S. troops without congressional authorization. Jenkins recorded the majority leader's demurrers:

MANSFIELD: I don't know how much good it will do. There is a sharp question between this and Cuba, Russia, and the United States. In this instance, Russia is remote. China is not involved directly. May be getting all involved with a minor third rate state. Then what is to come in response, if not Korea for China? The Communists won't be faced down. A lot of lives to mow them down.

PRESIDENT: Do you give me a formula?

MANSFIELD: Two, make them isolated acts of terror. Three, the United Nations, four, call on 54 countries to consider it a matter of urgency.

RUSK: Principal problem, however, is that China has not committed itself. It would be wonderful if she could get them to pull away. . . . If we concentrate in a limited fashion on the source of the attack, it gives the other side a chance to pull away.

MANSFIELD: In North Viet Nam there are jet airfields. In addition, have you considered actions that might happen in Formosa.

Toward the end of the meeting, Fulbright said, "I will support it." Mansfield was non-committal, saying: "it will go before the Foreign Affairs Committee." Aiken had the last word in the meeting and implied agreement with Mansfield: "by the time you send it up there won't be anything for us to do but support it."[38]

This was the first of three crucial meetings with congressional leadership during 1964 and 1965 when Mansfield stood alone in opposition.[39] Typically, despite his privately expressed reservations, Mansfield was publicly supportive of Johnson's response and the resolution. In a letter to a constituent, Mansfield wrote that "the President has acted wisely in connection with the situation that has developed and I am hopeful that the lesson will sink home." In a speech at the 1964 Montana Democratic Convention, Mansfield praised Johnson for using resolve and restraint in the Gulf of Tonkin, noting that he was one of the senators called in for consultation on the issue. Mansfield misled the delegates in saying that he wholeheartedly supported Johnson in that meeting. In 1988, when asked about his different responses in public and private, Mansfield responded that he did not recall the episode well enough to comment.[40]

Comments from the August 4 meeting with congressional leaders led to changes in the resolution drafted by the administration. At an August 5 meeting of congressional leaders in Mansfield's office, the majority leader argued that the resolution should be passed in Congress as it was submitted by Johnson. Pat Holt of the Foreign Relations Committee staff recalled:

> There was some fiddling around with words in the resolution but there wasn't any real discussion of substance. In the light of all of the soul searching that had gone on over similar resolutions with respect to Formosa and the Middle East in the 1950s, I listened to this with growing incredulity.[41]

On August 6, the joint hearings on the Gulf of Tonkin Resolution lasted less than two hours. Neither Mansfield nor Fulbright asked any questions. Later, Fulbright called the small amount of time spent on the Resolution "a disaster; a tragic mistake. The resolution would have passed anyway, but not in its present form. At the time, I was not in a suspicious frame of mind. I was afraid of Goldwater."

In the Senate debates on the resolution Mansfield said that Johnson "has acted with a cool head and a steady hand in a most critical situation. He has acted as the leader of a great free nation, fully aware of a great nation's responsibilities to itself, to freedom, and to the peace of the world." Mansfield was among the eighty-eight senators voting for the resolution; only Morse and Ernest Gruening (D-Alaska) opposed it.[42]

Johnson aide George Reedy suggested that Mansfield and others were

> misled by Fulbright's assurances and Fulbright had every reason to believe those assurances. I was in the room the night they had that meeting in which Fulbright got that big briefing. There is no doubt in my mind at all, I don't know if Johnson actually used the words but there is no question that he was saying this was a one-shot thing and it was only intended for this particular operation.[43]

George McGovern (D-S.D.) received Fulbright's assurances and considered his vote for the resolution the most regrettable one of his career. McGovern commented: "I commiserated with Bill Fulbright; he was just telling [Gaylord] Nelson (D-Wis.) and me what Johnson had told him."[44]

Mansfield's 1964 Reelection

In July, Johnson had leaked Mansfield's name with others as potential vice presidential candidates. Rowland Evans and Robert Novak speculated that Johnson was seriously considering Mansfield in order to make the "more aggressive, more skillful Humphrey" majority leader.[45] Possibly, Johnson saw the vice presidency as a way to further compromise and stifle Mansfield's dissent over administration Vietnam policy. Whatever Johnson's motivation, Mansfield made it clear to his mentor that he was not interested in leaving the Senate. However, publicity from the vice presidential boomlet played well in Montana, where Mansfield already had one of the safest Senate seats in the country.[46]

Mansfield worked hard to remain popular in Montana, answering all constituent mail and seeing as many Montanans visiting Washington as possible, once saying: "if I forget Montana, they're going to forget me. I know how I got here." One Republican said, "practically every living thing in Montana gets a Christmas card signed 'Mike.' I think he skips the elk and mountain sheep."[47] Mansfield routinely defeated his opponent, 180,643 to 99,367. Johnson campaigned for Mansfield in Montana, praising Mansfield's "reason and calm judgment." In his own campaign, Johnson attempted to ignore Vietnam. When the issue did arise, Johnson contrasted his restraint with Goldwater's belligerency.

Interestingly, Vietnam was not an issue in the Montana campaign. There was not enough correspondence on the issue to merit a file in Mansfield's papers, even though there had been a file in the 1958 election and would be substantial files in 1970. As long as U.S. troops were not committed, the nation concerned itself with other issues. After the Senate euphoria in passing the Civil Rights Bill, Republicans were reluctant to challenge Mansfield. Dirksen reportedly said that "he would go to the moon to help Republicans, 'but, please, don't ask me to go to Montana'" to campaign against Mansfield.[48]

MANSFIELD TRIES TO SLOW THE MOMENTUM FOR ESCALATION

During the autumn of 1964, the Johnson administration gradually reached the decision to escalate to a large-scale air war with the possibility of the eventual introduction of ground forces. On December 3, Maxwell Taylor, ambassador to South Vietnam, met with the Senate Foreign Relations Committee in an effort to begin to "touch bases with Congress."

As was often the case, Mansfield missed the meeting but undoubtedly was briefed on what Taylor said. Mansfield likely knew that the administration was making plans for further military action, but it was unlikely that he knew what decisions had been reached. Mansfield was the only member of the committee to follow up on the Taylor meeting when he sent a memo to the president. He feared what Johnson would do in Vietnam with the mandate handed him by his landslide victory.[49]

In his memo, Mansfield suggested the United States was moving "further out on a sagging limb" with an unstable government in Saigon. While the Diem government and even the Minh government had some claim to legitimacy, that was not true of the Khanh regime. The United States was now in a similar position to that of France during 1952-1954, one of putting together "make-shift" governments. The military situation was worsening, and Mansfield expressed fear that the war could move beyond the borders of South Vietnam.

Mansfield made a number of policy suggestions based on the premise that a negotiated settlement would eventually be needed to solve the problems in Vietnam. He favored face-to-face talks with the Chinese to get negotiations started and believed the United States should assist in creating a legitimate government in South Vietnam that would talk about the eventual "*peaceful* unification of all Viet Nam." Mansfield wanted to avoid any U.S. military action beyond the borders of South Vietnam, suggesting that the United States would weaken its negotiating stance if it played that card. Further, Mansfield cautioned that the administration had to quit underestimating Sihanouk, begin to negotiate with Cambodia, and keep U.S. and South Vietnamese forces away from the Cambodian border. He encouraged allowing Western countries to establish commercial and other contacts with Hanoi in order to reduce Chinese domination in North Vietnam. If the United States did not adopt a policy similar to his suggestions, Mansfield predicted that the commitment was likely to increase for "years and years and this should be spelled out in no uncertain terms to the people of the nation."[50]

McGeorge Bundy drafted a reply to Mansfield on December 16 that Johnson sent to Mansfield with his own letter on the 17th. The president thanked Mansfield for his memo and tried to minimize their differences:

> I think we have the same basic view of this problem and the same sense of its difficulties. The one suggestion in your memorandum which I myself would take direct issue with is that we are "overcommitted" there. Given the size of the stake, it seems to me that we are doing only what we have to do.

Bundy told Johnson that his memorandum was "designed to treat [Mansfield] gently. We could get into a stronger debate, but I doubt if it is worth it." Bundy wrote Mansfield that his memorandum was "characteristically thoughtful" and suggested that there was "no difference in fundamental purpose" between the senator and the administration. He pointed out that both saw the need for "a more effective and better supported government in Saigon" and "frugal use of American resources."

Bundy then rejected Mansfield's policy suggestions point by point. The administration did not feel that it could talk with China because the Chinese did not seem to have any interest in talks. While peaceful unification of all Vietnam might be a good goal, it was not practical for a government in the South with so many immediate problems. The administration was unwilling to commit itself to not expanding military action beyond South Vietnam. Communist infiltration and U.S. inability to dictate to the South Vietnamese would make Mansfield's suggestion of avoiding the Cambodian border difficult. The administration also disagreed with Mansfield's "very high judgment on Sihanouk." Johnson opposed "Free World friendliness to North Vietnam" because of what Hanoi was doing in South Vietnam. Mansfield was right that the United States faced "years of involvement in Vietnam," but the administration felt it had never hidden that from the public. Moreover, they disagreed with Mansfield that a "vast increase in the commitment" was likely.[51]

Since the reply to Mansfield disagreed with all of his specific proposals, it seemed odd that both Bundy and Johnson stressed their agreement with the senator. Whether or not it was a conscious strategy, it became Johnson's norm to minimize differences with Mansfield. It also became a norm for Bundy to respond to Mansfield's Vietnam memos.

Mansfield's quiet dissent in 1963-64 damaged his relationship with Johnson. In 1965 Mansfield faced pressures that would challenge his strategy. Yet he remained faithful to his belief in public support and private criticism, while he continued his futile attempt to change the nation's course.

CHAPTER 9

AMERICA GOES TO WAR

A t the beginning of 1965 President Lyndon Johnson confided to Adlai Stevenson that he was

> having trouble with Senator Mansfield, whom he considered "mean and small," who would not give [Hubert] Humphrey's wife a ticket to the State of the Union ceremonies, who refused to give Vice President Humphrey a suitable office in the Capitol, and who had once told Johnson that he, Mansfield, would run the Senate and that if Johnson sent Humphrey to run it Mansfield would oppose him.[1]

Humphrey later wrote "what friendship I had with Mike Mansfield had been damaged by my years as Vice President, when I worked the hill arduously, pushing Lyndon Johnson's 'Great Society' legislation, supporting the President on Vietnam, impinging, I'm sure, on the majority leader's prerogatives and power."[2]

Late in January, a new issue hinted at the strain on the relationship between the president and his majority leader. Johnson attempted to close a number of Veteran Administration facilities, including one in Miles City, Montana. Mansfield told Lawrence O'Brien to tell Johnson that he objected to this action and did not intend to accept it. The senator publicly called the move "an appalling, backward, and insensitive act." At a press conference, Johnson calmly stated that the decision was made by the Veterans administrator. He reacted defensively in private, telling O'Brien: "those hospitals should be closed and nobody's going to tell me they can't be."

Rowland Evans and Robert Novak reported:

> Johnson resented Mansfield's public display of anger. At meetings with his congressional leaders, the President repeatedly turned to Mansfield and, embarrassing the other Democratic leaders, mercilessly needled him about his opposition to the hospital closings. But it was not a laughing matter to Mike Mansfield. Tense and white-faced, he sat silent, puffing on his pipe and seething.

Although the Miles City hospital was ultimately spared, the incident clearly revealed the rift in the relationship.[3] It would seem that differences over Johnson's gradual escalation in Vietnam were at the center of this rift, for according to Mansfield aide Francis Valeo, the only long-standing "source of friction between Johnson and Mansfield was Vietnam."[4]

Mansfield's dissent disturbed Johnson, but did not persuade him. Doris Kearns pointed out why dissent like Mansfield's, Humphrey's, Richard Russell's (D-Ga.), and George Ball's did not influence:

> Those dissenters were significant figures in government, but none of them was among the inner circle of decision-makers. The institutional forms of the decision-making process made it difficult for those outside the process to prepare or present coherent arguments and rebuttals because those within the structure, the advocates of escalation, had daily contact with one another and access to secret information, which allowed them to prepare elaborately detailed predictions of the consequences, both immediate and far into the future, of a failure to escalate in Vietnam. Without adequate staff work and collective organization the dissenters could do little more than express personal judgments opposed to an extensively documented and argued opinion shared by nearly all the top officials in government.[5]

Ball, the person inside the administration with views closest to those of Mansfield, wrote that he was regarded in the Johnson circle with "benign tolerance," and others were uninterested in the "point-by-point discussion" on Vietnam that he tried to provoke. Secretary of State Dean Rusk recalled that Ball was the only senior advisor who stated unequivocally: "I think what we are doing in Vietnam is a mistake." In fall 1964 Ball prepared a sixty-seven page memorandum challenging the assumptions of American policy in Vietnam. Ball warned: "once on the tiger's back, we cannot be sure of picking the place to dismount."

The formalized role as devil's advocate was given to Ball, but his views were not taken seriously. In reading his memoirs, his lack of contact with Mansfield and other critics of escalation was noticeable. As Kearns suggested, each acted independently. When Mansfield was asked if he ever discussed Vietnam with Ball, he replied, "just informally." Rusk wrote that Johnson and his advisors appreciated Ball's pressing his case privately and not "gossiping with journalists or going public with his views." Johnson told Ball: "you can argue like hell with me against a position, but I know outside this room you're going to support me."[6] That loyalty, "outside this room," kept Ball and Mansfield available as voices of moderation.

While Ball and Mansfield remained accessible, the real influence in the administration came from the "Tuesday lunch" group. Early in 1964, the triumvirate of Rusk, Robert McNamara and McGeorge Bundy became the charter members of this group. Here the fundamental decisions about foreign affairs, including Vietnam, were made. Johnson and his three principal advisors were known as the "awesome foursome," and held similar views on Vietnam, at least until the end of 1965.

Where Presidents Dwight Eisenhower and John Kennedy had preferred to hear a wide range of views on various subjects, Johnson wanted his advisors to present a common front. President Johnson made his desire for conformity clear from the beginning of his administration. Thus, the triumvirate often met before the Tuesday lunches to find consensus and to present Johnson with one position. This decision-making pattern gave Johnson's three key advisors tremendous power to influence their leader. While those invited to the Tuesday lunches later expanded to include other officials and members of the military, the same closed format prevailed. William Bundy and Ben Read, who later attended some of the Tuesday lunches, "were increasingly appalled and frustrated by the unsystematic and narrow nature of inquiry."[7] Ball described McNamara's style in meetings: "McNamara brushed these caveats aside. . . . It was the quintessential McNamara approach. Once he had made up his mind to go forward, he would push aside the most formidable impediment that might threaten to slow down or deflect him from his determined course."[8]

John Burke and Fred Greenstein suggest that the questions raised by Mansfield and others in 1965 "were dissipated and diffused rather than addressed."[9] Valeo thought Rusk and Bundy had very little respect for legislative politicians. Thus, they easily ignored Mansfield's arguments. Johnson also ignored Mansfield's views. Valeo suggested that Johnson was used to controlling members of Congress, and he did not feel they had much to offer him. Rusk, McNamara, and Bundy were "the people who were supposed to know about . . . [foreign policy], Congress is supposed to know about other things."[10]

The power of Johnson's key advisors gave rise to the "last dove" theory: Johnson was a dove who gradually was persuaded to escalate by the advisors he inherited from Kennedy. The credibility of those men, in turn, was tied to a policy of escalation begun under Kennedy. Johnson aide Jack Valenti observed that Rusk and McNamara were the two Cabinet members Johnson most respected and that "he had a great belief in their judgment and in their general overall mental capacity to get the nettle of a problem and bring to it logic and intelligence."[11] When asked if he agreed with the assessment of Johnson as the last dove in the administration, Mansfield replied: "I do not know if this was the case."[12]

Mansfield diligently worked to counter the arguments of Rusk, McNamara, and Bundy in 1965. In January on *Meet the Press*, Mansfield cautioned: "I feel just as strongly that we cannot carry the war into North Vietnam because if you carry the consequences of that action to its ultimate conclusion, it means war with Communist China, and a situation will be created which will be worse than it was in Korea."[13] The majority leader was faced with the Johnson administration's decision to take the war to the North during the next month.

JOHNSON WAGES AIR WAR

In response to Vietcong attacks at Pleiku on February 7, 1965, and at Qui Nhon on February 10, the Johnson administration escalated U.S. involvement. The first bombing raids on the North were ordered on February 7 and became sustained on February 13. Johnson held meetings that included Mansfield on February 6, 7, 8, and 10. After these meetings, the president decided to wage an air war against North Vietnam. Most in attendance considered Johnson's decision to be the moderate course because it avoided a wider land war. Ball remembered Johnson listening to McNamara's arguments in favor of bombing during this period, over Mansfield's, Humphrey's, and his own calls for a more cautious approach. Yet Ball wrote that Mansfield's "voice carried special authority" with Johnson on the Far East due to his military service and academic specialty in the area.[14]

The February 6 meeting started four hours after the attack on Pleiku. Mansfield and Speaker of the House John McCormack (D-Mass.) were the two congressional representatives. Everyone at the meeting except Mansfield agreed that retaliation was necessary. The need for a congressional resolution to guarantee that the administration was acting constitutionally was addressed. At the end of the meeting, Mansfield looked directly at Johnson and said forcefully, the "attack has opened many eyes. We are not now in a penny ante game. It appears that the local populace in South Vietnam is not behind us, [or] else the Viet Cong could not have carried out their surprise attack." Johnson wrote that Mansfield "proposed no alternative." He recalled responding: "we have kept our gun over the mantel and our shells in the cupboard for a long time now, and what was the result? They are killing our men while they sleep in the night. I can't ask our American soldiers out there to continue to fight with one hand tied behind their backs."[15] William Bundy recorded that Johnson

> did not try to draw the Majority Leader out, as he might have done in a setting of more privacy and less tension. Instead, his reply was terse and quite biting. It was not a rational attempt to persuade. Hours and hours of private talk lay behind the difference now nakedly revealed. My impression was that the Senator would have given anything to be alone with the President; finding that he had to speak in front of others, he did so with typical courage and frankness.[16]

Perhaps stung by Johnson's reaction, Mansfield had little to say at the February 7 meeting. At the beginning of the gathering, Mansfield merely asked "why cannot we handle this matter through the United Nations? Can't the Geneva powers act?" Johnson replied that "this cannot be done."

On the following day, Ball discussed the letter the administration had sent to the U.N. secretary general to "preempt" a discussion of the U.S. bombing by the Security Council. While the administration was willing to discuss the bombing at the United Nations, they wanted to "control the circumstances" of the discussion. McGeorge Bundy argued that U.S. credibility was on the line. A pull-out from Vietnam would have serious ramifications, "even to the extent of affecting the morale in Berlin." Johnson admitted a "bad governmental situation in Saigon" but hoped that U.S. bombing "may pull together the various forces in Saigon and thus make possible the establishment of a stable government." He argued that the Tonkin Gulf Resolution, combined with the constitutional power of his office, gave him the legal right to wage the air war. Johnson planned to use the resolution "carefully but effectively," but he would not let the views of several senators control his actions. He said: "we face a choice of going forward or running. We have chosen the first alternative. All of us agree on this but there remains some difference as to how fast we should go forward."

Johnson knew that Mansfield did not agree, but the majority leader remained silent. Perhaps he was intimidated by Johnson's reaction two days earlier. Mansfield also knew that he could better develop his position in writing and was more comfortable disagreeing in private. So Mansfield gave Johnson a memorandum summarizing his views: he was concerned that the U.S. bombing would bring the Soviets and Chinese closer together; he feared the possibility of Chinese intervention; he expressed concern for lax security that allowed the attack at Pleiku; he cautioned that General Vo Nguyen Giap's army of 350,000 would be formidable; and he believed that the United States was stretched too thinly around the world. Mansfield was also disturbed that the United States retaliated before consulting with the government of South Vietnam. He warned:

> I have grave doubts about the ability of General [Nguyen] Khanh's government. I have no doubt but that the great majority of the population of South Vietnam are tired of the war and will give us no significant assistance. I appreciate your repeated statements that it is not your desire to spread the war. However, the prospect for enlargement now looms larger and I think it is only fair that I give you my honest opinions, as I did on Saturday and Sunday, because to do otherwise would be a disservice to you and to the Nation.
>
> I am persuaded that the trend toward enlargement of the conflict and a continuous deepening of our military commitment on the Asian mainland, despite your desire to the contrary, is not going to provide . . . [an answer].

The senator recommended that Johnson take the issue to the United Nations, reconvene the Geneva powers, talk with the Soviets and Chinese, or seek any other forum that might resolve the issue. Characteristically, Mansfield ended his memo by affirming that the decision was LBJ's and assuring Johnson that he would support him in the exercise of his "grave responsibility."

McGeorge Bundy again rebutted Mansfield's memo. Bundy was polite, writing that "your careful questions deserve a prompt reply." He disagreed that U.S.

bombing would bring the Soviets and Chinese closer together. Bundy assured Mansfield that Johnson was also deeply concerned about the possibility of war with China. He agreed that the government in South Vietnam was a weak one, but thought Mansfield was harsh in his judgment of the support the United States could expect from other nations and the South Vietnamese people. Bundy explained that the problem of military security was being addressed, and argued that the U.S. response to Pleiku was not unilateral. He differed with Mansfield over whether the United States was "stretched too thin" around the world. Then, Bundy turned to the issue of the United Nations:

> From the Secretary General on down, we are unable to find any expert on the UN who sees any prospect that it can act effectively in the present situation in Vietnam. Neither is the President aware of any prospect that any other conference or forum would currently lead to an agreement by the Communists to end the fighting on any terms other than those of surrender.

Bundy ended his response by calling Mansfield "one of the outstanding public servants of our time," adding:

> I therefore regret that your judgment and that of the Administration should be at variance on this most important issue, and I beg you to understand that while I have tried to write directly and straightforwardly, I have done so with a feeling of deep respect not only for you but for your deeply held convictions.[17]

In a 1965 interview Bundy claimed that Johnson listened intently to views in opposition to the February bombing. For support, Bundy mentioned memoranda from Mansfield and J. William Fulbright (D-Ark.) that the president "read with care," as well as conversations with columnist Walter Lippmann.[18] A more objective examination of Johnson's papers led Burke and Greenstein to conclude that while "Johnson regularly asked his aides to draft point-by-point replies to Mansfield," they "show no evidence that the substance of his critiques was debated."[19]

After the February 10 attack on Qui Nhon, Johnson held two meetings. At the first meeting, which did not include members of Congress, Humphrey, Ball and Llewellyn Thompson expressed reservations about the retaliation. John McCone (CIA director), C. Douglas Dillon (secretary of the Treasury), and Carl Rowan (director of the U.S. Information Agency) were all in agreement with LBJ's decision. Johnson assistant Bill Moyers argued that the air strikes "should be made to meet domestic public opinion requirements."

Humphrey followed up on his dissent with two memoranda that the vice president reported "infuriated" Johnson, who told him that: "we do not need all these memos." Several writers indicated that Humphrey's dissent caused

Johnson to ban his vice president from Vietnam decision-making for a number of months.[20]

Mansfield came to the second meeting on February 10 with a prepared memorandum. Johnson assistant Lawrence O'Brien sat next to Mansfield and thought the majority leader was about to read his prepared statement, but decided "at the last second not to bring the memo into discussion at the meeting."* Rather, he handed the memo to Valenti to give to the president. Mansfield told Johnson what to anticipate after the Qui Nhon attack: the North would strengthen air defenses; the United States should anticipate that the Vietcong would also escalate in response to the air strikes and "play their strength against our weakness. . . . [which] is on the ground in Viet Nam, where isolated pockets of Americans are surrounded by, at best, an indifferent population and, more likely, by an increasingly hostile population." He warned that U.S. outposts in Vietnam would "have to be *vastly strengthened by American forces* or pulled into and consolidated in the Saigon area." With the U.N. option rejected, Mansfield shifted to a French proposal to reconvene the 1954 Geneva Conference in the hope of obtaining a cease-fire.[21]

The following day, McGeorge Bundy once again replied to Mansfield. Bundy assured Mansfield that Johnson "values your continuing counsel on this very difficult problem" and again responded to Mansfield point-by-point. He agreed that the question of North Vietnamese air defenses was of critical importance. The administration did not expect the air strikes to immediately "cool off the situation," but air strikes were superior to the alternative of not responding to the communist attack. Vietcong harassment of Americans on the ground was anticipated, but such activity would be expected without the air strikes. Bundy believed it was too soon to reach Mansfield's "pessimistic conclusion" about help from the South's population, and while Mansfield's call for an international conference was an interesting one, Bundy posited that

> if the cease-fire were to apply to all forces in South Vietnam, it would seem to me to be an effort to apply equal standards to the cops and to the robbers; but if it is a matter of saying that any replies we make in the North can be stopped the minute there is an end to aggression in the South, I can see great merit in it.[22]

Clearly, Mansfield's desire for using the United Nations, Geneva Conference, or any international body with legal status to foster negotiations was not treated seriously by the administration. Johnson's advisors still sought a military victory and they rejected any international involvement.

Even with his ideas rebuffed, Mansfield followed his rhetorical strategy of private, but not public, dissent. On February 9, even as he must have been writing his February 10 memo to Johnson, he told the press that "in the circumstances, the President has had no choice but to respond as he did to the military developments in Viet Nam." In answering a constituent, Mansfield defended the president's retaliatory bombing: "I believe that the President was acting with restraint in this matter and that what he was seeking is to restore the independence and integrity of South Viet Nam in accord with the 1954 Geneva agreement." He did not criticize Johnson, but pursued his separate agenda. On February 11, Mansfield had Senator Claiborne Pell (D-R.I.) read a prepared statement into the *Congressional Record* that emphasized the need to reconvene the Geneva Conference of 1954 or 1961, a position rejected by the administration in Bundy's memo to Mansfield one day earlier.[23]

Johnson's bombing decision led to a public outcry that caused the administration to issue a "White Paper" defining U.S. objectives in Vietnam and attempting to document Hanoi's involvement in the South. While a number of war critics attacked the Johnson justification, Mansfield defended the president in the Senate on March 1: "the paper helps to make clear why this Nation has been compelled to take steps which it has in recent weeks." He added, "it should satisfy those who have been insisting that the President should address an explanation to the American people as to what is involved in Vietnam. The President, so far as I can see, is trying to keep a lid on a dangerous volcano in Southeast Asia. He is not trying to blow it off."[24]

Mansfield lost the private battle over escalation to an air war. He then geared up to oppose the ultimate escalation, the commitment of U.S. ground forces.

MANSFIELD SEEKS A "REASONABLE OUT"

On March 6, McNamara called Mansfield to check his views on sending 3,500 Marines to Vietnam to protect the air base at Da Nang. Mansfield responded that doing so would make the situation "more delicate" and "dangerous" by creating the impression of further U.S. escalation, and countered that sending troops already stationed in Saigon would be more appropriate. Once again, Mansfield admitted that the responsibility was McNamara's and the president's, and he assumed that the decision had already been made to commit the Marines. McNamara denied that, and said that he assumed Mansfield opposed sending Marines. The senator replied, "yes," and McNamara thanked him. The first contingent of the 3,500 Marines was sent to Vietnam two days later, on March 8, 1965. These were the first U.S. combat troops on the Asian continent since the Korean War, and the decision to send them was one of the more crucial ones of the war. Yet the decision was virtually ignored in the United States.[25]

Johnson remained concerned about America's gradual drift toward war. At a meeting with three advisors in mid-March, McGeorge Bundy's notes reflect Johnson admitting that "I did cross [the] bridge" to increasing the use of American forces in December. He said, "to give in = another Munich, *if not* here—*then Thailand."* The president added, "if you can show me any reasonable out I'll grab it."[26]

Mansfield sensed Johnson's mood and tried to supply that "reasonable out." Clark Clifford claims that once the bombing started, McNamara and the Joint Chiefs of Staff knew that troops would be needed, initially to protect air bases, but inevitably to launch offensive operations. Johnson was not told because he would have been hesitant to begin the bombing. Mansfield had tried to warn Johnson of that likelihood as early as his February 10 memo. He delivered a memo solicited by LBJ on March 18 that suggested how to use the Marines in Da Nang: the number of ground forces should be strictly limited to the number necessary; "such American-guarded installations, preferably, be on the coast or otherwise readily accessible from the sea"; and "Americans scattered elsewhere in Viet Nam [should] be drawn into those American-defended installations." He provided rationales for his suggestions, including the belief that the deployment of U.S. troops strengthened the hand of the Vietcong because it allowed them to pick American targets "at times and places of their choosing."[27]

Following a March 23 meeting between Johnson and Democratic congressional leaders and a telephone call from the president, Mansfield sent a letter to Johnson on March 24, in which he reviewed his "main lines of thought" in memos to both Kennedy and Johnson. This memo seems to have been a last-ditch effort to change the direction of U.S. escalation.

Mansfield acknowledged that his positions would lead to the charge of "a return to isolationism," but argued "that there is no automatic virtue in an ubiquitous and indiscriminate internationalism, particularly when it leads to the kind of isolated internationalism in which we presently find ourselves in Viet Nam." He emphasized that he was writing without "rancor or criticism." Mansfield asserted that his opinions since 1963 had "received careful attention." Then, in a line that would smack of sarcasm coming from anyone but Mansfield, he added that "your assistants and the bureaucracy have studied them and occasionally even have concurred in an idea expressed in them."

The senator demonstrated how present policy ran counter to the opinions he had developed over the years. The United States was moving toward the attempt to exercise primacy in Vietnam, even if it meant "going into North Viet Nam and beyond." Current policy was trying to obtain the "unconditional capitulation" of the Vietcong. Mansfield expressed fear that important military decisions would be made in Vietnam instead of at the White House. The president had told him that morning that he had been unaware that "gas" was used in Vietnam. Mansfield thought the use of napalm and the bombing of "targets of convenience," which harmed civilians, were also decisions Johnson may not have made.

Mansfield sounded pessimistic in suggesting policies, with "no great hope" that they would prove useful to Johnson. He lacked hope because his suggestions to reconvene the 1961 Geneva Conference group and involve the United Nations had been previously rejected. Mansfield absolved the president of guilt, writing that the United States was too deeply involved by the time Johnson assumed office. He then equivocated, saying that only Johnson knew "the whole situation on a day-to-day basis and I most certainly respect the decisions which you have felt compelled to make in this connection." Mansfield emphasized Johnson's great responsibilities, writing about the different viewpoints that the president must consider. He ended by offering his assistance and pledged: "I shall not trouble you further with memorandums on this situation and I do not expect an answer to this letter."[28]

Johnson replied anyway. He once again denied serious disparity with Mansfield, saying that there was "more agreement than differences between us." Johnson ignored Mansfield's main arguments, but commented on several points he thought Mansfield had overstated.

> We have no desire to exercise "a primacy" over what transpires in South Vietnam. . . . I do not agree with the suggestion that the military authorities in Vietnam should have sought my personal approval before making the limited, specific use of riot-control gases which they authorized in an effort to save lives.
>
> You will agree that I should be careful in responding to your specific proposals for future action, simply because of my obligation to maintain freedom of choice as the situation develops.[29]

On March 26, George McGovern (D-S.D.) talked to Johnson about Vietnam and reported the president as saying: "don't give me another goddamn history lesson. I've got a drawerful of memos from Mansfield. I don't need a lecture on where we went wrong. I've got to deal with where we are now." McGovern recalled that in leaving the White House that night, "I literally trembled for the future of the nation."[30]

In late April, though, Johnson called Mansfield to apprise him of the current situation in Vietnam. Mansfield recorded that Johnson sounded desperate. The president contradicted what he said to McGovern in March by saying "he would appreciate receiving any ideas or any suggestions for initiatives and would appreciate any memorandums that might be sent to him." Johnson also suggested that Mansfield visit him to discuss Vietnam and complained that "he was being criticized for not being liberal enough on the one hand and for not being warmongering enough on the other."[31]

Clearly, Johnson was bothered by the criticism from Mansfield and Fulbright as he moved toward committing U.S. troops. At a May 2 meeting with congressional leaders, Johnson glared at his old friend, Fulbright, who had called for a bombing halt. Johnson "implied that Congress ought to show the world it really backs up his policies." The president did initiate a bombing pause on May 12 that lasted until May 18. At a May 16 meeting where it was decided to end the pause, Johnson said: "my judgment is the public has never wanted to stop the bombing. We have stopped in deference to Mansfield and Fulbright. We tried out their notions and got no results." McNamara interjected: "Mansfield ought to know Hanoi spit in our face." Johnson, however, believed that the *New York Times*, Mansfield, and Fulbright would oppose the lifting of the bombing pause. In a May 31 memo to Johnson, Bundy wrote of Mansfield's "somewhat mousey stubbornness" in opposing intervention.

Yet Mansfield continued to walk the fine line between support and criticism. He became an administration spokesperson at a national teach-in on May 15, saying in part that Johnson would not be "goaded by the voices of an impatient arrogance" into withdrawing forces from Vietnam.[32] Fulbright chose a different path.

FULBRIGHT BREAKS FROM LBJ

Fulbright was in basic agreement with Johnson's Vietnam policy through most of 1964. On March 25, he delivered the most discussed speech of early 1964. In "Old Myths and New Realities," Fulbright became the first prominent official since the beginning of the Cold War to challenge seriously the rationale behind U.S. foreign policy. Despite this radical departure from administration policy, Fulbright rejected any call for negotiation in Vietnam until the U.S. bargaining position was stronger. Fulbright was working closely with Johnson, and it was at his request that Fulbright repeated the official administration position on Vietnam.[33]

Fulbright started to privately urge Johnson to withdraw from Vietnam before the 1964 presidential election, but he feared that any public criticism would end Fulbright's effectiveness at the White House. He was probably not atypical in writing that in February 1965 he still felt insecure about the issue because he was just "in the process of learning about Vietnam."[34]

Carl Marcy, Chief of Staff to the Foreign Relations Committee, said that once he started reading about it "Fulbright immersed himself in that area in a way that surprised me."[35]President Johnson issued a statement on March 25, 1965 that sounded as if he were moving toward negotiation on Vietnam. On April 5, Fulbright sent Johnson a memo suggesting that a strong communist government under Ho Chi Minh was preferable to a democratic one that could not survive. Fulbright compared Ho to Tito of Yugoslavia, and said that a nationalist government could prevent Chinese domination of Southeast Asia. Johnson did not respond to Fulbright's memo, but he invited Fulbright and Mansfield to the White House on April 6 to discuss the Johns Hopkins speech which Johnson delivered the next day. Fulbright came to believe that the meeting was an effort to get Fulbright and Mansfield "on board." In the speech, Johnson said the

United States would not be defeated or withdraw, but he offered to finance a huge Mekong development project if the North would agree to "unconditional discussions." On April 8, Mansfield had Johnson's Johns Hopkins speech entered into the *Congressional Record* and praised Johnson's address as a "profoundly moving and constructive statement which reveals both the great strengths of President Johnson's resolve and his deep concern for the welfare of all people." Fulbright delivered a Senate speech praising Johnson's willingness to negotiate and suspend bombing. Both Mansfield and Fulbright thought the Johns Hopkins address proved that Johnson was listening to their private advice against escalation.[36]

One Fulbright biographer wrote that Senator Fulbright followed a rhetorical strategy similar to Mansfield's, in which he curbed his public statements because Johnson had convinced him that his advice was welcome. Fulbright wrote in 1965: "personally, I have not believed that my making public statements about it [Vietnam] would result in any beneficial change." In 1966 Fulbright suggested:

A Senator who wishes to influence foreign policy must consider the . . . results of communicating privately with the Executive or, alternatively, of speaking out publicly. I do not see any great principle here: it is a matter of how one can better achieve what one hopes to achieve.[37]

In 1989 Fulbright wrote about his 1965 dissent:

I kept thinking that I could influence [Johnson] privately. I saw him quite often. He was very friendly to me, and as long as I didn't make a *public* statement, he was willing to talk. Not only was he willing to talk, but he had Dean Rusk talk to me and he sent other people to talk to me. I kept thinking, as long as people were doing that, that one of these days I might influence them.[38]

Fulbright's situation was analogous to Mansfield's in many ways. Both men were close friends of President Johnson. Both were members of Johnson's political party. Both had powerful Senate positions that Johnson aided them in obtaining: Johnson helped Fulbright gain his position as Chairman of Foreign Relations; he also interceded with Kennedy in 1960 in an effort to make Fulbright secretary of state.[39] Johnson respected Mansfield's expertness on Vietnam because of his background, and he respected Fulbright as a foreign policy expert, telling Fulbright, "you're my secretary of state" when Johnson served as majority leader.

When Pat Holt of the Foreign Relations Committee staff was asked why LBJ did not listen to Fulbright, he replied: "but you know, Johnson didn't listen to Mansfield either. According to his [Johnson's] memoirs, Mansfield was dissenting more strongly and earlier than Fulbright."[40] Both Fulbright and Mansfield followed a similar rhetorical strategy of criticizing the president in private, but supporting him in public. So when Fulbright went public with his criticism of administration policies, he provided an interesting counterpoint to the Mansfield strategy.

When Fulbright became convinced that his ideas were not persuasive within the administration, he went public with his views, hoping to at least open debate on Vietnam. On June 14, 1965 Johnson once more asked Fulbright to defend presidential policies in a speech. Fulbright gave the speech in the Senate the next day.[41] The senator's speech was quite moderate. He opposed a U.S. withdrawal but also opposed escalation, and he believed that negotiations must include the Vietcong. Johnson thought Fulbright's speech shifted the senator from a private critic to a public one on both the Dominican Republic and Vietnam. As a result of this incident, when Johnson made the crucial decisions to commit ground troops to Vietnam in late July, Fulbright's views were no longer considered. Holt said that after this speech, "Johnson sort of scratched Fulbright off his list."

Fulbright admits that Johnson's treatment of him pushed him toward a stronger position against the war. But Fulbright concluded that he could not exert influence on Johnson in private with "quiet persuasion." Members of Fulbright's staff continued to believe that Fulbright erred in going public with his dissent, and that he might have been more persuasive with Johnson in private. Marcy "thought it more important for him [Fulbright] to keep a close relationship with Lyndon than to do anything that would break that relationship. I felt Fulbright still had access to and influence with the president, something one does not throw away lightly."[42]

Mansfield, however, continued to voice his dissent only in private. Thomas Eagleton (D-Mo.) commented on Mansfield's strategy:

> Fulbright became absolutely *persona non grata* with Johnson. It is just amazing to me that Mansfield didn't. It was a function of his personality, his style, the office that he held, and his conception of that office. So, Johnson could say, "I can even afford to break with Bill Fulbright, the chairman of the Foreign Relations Committee, but, my God, I can't afford to break with the man who succeeded me as majority leader."[43]

Years later, George Ball explained why he chose the same strategy as Mansfield: "I figured that I could do better by remaining on the inside. Had I quit, the story would have made the front page of the *New York Times* next day—and then I would have been promptly forgotten."[44]

PRELIMINARY DECISIONS TO COMMIT U.S. GROUND TROOPS

Early in June, Mansfield actively tried to dissuade Johnson from the escalation he was considering, and Johnson held off the escalation for a time. Kahin believed that Johnson's concern over questions by Mansfield, "for whom he had great respect," led him in turn to consider Ball's arguments, since Ball was his advisor with views closest to Mansfield. Like the senator, Ball was arguing against escalation by drawing an analogy to the French experience in Vietnam, but Rusk and the rest of Johnson's inner circle rejected the comparison. Kahin added that "McGeorge Bundy, from his position of proximity in the White House, appears to have interacted most frequently with the president and clearly spent considerable time in undercutting the arguments of Ball and Mansfield."[45] Burke and Greenstein concluded that Bundy functioned as both Johnson's policy advisor and his process manager. As such, "Bundy consistently brought differences of viewpoint to Johnson's attention . . . [but] in advancing his own views he sometimes failed to do justice to the views of others."[46] Johnson aide Harry McPherson agreed, Bundy would "push . . . [his policy] subtly."[47] Most of the debate to which Johnson was exposed during this crucial period was that of his inner circle of advisors, including Rusk, McNamara, Bundy, Taylor, and Ball. Even though he served in a different branch of government, Mansfield was trying to crack that circle through memoranda.

On June 3, Johnson held a leadership meeting attended by Mansfield. In a memo for his files on the meeting, Mansfield reported that Johnson was pessimistic about Vietnam and was stalling the Joint Chiefs of Staff on their desire to bomb Hanoi, because Johnson feared Chinese entry into the war. The president admitted that there were not many targets in the North left to bomb and "mentioned the possibility of sending up another [Gulf of Tonkin-type] Resolution" on bombing. When Senator Russell Long (D-La.) suggested bombing China at the meeting, Mansfield recorded: "I said as emphatically as I could, 'I disagree with you completely and absolutely.'"

Two days later Mansfield violated his March 24 pledge not to send further correspondence on Vietnam to the president. Mansfield thought that Johnson was receiving bad advice from his inner circle. After expressing support for Johnson's "resistance to pressures for an irreversible extension of the war in Asia," the majority leader suggested:

> I think it is about time you got an accounting from those who have pressured you in the past to embark on this course and continue to pressure you to stay on it. It is time to ask, not only what immediate advantages it has in a narrow military sense, but where does it lead in the end: What was promised by the initial extension of the war in the air over the North? And what, in fact, has it produced to date?

Mansfield further argued that Johnson was on "sound historic and realistic grounds" in resisting such pressure. President Dwight Eisenhower had resisted "getting in deep in the Asian mainland." Bombing Hanoi and Haiphong would be of "no significant value to the military." It would forestall discussion and cause the world community to disassociate itself from the United States. Such bombing would bring about Chinese domination of North Vietnam and freeze Russia into a role of principal provider of military supplies to the North. This would lead to "acceleration of the ground war in South Viet Nam," creating the need for more U.S. troops and the necessity of pushing the war into the North, which would instigate war with China. Then McNamara's estimation of a needed 300,000 Americans to combat General Giap would escalate into millions.

Rather than moving in that direction, Mansfield suggested that the United States "throw out some signs and signals of our own instead of waiting for the other side" to initiate getting to the conference table. Such "signs and signals" might include: the favoring of a non-involved Cambodia and consideration of international guarantees for its frontiers; "an immediate cease-fire and stand-fast" in all of Vietnam; clarifying that the United States would "not foreclose any ultimate political solution, *provided*" it be based on free choice by the people of Vietnam; and amnesty for both sides enforced by an international peace force including the United States.

Johnson called Mansfield on June 8 to inform him of General William Westmoreland's request for additional troops and to seek his advice on the congressional resolution under consideration. Mansfield responded on June 9.[48] After the recent overthrow of the Dr. Phan Huy Quat government in South Vietnam, Mansfield was concerned with Westmoreland's authority to commit American combat troops:

> As I understand it, Westmoreland will respond to requests from the Vietnamese *military* not the Vietnamese *government*. This underscores the fact that there is not a government to speak of in Saigon. In short we are now at the point where we are no longer dealing with anyone who represents anybody in a political sense.

Mansfield attempted to clarify Johnson's options through three alternatives. The first was for the United States to stay until South Vietnam prevailed south of the 17th parallel; but Mansfield warned that achieving this goal would require decades and millions of American troops, even assuming that China did "*not*" become involved with forces. His second alternative was to maintain the status quo, retaining "the provincial capitals, the larger towns in the interior, Saigon, and the coastal cities" as well as maintaining "tenuous . . . communication on the ground in between." He argued that McNamara's estimate that 300,000 troops would be needed was too low, and that a "range of 500,000 might do it, at least if Giap's army does not move in full and open force across the 17th parallel."

Mansfield based his third alternative on the goal of a negotiated settlement, some protection of allies, and eventual self-determination with the withdrawal of foreign troops. In that case, he suggested a withdrawal to Saigon and the coast. With U.S. naval and air power plus 100,000 combat troops, Mansfield felt they could hold out "at least for a year or so," while attempting to get to the negotiation table. He rightly deduced that Johnson's advisors were pushing for the second course, while Mansfield argued for the third. Kahin called Mansfield prescient in cautioning that "a course once set in motion often develops its own momentum and rationale whatever the initial intentions."

Mansfield argued against a Gulf of Tonkin-type resolution, which would give Johnson leeway in the use of ground forces. He wrote that "the Senate cannot direct you in the conduct of foreign relations even if it wanted to," but that the Senate's reaction would be critical. Mansfield added that the Gulf of Tonkin Resolution had been passed with "grave doubts and much trepidation on the part of many Senators. It has been done largely on faith, out of loyalty to you and on the basis of the general view that when the President has the responsibility and when he requests legislative support in a crisis, he should have it."[49] Johnson read Mansfield's June 9 memo at an administration meeting on June 10, 1965, and McGeorge Bundy's notes indicate that those present "answered [it] line by line."[50] Johnson clearly understood, as he told George Ball several days later, that "Mansfield is unhappy," but the president was not willing to take the steps Mansfield endorsed.[51]

On June 14, Mansfield wrote out some suggestions for how to get to the negotiation table. He apparently held them, waiting for a response from Johnson to his earlier memos, but when no response came Mansfield sent the June 14 memo to Johnson with a cover letter. The memo reiterated Mansfield's recommendations from June 5 to send "signs and signals" to North Vietnam of American readiness for serious negotiation. Mansfield suggested that Johnson call for the reconvening of the Geneva Conference, and that world opinion would be favorable even if the proposal did not lead to the conference table. Mansfield was not present when his plan for negotiation was discussed but rejected at a White House meeting on June 23.[52]

Once again McGeorge Bundy responded to Mansfield's June 5, 9, and 14 memoranda, and he directly refuted all three. Concerning the June 5 memo, Bundy pointed out that Eisenhower supported the administration's Vietnam policy and that the air war had accomplished its objectives: it made infiltration more difficult, it helped South Vietnam's morale, and it hurt the morale of the Vietcong. He did not respond to Mansfield's warnings on bombing Hanoi/Haiphong because such action had not been taken. The administration agreed with Mansfield on the need to get to the conference table.

Bundy viewed Mansfield's June 9 memo as "unduly pessimistic." He refused to make a choice among Mansfield's three alternatives and was critical of the levels of force predicted by the senator. Bundy did not feel qualified to comment on Mansfield's position on a congressional resolution. He interpreted Mansfield as indicating that South Vietnam would choose communism in a free election, an assessment with which the administration disagreed.

As for Mansfield's June 14 memo, Bundy assured him that the administration had sent out "signs and signals," both in a recent Rusk speech and through diplomatic channels. The administration agreed with Mansfield on Cambodian neutrality, amnesty, and the withdrawal of foreign troops. They also concurred that free choice by the South Vietnamese people was the key ingredient to any peace settlement. However, they did not think a "cease-fire and stand-fast" was practical before a conference. Bundy ignored Mansfield's arguments that Johnson was receiving bad advice and that there was no government in South Vietnam that represented anyone in a political sense. As was the norm, the administration minimized its differences with Mansfield. Johnson had the audacity to proclaim to Mansfield that "Bundy's comment persuades me once again that we agree much more than we differ."[53]

On June 30, McGeorge Bundy wrote Johnson that the public accepted the American role in Vietnam. Elements of the academic and church communities were the most "articulate critics," but they were usually minorities within their own groups. The press and Congress generally supported the president:

> The most vocal current comment on the Vietnam situation is coming from the Congress. Senators Morse and Gruening remain convinced that we must pull out. There is another group, somewhat larger, which could be termed "reluctant realists" whose viscera says get out but whose heads tell them the present policy is unavoidable. Senators Mansfield, [Frank] Church (D-Idaho) and Fulbright seem to fall in this category. Once again, the problem is one of *offering a plausible alternative that would assure the existence of a non-Communist South Vietnam*.[54] [Emphasis added.]

Bundy's last line indicated why Mansfield was destined to fail. The administration talked of self-determination, but the reality was that self-determination would not be allowed unless it could be certain that the choice would lead to an anti-communist South Vietnam.

JOHNSON DECIDES TO COMMIT U.S. GROUND TROOPS

The decision to commit U.S. troops was made in late July. George Ball remembered that he, Mansfield, and Johnson advisor Clark Clifford were the principal opponents of escalation since Fulbright had been "written off." Mansfield started the week with a Senate speech on July 21. He spoke of the worsening situation in Vietnam and called for a reconvening of the 1961 Geneva Conference, a recommendation recently broached by both Norodom Sihanouk and Souvanna Phouma. Mansfield feared a war that could last up to ten years, and claimed, "we are in for an ordeal of indefinite duration and increasing sacrifice which will persist until the problem can be resolved at the conference table."[55]

Johnson's top advisors met on the same day Mansfield delivered his speech. In the discussion prior to the president's arrival, these men revealed their expectation that Johnson would approve McNamara's request for ground troops. Yet Johnson seemed to agonize over the decision. He insisted that Ball suggest alternatives even though Ball said, "I have had my day in court." When prodded, Ball stated, "we cannot win, Mr. President." He suggested making proposals to South Vietnam that they could not accept. In the Ball scenario, South Vietnam would then ask the United States to leave, take a neutralist position, and eventually come under the control of Hanoi. Johnson feared the loss of U.S. credibility that would result from Ball's alternative. Bundy, Rusk, and Lodge agreed with the president. It was likely that Johnson made up his mind prior to this gathering and just wanted Ball to play his role as devil's advocate. Even if Johnson had any doubts going into this meeting, he certainly stacked the assembly with advisors who favored committing troops.

The president met with his military leadership and top aides on July 22. Johnson still gave the impression that he was struggling with his decision. Yet the president's description of his three alternatives clearly showed the direction in which he was leaning. Johnson called Ball's alternative "the 'bugging out' approach," and labeled maintaining the present force as a way to "lose slowly." The third approach called for adding "100,000 men—recognizing that may not be enough—and adding more next year." The military men agreed with the third approach, and the potential loss of prestige was a primary reason. While Johnson's military advisors favored escalation, none guaranteed success. Admiral David McDonald hoped "that sooner or later we'll force the enemy to the conference table. We can't win an all-out war." McNamara offered "the most extreme version of the domino theory" that Clifford had ever heard. McNamara's view was strikingly similar to what Mansfield had said in 1953-1954. While Mansfield had reassessed his view of the domino theory, Johnson and most of his advisors had not.

After this meeting, the president met with his senior aides and several civilian advisors. By the end of this meeting, Johnson had decided to commit ground forces. The lack of foresight on the potential outcome of this decision was suggested when John McCloy asked: "would we be willing to take a Tito government or a VC victory?" Bundy replied, "that's where our plan begins to unravel." Johnson included Clifford at this meeting, who he knew opposed escalation. Pleased to have an ally in attendance, Ball and Clifford talked afterwards.

Clifford was not optimistic. He referred to Johnson's advisors by saying, "individuals sometimes become so bound up in a certain course it is difficult to know where objectivity stops and personal involvement begins." Rusk suggested that Johnson meet with congressional leaders on July 27 to announce his decision. That same day, Johnson predicted to some advisors, "you'll never hold Fulbright, Mansfield, Church."[56]

Unaware that Johnson had reached his decision, Mansfield continued his efforts to influence from the outside by sending a memo to the president on July 23. One hint of the panic Mansfield felt was that for the first time he wrote a memo to a president that lacked an introduction; Mansfield simply plunged into his ten points that were largely designed to get to the bargaining table. He asked Johnson to re-examine the meaning of the Viet Cong's condition of American withdrawal in order for negotiations to occur. If the Vietcong meant "withdrawal in fact, it is not acceptable. But if it is a principle, as a means of leading to an eventual withdrawal of all foreign troops based on satisfactory negotiations, then it is something else."

Mansfield asked Johnson to keep in mind a recent Walter Cronkite interview with Premier Nguyen Cao Ky, in which Ky said that "South Viet Nam troops should, in effect, form the rear guard." He cautioned Johnson, as he had Kennedy, that the war was already considered an American war, and could eventually be called "Johnson's war." Mansfield warned Johnson that divisiveness over Vietnam would affect the Great Society programs. The talk of 200,000 to 300,000 U.S. troops continued to be considered low by Mansfield, who felt that one million might be conservative. He also argued that the "pressure to pull out all military stops" would create the momentum to increase U.S. ground forces. This time, Ball prepared the administration response to rebut Mansfield's arguments.[57]

On July 25, Johnson met with McNamara, Clifford, and Arthur Goldberg, ambassador to the United Nations, at Camp David. Even though his decision seemed to have been made by the 22nd, Johnson did not disclose that. Perhaps he felt insecure about the decision, or he may have been attempting to demonstrate his reluctance to escalate for future historians. Clifford prophetically argued that the United States could lose 50,000 men and billions of dollars that would "ruin us." Johnson read a letter expressing similar views, which was probably Mansfield's. Clifford had hoped to debate McNamara on every point, but the president ended the discussion. His decision was made.[58]

MANSFIELD'S LAST-DITCH EFFORTS TO PREVENT ESCALATION

On July 26, Johnson met with his top advisors and announced his decision to commit U.S. ground troops. When informed of the decision, Mansfield worked to change Johnson's mind. He talked to the president on the morning of the 27th, and then met with Senators Fulbright, Russell, George Aiken (R-Vt.), John Sherman Cooper (R-Ky.), and John Sparkman (D-Ala.).[59] Their meeting led to a nineteen-point memo sent to Johnson later that day. Although the nineteen points expressed many views articulated by Mansfield earlier, Kahin called the "semi-consensus" in the memo "considerably more moderate" than the position Mansfield had expressed that morning.[60]

The senators expressed "a general desire to support [Johnson] in this course." Yet they pointed to the need for a negotiated settlement, and they voiced concern for the use of American conscripts, as well as disappointment in McNamara's handling of the Vietnamese situation. The sixth point predicted:

> The country is backing the President on Vietnam primarily because he is the President, not necessarily out of any understanding or sympathy with policies on Vietnam; beneath the support, there is deep concern and a great deal of confusion which could explode at any time; in addition racial factors at home could become involved.

The seventh point suggested a dilemma: "the main perplexity in the Vietnamese situation is that even if you win, totally, you still do not come out well. What have you achieved? It is by no means a 'vital' area of U.S. concern." The senators ended by admitting a lack of unanimity, but "full agreement that insofar as Viet Nam is concerned we are deeply enmeshed in a place where we ought not to be; that the situation is rapidly going out of control; and that every effort should be made to extricate ourselves."[61]

Gibbons suggested that these six Senate "'Wise Men' . . . constituted an extraordinary 'privy council.'" If Johnson had been seeking a way to avoid escalation, they offered him justification for such a path.[62]

Johnson did not heed their advice. Instead, he had McNamara prepare a response to eighteen of the points, and the president wrote a note to Mansfield in which he answered the nineteenth point, calling McNamara "the best Secretary of Defense in the history of this country." McNamara argued that conscripts were needed, and that "South Vietnam *is* vital to the United States in the significance that a demonstrable defeat would have on the future effectiveness of the United States on the world scene."[63] McNamara's credibility with Johnson won out over Mansfield and these Senate wise men.

Just before 6:00 p.m. on July 27, 1965, Johnson met briefly with the National Security Council prior to his scheduled meeting with the congressional leadership. The meeting notes make it clear that the decision had been made by this time, and that Johnson used the fifteen-minute NSC session to work out his thoughts before announcing them to the leadership.[64] At 6:30, Johnson and his senior advisors met with elected congressional leaders, including Mansfield.[65]

Johnson began by outlining the five options open to the United States. He rejected three of them: all-out war, pulling out of Vietnam, and staying at the current level of 80,000 troops. The fourth choice was to call a state of emergency, ask Congress for money, request the authority to call up reserves, and send more combat battalions. Johnson rejected that option, too, because it would alarm the Soviets and Chinese and cause them to increase their commitments to North Vietnam. The final option was the one Johnson had chosen. The president was committing only the number of troops requested by the military. No additional money would be requested until January. During the interim, Johnson stressed, he would seek a diplomatic solution. The president said, "if the Russians did not come in and if China was not gambling we might be able to say 'cut out your foolishness and come to the conference table.'" The minutes continue:

PRESIDENT: So the fifth alternative is the one that makes the most sense. We don't know if this will be 2 years or 4 years or what. We didn't know World War I was going to be one year or five years.

RUSK: The attitude of the Communist world is the key question.

SMATHERS: We are denying the VC [Vietcong] the victory aren't we? Is not our purpose not to be driven out—and avoid WW III by not bringing in China and Russia. Is this a change of policy?

PRESIDENT: As aid to the VC increases, our need to increase our forces goes up. There is no change in policy.

LONG: If we back out, they'd move somewhere else. Ready to concede all Asia to Communists? Not ready to turn tail. If a nation with 14 million can make Uncle Sam run, what will China think?

McCORMACK: I don't think we have any alternatives. Our military men tell us we need more and we should give it to them. The lesson of Hitler and Mussolini is clear. I can see five years from now a chain of events far more dangerous to our country. [At this point in the meeting, McGeorge Bundy recorded in his notes: "the Leadership seems mighty hawky so far."]

The discussion then turned toward justifying option five over four.

ARENDS: How many men?

McNAMARA: We don't know—we will meet requirements. Right now 50,000 additional. We will ship NOW—as soon as the decision is made.

PRESIDENT: Let me appeal to you as Americans to show your patriotism by not talking to the press. I'm going to do everything I can, with honor, to keep Russia and China out.

DIRKSEN: I quite agree with your premise. The first business is to peel off dramatics. Tell the country we are engaged in very serious business. People are apathetic. Afraid we are stripping Europe components.

McNAMARA: Baloney on stripping. We are not stripping. . . .

DIRKSEN: We don't need to withhold information.

PRESIDENT: We won't withhold. We want to announce as soon as troops arrive. In the morning I will consult Ike [former President Dwight Eisenhower] and tell him what we hope to do and get his view. I will see the Chairmen of Foreign Relations, Appropriations and Armed Forces. Then announce decision in press conference.

Mansfield sat silently through the discussion until this point. As usual, he was offered the opportunity to speak near the end of the meeting. For the third time in less than one year, Mansfield became the only person to speak out against Johnson's escalation decision. He wrote later: "I was not convinced by those who spoke before me. I wanted my views, in opposition, on the record."[66]

Puffing on his pipe, Mansfield pulled a three-page prepared statement from his pocket and repeated his major arguments from numerous memoranda and conversations with the president:

> As the Minority Leader has said, there is apathy among the people & I would add disquiet & concern as well & it applies to the Senate also.
>
> The decision was yours to make and you have made it or will make it shortly. That is understood fully and clearly. I will support this decision to the very best of my ability. I would do that, as a Senator, even if I did not have the additional requirement of circumspection which goes with Leadership in the Senate.
>
> However, I would not be true to my conscience, to the people I represent or to my oath, if I did not, now, in the confidence of this room, make known to you my feelings on this matter. I would not want it said that the opportunity to speak was offered and that it was met with silence on my part.

Mansfield proceeded to develop eight points, most of which he had previously articulated: no government in Saigon had represented the people in any real sense; any commitment that the United States had previously "was abrogated with the assassination of Diem"; a total victory would be a loss, leaving behind a decimated Vietnam with huge reconstruction costs; no other nation would aid the United States; the American people would not support the war for 3-10 years as racial issues, drafted manpower, and partisan politics came into play; America lacked the national interest for this kind of involvement; the United States had not done enough to bring about negotiations and failed to use France for that purpose; escalation would beget more escalation and "as we go more deeply into this conflict, in short, I think it most advisable, at least, that we go in with our eyes open."

The president did not respond to Mansfield's statement, but later wrote: "as always, he expressed his opinion candidly."[67] Jack Valenti remembered that after

Mansfield's comments, "the President nodded to Senator Mansfield, his old colleague and friend, possibly feeling as I did, that this nation has managed to withstand the bloody assaults which threaten its survival because of men like Mansfield." Valenti added:

Mansfield's discontent was remarkably prophetic. The majority leader never wavered in his assessment of Vietnam and its deadly impact on the nation. What might have happened if the president had listened to Mike Mansfield and given his views more weight in his own mind? Mansfield's assay of Indochina was probably closer to the mark than other public men, with the possible exception of George Ball.

With Mansfield's comments to the president, the meeting had come to its end. The die was cast. The decision taken.[68]

CHAPTER 10

MANSFIELD'S FIFTH VISIT TO VIETNAM AND EARLY EFFORTS TO GET TO THE BARGAINING TABLE

When President Lyndon Johnson announced his decision to commit ground troops on July 28, 1965, reactions were generally favorable. There was little opposition to the president's decision from his defense advisors, academicians who served as civilian strategists for the Pentagon. A search through the *Congressional Record* shows only praise for the president's decision. Mansfield continued his strategy of public support for the president, responding to Johnson's address by saying that the president was "doing his very best, and that is all that any one man can do." He put a positive spin on Johnson's openness, asserting "I know of no President who has consulted more with Congress than has Lyndon Johnson."[1]

Despite his public support, Mansfield did not wait long after losing the debate on the July 1965 escalation before returning to his familiar role as quiet critic. Mansfield's new strategy was to try to influence the administration to get to the negotiation table as quickly as possible. On August 13, Mansfield delivered a Senate speech in which he praised the "virtues of seeking solutions by way of negotiations." At the end of August, Mansfield engaged in a debate with J. William Fulbright (D-Ark.) over the administration's interest in negotiation. Fulbright claimed that the Johnson formula was negotiation, but "the other side must stop doing what it is doing." That equaled surrender, which was not likely to happen. Fulbright's perception of the anti-negotiation sentiment in the administration was correct, which doomed Mansfield's new strategy to failure.[2]

MANSFIELD FLOATS AN ADMINISTRATION TRIAL BALLOON

On August 30, Mansfield pursued his new strategy by sending Johnson a package of material including a cover letter, a memo, a copy of an editorial he had written for the *Great Falls Tribune,* and a statement on Vietnam which he planned to deliver in the Senate. In the letter, he asked for Johnson's comments on his proposed statement, promising to

163

make the statement entirely on my own, without reference to you or this exchange. That will leave you completely free to react as you see fit to a Communist or other response to the statement. I am hopeful that this statement will be helpful in moving us towards your objective of opening discussions. Then again, it may come to nothing. In any event, I believe that it is worth a try.

Mansfield then went on to discuss his oft-stated position of supporting the president as much as possible in public, predicting:

> I may well be criticized in some quarters for the statement but my own feeling is that, in the present situation, it is necessary to set forth our basic conditions for bargaining if we are to have an opportunity to get negotiations underway.[3]

In the remainder of the memo and in the proposed speech, Mansfield argued for three points that were compatible with recent statements from Defense Secretary Robert McNamara and the president: the people of South Vietnam must be allowed to choose their future through the ballot box under the Geneva guidelines; the choice must be "free of terrorism, violence, and coercion from any quarter"; and "there shall be a withdrawal of all foreign forces and bases throughout Viet Nam."

Mansfield offered two additional conditions he deemed necessary to begin negotiations: first, "there needs to be provision for a secure amnesty for those involved in the struggle on all sides in Viet Nam." Second, "there needs to be a willingness to accept, on all sides, a cease-fire and stand-fast throughout all Viet Nam which might well coincide with the initiation of negotiations."[4] Johnson and Mansfield apparently talked about the two points as the senator added in the draft of his speech: "I can say, on the basis of many conferences with the President on this matter, that the following two points have always reflected his view and do so now."[5] U.S. News and a French historian concluded that Mansfield expressed Johnson's views in this speech.[6]

Mansfield received the criticism that he had predicted in his memo to Johnson. Time editorialized heavily in a news story about the speech:

> Almost as hard to swallow was Mansfield's apparent assumption that the U.S. could withdraw . . . from South Viet Nam, in the belief that the Viet Cong—most of whom are not "foreign"—would do likewise.
>
> White House Press Secretary Bill Moyers maintained that the speech "reflects the sentiment of the Johnson Administration," which was the only polite thing to say, since Mansfield had discussed it with Johnson before he made it.[7]

The Reporter was incensed by Mansfield's speech. It suggested that Mansfield was naive in believing that elections could solve the problem in Vietnam. Later, it asserted that Mansfield had an "unerring gift for carrying ideas he espouses to solemn absurdity," using the September 1 speech as an example.[8]

MANSFIELD'S VISIT TO LAOS AND CAMBODIA

By mid-September, Johnson had become concerned that the bombing and troop buildup were not having the successful effect on the enemy predicted by the military. Mansfield campaigned for several months to get Johnson to send him to Indochina. Undoubtedly, Mansfield sought the trip to offer Johnson a fresh perspective, in an attempt to moderate policy. As with Kennedy, administration visits to Vietnam went with preconceived notions of what they wanted to find. Chester Cooper suggested that it was a norm to write recommendations based on a visit to Saigon on the way *"out."*[9] Mansfield was not about to do that.

Johnson finally relented, inviting Mansfield to make his fifth visit to Indochina in November. Mansfield was joined by Edmund Muskie (D-Maine), Daniel Inouye (D-Hawaii), George Aiken (R-Vt.), and J. Caleb Boggs (D-Del.). It is not clear why Mansfield wanted the trip to be sponsored by the president and not by the Foreign Relations Committee. Fulbright was annoyed by that.[10] Perhaps Mansfield believed that a presidentially sponsored report was more likely to be considered seriously at the White House. Mansfield said that the group was going "to see, to ask, to listen, and to report. To the extent that we speak abroad, it will be solely to stress the essential unity of this government in the search for an equitable and lasting peace in Viet Nam."[11]

The Mansfield party spent November 28 in Laos where they were briefed by U.S. Ambassador William Sullivan and met separately with Laotian King Sri Savang Vatthana and Prime Minister Souvanna Phouma. The U.S. Mission in Laos reported that Mansfield's "repeated visits to Southeast Asia . . . and understanding of Lao problems, makes him a welcome guest and conveys a favorable image of strong United States interest in this troubled Kingdom."

Sullivan viewed Laos as "a holding operation"; the future of Southeast Asia would be determined in Vietnam. The North Vietnamese and Chinese were using Laotian soil. Sullivan stressed that North Vietnam did not want Chinese intervention in Southeast Asia because of the historical enmity between Vietnam and China, but that the North Vietnamese were becoming highly dependent on China.

The King indicated that the North Vietnamese were violating Laotian neutrality to filter troops and equipment to the South. He thought there was little direct Chinese involvement in Laos but that China was behind Pathet Lao [Laotian communist] activities. Sri Savang Vatthana impressed upon the delegation that the Lao people considered U.S. military action in Vietnam "moral" and not a form of imperialism or of "using its great power to oppress smaller countries."

The Prime Minister thought that the military situation was not going "too badly," but wished that North Vietnam would withdraw its troops from Laos. Souvanna believed that U.S. military action in Vietnam had saved Laos and would force North Vietnam to the conference table. When asked about Cambodia, Souvanna suggested that Prince Norodom Sihanouk might be seeking an accommodation with the United States. He thought that Mansfield should explore Sihanouk's idea for a Southeast Asian Conference because the problems of Laos and Cambodia could not be solved until those of Vietnam were resolved as well.[12]

Mansfield flew to Cambodia for a secret meeting with Sihanouk on November 30. Sihanouk had broken diplomatic relations with the United States in May 1965 because of border violations by the United States and its allies. The Prince's invitation was intended only for Mansfield, so Mansfield and Valeo initially met the Cambodian leader without the rest of the party.

The senator was received with "great courtesy and attention." He was one of the few Americans that Sihanouk trusted. Sihanouk proclaimed: "like General de Gaulle, you represent to Cambodia Justice in the Occidental world. That is why we love you both." A handwritten and unsigned note in Mansfield's files indicated that a street in Cambodia was being named for Mansfield.

At the November 30 meeting, Sihanouk explained his philosophy of neutrality, and Mansfield expressed high personal regard for Sihanouk, while avoiding substantive comment. Mansfield sent a telegram to Johnson and Secretary of State Dean Rusk summarizing the meeting:

> [Sihanouk] wants to rebuild relations between the U.S. and Cambodia. . . . In order to rebuild relations on a firm basis three conditions must be met for the resumption of diplomatic relations: a) The U.S. government should recognize the frontiers of Cambodia. b) There should be an indemnity paid by the U.S. for Cambodian lives lost, even though this indemnity might be only token or symbolic. c) Cambodia's frontiers would be respected and . . . there would be no more bombings or incursions.
>
> Sihanouk said he did not care what the United States did in South Viet Nam . . . but he wanted the bombing of Cambodian territory stopped.[13]

In his reports on his visit, Mansfield was emphatic about keeping the war from "spilling over into Cambodia" and continued to labor for American acceptance of Cambodian neutrality.[14] His friendship with Sihanouk became central during the Nixon administration when Cambodia was finally dragged into the Indochina war.

MANSFIELD'S FIFTH VISIT TO VIETNAM

The Mansfield party met with Ambassador Henry Cabot Lodge, General William Westmoreland and other American representatives on the afternoon of December 2, 1965. Westmoreland, Lodge and the other U.S. officials were optimistic about South Vietnam's future now that U.S. troops were involved in the conflict because of the morale boost it had provided the South. Lodge asserted that U.S. troops had changed the stalemate that had existed before their arrival, while admitting that units of the North Vietnamese army were first sent south as a reaction to the U.S. escalation. Westmoreland was blunt in predicting that the "intensity of military action will continue to increase. I foresee the need for a great number of additional U.S. forces. I foresee a protracted conflict. We cannot afford this time to underestimate the enemy. And, as I see it, this war is beginning to take on an attritional character." Responding to a question from Senator Inouye, Westmoreland defined attrition as inflicting "such heavy losses on the Viet Cong that we destroy his forces faster than he can destroy the ranks of the Government forces and the forces that the U.S. is able to bring in the country." Indeed, Westmoreland reported that in the previous week "the intensity of the war was the highest on record"; 448 Americans were killed in November (which was 35 percent of all Americans killed up to that point), compared to 5,300 of the enemy. The General believed the figures validated his point on attrition. Westmoreland wanted to entice the Vietcong and North Vietnamese to stand and fight instead of using traditional guerrilla warfare methods of hit and run. Mansfield thanked Westmoreland for his candor and suggested that the American people needed to be told that the war would be long and that it would cost many Americans lives.[15]

Mansfield avoided substantive comment through more than a third of the meeting. Then, however, he took control of its direction through his questions. Mansfield's questions were tough and pointed, showing his doubts about the war and the accuracy of the information being provided.

The senator's cross examination of Westmoreland was particularly sharp. He demanded statistics on how much of the countryside was controlled by the Vietcong. Westmoreland argued that land was not a good indicator; he was only willing to share statistics on population. The Saigon government controlled sixty percent of the population because it held the cities, with another eighteen percent of the people "contested." Mansfield referred to a briefing from McNamara who conceded that the Vietcong controlled two-thirds of the land in South Vietnam. Westmoreland and Lodge were unwilling to accede to that estimate.

Mansfield then questioned Westmoreland closely as to his estimation of needed U.S. troop levels. The general was evasive in his responses, but indicated the need to double the current level of troops, then at 170,000. Mansfield pressed Westmoreland, trying to get him to admit that he was looking to expand the U.S.

presence to 500,000 troops. Westmoreland refused to concede that number, indicating instead an expected ceiling of 350,000 to 380,000. Mansfield nonetheless concluded from this exchange that 500,000 troops would be required, and that "all his worst fears about American involvement in Indochina were being realized, step by step."[16]

The "fatigue" of the Army of South Vietnamese (ARVN) after so many years of warfare was also discussed at this meeting. Westmoreland praised the ARVN's fighting ability, but admitted that U.S. troops were more effective. The senators expressed concern with the number of desertions in the ARVN. Mansfield prodded the general until he conceded that 90,000 per year deserted. The majority leader pointed out a dilemma. Vietcong main force strength had been 35,000 during his 1962 visit, but had now risen to 56,000, not including the 14,000 North Vietnamese regular troops who had moved into South Vietnam since the U.S. escalation.[17] So the Vietcong were increasing their numbers while the South Vietnamese military was experiencing a serious problem with desertions. Mansfield asked of the added numbers in the Vietcong, "are these volunteers, kidnappings, hostages?" Westmoreland did not answer that question.

Mansfield used other questions to try to expose the lack of allied support for U.S. involvement in Vietnam, asking Lodge for a detailed account of how the thirty nations the administration claimed to be "helping" in Vietnam were contributing to the effort. He gained an admission that the Korean forces were funded by the United States, as the Philippine forces would be when they arrived. Lodge was unsure of the arrangements with Australia and New Zealand.[18]

The following day, the Mansfield party and Lodge visited separately with members of the South Vietnamese leadership, General Nguyen Van Thieu, Chairman of the National Leadership Committee, Prime Minister Nguyen Cao Ky, and Foreign Minister Tran Van Do. Foreign Minister Tran emphasized that the U.S. commitment of troops had increased morale. Before July, South Vietnam had feared that the United States would withdraw as France had in 1954. A coalition government would not be acceptable because the communists were better organized and would squeeze other nationalists out of such a government. Tran believed that the North was under the control of China and could not cease hostilities even if it wanted to. He justified corruption in South Vietnam: "during a long war nobody is sure to whom they belong or whether they will be killed in a change of regime. So they assure their own interests first."

Ky agreed that China was the real source of the war, and believed that 4,000 years of Vietnamese experience made war with China inevitable. The Prime Minister emphasized that his government was moving toward democracy, which would solve the religious conflict between Catholics and Buddhists. Ky hoped to solve the problem of military desertions by emphasizing better pay and conditions for the troops, as opposed to officers, and to "indoctrinate" them better as to why they were fighting.

In the meeting with Thieu, Senator Aiken expressed concern about economic and social development. The general responded that the lack of security was responsible for the failure of such programs and he expected the military situation to improve. Senator Muskie indicated that his constituents always asked the question, "does the government of Viet-Nam really represent the people, and have their support?" Thieu explained his government's desire gradually to become democratic, but in doing so, showed his lack of appreciation of democratic processes: "we need time to educate the people; brainwash them. We do not need to impose democratic institutions that they cannot use. We are not like the United States. Our people have not had time to be educated." Mansfield responded, we "do not insist that you model yourself on us, but on the Viet-Nam that you understand." The senator emphasized, as he had with Westmoreland, Lodge, Tran, and Ky, that the war was a Vietnamese one and the U.S. role was secondary, to assist and advise.[19]

Lodge cabled Rusk on December 3 that Mansfield "has expressed satisfaction on the quality of American Mission personnel and the briefings he and his colleagues have received. Mansfield also informed me that he was impressed by the maturity of views of both Thieu and Ky."[20]

MANSFIELD'S PRIVATE AND PUBLIC REPORTS

Although Lodge's characterization of Mansfield's attitude seemed positive, the majority leader proved to be less optimistic in the private report that he submitted to Lyndon Johnson the week before Christmas. He discussed his report not with Johnson, but with McNamara and Rusk. That may have been because Johnson did not focus on foreign affairs as Kennedy had. It might also have indicated Johnson's impatience with listening to Mansfield's pessimism about Vietnam. Mansfield knew that Johnson did not like to read lengthy reports, so he submitted a three-page memo that Johnson was more likely to read which summarized his private report.[21]

The private report was negative. Mansfield was complimentary of the Ky government, although he still perceived the "apex of success" of Vietnamese government came under Diem. The senator's major conclusions were prophetic: the war was "at the very beginning of a beginning" (as he had warned Kennedy in 1962); the United States was likely to become more deeply committed with large troop increases and increased pressures for bombing; and the war would likely spill over into Laos, Cambodia, Thailand, and possibly China. He warned that "a military step once taken compels a militarily logical second step and if the process goes on for any length of time the limited initial objectives are easily lost in the expanded dimensions which the conflict assumes." Mansfield saw the final number of U.S. troops "not as 170,000 men or 300,000 men or even double that figure but, rather, an open-end requirement of unpredictable dimensions." He accurately cautioned that the "civilian discomfort with the impact of the arrival of great numbers of Americans could grow into outright bitterness, with the only remaining semblance of a believable Vietnamese leadership that of the Viet Cong."

Mansfield's deescalation suggestion was to pursue the more limited objective of indefinitely holding on to either territory currently controlled or just the coastal enclaves. Then, he proposed the United States wait for North Vietnam and the Vietcong to negotiate. The senator argued that America could protect its allies from such enclaves, provide a positive bargaining position, and save lives and resources. He ended his private report by assuring Johnson he knew the president was trying to move to the bargaining table, but he cautioned:

> Until that moment arrives, I believe every effort must be made to restrain rather than extend our involvement on the Asian mainland. . . . This is a conflict in which all the choices open to us are bad choices. We stand to lose in Viet Nam by restraint; but we stand to lose far more at home and throughout the world by the pursuit of an elusive and ephemeral objective in Viet Nam.[22]

Regardless of Mansfield's private rhetoric and Johnson's public utterances, the senator knew that Johnson's policies were not designed to get to the bargaining table. Mansfield believed that Johnson wanted negotiations, but was being swayed by advisors who did not. In 1990 Mansfield admitted that most of Johnson's advisors seemed to oppose negotiation.[23] For the remainder of LBJ's presidency, Mansfield continued to prod Johnson toward the bargaining table.

Although Johnson may not have cared for Mansfield's private report, the senator's colleagues found it admirable. Aiken described the private report as "more open, more factual, plainer talk than the one which was made public." He continued to believe "it was a very accurate report." Inouye thought the conclusions were correct. Eugene McCarthy (D-Minn.) wrote that it "proved to be not only accurate in its noting of facts, but prophetic as well."[24]

The public report, released on January 6, 1966, reflected the "unity" Mansfield announced at the time of his departure. All five of the senators are listed as authors, but Mansfield appears to have been the primary contributor. While its conclusions were not optimistic, it was more upbeat than the private report. The public report ended by suggesting a dilemma. On the one hand, if negotiations came "accompanied by a cease-fire and standfast," the government would control most of the population, but the countryside would be controlled by the Vietcong. There would be no guarantees of how such a negotiation would turn out. The second scenario called for the "indefinite expansion and intensification of the war which will require the continuous introduction of additional U.S. forces." That scenario also provided no guarantees for a quick resolution of the conflict.[25]

Mansfield was much more forceful in private about the lack of allied support, saying that to imply that over thirty nations were assisting in Vietnam was "grossly misleading and, as propaganda, fools nobody except ourselves." His private report also emphasized the potential dangers stemming from our involvement in Vietnam much more than did the public report. The danger of war with China, the Soviet Union's advantage of sitting on the sidelines, the threat to the Western Alliance, and the danger to Japanese-American friendship were all emphasized in the private report, but not in the public one. Mansfield supported the enclave approach in his private report while the January report listed two alternatives: the defense of enclaves or continued escalation. The senators made no recommendation between the two alternatives. Undoubtedly, the senators wanted to show a united front to the communist adversary if Johnson continued to escalate.[26]

Mansfield's trip to Southeast Asia did not receive as much media attention as earlier visits had. That may have been because visits to Vietnam by members of Congress were becoming commonplace. When Mansfield made his three trips to Southeast Asia in the 1950s, he was one of only a few to do so. Even when Mansfield visited the area for President Kennedy in 1962, such trips were not common. By the time the January 1966 report was issued, over one hundred members of Congress had visited Vietnam, most of them between the 1965 and 1966 sessions.[27]

Mansfield's public report did receive some coverage. *U.S. News* called it "one of the gloomiest reports to come out of the Vietnam war." *Newsweek* noted that it "carefully avoided direct criticism of administration policy but was bleakly pessimistic about the war."[28] Writing in the *New York Times,* E. W. Kenworthy called the report bleak and said that the "inference can be drawn from the way the report describes the situation in Vietnam that the United States should take the best peace settlement it can get that is consistent with honor." Rumors about Mansfield's private report must have been circulating since Kenworthy referred to the private report as a "longer, more detailed, franker and tougher version of the public report."[29] The article concluded that the report did not please Johnson or Rusk, that it would become a rallying point for senators opposed to escalation, and that Senate debate would increase on Vietnam.

One of the article's claims is supported by archival evidence. Kenworthy posited that "officials agree" that the private report "was a strongly contributing factor in Mr. Johnson's decision to order the pause in the bombing of North Vietnam."[30] It is true that Mansfield was involved in the administration's decision for a bombing pause. Rusk had asked Francis Meloy, a foreign service officer traveling with the Mansfield party, to "very privately" seek Mansfield's reaction to a bombing pause. Mansfield consulted with Aiken and responded that while Ky might look at the bombing pause with disfavor, it was less psychologically important to South Vietnam since the arrival of U.S. ground troops.

The bombing was not halting the flow of men and material, and was likely hardening the will of the North Vietnamese to fight.

In Mansfield's conversations with Russian, Rumanian, and Polish officials, it was indicated that they could do nothing to help end the hostilities as long as the bombing of the North and "U.S. aggressive actions" continued. Such a pause might "smoke out" whether the Soviets were willing to be helpful. While he had initially opposed the bombing, Mansfield consistently believed that it was a mistake to suspend bombing only to resume and extend it later. If the bombing were suspended, Mansfield called for direct U.S. initiatives with the Soviets, Rumanians, Poles, and even the Chinese to find a solution to the conflict. Besides a suspension of bombing, the senator suggested that Johnson call for a termination of all hostilities in Vietnam based on a Vietcong offer of a twelve-hour cease-fire on Christmas. Indeed, he thought it advisable to call for a cease-fire through Tet, the Vietnamese New Year, which would make the ceasefire last almost one month.[31]

At the end of December, Johnson told George Ball that the administration did not have "great hope" that the bombing halt would lead to negotiations, but they "in effect are doing what Mansfield has said." The administration kept Mansfield apprised of its efforts to use the pause to open talks with North Vietnam.[32]

Mansfield's trip helped to achieve a bombing pause, but his goals were much higher than that. He hoped to stem the flow of American forces moving to South Vietnam, to move those remaining to enclaves, and hold out for negotiations with the enemy. Mansfield failed to achieve those goals. For the rest of the Johnson presidency, Mansfield explored every avenue through which he could work to speed up the onset of the inevitable negotiations. Mansfield would not return to Vietnam until after the war had ended, and he would not return to Indochina until 1969.

Chapter 11

"Tugging" at Johnson's Coat

Mansfield Fails to Lead Senate Opponents of the War

Lyndon Johnson and Mike Mansfield got along reasonably well when serving as leader and whip in the late 1950s. When LBJ became vice president and Mansfield majority leader, the relationship remained cordial. The real strain started when Johnson moved to the White House, and differences over Vietnam policy were the major cause for the split. Mansfield's 1965 report seems to have contributed to a cooling in his relationship with the president. James Rowe knew Johnson since the Roosevelt administration and Mansfield since his days in Butte, and no one knew the pair better than he. Rowe described them as "temperamentally two different men" and concluded that LBJ and Mansfield "didn't like each other much."[1] Mansfield would never agree with Rowe's assessment and typically claimed that differences with Johnson over Vietnam "did not chill our personal relationship."[2] The bulk of the evidence refutes Mansfield.

When asked if there was a chill in Mansfield's relationship with Johnson by early 1966, both George Reedy and Francis Valeo agreed such was the case. David Halberstam reported that Johnson sent Vice President Hubert Humphrey on a trip to Asia in 1966 with orders to "brand China as *the* aggressor"— a report which, in Johnson's words, would "nail Fulbright, Mansfield and the *New York Times* editorial board to the wall." Rowland Evans and Robert Novak indicated that the Johnson/Mansfield relationship was strained by the beginning of the 1966 term, and hinted at Mansfield's failure as an opponent of the war. They speculated that about one-half of the sixty-six Democratic senators had become opponents of the Vietnam War, "but there was no leadership, no cohesion, and little willingness to take an exposed position against the President."[3]

Could Mansfield have provided that leadership and organized Senate opposition to the war in 1966? Certainly his elected leadership position and perceived expertise on Asia gave him the credentials to lead the opposition to a war that he later called a mistake and a tragedy. Mansfield's 1965 visit to Vietnam and the report he wrote gave him the impetus to lead Senate opponents of American

173

involvement in the conflict. Senator Eugene McCarthy (D-Minn.) complained that after Mansfield filed his "very negative" 1965 report, "that's sort of where he left it." Montana's junior Democratic senator, Lee Metcalf, found this reticence to be a problem when he ran for reelection in 1966. Metcalf felt that he could not break with the president over the war until Montana's senior senator and majority leader had broken with the administration.[4]

Yet Mansfield's personal philosophy prevented him from assuming the leadership in this battle. In 1966 he noted that "I always ask myself when I attempt to criticize people in high positions just what would I have done had I been in their position, and sometimes even on the basis of hindsight I don't know that I could have done any better."[5] Mansfield's reluctance to criticize, his friendship with Johnson, his respect for the presidency, and his party position made him an unlikely candidate to organize Senate opposition to the war. On two different occasions when discussing the Kennedy administration, Mansfield said that he would have resigned as majority leader if he had fundamental differences with Kennedy.[6] Yet he never considered resigning the post during the Johnson administration and continued to believe that he could influence the president.[7] Just as Johnson's Vietnam escalation was gradual, the severity of the gulf between the two men slowly widened.

The senator's belief that Johnson's views could be reconciled with his own was challenged late in January. At a White House meeting on January 25, 1966, Mansfield declared his opposition to the end of the bombing pause, declaring, "the best chance of getting to the peace table is to minimize our military action." Evans and Novak reported that Mansfield "was finding it increasingly difficult to harmonize his loyalty to the president with his desire for a soft line on Vietnam and now made no secret of his opposition to ending the pause." Mansfield expressed regret at Johnson's ending of the thirty-seven day bombing suspension in a letter to a constituent, but as majority leader, he was not willing to organize the Senate opposition. He left that to Vance Hartke (D-Ind.), who attempted to lead the opponents of the war through a January 27 letter to Johnson that endorsed Mansfield's call for an indefinite suspension of bombing. Mansfield was not among the fifteen Democratic senators signing the letter.[8]

Earlier, Johnson would have attempted to persuade former allies like Hartke, Fulbright, and Mansfield of the correctness of the administration position. By 1966, though, Johnson shunned his old friends and sought new allies. Johnson started to work with Minority Leader Everett Dirksen (Ill.) and such Democratic allies as Gale McGee (Wyo.), Birch Bayh (Ind.), Fred Harris (Okla.), and Paul Douglas (Ill.). Johnson's new allies replaced the old at formal and informal visits to the White House. One journalist reported that "in 1966 and 1967, as Mansfield's opposition hardened, Mansfield would be seated for White House state dinners at a table in one of the far corners of the dining room, and Dirksen would be seated at the President's table. Fulbright would not be invited to attend."[9]

At this time, Johnson described Mansfield as a cross between Jeanette Rankin and Burton Wheeler, Montanans known for their pacifism and isolationism, respectively. That unfriendly characterization found its way back to Mansfield. By rhetorically branding Mansfield with the pejorative term of "isolationist," Johnson's inner circle was able to discount Mansfield's misgivings without thoroughly airing them. Walt Rostow, for example, called both Mansfield and Frank Church (D-Idaho) "isolationists or neo-isolationists" in his memoirs, without bothering to define those terms.[10]

Mansfield struggled to reconcile his loyalty to Johnson and his opposition to the war. On March 1, Wayne Morse (D-Ore.) moved to debate the war on the floor of the Senate. Mansfield had the amendment tabled. Senator McCarthy recalled: "the move of Senator Morse was clearly within the range of Senate rights and responsibility, and the Mansfield motion was clearly in the service of the Johnson administration." After March 1, McCarthy became convinced that the war could not be challenged in the Senate, but would have to be contested in the 1968 presidential election.[11]

Senator Mansfield offered a new peace formula in April, calling for "direct confrontation across a peace table" by the United States, China, North Vietnam, and "essential elements from South Vietnam." By excluding the government of South Vietnam from his proposal, Mansfield suggested a compromise with the North. If the war were lost, he thought it would be because of the lack of a stable government in Saigon since Diem's fall. Mansfield received considerable support, including that of some Republicans and the administration. Hanoi, however, rejected it.[12]

MANSFIELD PUSHES FOR THE ENCLAVE APPROACH

On June 13, 1966, Mansfield wrote a memo in response to a Johnson communiqué listing the advantages and disadvantages of five possible alternatives in Vietnam. Mansfield rejected option I (immediate withdrawal) and alternatives IV and V (which both called for massive U.S. escalation). He implicitly attacked option III, which was the status quo, because the gradual escalation had increased American manpower "tenfold" and costs "fifteen-fold," which was leading toward options IV or V. Mansfield said that the current policy "requires us to run even faster just to stay in the same place, militarily." He believed that option II, the enclave approach, was the best policy. He had first proposed an enclave approach in his December 1965 report to Johnson, and believed that Johnson's goal must be to limit U.S. involvement while seeking negotiations, which would be made possible by defending enclaves. According to the senator, the approach would "provide a believable U.S. bargaining position for negotiations, more commensurate with U.S. interests on the Asian mainland."[13] The administration never saw the approach as viable.

Rostow replaced McGeorge Bundy as national security advisor, and as rebutter for Mansfield's arguments, in 1966. When Rostow analyzed Mansfield's memorandum for the president, his letter showed the degree of difference between Mansfield and the administration. The draft suggested two "gut" questions: "do we want a settlement that is going to leave South Viet Nam independent or do we just want to get out with as much as we can salvage?" Second, "if we want meaningful negotiations, which course is more likely to convince Hanoi of our seriousness of purpose; that is, are we trying to convince them they can't win, or are we trying to make it so costly they will call off the aggression?" Rostow claimed that Mansfield's enclave suggestion would be like "hunker[ing] up like a jackass in a hailstorm," and would lead to a bad settlement. Johnson's advisor believed that American goals were less narrow than Mansfield implied, and he expressed the unrealistic desire of getting the North Vietnamese to "either negotiate or simply fade away."

Johnson sent Rostow's written response to Mansfield on June 22. As usual, Johnson emphasized their areas of agreement, but this time he accused Mansfield of "nit-picking" and indicated that he disagreed sharply with some of Mansfield's points. He opposed the enclave approach, suggesting that it would lead to the type of settlement the United States could have had in Korea in 1950. The president also drew an analogy to WW II. He disagreed that the United States was "running faster to stay where we are," arguing that the military situation had improved since 1965. Johnson then articulated his vision for a Vietnam settlement, a vision that hoped not for a negotiated settlement, but for an outright victory:

> Once [the communists] become convinced that we are not weak; that we are not impatient; that we are not going to falter; that they cannot win; that the cost to them of their continued aggression is rising; that their bargaining position at a conference is getting weaker every day—then peace will come, whether at the negotiating table or not.[14]

Mansfield responded with attacks on the analogies to Korea and WW II. America operated "unilaterally" in Vietnam and had allies in both WW II and Korea. There was no United Nations support for the U.S. position in Vietnam as there had been in Korea. Ho Chi Minh was hardly Hitler and 40,000 North Vietnamese troops operating with small arms in the South was not comparable to Nazi's "goose-stepping" through Europe, or Japan invading much of Asia. Since there was not "the remotest possibility" that the United States could withdraw quickly, the real question was whether to continue the status quo course of "steady, expanding U.S. involvement" (option III), which Mansfield saw as "a kind of grim game of 'Uncle'" for which costs and length could not be predicted.[15]

Rostow prepared a response for Johnson that gently tried "to put a bit of the monkey" on Mansfield's back. The memo asserted that North Vietnam "watch[ed] our debates at home for signs of wavering" and declared that Mansfield's "potentiality for leadership in helping create the conditions for an honorable peace are almost as great as mine."[16]

The Johnson/Rostow appeal to guilt had no discernible effect on Mansfield's strategy. He continued to try to balance his role as leader with his independent one as a senator. In August, Mansfield annoyed Johnson by introducing a Senate resolution calling for a reduction in U.S. troops stationed in Europe. Yet in September, Mansfield aided the administration when Johnson prepared to denounce Fulbright publicly "for giving aid and comfort to our enemies," because Fulbright planned to use the Foreign Relations Committee to hold hearings on the U.S. involvement in Thailand. Mansfield and Russell Long (D-La.) dissuaded Johnson from his denouncement by promising to attempt to prevent Fulbright from making the hearings "another televised attack on Vietnam."[17]

On October 13, Mansfield proposed to the president methods to get to the bargaining table and "reduce the intensity of the struggle." He called for a bombing halt and a "fire only if fired upon" order in South Vietnam, in an effort to obtain a "cease-fire and stand-fast." Mansfield wanted a unilateral withdrawal of 30,000 U.S. troops at the onset of negotiations and a willingness "to work out a time-table for joint and total withdrawals of all forces alien to South Viet Nam as part of a settlement." He preferred the involvement of U.N. Secretary General U Thant to bring the proposals to Hanoi. Mansfield offered his suggestions "to use or discard as you see fit." Johnson discarded them, responding that Hanoi did not share U.S. objectives to deescalate and negotiate.[18]

THE MANSFIELD/GOLDBERG U.N. SOLUTION

A number of times in 1966 Mansfield publicly praised U.N. Ambassador Arthur Goldberg's efforts to bring the Vietnam conflict to an end. Goldberg had accepted the appointment as U.N. ambassador in the hope that he would be able to help negotiate a settlement in Vietnam. The two men worked together in an attempt to find such a formula. In a phone conversation in October, Goldberg said, "Mike, thank God you are where you are." Mansfield replied, "thank God you are where you are, Arthur."[19]

The contact with Goldberg contributed to ideas for Mansfield's Johns Hopkins University address in early November. The speech praised the domestic successes of the past session, but said they were "obscured in the shadow" of Vietnam. Mansfield's major thrust was the need to involve the United Nations in the settlement of the war, as it had been involved with

Korea. He admitted the flaws in the United Nations, but argued that the Security Council needed to be actively involved in any settlement.[20] The need for U.N. involvement continued to be the main focus of Mansfield's Vietnam rhetoric for the next year.

Johnson and Goldberg both called Mansfield after his Johns Hopkins address, the president saying he was interested in Mansfield's proposals. This interest was perhaps spurred by McNamara's private but profound change of position on the war, as the secretary of defense concluded that the war could not be won militarily. Johnson's interest set the stage for a Mansfield trip to New York to discuss the matter with Goldberg and U Thant. U Thant preferred quiet diplomacy to the involvement of the Security Council, but the quiet diplomacy he undertook with Goldberg ultimately failed.[21] Mansfield undeterred, continued to fight to involve the United Nations.

On December 13, Mansfield issued a press release in response to North Vietnam's call for two forty-eight hour cease fires during Christmas and the New Year. As in 1965, Mansfield wanted the United States to counter the offer with a "cease-fire and stand-fast throughout Viet Nam, north and south." The White House did not comment on Mansfield's press release. The *New York Times* concluded that it was "the firmest indication that critics in Congress of the conduct of the war would try again to press for American diplomatic initiatives to prolong the holiday truces."[22]

Johnson called Mansfield again to express continued interest in utilizing the United Nations and in a bombing halt:

> President Johnson called me at home and said Ambassador Goldberg was coming out to see me.
>
> [Goldberg] came to my house about one-half hour later and discussed in brief the meeting just held at the White House, attended by Lodge, McNamara, Rostow, Goldberg and others and he was very much disturbed. He said he and McNamara advocated the following up of the Mansfield proposal for a truce thru Tet and that Lodge was noncommittal and others not sympathetic.
>
> [Goldberg] was . . . distressed and seemed to indicate that he was getting very fed up with his job at the U.N., but I told him that he could not consider leaving, that some of us had to keep on making our voices heard even though they were overshadowed and that he had responsibility there just as I had responsibility here.[23]

The failure of his 1965 Christmas bombing halt to bring Hanoi to the bargaining table made Johnson leery of future ones[24] and the extended bombing halt envisioned by Mansfield, McNamara, and Goldberg was rejected by the president.

AN IMPROVED JOHNSON/MANSFIELD RELATIONSHIP

Perhaps the late 1966 telephone conversations between Johnson and Mansfield broke the ice between them. The chill from early 1966 seemed to end by 1967, and contact between Mansfield and LBJ became more frequent. Johnson might have been seeking ways out of Vietnam and wanted to encourage Mansfield's suggestions. Or Mansfield's U.N. proposal may have seemed to offer possibilities. Conceivably, Johnson came to appreciate Mansfield's public support as the attacks on the president increased from other quarters. More likely, LBJ strategized that by providing Mansfield with a private forum for his dissent, the majority leader would tone down any public criticism.

A January 6, 1967 telephone conversation led Mansfield to write the president a memorandum on that same day. Mansfield was convinced that the North Vietnamese were sending signals that the North was hurting from the bombing and wanted it stopped, but was unwilling to say "Uncle" to the United States. While the Hanoi government was still capable of discussing a settlement of the conflict without Russian or Chinese permission, their dependence, especially on China, was increasing. Hanoi was willing to talk about a settlement, but not without assurances of a U.S. troop withdrawal in a reasonable amount of time. The North could afford to wait until America viewed the war as Hanoi did because the North was winning. Mansfield argued that the United States was at the "second level" he had suggested on June 9, 1965 (holding the military situation where it was in the status quo), and was moving toward the first level (fighting until the United States prevailed below the 17th parallel). As long as those were U.S. goals, he argued that no useful negotiations with Hanoi could be expected.[25]

Johnson was warm in his response, writing, "I greatly value your telephone conversation and memorandum." He assessed Mansfield's analysis: it was not clear if Hanoi wanted to negotiate or simply wanted U.S. bombing stopped. Johnson agreed that Hanoi wanted to know about troop withdrawals and ultimate Vietnamese unity before publicly committing to negotiations, but questioned whether Hanoi would "accept honest self-determination by the people of South Vietnam in an environment freed of aggression and terror." While North Vietnam may have announced its expectations for negotiations, the United States had done so much more explicitly. In referring to the June 1965 memo, Johnson stated that U.S. force was only being used to ensure self-determination. He concluded his remarks by attempting to force agreement: "and in this, I believe you and I deeply agree. I'm sure you have derived encouragement over the past year, as I have, in the real progress towards constitutional government made in South Viet Nam."[26]

Mansfield knew that self-determination was not the real goal of the White House and that little progress toward constitutional government had been made in South Vietnam. The senator expressed his personal goal to a constituent: "every bit of influence I have will be used to help the President reach the negotiation table [so] an honorable settlement can be achieved."[27] To reach that goal, Mansfield needed to be heard at the White House. While it was his nature to be balanced in his rhetorical strategies, he also wanted to avoid being "written off" as Fulbright had been. Thus, Mansfield's speeches and correspondence show a contradiction. Mansfield attempted to protect the president from his attackers, but his arguments often contained veiled criticism of Johnson's efforts to negotiate. For example, in a North Carolina speech, Mansfield recommended pursuing "any avenue, byway, route or whatever, which might lead to the negotiation table." Mansfield outlined the many proposals he had made in the past to get to the conference table and suggested Johnson concurred with some and "had them pursued by his diplomats." With the proposals Johnson rejected, Mansfield "could only conclude that there have been sound reasons for not pursuing them."[28] It is doubtful that Mansfield seriously believed this statement.

Mansfield introduced two new ideas in North Carolina: "that the Security Council invite all belligerents, direct and indirect, including China and North Viet Nam, to participate in an open discussion of the conflict in Viet Nam and ways and means of ending it," and "that the Security Council request the International Court to render an advisory opinion on the current applicability of the Geneva Accords of 1954 and 1962 and the obligations which these agreements may place on the present belligerents in Viet Nam."[29] Introducing these ideas in a public forum indicated his lack of faith in the treatment such proposals would receive at the White House.

Yet Mansfield publicly insisted that the president was doing everything he could to end the conflict. In two speeches, Mansfield quoted Johnson as saying: "I go to bed every night feeling that I failed that day because I could not end the conflict in Viet Nam." Mansfield argued that the failure did not belong solely to the president, but to everyone. He opposed criticism of Johnson that "goes far beyond the merely ungracious and borders on the disgraceful." Mansfield contended that the conflict "cannot be settled from the Congress or from the campus." Johnson listened to advice from the Senate, but while "a Senator lives with a Constitution, a constituency, and a conscience . . . it is the President who makes the fundamental decisions on foreign policy."[30] Mansfield's belief in executive supremacy in foreign affairs constrained his ability to criticize the sitting president. His party position made it more difficult with a Democrat in the White House.

Mansfield demonstrated this philosophy in late February 1967. Senator Joseph Clark (D-Penn.) introduced an amendment to the military procurement bill urging a negotiated settlement and limiting U.S. personnel in South Vietnam to 500,000 unless Congress declared war. Clark's amendment was sure to be defeated, but a large vote would have embarrassed Johnson. Mansfield came to

Participation in Mrs. Eleanor Roosevelt's TV program Prospects of Mankind, 10/13/60.
Photograph by Ralph Norman. Mike Mansfield Mss., Mansfield Library, University of Montana.

Secretary of State Kissinger and Senator Mike Mansfield - Capitol, Rm. S-116 (For. Rela.
Comm. Room) - 4-10-74. Mike Mansfield Mss., Mansfield Library, University of Montana.

China trip, 1974. Left to right: Premier Zhou Enlai, Mike and Maureen Mansfield. Mike Mansfield Mss., Mansfield Library, University of Montana.

With General Secretary Leonid Brezhnev and President Richard and Pat Nixon at the State Dinner in honor of Brezhnev, July 1973. White House official photograph. Mike Mansfield Mss., Mansfield Library, University of Montana.

From left, Undersecretary of State Herbert Hoover, Jr.: Sen. Mike Mansfield, (D) Mont., Chairman of a Senate Foreign Relations Subcommittee on Technical Assistance: Secretary of State John Foster Dulles and Sen. John Kennedy, (D) Mass., as they conferred shortly before Dulles and Hoover testified before the Subcommittee [1/23/56]. INP soundphoto by Al Muto. Mike Mansfield Mss., Mansfield Library, University of Montana.

Left to right, Lawrence Spivak and Mike Mansfield on Meet the Press, July 27, 1975. Photograph by Reni Newsphotos Inc. Mike Mansfield Mss., Mansfield Library, University of Montana.

Michael Manfield, Secretary of State Dean Rusk, Malayan Ambassador Dato Ong, and Senator J. William Fulbright, 1963. Photograph by Reni Newsphotos Inc. Mike Mansfield Mss., Mansfield Library, University of Montana.

Mike Mansfield with President Gerald Ford, Feb. 5, 1976. White House official photograph. Mike Mansfield Mss., Mansfield Library, University of Montana.

Mike Mansfield, n.d. Photograph by Robert Stiles. Mike Mansfield Mss., Mansfield Library, University of Montana.

Dec., 1963. Left to right: Hubert Humphrey, Everet Dirksen, Mike Mansfield, President Johnson. Mike Mansfield Mss., Mansfield Library, University of Montana.

Left to right: LBJ, JFK, Sam Rayburn, Mike Mansfield, Florida, 1960. Mike Mansfield Mss., Mansfield Library, University of Montana.

Wesley Fishel with Ngo Dinh Diem. Michigan State University Archives and Historical Collections.

Mansfield at MSU Commencement, 1962. Michigan State University Archives and Historical Collections.

the administration's defense. He amended Clark's amendment by removing the 500,000 troop barrier. In that form, it easily passed. True to his philosophy, Mansfield upheld the hand of the executive over his own branch of government.[31]

Just as Johnson minimized his differences over Vietnam with Mansfield in their communication, the majority leader denied the severity of his disagreement with the president. Mansfield sincerely believed that there was no contradiction in his supporting the president while disagreeing with his Vietnam policy. This was illustrated on March 2 when Robert Kennedy (D-N.Y.) delivered a Senate speech that broke with Johnson's Vietnam policy. Virtually all observers except Mansfield viewed the Kennedy speech as a strong repudiation of Johnson. Mansfield chose to emphasize the areas in which Kennedy and Johnson were in agreement. An advance copy of Kennedy's speech was located in Mansfield's papers with the majority leader's written comments: "many will read into this speech a divergence with present U.S. policy & its administration. *Not so*—advice but not necessarily dissent. President & Sen. agree on suspension of bombing— the ? is how & on what basis."[32] When Johnson reacted negatively to Kennedy's March 2 message, Mansfield claimed that "Lyndon embarrassed his friends in the volcanic way he reacted to this speech by Bob."[33]

On March 17, 1967 Mansfield wrote to Johnson about his hopes to visit the Soviet Union and China. One reason for the proposed trip was to inform himself of "the actions and objectives of China and the Soviet Union respecting Viet Nam, and the implications for us of the two positions as well as of any interplay between them." Mansfield wanted Johnson's reactions, but would state explicitly that the trip to each country was his own idea. Johnson replied the next day, "I frankly doubt that the Chinese will admit you at the present time." The president wished him well and indicated that he and Secretary of State Dean Rusk would like to talk with Mansfield before the trip, if it materialized.[34] Although Mansfield continued to push for a trip to China, he would not succeed in going until President Richard Nixon sent him in 1972. Nixon, Mansfield and Henry Kissinger came to appreciate the role China could play; Johnson and Rusk did not.

MANSFIELD'S U.N. INITIATIVE GETS NEW LIFE

Mansfield's "shotgun approach" to ending the U.S. role in Vietnam involved more than playing the China card. At Johnson's request, Mansfield met with him for one and one-half hours on Saturday, April 29, 1967, at which time he once again presented the president with a memorandum that he had prepared that morning. Mansfield obviously felt more comfortable with written communication. In the memo, Mansfield suggested making "a quiet and clearly conciliatory approach to China," possibly through a presidentially arranged Mansfield trip to Beijing. He also reaffirmed his support for the two-step U.N. approach that he first suggested in his North Carolina speech the previous March. Finally, Mansfield indicated his support for the idea of barricading the area from the South China Sea across the 17th parallel of Vietnam and Laos to the Thai border. The idea for a defensive barrier had been explored as early as 1961 and the army first proposed such a barrier in 1965. McNamara and Rusk were two members of the administration who were intrigued by the corridor concept. Mansfield had been talking up the idea in the Senate, and he spent considerable time in the memo refuting potential disadvantages.[35]

Mansfield argued that following the status quo of steady escalation would lead to war with China, and "the wide and deep gulf which now exists between the Soviet Union and Peking [Beijing] will be 'papered' over and they will unite against us." He then wrote an appeal based on nostalgia and his oft-stated philosophy of executive supremacy in foreign policy:

> You may recall that when you were the Majority Leader and I was your Deputy sitting next to you, that on occasion *I would lean over and tug at the back of your coat* to signal that it was either time to close the debate or to sit down. Most of the time but not all the time you would do what I was trying to suggest. Since you have been President I have been figuratively tugging at your coat, now and again, and the only purpose has been to be helpful and constructive. I am sure that every suggestion I have made has been given consideration by you and I appreciate their cautious consideration. One last word—in my personal opinion, *the hour is growing very, very late*.[36] [Emphasis added.]

Johnson ignored the appeal, taking his usual tack of expressing agreement with Mansfield. Rostow responded for Rusk to Mansfield's memo in a note to the president. On the basis of his conversation with Goldberg, Rusk told Johnson that the U.N. ambassador was ready to take Mansfield's proposals to the Security Council; that U Thant and other members of the Security Council would oppose U.N. involvement because Hanoi did not want it; and that Rusk "strongly opposed" a Mansfield visit to China because it would make the Soviet Union "upset and suspicious" and lead to the belief among our allies in "free Asia" that the United States was "about to sell them out." Rusk believed that "Mansfield should remember that he is 'an officer of the United States Government,' as a member of the legislative branch." Finally, Rusk argued that the World Court lacked jurisdiction to deal with the problem and would duck such responsibility.[37]

It is unlikely the administration ever considered the United Nations as seriously as Mansfield had hoped. Rostow called the idea a gimmick in a note to Johnson on April 30.[38] Yet the next day, apparently to appease the senator,

Johnson held a breakfast meeting on the proposal at which he and Mansfield were joined by Rusk, Goldberg, Rostow, Senator Morse, Nicholas Katzenbach, and Joseph Califano. When Johnson asked Mansfield to "lead off," the senator reviewed his earlier efforts at getting the United Nations involved with the peace process through U Thant. Mansfield proposed a U.S. resolution before the Security Council that would bring the combatants, including China, before the United Nations. Mansfield recalled:

> Ambassador Goldberg supported me strenuously; Rusk supported me with a proviso that he thought it might be a good idea to make the question an Indo-China one, thereby include Cambodia and Laos. Katzenbach seemed to think that this might be considered a "phony" approach. I immediately dissented and said it was not a phony proposal but something that should be laid before the United Nations in good faith.
>
> Rostow, in general, agreed to the suggestion. He said he thought the possibility of getting somewhere was against us. Goldberg went over the list of the members of the Security Council, because of the composition this year, it would be a little more difficult for us to have it placed on the agenda for discussion.
>
> The President . . . said that this might have merit but how would we look in the eyes of the world? Would it be a decline in our prestige? Would it make us look weaker and more foolish than we are? Would we keep on fighting while this was happening, and to that the answer was yes all around.[39]

On 3 May substantially the same group held a follow-up breakfast meeting. Mansfield wrote a memo to Johnson based on the earlier meeting that he likely delivered on the 3rd. He was concerned with Katzenbach's charge of "phoniness" and Johnson's concern of "looking foolish or weak." Mansfield argued that it was imperative that the initiative be enthusiastically endorsed by the administration. If not, "some unwitting action or ineptitude in its pursuit" would give the appearance of being "phony." If that "pitfall" could not be avoided, it was better not to pursue Mansfield's proposal. If the United Nations were utilized, rather than "looking foolish or weak," the United States would look "willing to walk the extra mile" for peace.[40] Johnson's papers labeled the May 3 conversation "off the record" but indicated that Mansfield's U.N. proposal was discussed by the participants.[41]

As the meeting of May 1 revealed, the loss of credibility for the nation and himself was the dominating issue for Johnson, so Mansfield's U.N. proposal never received serious attention in the administration. Rostow pointed to timing as the key element: once involved with the United Nations, escalation on the battlefield would be more difficult.[42] That was the very reason why Mansfield favored the approach, but it gave the administration reason to reject it.

The United Nations remained on Mansfield's front burner, but quickly moved to the back for Johnson. On May 15, Mansfield delivered a Senate speech that summarized the positions he had been pursuing for a number of months. Morse led discussion on Mansfield's speech, hinting at the May 1 U.N. initiative and thanking Mansfield for his "public discussion." He added: "this man, may I say, has been at work for a long time, trying to help bring about a peaceful solution of this problem within the framework of the existing peacekeeping procedures of international law." When George Aiken (R-Vt.) asked Mansfield if Johnson would "be willing to take this step toward the United Nations," Mansfield replied that the president "would look with favor on the proposal."[43] The *New York Times* missed Morse's subtle praise and called the criticism from the Senate on May 15 "the most prolonged that the Senate has had in several weeks. The tone was one of sad resignation that President Johnson seemed committed to a larger war."[44]

The newspaper was inaccurate in May, but by July it sensed Mansfield's mood. On July 11, 1967 Mansfield delivered a Senate speech that the *New York Times* called "the most bitter speech he has made on Vietnam policy." The speech was written earlier, but delivered to coincide with McNamara's return from Vietnam and his expected request for 100,000 additional troops. Mansfield was angry that the administration was ignoring his U.N. initiative. He asked the Senate to be skeptical about reports of progress in Vietnam, which had been heard since the time of the French. He addressed Johnson abruptly, saying, "yes, Mr. President," we can escalate, but he warned of the repercussions, including a third world war that could be "incubating" in Southeast Asia.[45]

Two days later, Mansfield wrote a statement based on his July 11 Senate speech. It was intended for Johnson, but it may not have been delivered. Mansfield mentioned in his memo that Johnson had told him more than one month before that they were running out of bombing targets in North Vietnam. That left Johnson and McNamara with difficult choices: escalation in the bombing of new targets, deescalation, or a cessation or suspension of the bombing in the North. Mansfield feared the rumors and leaks from the "usual channels" that suggested an increase of 100,000 to 200,000 more troops and "more effective" use of air power, which Mansfield took to mean bombing Hanoi, Haiphong, and airfields closer to China. Mansfield feared that those new targets would increase the probability of confrontation with China.

Mansfield repackaged three proposals that he "thought might be helpful in curbing the ever-growing involvement, without adverse consequences to our present position." First, he argued for the defense perimeter he had pursued in April. Mansfield thought that such a barrier would compensate for the failure of the bombing in the North to cut the flow of supplies to the South, as well as its failure to force Hanoi to the bargaining table. Second, Mansfield advocated the use of the "Cooper formula." Senator John Sherman Cooper (R-Ky.) had proposed cessation of the bombing of the North and a concentration of bombing along the infiltration routes of the Ho Chi Minh Trail and the 17th parallel.

Finally, Mansfield recommended that Johnson pursue his U.N. initiative. A vexed Mansfield asserted: "I had thought this possibility had been thoroughly examined some weeks ago and was found to have merit."[46]

There is no extant communication from Johnson about the July 13 memo. Indeed, it is not clear that he received it. Yet Johnson was concerned with Mansfield's speeches about his U.N. initiative, asking White House aide Mike Manatos to raise the issue with Mansfield. Manatos reported "a noticeable raising of eye brows" when he broached the subject: "for a moment I thought the Senator might go through the ceiling." Mansfield was puzzled, thinking Johnson had approved of the U.N. approach based on the April 29 and May 1 meetings with him.[47]

The Johnson administration's positive reaction to Mansfield's U.N. initiative in spring 1967 seems an attempt to placate him. By then, Johnson had terminated communication with all Senate doves except Mansfield.[48] Because of the combination of Mansfield's party position and their long relationship, the president apparently felt the need to deal with Mansfield. In August, James Rowe wrote to Johnson, suggesting that he attend a Montana Democratic dinner in honor of Mansfield: "I feel Mike would be touched and pleased—and there might be speculation if you do not appear." Rowe suggested that Mansfield needed "cultivation" and the hand holding of the president. Years later when asked if he had tried to "neutralize" Mansfield, Rowe responded: "I don't think so. I don't know."[49] Yet "neutralize" seems an apt description of Johnson's strategy. He continued to toy with Mansfield's U.N. initiative, and in so doing, toyed with Mansfield. Goldberg ultimately concluded, "I was being used about Vietnam, there can be no doubt."[50] Mansfield, too, was being used. By keeping him busy pursuing his U.N. initiative, LBJ constrained Mansfield's criticism of administration policy.

In August, at Johnson suggestion, Mansfield recruited Senator Cooper to help get the initiative rolling. As the former ambassador to India, Cooper sought India's assistance in getting the Mansfield initiative before the Security Council. Cooper reported to Mansfield on his meeting with Indian Ambassador Nehru on August 28:

> there is no doubt that the Government of India would vote to place the matter of Vietnam on the agenda of the Security Council. As to the matter of India joining with the United States in a resolution, he said that he did not believe India would be willing to do so unless it was assured that the United States would be willing to accept the recommendation of the Security Council.
>
> I told him . . . I believed . . . it would accept the UN's decision. He suggested that Russia might not veto a recommendation by the Security Council if it were convinced that the United States was submitting the item without reservation.[51]

Despite this initial step, Nehru had a back problem that prevented his meeting with Mansfield.[52]

In mid September 1967, when Mansfield visited Japan to address the Japanese-American Assembly in Shimoda he used the occasion to push a different peace proposal. The *New York Times* summarized the Shimoda speech, mentioning that Mansfield conferred with Johnson on the speech before departing. The article claimed that Rusk deflected Mansfield's major proposal—that Japan, the United States, and possibly the Soviet Union consider the security needs of the western Pacific. Japan was skeptical of such discussions. Mansfield's report talked of the importance of the establishment of normal relations with China: "an absence of trade relations distorts the general relationship between countries and constitutes a barrier to communications and to knowledge"; talking to China was the way to "prevent future Vietnams" in Asia.[53]

MANSFIELD'S U.N. RESOLUTION PASSES

In late September, President Johnson made a peace proposal in a speech delivered in San Antonio. The San Antonio formula offered a bombing halt without the precondition that Hanoi halt its infiltration into the South. Ho rejected the proposal. With the American elections coming up, there was no incentive for North Vietnam to negotiate. Larry Berman claims: "the President was almost desperately looking for a way out that would not involve humiliation for the allies and his administration."[54] Mansfield continued to try to help Johnson find such an out.

At an October 23 meeting with the Democratic leadership, Johnson had "a very confidential discussion on Vietnam" with McNamara, Rusk, CIA Director Richard Helms, and Republican congressional leaders. This meeting was called two days after 50,000 antiwar protesters marched in Washington. Johnson described Hanoi's position as rigid, gave a history of administration efforts to get to the bargaining table, and explained why all of his principal advisors believed that a bombing halt would not lead to "productive negotiations." Johnson was convinced that Hanoi did not want peace and added, "I recognize that there will continue to be people who will urge—despite the evidence—that a change in our bombing policy could lead us toward peace. But I am not prepared to act simply on hope."

Senators Dirksen, Bourke Hickenlooper (R-Iowa), and Representative William Bates (R-Mass.) expressed support for Johnson's policy. Bates asked McNamara what the effect of the bombing had been, since "there has been great misunderstanding about what the Secretary has said on the matter." McNamara responded: "we cannot win the war with bombing the north. We need action in South Vietnam supplemented by bombing in the north with limited objectives. . . . The great danger is to lead our people to think we can win the war overnight with bombing. We cannot." Johnson's retort to his secretary of defense was, "we do have differences of opinion."

A number of congressional leaders jumped on the Johnson bandwagon. As had been his pattern, Mansfield spoke near the close of the meeting, becoming the only one in attendance to agree with McNamara and not the president:

> We could bomb North Vietnam into the stone age if we wanted to. I do not believe we have reached the objective which was stopping the flow of men and material into the South. We have lost many planes and we are flying within 24 seconds of China. We should think of contact between the NLF and Saigon to try to cut them out from North Vietnam.[55]

McNamara had changed 180 degrees. A staunch hawk during the Kennedy administration, he may have had more responsibility than any person for U.S. Vietnam policy, but gradually he changed his mind about the war. The defense secretary became a voice of moderation within the administration.[56]

With McNamara as a new-found ally in the administration, Mansfield pressed hard for his U.N. resolution in October, sending a five-page letter to all senators, Goldberg, and Rusk. The letter explained the history of the resolution and provided a rationale for its adoption. At least twenty-two senators responded to Mansfield's letter. Walter Mondale (D-Minn.) called Mansfield's letter magnificent and "as valuable as any document I have read concerning the Vietnam war." Frank Moss (D-Utah) wrote that the war must be resolved or the Democrats would face disaster. Joseph Clark added a postscript that pointed out a potential problem to Mansfield's approach: "I don't see how you get N. Vietnam and the Chi coms [Chinese Communists] to pay any attention to the U.N." Peter Dominick (R-Colo.) put it more strongly: "the North Vietnamese have rejected any U.N. action in this conflict and that the South Vietnamese would be amenable if we insisted, but not enthusiastic. Once again, we seem faced with the age old problem of needing two parties for peaceful solutions and only having one in hand."[57]

Goldberg battled Rusk to gain Johnson's support for Mansfield's resolution.[58] On October 30 Goldberg called Mansfield:

> GOLDBERG: I have prepared testimony in conjunction with my appearance before the [Foreign Relations] Committee endorsing your proposal. The reaction will be against us in the U.N. but I see no choice. I cannot predict the outcome and only hope that it will be helpful. The President is as nervous as a kitten.
> MANSFIELD: I [do not[59]] know why the President is as nervous as a kitten. In effect, this is his idea. I think it is Rusk.[60]

Johnson was "nervous as a kitten" because any involvement by the United Nations or the Foreign Relations Committee threatened administration control of the situation. Concerned as well about Goldberg's appearance before the committee, the president called Mansfield on November 1 to discuss the matter. Mansfield recalled:

> I emphasized the *initiation* of procedures . . . not the *resolution* because I felt that the U.N. would dodge its responsibility in that respect. My reaction is that he seemed to be a little excited. He talked loudly and seemed to be disturbed about what the Senate was attempting to do and the consequences which might well be tributed [sic] to him should the . . . Resolution fail. I did not see fit to recall to him that it was he who started this discussion about going to the U.N.[61]

On the same day as Johnson's phone conversation with Mansfield, the president held a news conference in which he attributed U.S. involvement in Asia to the SEATO Treaty, saying that it was "signed by Senator Mansfield." The fact that Mansfield was a signatory in 1954 and opposed the war in the late 1960s seemed contradictory to Rusk and gnawed at Johnson. In a later interview, Johnson recalled that "SEATO had been approved 83-1. I didn't sign it, Dirksen didn't sign it, John Kennedy didn't sign it. But Mansfield signed it like John Hancock."[62] The president could not accept Mansfield's change of mind. He expected the unqualified support of his majority leader.

At the time of the Foreign Relations Committee hearings in late October and early November, fifty-four senators were sponsoring Mansfield's resolution. He had little to say at the hearings except to emphasize that his resolution was entirely advisory, and that he did not want to place a straitjacket on the president. The star witness was Goldberg, who said on two occasions: "Senator Mansfield's resolution at this time will support the efforts I have been making at the United Nations at the direction of the President to enlist the Security Council in the search for peace in Vietnam." On November 30, the resolution passed 82-0. Yet because Johnson was unwilling to change the American position, there was little chance that the Security Council would consider the issue.[63]

Mansfield later complained that "circumstances have apparently not permitted the taking of the initiative which was urged by that resolution."[64] Even after this presidential rebuff, though, Mansfield stuck with his strategy of quiet criticism, and he continued to toss out ideas to get to the bargaining table.

In a November 20 Senate speech, Mansfield proposed a new idea on how to settle the war. Saying that the United States had exhausted possible approaches to ending the conflict, he argued: "negotiation between Saigon and the Vietcong might prove fruitful. This is one possibility which has not been recognized, except intermittently and haphazardly." John Finney interpreted this speech as

Mansfield's splitting still further with Johnson and emphasized his challenge of administration optimism.[65]

MANSFIELD AND THE FOREIGN RELATIONS COMMITTEE

Johnson and his supporters viewed Fulbright and the Foreign Relations Committee as enemies. Dean Acheson, secretary of state under President Harry Truman and an unofficial advisor to Johnson, told the president: "the cross you have to bear is a lousy Senate Foreign Relations Committee. You have a dilettante fool at the head of the committee."[66] Opposition to the war began there and eventually spread to the rest of the Senate. Once Fulbright concluded that he could not persuade Johnson to change the course in Vietnam, he used his committee as a means to educate the public, starting in early 1966 with hearings on Vietnam. Fulbright became a difficult adversary for Johnson, and later for Nixon.[67]

As party leader and member of the committee, Mansfield seemed to view his role as a conciliator between Johnson and Democratic Senate doves. Beginning in late November 1967, Johnson battled the committee over a request for Rusk to testify in open session. Rusk's relationship with the committee had been good until the Dominican Republic invasion in April 1965. Following that, according to a member of the committee staff, Rusk's relationship "followed a constant downward trend, due almost entirely to Vietnam." Rusk was vague and evasive with both the committee and the press on the subject, never disclosing options under consideration, admitting only what was absolutely necessary. One Rusk biographer concluded that Rusk's "half-truths and incomplete answers were frequently misleading," which contributed to the administration credibility gap.[68]

Mansfield protected the president by working with Aiken, Hickenlooper, and Frank Lausche (D-Ohio) to prevent a confrontation with the committee. On November 21, Mansfield sent a memo to Johnson urging that Rusk accept an invitation to appear in open session. By this time, war protesters goaded Rusk, shouting him down wherever he spoke. Mansfield said he found the treatment that Rusk had received deplorable. He promised that Rusk would not receive "personal harassment," nor would he be subject to a "circus atmosphere" in a Senate appearance. Questions would not be tougher than those asked by the press, which Rusk always handled with "deftness." Besides, Mansfield insisted, he could always refuse to answer on the grounds of security or, "better yet, offering to answer later in executive session." Mansfield regretted the "anomalous" relationship between Rusk and the committee, especially among Democrats. He ended the memo with an appeal:

It would not be helpful if the Secretary refuses to appear, if he delays unduly in accepting the invitation, or if he seeks to establish conditions in advance for his appearance. You know . . . how Senators tend to react in such circumstances. There is nothing to be lost and everything to be gained from Rusk's acceptance.[69]

Yet when Johnson aide Harry McPherson attempted to gain Mansfield's support on a procedural matter to prevent Rusk's appearance, Mansfield reluctantly agreed: "all right, I'll try to support him. I think he is wrong, but I'll try to support him. But you ought to be aware that this could develop into a Constitutional crisis."[70]

Some believed that Mansfield leaked information to the president. William Berman suggested that Mansfield and Aiken kept Johnson informed as to what was happening on the committee:

> Although [Mansfield] was a staunch dove on the inside, he could never compromise his leadership position in the Senate or higher loyalty to Johnson, which may be why Fulbright, years later, referred to him as "Johnson's alter ego." According to Marcy, Mansfield was no favorite of the committee, as he often received information from the White House which was not shared with his colleagues. Frank Church confirms that there was "tension" between Fulbright and Mansfield, despite their similar positions on the war.[71]

The degree of that tension is difficult to measure. Marcy did not shed any light on it in his oral history. Mansfield flatly denied keeping Johnson informed of committee activities. Valeo was also unaware of the tension Berman claimed. Mansfield's aide recalled:

> I never thought there was any tension between Fulbright and Mansfield. Certainly it wasn't true on Vietnam. As for Mansfield giving information to Johnson out of the committee, Mansfield rarely attended the sessions of the committee, so he would have been a poor source of information. If you knew Mansfield at all, he would be the last man to be a channel to Johnson or anyone else for that matter. He doesn't talk much.[72]

Andrew Glass corroborates Valeo's position, suggesting that Mansfield was "an extremely poor 'leak' on Senate matters that have not been publicly announced."[73]

Mansfield's personality was such that he likely tried to mediate between Fulbright and Johnson, as he did with Rusk's appearance. He was uncomfortable with conflict and was disturbed by the hostility between the administration and the committee. Mansfield viewed his role as conciliator, not as spy. Yet some members of the committee apparently believed that he kept Johnson informed of their activities. His chosen role of conciliator and private critic became a frustrating one for Johnson, too. McPherson wrote that as Mansfield's "active support was needed, silence was almost as irritating to the White House as an exposed confrontation; it was not enough for a Democratic leader to look the other way as the line was being drawn in the dirt."[74]

In the case of Rusk's appearance, Mansfield continued to try to mediate the dispute. On February 7, 1968, Manatos reported to Johnson that "Senator Mansfield filled me in on what happened in the Foreign Relations Committee today." Mansfield, Aiken, Hickenlooper, and John Sparkman (D-Ala.) opposed trying to force Rusk's appearance. An accommodation was reached and Rusk finally testified on March 11-12, 1968.[75]

MANSFIELD REMAINS LOYAL TO THE END

Mansfield tried to remain a team player. In a memo to Johnson in early 1968 about a Mansfield foreign policy speech, Manatos concluded: "he made a conscious effort to associate himself with Administration policy rather than articulate the differences he has with it."[76]

The Tet offensive, which started on January 31, destroyed the rural pacification program that was considered vital to the long-term successful outcome of the war. It may have been a military victory for U.S./South Vietnamese forces, but it was a great psychological victory for the Vietcong. Mansfield had little to say about Tet in public or private, but labeled Tet "neither a defeat nor a death rattle for our opponents. It was, if anything, a confirmation of a stalemate."[77]

In the wake of Tet and the North Korean capture of the American ship *Pueblo*, Johnson held a Democratic leadership breakfast on February 6 at which the mood was tense. The president set the tone when he challenged, "if a man has nothing to offer as an alternative, I advise that he say nothing. Anybody can kick a barn down. It takes a good carpenter to build one." Nonetheless, Senator Robert Byrd (D-W.Va.) and others asked Johnson some tough questions concerning Tet. In his responses, Johnson showed defensiveness about the criticism emanating from Mansfield's speeches:

> I am of the opinion that criticism is not worth much. I look at all these speeches, . . . I look at all the people who are going around the country saying our policy is wrong. Where do they get us? Nowhere. . . . I wish Mike would make a speech on Ho Chi Minh. Nothing is as dirty as to violate a truce during the holidays. But nobody says anything bad about Ho. They call me a murderer. But Ho has a great image. . . . Fulbright, Young and Gruening haven't helped one bit.

The president indicated why he had not been influenced by such congressional critics as Fulbright and even Mansfield: "I believe that our military and diplomatic men in the field know more than many of our Congressmen and Senators back here." Mansfield was silent during the meeting.[78]

Despite his restraint in this session, Mansfield was motivated to speak on the floor of the Senate when rumors indicated a planned troop increase of up to 100,000 men. Mansfield understood the hopelessness of the situation. The United States had 510,000 troops in South Vietnam while North Vietnam had only committed 60,000 of General Vo Nguyen Giap's 474,000 troops to the South—only one-eighth of the North's total. Any U.S. troop escalation could easily be matched. When Mansfield indicated that the president had not talked with him about the increase, Fulbright concluded that if Johnson had not discussed it with Mansfield, he had not discussed it with any member of the Senate. Fulbright was disturbed that Johnson might commit that many additional troops without consultation with the Foreign Relations Committee. Mansfield attempted to defend Johnson, yet argued against any troop increase since previous ones had only increased the carnage. Mansfield explained his position, which seemed a contradiction to Fulbright and others: "it is my intention to uphold the hand of the President as much as I can, and at the same time stick to my own convictions."[79] In Mansfield's mind, this was not a contradiction at all.

Eugene McCarthy (D-Minn.), a fellow war critic, solicited Mansfield's support for the Democratic presidential nomination. Mansfield's loyalty and party position, however, kept him in LBJ's camp.[80]

LBJ SEEKS PEACE

On March 8, 1968, Clark Clifford, McNamara's replacement as secretary of defense, and General Earle Wheeler met with Senate leaders to discuss a military reserve call-up leading to increased troop strength in Vietnam. They met with Stennis, Henry Jackson (D-Wash.), Stuart Symington (D-Mo.) and Richard Russell (D-Ga.), and then met separately with Mansfield. None supported the call-up. Mansfield told Clifford and Wheeler in his "gentle manner" that Congress "had reached the end of the line" on troop levels. Clifford reported: "Johnson realized the implications of the congressional consultations immediately, and, for the first time, showed serious doubt about sending more troops to Vietnam."[81]

Later that month, Johnson met with his senior foreign policy staff, a remarkable group of men dubbed the "Wise Men" because of their vast experience in diplomacy and the military. The group was composed of Acheson, Goldberg, George Ball, McGeorge Bundy, Douglas Dillon, Cyrus Vance, Arthur Dean, John McCloy, Robert Murphy, Henry Cabot Lodge, Abe Fortas, General Omar Bradley, General Matthew Ridgway, and General Maxwell Taylor. When the

Wise Men had last met on November 1, 1967, they were virtually unanimous that the United States must stay in Vietnam. Ball reportedly said that he no longer favored withdrawal.

These men returned for briefings on March 25 and learned of the devastation of Tet. They were told that pacification would take at least five to ten years. Johnson counted on this group of advisors, but the group had changed its mind in less than five months. While the Wise Men were not unanimous in their opinion, after Johnson's meeting with them on March 26, disengagement seemed the only option.[82]

The next day, Mansfield met with the president, discussing Vietnam and the address Johnson was to deliver on March 31. The president's account of that meeting differed substantially from Mansfield's. Johnson recalled: "In the hours we were together, we discussed many things, including my planned statement. I read to him portions of my address and told him I intended to end all bombing north of the 20th parallel."[83]

While the president's recollection focused on the bombing halt, Mansfield remembered Johnson's plan to commit more U.S. troops: "I went down to the White House . . . very reluctantly, after mutual friends repeatedly urged me to go see the President and talk to him about Vietnam. I didn't think it would do any good." Mansfield continued:

> I told him that I thought it would be a mistake to make the speech because it offered no hope to the people and it only indicated a further involvement. He did mention the possibility of ending the bombing north of the 20th parallel. He asked my opinion about sending 40,000 more troops. I said, "no, we've got to get out, should not have been there in the first place." I urged him as strongly as I knew how to bring this tragic war to an end because it was an area which was not and never had been vital to our security. I spent three and a half hours there that night with Johnson and as I finally got to the door, he said, "Mike, I wish my leader would support me." Well, I was *not* his leader, I was the Senate's leader. "But," he said, "I want you to know I appreciate your honesty in telling me how you feel about it."
>
> Three days later, I heard him deliver that Sunday night TV speech—which he had been working on that night—and I heard him add that he would not run for reelection. I was surprised.[84]

In Johnson's speech on March 31, he announced a troop increase of only 13,500, which kept troop levels below the authorized level of 525,000. This increase was considerably below the 40,000 he discussed with Mansfield on March 27, and the lower number must have pleased the senator. Johnson also called for reconvening the Geneva conferences and involving the Security Council in the war, frequent Mansfield themes.

There is no evidence to suggest Mansfield's meeting with Johnson directly influenced his speech. The last major revision of the speech was made on the evening of March 28, at which time the peace proposals were moved to the beginning. Rostow, Rusk, Clifford, McPherson, and William Bundy were involved in that last revision. Clifford and McPherson successfully worked to change the original strident draft to a conciliatory final one. McPherson said that he felt like "an engineer assembling an erector set" in crafting the speech through five or six drafts. The president did not make up his mind on the bombing halt until after the March 28 meeting. That decision was based on the meeting with the Wise Men and the public's dissatisfaction with the war.[85]

Johnson's speech was a turning point in the war. Clifford argued: "it marked the end of the era of escalation, and the first step, however ambiguous, toward de-escalation and disengagement."[86] Typically, Mansfield praised Johnson in public for his policy change, engaging Fulbright in debate on April 2 over the meaning of the president's announcement. Fulbright derided the president's statement as limited and "no inducement to the North" to negotiate. Mansfield claimed the change in policy was substantial, even though he acknowledged that he preferred a more complete bombing halt. In words quite strident for Senate debate, Fulbright chided Mansfield and Russell:

> It is perfectly evident from those who participated prior to the speech—the leading Members of the Senate who really control the Senate and who have spoken here today—that there was no such puropse. There was no such purpose in asking for a conference with Hanoi because, obviously, what has been said here is no inducement to have a conference based upon Geneva.

Morse was the only senator to side with Fulbright in the debate, but Gordon Allott (R-Colo.) joined Fulbright in expressing frustration that only a few senators had access to the White House: "unfortunately, most Senators are not privy to these White House councils. We are not privy to the inside situation of the war." Typically, Mansfield denied the open conflict with Fulbright, referring to the cynicism of those who attacked the motives of the president yet exempting all senators, "because we are all aware of the significance of the speech made by the President."[87] Fulbright had clearly attacked that very significance.

Mansfield expressed hope in Johnson's peace initiative and asked for the support of all Americans.[88] His greatest fear was that Johnson would become frustrated and extend the war. In May, he cautioned the president: "we have tried to end this war by military means for about three years, at great cost and without success, and the negotiations have been at it for not much more than three sessions."[89]

By the end of the summer, Mansfield was disappointed with the lack of progress in Paris, and he issued a blunt press release for his colleagues: "Others may indulge in pietisms and pomposities on Viet Nam. . . . As Democrats we cannot. Ours is the responsibility for getting in. Ours should be the responsibility for getting out."[90]

After the election, Mansfield predicted that Johnson had reversed "this ever-deepening enmeshment." He also pledged Democratic support for President-elect Richard Nixon.[91]

CONCLUSION TO THE JOHNSON YEARS

Before the 1954 fall of Dien Bien Phu, Secretary of State John Foster Dulles prophetically told French General Paul Ely: "if the United States sent its flag and its own military establishment—land, sea or air—into the Indochina war, then the prestige of the United States would be engaged to a point where we would want to have a success."[92] Initially, Eisenhower had committed the United States to Diem. Kennedy increased the original commitment to South Vietnam, and Johnson took the ultimate plunge in July 1965. The credibility of the nation, as well as that of the sitting president, were considered to be the stakes. That would not change with the coming of the Nixon administration.

Mansfield tried to end the escalation throughout the Kennedy and Johnson administrations. His political philosophy mandated that he be a quiet critic, attempting to persuade Johnson in private while supporting him in public whenever possible. Mansfield did so because he believed the war must be ended by the president. His position as majority leader made Mansfield's stance a difficult one. Further, Mansfield's personal style found face-to-face interpersonal conflict repugnant. Fulbright came to regret that he was not more effective in opposing the war. Mansfield has concluded that his strategy of presenting his views privately to Johnson while trying to be supportive in public, "evidently did not help."[93]

Many saw Johnson as a dove who was reluctantly persuaded to escalate through the weight of opinion of the advisors he inherited from Kennedy. That premise seems valid, but Mansfield provided Johnson with another option, an option that the president tragically chose to ignore. Once the majority leader lost the battle on committing ground troops, he worked diligently to help LBJ find some way to the bargaining table.

As majority leader and chairman of the Foreign Relations Committee, Mansfield and Fulbright were among the most powerful members of government. Following different rhetorical strategies, both failed to directly influence policy in Vietnam. An argument can be made that beginning in 1966 anti-war senators needed the leadership of a Mansfield or Fulbright, leadership that was not forthcoming. Neither man felt comfortable in that role, believing that each senator must decide individually.[94]

Like most Americans, Mansfield and Fulbright had been cold warriors in the 1950s, but both moderated their cold war vision when events showed it to be flawed. Both Rusk and McNamara, Johnson's principal advisors, misjudged Chinese intentions and did not change their 1950s view of the world.[95] In keeping Kennedy's advisors, the men who started the United States on the path to escalation, Johnson made it unlikely that he could change course.

Although there is no direct evidence linking the dissent of either Mansfield or Fulbright to Johnson's eventual decision to cease American escalation and seek peace, it seems likely that the pressure both men kept on Johnson contributed to his decision to change direction in March of 1968. In comparing the rhetorical strategies of Mansfield and Fulbright, an important difference is that, unlike Fulbright, Mansfield continued to be heard at the White House. After a cooling in the Johnson/Mansfield relationship in early 1966, they resumed their frequent contacts. One can never know the complexities that led to Johnson's decision to give up the presidency and to concentrate on ending the war. Mansfield's "drawerful" of memos and personal conversations with Johnson likely exerted some constraints on the president's policies and practices.

When asked if Mansfield could have been more effective had he been more vocal in his public dissent, former Senator William Proxmire (D-Wis.) responded, "no way. Any such outspoken dissent from Mansfield if anything could have made Johnson harder to handle, not easier. Johnson's position on the Vietnam War could not be influenced by Mansfield or any other member of the Senate or the Congress or the administration." Johnson aide George Reedy answered the same question: "critics reinforced Johnson, locked Johnson into a position. Public criticism wouldn't have worked with Johnson." Valeo concurred: "he would not have been more effective [with public criticism]. . . . Mansfield believed the involvement could be brought to an end, as a practical matter, only through the presidency and he felt his influence could best be registered there."[96]

Johnson's decision to seek an end to U.S. involvement locked Richard Nixon into deescalation. Nixon himself wrote that Tet and the November 1968 bombing halt: "foreclosed the option of committing ourselves even deeper. Whatever the merits of our cause and whatever our chances of winning the war, it was no longer a question of whether the next President would withdraw our troops but of how they would leave and what they would leave behind."[97]

Events during the Nixon administration would challenge Mansfield's view of executive supremacy in foreign affairs. In May 1970, Mansfield decided that he could wait no longer for executive action, and that the war must be ended by the Senate.

Part IV

1969-1975

Cambodia and the End of Mansfield's "Quiet" Criticism

CHAPTER 12

NIXON, CAMBODIA, AND THE
SECOND INDOCHINA WAR

M ansfield faced unfamiliar challenges in 1969-1970. The Montanan had
served for eight years as majority leader, but always with a Democratic
president. With the election of Richard Nixon, Mansfield became an "out" for
the first time since his election to the leadership. Furthermore, Mansfield lacked
the personal clout that he enjoyed based on friendships with presidents John
Kennedy and Lyndon Johnson. The positive side of having a Republican in the
White House was Mansfield's freedom to criticize without constraint by his
elected party position.

Another challenge involved Mansfield's old friend, Prince Norodom
Sihanouk. Since Mansfield's 1953 visit to Indochina, Cambodia had been the one
former French colony given a reasonable chance for success in remaining non-
communist. After almost two decades of relative stability, Cambodia was
dragged into the Indochina war.

NIXON'S INDOCHINA BACKGROUND AND RELATIONSHIP
WITH MANSFIELD

Vice President Nixon visited Indochina in 1953, shortly before Mansfield's first
trip. Nixon agreed with Mansfield after their 1953 visits that the Vietnamese
needed a nationalist leader, yet he feared that if the French withdrew, "Vietnam—
and possibly Laos and Cambodia as well—would fall like husks before the fury of
the communist hurricane." The vice president was not impressed with King
Sihanouk, who he found to be an intelligent man, but "vain and flighty."[1]

Stephen Ambrose suggested that Nixon's 1953 Far East trip increased his
interest in foreign policy. Stopping the advance of communism and preserving
a non-communist Indochina became his goal for more than two decades.
Nixon became a hawk within the Eisenhower administration and favored U.S.
intervention to save the French at Dien Bien Phu, even if it meant the use of
several atomic bombs and the introduction of U.S. ground forces.[2] He believed

that Vietnam would quickly turn communist without U.S. intervention because "the Vietnamese lack the ability to conduct a war by themselves or govern themselves," ironic positions given his later policy of "Vietnamization."[3] In 1954 Nixon supported the Southeast Asia Treaty Organization (SEATO), but wanted it toughened to deal with subversion as well as overt aggression. Like Mansfield, Nixon opposed the agreements made at Geneva to end the first Indochina war.[4]

In 1956 Nixon traveled to South Vietnam for the second anniversary of Ngo Dinh Diem's assumption of the presidency. By that time, Nixon was a strong supporter of Diem, and, like Mansfield, was making himself an expert on Asia.[5] By October 1963, private citizen Nixon criticized the Kennedy administration for withdrawing its support from Diem, arguing as Mansfield might have: "I would say that in Vietnam today the choice is not between Diem and somebody better, it is between Diem and somebody infinitely worse." After Diem's assassination, Nixon wrote Eisenhower: "I think our complicity in Diem's murder was a national disgrace." Nixon never attacked Kennedy for increasing the U.S. commitment to South Vietnam, but did criticize him for limiting the use of U.S. force to aid the country.[6]

During President Johnson's 1964 presidential race with Barry Goldwater, Nixon took a more hawkish position than did Goldwater, favoring U.S. escalation and criticizing Johnson's cautious approach. Nixon called the neutralization course favored by Mansfield "another name for appeasement, surrender on the installment plan," and said that Vietnam was the place "to stop the Communist advance." The former vice president supported Johnson on the Gulf of Tonkin Resolution. Nixon also continued to believe in the domino theory, writing in the *Reader's Digest* in August of 1964: "on the fate of Vietnam, depends the fate of Asia. For South Vietnam is the dam in the river."[7]

After Johnson's reelection, while Mansfield was urging caution in Vietnam, Nixon pushed Johnson to escalate, suggesting that Republicans would never criticize the president for increasing the stakes in the war. While Mansfield opposed the February 1965 bombings of North Vietnam, Nixon criticized the administration's response as inadequate. Nixon continued to favor increased bombing and more U.S. troops, and claimed that Johnson's talk about negotiation would prolong the war. This pressure from Nixon and from the Republican right contributed to Johnson's decisions to pursue the war. Ambrose concludes that the Vietnam policies Johnson had followed were really the exact policies Nixon had advocated.[8]

Like most Americans, Nixon was surprised by the success of the communist Tet offensive in 1968, which led him to pledge to end the war if elected. His plan, which became known as "Vietnamization," was designed to gradually turn the fighting over to the South Vietnamese and had actually commenced at the end of the Johnson administration.

Mansfield and Nixon had little contact before 1969. Nixon grouped Mansfield with the "real" and not the "radical" Democrats. Perhaps that assessment is the reason that despite the request of Mansfield's opponent in the 1958 Senate race, the vice president told Mansfield that he would not come to Montana to campaign against him. Even so, in 1967 Nixon condescendingly called Mansfield "misinformed but well intentioned" about the war in Vietnam.[9]

The Johnson administration's briefing with President-elect Nixon revealed no important differences on Vietnam. Nixon accepted Clark Clifford's plan to pressure South Vietnamese President Nguyen Van Thieu to come to Paris and join the negotiations and to begin the withdrawal of U.S. troops.

Upon his arrival at the White House, Nixon had the perfect opportunity to end the war quickly, with little political risk to himself or to the Republican Party. The new president could have admitted that Vietnam had been a mistake, since he had not been directly involved in those decisions. Nixon let the opportunity slip by, and once his honeymoon period had ended, the war became his responsibility.

Initially, Nixon gave the distinct impression that he would quickly end the war. In his inaugural address, the new president said: "the greatest honor history can bestow is the title of peacemaker. This is our summons to greatness." Mansfield was heartened by the president-elect's conciliatory approach, which led him to say that he anticipated a stronger Senate role in foreign affairs during the new administration. Nixon did plan to end the war. His aide, H. R. Haldeman, reported Nixon saying: "I'm not going to end up like LBJ, holed up in the White House afraid to show my face on the street. I'm going to end that war. Fast."[10]

The new president knew that Mansfield shared his fascination with Asia—particularly with China. Nixon was privately exploring possible rapprochement with China. In early February 1969, in their first of many breakfast meetings, Nixon confided to Mansfield that he was going to attempt to "open the door" to mainland China, claiming: "you can't ignore China, it's too big. It's there. You have to live with it." Marvin and Bernard Kalb reported him promising: "when the door is open, Mike, I want you to be the first high level American to visit China. I'd like to go myself, but that doesn't seem quite feasible for the moment." Mansfield was flattered.[11]

In June 1969, Nixon instructed Henry Kissinger, his National Security Advisor, to tell Mansfield to pursue his plan to seek a visa to visit China. Kissinger encouraged Mansfield to go public with his efforts. The original trip that Mansfield had tried to arrange in 1967, which had been thwarted by Secretary of State Dean Rusk, was now a possibility during a Republican administration. Mansfield immediately set out to make this trip a reality. He wrote a letter to Sihanouk, using him as an intermediary in order to deliver a second letter to Chinese Premier Zhou Enlai. Mansfield made sure that "the President knows every significant move I make in regard to this trip."[12]

Nixon was anxious to establish a good working relationship with Democrats in the Senate, so he asked John Sherman Cooper (R-Ky.) if there was a Democrat he could trust to help him. While he strongly recommended Mansfield, Cooper told Nixon that if he "wanted to establish a bonafide relationship with Mansfield, he would have to see him *alone* and frequently, and of course he would have to handle the relationship with complete confidentiality." Rowland Evans and Robert Novak reported that the relationship never became as close as the relationships between Eisenhower and Majority Leader Lyndon Johnson (D-Texas) and Speaker of the House Sam Rayburn (D-Texas), or the relationship between Johnson and Minority Leader Everett Dirksen (R-Ill.). Evans and Novak called the meetings between Nixon and Mansfield "sterile as a source of Nixon power or even influence in the Senate."[13]

By spring, though, Nixon had established frequent breakfast meetings with the majority leader. Although Mansfield rarely recorded his thoughts about these meetings,[14] he did describe the breakfasts later:

> I met with President Nixon on at least a once-monthly basis . . . apart from the regular leadership meetings. These breakfast meetings began with Nixon's first month in office. They were held at his request and they were . . . just between the two of us, except for one.
>
> It was at those meetings that we began to discuss foreign policy matters and we initially started out considering ways and means of achieving a better status with the PRC [People's Republic of China], which eventually resulted in Kissinger's secret trip to Beijing, followed by Nixon's trip in February, 1972.[15]

In addition to China, the subject of Vietnam arose; as Mansfield wrote a constituent: "I am doing my best to counsel the President, when I get the opportunity, to do everything in his power to bring this war to a conclusion."[16] After he left office, Nixon wrote to Mansfield: "our breakfasts were particularly helpful to me—because you were one of those rare men in public life who never breaks a confidence."[17]

Mansfield characterized his relationship with President Nixon as good and said that in addition to the breakfast meetings, they talked on the phone. He claimed that Nixon understood his position on Vietnam. Francis Valeo said that Mansfield "spoke with him often; Nixon liked to talk with him on Asia generally." Valeo described the relationship as "on the whole good, but very cautious on the part of Mansfield. Very, very cautious, and I would assume on the part of Nixon as well." Mansfield's aide believed that the senator was

> concerned about Nixon's stability and he did not want to upset him in any way, especially after the Watergate thing. Nixon was not an easy person for anybody to get to know let alone to get friendly with. They were not friends in the kind of way

you could be with somebody like Jerry Ford. . . . He was accommodating, whenever Mansfield wanted anything he would do what he could to respond to it.[18]

MANSFIELD TRIES TO SUPPORT NIXON'S VIETNAM POLICY

Cognizant of Nixon's opportunity to conclude the American involvement in the war quickly, Mansfield gave the president some time before beginning to speak out against his Indochinese policies. In January, Mansfield responded to a soldier: "I am in accord with President Nixon's views" on bringing the war to an end.[19] The Foreign Relations Committee also was willing to support the new president during his honeymoon period. When George McGovern (D-S.D.) suggested in March that Nixon lacked moral courage for failing to reverse Johnson's policy, he was admonished by Mansfield and Edward Kennedy (D-Mass.), who wanted to give Nixon more time to end the conflict.[20]

By spring, however, Mansfield was getting impatient. Stanley Karnow concluded that the majority leader had "muted his misgivings during the Johnson era, [but] was now speaking out." Mansfield was especially sensitive to the White House dismissing the Vietnam debate in the Senate as "irrelevant or less." When asked if he found it easier to be the majority leader under a Republican president, Mansfield replied, "I certainly do." Yet Mansfield's rhetoric remained typically cautious.[21]

On May 14, Nixon spoke to the nation, proposing a simultaneous withdrawal of U.S. and North Vietnamese forces. Mansfield praised the new position. Nixon had always kept his opponents off balance and followed the May 14 speech with one in Colorado Springs that became known as the "new isolationist" speech. That address reminded many of the "old" Nixon and put war critics on the defensive. In assessing the speech's impact with his advisors, William Safire reported that Nixon attacked J. William Fulbright (D-Ark.), but added: "Mansfield is different, of course."[22]

For his part, Mansfield tempered his support for Nixon with a number of warnings. At a Democratic dinner, he employed a carrot-and-stick approach in promising that the Senate "will join with the President in an effort to end the war in Viet Nam. As far as conscience permits, we will uphold the President's hand in that situation; he is the President of all Americans—Democrats no less than Republicans. But we cannot and we will not acquiesce in the indefinite absence of peace."[23] Mansfield offered the carrot because he was pleased that Nixon was changing the role of American ground troops to a more defensive one, thus decreasing the number of U.S. casualties. Yet he warned Nixon that there was a time constraint on extricating U.S. forces.

On July 25, when Nixon spoke in Guam, he said that Asians did not "want to be dictated to from the outside, Asia for Asians is what we want." He added, "we must avoid that kind of policy that will make countries in Asia so dependent upon us that we are dragged into conflicts such as the one that we have in Vietnam." Mansfield enthusiastically embraced Nixon's words and became the leading proponent of the new approach. He was especially pleased that Nixon seemed to accept his oft-stated position that the United States was a Pacific power, rather than a power on the Asian mainland. The Kalbs suggested that Mansfield even "dubbed" Nixon's words the "Nixon Doctrine."[24] The senator rhetorically elevated Nixon's simple statement of policy to the status of a doctrine. He spent the rest of the Nixon administration trying to persuade the president to live up to Mansfield's interpretation of the new doctrine.

THE CAMBODIAN SITUATION

Cambodia had broken off relations with the United States in May of 1965. As North Vietnamese incursions into Cambodia increased, Sihanouk had little choice but to ignore them. China was unable to help during its cultural revolution, so Sihanouk tried to mend his fences with America. In 1967 Sihanouk invited Jacqueline Kennedy to visit the Angkor temples and treated her as a state dignitary. In an interview with the *Washington Post* in late 1967, Sihanouk requested that President Johnson send a special envoy to discuss problems, suggesting Mansfield as "a just and courageous man whom we consider a friend."[25] Recognizing Mansfield's unique relationship with Sihanouk, the Johnson administration had already considered using that friendship to further policy aims with Sihanouk.[26]

In early 1968, however, Johnson sent Chester Bowles, then U.S. ambassador to India, to persuade Sihanouk to press for a more active and better equipped International Control Commission (ICC) to check for Vietcong and North Vietnamese intrusions into Cambodia. In return, Sihanouk wanted a clear American statement rejecting the concept of "hot pursuit." Bowles could not provide that, but believed he persuaded the prince that hot pursuit would not be necessary with a stronger ICC presence.[27]

Karnow and others accepted the State Department version of Bowles's meeting with Sihanouk, in which the prince supposedly told Bowles that he "was not opposed to hot pursuit in uninhabited areas" that "would be liberating us from the Vietcong."[28] Mansfield's correspondence with Bowles and Sihanouk denies that interpretation, a disparity that would later lead to controversy.

After his trip, Bowles had written Mansfield: "I was given instructions by Prince Sihanouk to send you his warm personal greetings and to tell you once again that he hopes you will be able soon to pay another visit to Cambodia."[29] Mansfield thanked Sihanouk for the invitation, but was unsure when such a trip would occur. He praised Sihanouk's efforts to restore good relations between

Cambodia and the United States, but understood how difficult that would be. Sihanouk complained that U.S. and South Vietnamese incursions into Cambodia were continuing and those killed were always Cambodian soldiers and peasants, not Vietcong. The prince outlined his two conditions for reconciliation with the United States: a cessation of border incursions and the recognition of Cambodia's present borders. Sihanouk realized that border incidents were inevitable with war in South Vietnam, but wanted apologies and compensation for families when they occurred. Both Thailand and South Vietnam claimed part of Cambodia's territory, and Sihanouk complained: "All big powers have now recognized our borders, or at least proclaim their inviolability. I must tell you that such a recognition does not imply . . . a political choice between Cambodia and her neighbors, but a choice between international law and the 'law of the jungle.'"[30]

Valeo believed that Mansfield had persuaded Johnson not to involve Cambodia in the conflict, even though many in the military wanted to attack the enemy sanctuaries in Cambodia.[31] This policy of restraint during the Johnson administration changed with the election of Nixon. The communist Khmer Rouge rebellion in Cambodia, dormant since 1954, resumed in 1968 with aid from North Vietnam.

NIXON, SIHANOUK, AND MANSFIELD'S SIXTH TRIP TO INDOCHINA

Mansfield attempted to persuade Nixon to continue to protect Cambodian neutrality. In March 1969 he cautioned Nixon from the Senate not to listen to reported military requests for permission to attack enemy sanctuaries in Cambodia. Mansfield doubted reports that Sihanouk would not object to the U.S. bombing of communist targets and prophetically predicted: "an attack on Cambodia would very possibly bring that nation into the conflict." Nixon had ordered the secret bombing of Cambodia to begin in March, but the first press reports of the B-52 raids did not come until May. Appearing on *Face the Nation* after those press reports, Mansfield deplored the attacks on Cambodian territory as uncalled for and unnecessary because they were likely to broaden the war.[32] Mansfield remained ignorant of the systematic and widespread nature of the bombing campaign until 1973.

Yet Mansfield was pleased that Nixon planned to reestablish relations with Sihanouk's government. On May 2, disturbed by reports that Nixon was backing away from recognition, Mansfield wrote the president. He praised Nixon's recognition of Cambodia's territorial integrity, but noted that the interpretations by other officials of what Nixon meant by territorial integrity was what had upset Sihanouk. This pattern had occurred in the past when improvements in relations seemed imminent. Mansfield advised:

When the President issues a statement in situations of great delicacy, it seems to me that, unless otherwise instructed, the standard answer throughout the Executive Branch to further queries should be: "The President's statement speaks for itself."

If it is imperative for our national interest, as I believe it is, that the Vietnamese war does not spread over Cambodia and the rest of Southeast Asia, the continued diplomatic estrangement with Phnom Penh is most unfortunate.[33]

In March, before the problems with recognition were resolved, Nixon had raised the possibility of Mansfield returning to Cambodia. After Nixon returned from his July trip to Asia and Rumania, he repeated the request, asking Mansfield to assess reactions to the Nixon Doctrine. The resulting trip included a stop in Laos, but not South Vietnam. Valeo recalled: "it was [Mansfield's] decision not to go back to Vietnam and I'm not so sure why. He just said I want to stay away from it or something to that effect. He probably felt he could do nothing by going to Vietnam."[34]

By the time of Mansfield's sixth trip in 1969, Laos was, in many ways, more of a U.S. client state than South Vietnam. It received more U.S. aid per capita than any other nation. While there were no American ground troops in Laos, numerous CIA agents were present, and U.S. planes systematically bombed communist forces in Laos in this so-called "secret war." Royal Lao and Hmong forces were used on the ground to oppose the Pathet Lao and North Vietnamese troops, while U.S. air power based in Thailand provided support. Many congressional visitors left Laos impressed because of the low cost of U.S. operations there. Mansfield was not among them.

Valeo said that the situation had changed since 1965, Laos "was completely immersed in the war, and the American Embassy was practically running the whole campaign." Mansfield's aide recalled that the senator met King Sri Savang Vatthana in the 1950s when the king was crown prince: "he was a man of considerable self confidence at the time, young and impressive." The king held a luncheon for the Mansfield party in Luang Prabang and met with the senator for several hours. Valeo described the king as "worried" by 1969. He was deeply concerned about the "Chinese pressures" and the way the United States had made Laos a battleground. The Laotian press reported that Mansfield delivered a letter to the king from Nixon. Prince Souvanna met with Mansfield in Vientiane for no more than one hour.[35]

The Mansfield party arrived in Phnom Penh on August 21 and was met at the airport by Sihanouk, who designated the trip a "state visit." Mansfield became the first official American visitor to Cambodia since relations had been restored, and he received full military honors, a distinction usually bestowed only on heads of state.

That evening, the party attended a formal dinner. Sihanouk toasted Mansfield as "one of [Cambodia's] greatest and most faithful friends, the courageous advocate of Cambodia's just cause," and he praised the senator's "ability to understand our point of view." The Cambodian leader also complimented Nixon's friendly attitude. Mansfield said he was delighted with the Nixon Doctrine, interpreting it to mean that "American forces will not be used on the mainland except in the most extreme circumstances," and calling it "a shift from a vested policy good 20 to 25 years ago but not valid today." Mansfield added, "when you think of Cambodia you think of Prince Sihanouk," and he commended Nixon for an end to the "tragic misunderstanding" between the nations.

Valeo was surprised when Sihanouk said after this dinner that "he didn't know how long he could hold out, but he was determined to leave the Cambodian people with the impression of the monarchy as being the golden age in Cambodian history." Cambodia was still considered stable and Valeo said the people adored Sihanouk. Mansfield's aide recalled meeting the new prime minister, Lon Nol, who seemed a loyal supporter and whom Sihanouk considered as a brother.[36]

The following morning, Sihanouk and Mansfield held their official meeting, which was also attended by Valeo, U.S. Chargé d'Affaires Lloyd Rives, and James Lowenstein from the Foreign Relations Committee staff. Sihanouk started the meeting by saying he was at Mansfield's disposal, at which point Mansfield asked for Sihanouk's views on the situation in Indochina, his feelings about China, and his thoughts on the Nixon Doctrine. Sihanouk "proceeded almost without pause ... for over two hours."

As a great power, Sihanouk thought that China could not be "avoided." Cambodia's relations with China had been "alright" [sic] until 1967 when China tried to export her cultural revolution. Those problems had been worked out and the two countries were on good terms. Yet relations never totally recovered from 1967. He suggested that the Chinese "cannot be pleased that Cambodia has resumed diplomatic relations with the United States" but noted that they had "made no comment."

According to the prince, Vietnamese communism presented a greater threat than did Maoist communism. The current communist insurgency in Cambodia was blamed on North Vietnam. North Vietnam's violations of Cambodian neutrality now exceeded those of Americans. Since the United States could not defeat North Vietnam, neither could Cambodia with an armed forces of 36,000. Lowenstein's notes indicated Sihanouk saying that he had

protested to Ambassador Bowles against American bombing [in Cambodia], but not against bombing sanctuaries in areas of Cambodia not inhabited by Cambodians. American intelligence people know where these sanctuaries are. They have been bombed many times. "I never protest against such bombings," the prince said. He added that he learned of such bombing when he read Time or Newsweek, but he never protested. It is in one's own interest, sometimes, to be bombed—in this case, the United States kills foreigners who occupy Cambodian territory and does not kill Cambodians.[37]

But the prince continued, he did protest the bombings of Cambodian peasants. Sometimes the United States has false information and bombs places where there are not Viet Cong.[38]

The prince's solution was for the United States to leave South Vietnam. He recommended that America should concentrate on helping Cambodia, Thailand, Malaysia, and Burma to stabilize the region. Sihanouk prophetically said: "a socialist Vietnam cannot be avoided in the future. Some day, the United States will withdraw from Vietnam, as the Prince has always thought." By the same token, Sihanouk argued that there was only one China: "Chiang Kai Chek could be perfectly happy in comfortable retirement in Hawaii or California, once [the] U.S. decides [to] abandon Taiwan." Sihanouk emphasized the need for improved U.S.-Chinese relations, saying: "Cambodia cannot lead a tranquil life when there is rivalry and hostility between the U.S. and China." He said that the United States needed to be realistic and accept the inevitability of Hanoi and Beijing. Hanoi, he noted, at least recognized Cambodia's borders, while Saigon made claims on Cambodian territory.

Between 1965 and 1969, it had been difficult to resolve problems with the United States. Sihanouk pledged: "I promise not to cut again our relations with you; it is better to have frank and direct relations." However, Cambodia could not establish relations with South Vietnam as long as Thieu claimed Cambodian territory.

The prince was conciliatory: "for many years we have watched for a way to shake hands again," and "thanks to the new U.S. policy of Nixon," that would be possible. He had received "many friendly messages" from Nixon and was very touched. He called the Nixon Doctrine wise, and professed to be very satisfied with it.[39]

Rives cabled Secretary of State William Rogers that the "visit was [a] personal triumph for Senator, who [is] genuinely admired by Cambodians. However, in official circles [it] was also success for new U.S. policy enunciated by President Nixon." Rives said that the combination of Nixon's letter to Sihanouk and Mansfield's "kind and public words" about Rives, would "launch the embassy in sea of good will."[40]

Mansfield also used his contact with Sihanouk to explore a potential visit to China. He received a letter from Sihanouk after his trip that included a copy of a letter from Zhou Enlai to Sihanouk, in which the Chinese premier turned down Mansfield's request for a visit to China. Mansfield responded:

> While the response was not what I had hoped for, it was not unexpected. In fact, it was foreshadowed during our recent conversation in your analysis of the significance of Taiwan to U.S.-Chinese relations.

However, in writing to the Chinese Premier I was persuaded that a point of beginning, a point of fresh contact, had to be found sooner or later if there was to be a peaceful soluation (sic) [solution] respecting not only Taiwan but other issues between the United States and China.[41]

MANSFIELD'S REPORT DEFINES THE NIXON DOCTRINE

On August 27, 1969, Mansfield met for one and one-half hours with Nixon and Kissinger at the western White House in San Clemente, presenting both an oral and a private written report on his trip.[42] Mansfield argued in his report that the 800,000 U.S. troops stationed in Asia and the $3 million spent each hour in Vietnam were not justified when money was needed at home. The U.S. commitment was based on the fear of Chinese invasion, but none of the countries Mansfield visited expressed such a concern. The real threat to existing governments was caused by "local grievances and conflicts." America had become a "self-appointed great power protector" in an era when nationalism opposed foreign intrusion. America had legitimate national interests in the Pacific, but our interests on the Asian mainland were peripheral.

Cambodia and the United States were "at a threshold that offers an opportunity to make a clean beginning." Mansfield praised Sihanouk for leading Cambodia to independence before 1954, for preserving Cambodia's unity, and for mobilizing her "energy in the building of a progressive and peaceful state." The four people serving in the new embassy were the same number Mansfield encountered on his 1953 trip. While that number would grow, Mansfield hoped to avoid the "overweening official presence with the extensive paraphernalia of programs that has become so characteristic of official U.S. establishments in Asia during the past decade." It was important to maintain "this oasis of peace in a war torn Southeast Asia." Mansfield's report was critical of the government of South Vietnam for its failure to recognize Cambodia's borders.

The U.S. presence in Laos had grown to disturbing proportions in Mansfield's view, which differed with the Nixon Doctrine. The dilemma was that continued U.S. aid was necessary to stave off defeat, but continued aid threatened the government's credibility with the population. Mansfield feared that the United States was moving toward the direct involvement Kennedy had rejected. Mansfield cautioned: "every effort must be made to avoid any further magnification of the American presence in Laos." His trip had convinced him that the king was the key to any settlement. Mansfield had lost faith in Souvanna Phouma's ability to successfully cope with the situation. Valeo said Souvanna was tired and had lost his enthusiasm by the time of the 1969 visit.

Mansfield made the conscious rhetorical choice of interpreting the Nixon Doctrine in an effort to determine policy. First he branded the concept a "doctrine," and then he supplied his own definition of what Nixon meant by it. It then became difficult for Nixon to deny Mansfield's interpretation after it had been shared with a number of Asian heads of state. Valeo said that Mansfield

> pushed [the Nixon Doctrine] to make sure it stayed in and hammered in because as he interpreted it, the Doctrine implies a reduction of U.S. involvement in Asia. He continued to interpret it that way whether Nixon meant it that way or not. . . . That was a very important point with him.

Mansfield defined his interpretation of the doctrine's points to various leaders: the United States would honor treaty commitments and provide military assistance, but manpower should be provided by the affected nation. Nuclear threats were a different matter. But nations in the Western Pacific and Asia "will not be denied a concerned . . . ear in this Nation." The United States would avoid situations where Asian nations become over-dependent on it for support. More emphasis was to be placed on economic than military aid, and while America would continue to play an important role in Asia, it would be more multilateral in nature. Rather, the United States would assist Asian nations to develop "multilateral political, economic, and security arrangements" among themselves.

The majority leader argued in his report that to invoke the Nixon Doctrine, it would be necessary to end the war in Vietnam and to fight the bureaucratic tendency to expand U.S. presence. With the exception of Laos, the leaders with whom he spoke favored the shrinking of the U.S. role on their continent, but were uncertain as to what the doctrine would lead to in specific terms. Mansfield deplored the fact that some U.S. missions still called the Asia mainland vital to U.S. interests, wanted an expanded presence, and seemed out of step with Nixon's new outlook. It was necessary for the administration to make the new policy clear to overseas departments and agencies and to begin the implementation of that policy. As a first step, Mansfield called for a freeze on military and civilian personnel in the area by presidential order, with congressional support. Congress and Nixon could then examine programs to get rid of those that they deemed "ill-fitted or ill-scaled" to present conditions.[43]

Nixon responded that Mansfield's private report "was of considerable interest to me and you may be sure that your insights will be very helpful in considering U.S. policy goals and the means of carrying them out in that area in the coming months."[44] In his memoirs, however, Nixon made it clear that he explained the doctrine to Mansfield; the senator simply chose to interpret it in his own way:

> The Nixon Doctrine was misinterpreted by some as signaling a new policy that would lead to total American withdrawal from Asia and from other parts of the world as well. In one of our regular breakfast meetings Mansfield articulated this misunderstanding. I emphasized to him . . . that the . . . Doctrine was not a formula

for getting America *out* of Asia, but one that provided the only sound basis for America's staying *in* and continuing to play a responsible role in helping . . . our Asian allies to defend their independence.[45]

Interestingly, the *New York Times* definition at this time was closer to Mansfield's interpretation: "the doctrine proposed that while the United States would continue to honor its treaty commitments, it would expect the Asian nations to handle their own defense without assistance from American troops."[46] Mansfield's rhetorical strategy seemed to be paying dividends with the press, if not with Nixon. In truth, Mansfield's definition of the Nixon Doctrine was almost identical to Nixon's. The difference was one of timing. Nixon wanted the doctrine implemented *after* he straightened out the mess he inherited in Indochina. Mansfield wanted a rapid ending of the conflict so the promise of the new doctrine could immediately bear fruit.

By the time of the public report, the Senate had learned more about the extent of U.S. military involvement in Laos's "hidden war." Members of the Foreign Relations Committee believed the administration had not informed, and had even misled them. Mansfield knew the administration was bombing to stop North Vietnamese infiltration, but he was upset that the United States was also bombing in support of Royal Laotian forces. Such measures violated the spirit of Senate legislation.

Premier Souvanna visited Washington shortly after Mansfield's report was issued. Nixon had a stag dinner for the prince, to which he invited Joseph Alsop and Walter Cronkite. The *New York Times* reported that a "notable omission" from the party was Mansfield, who had "cautioned against any increase in the United States involvement in Laos." In a comment that seemed to be pointed at Mansfield, Souvanna scoffed at Americans who doubted the need for a U.S. presence in Laos.[47]

MANSFIELD BEGINS TO BREAK WITH NIXON

U.S. News noted that Mansfield seemed unleashed with a Republican in the White House. They claimed that he was speaking out and taking firmer stands than he had under Kennedy and Johnson. This caused headaches for the administration, especially on Vietnam. The magazine speculated that Johnson had called the shots in the Senate, and that Mansfield was now able to be his own man. An anonymous source claimed Mansfield's "relations with President Nixon are correct and business-like, each respecting the other's official position. They are unlikely ever to be warmer."[48]

While we do not know what was said between them in private, Mansfield publicly pressured Nixon in September to join North Vietnam and the Vietcong in a three-day cease-fire. He hoped that this could lead to a "stand-down" that could break the impasse between the two sides.[49] Yet he was torn by his philosophy of presidential power and his inherent fairness. In a one and one-half hour secret meeting with Nixon in October, Mansfield had been impressed by the president's determination "to find a responsible way out of Vietnam." When Nixon wanted Foreign Relations Committee hearings with Secretary of State Rogers and Secretary of Defense Melvin Laird delayed until after his November 3 address, Fulbright "closeted" himself with Mansfield and George Aiken (R-Vt.) and was persuaded to delay the hearings. All three members of the committee were pleased that the level of fighting in Vietnam had tapered off and wanted to give Nixon a fair chance to end U.S. involvement.[50]

Before Nixon delivered this address, Mansfield sent a memo that he asked the president to read before committing himself to his final message. Nixon took the correspondence to Camp David and read it while finishing the speech. Nixon referred to Mansfield as "a personal friend for over twenty years . . . whose views on foreign policy I greatly respected."[51] Yet Nixon ignored Mansfield's advice and used this address to break with him. Nixon reported Mansfield writing:

> "The continuance of the war in Vietnam, in my judgment, endangers the future of this nation." He said that it was more than just the loss of lives or the waste of money and resources that concerned him. "Most serious," he wrote, "are the deep divisions within our society to which this conflict of dubious origin and purpose is contributing."
>
> He said that he would give articulate public support to "any or all of the following decisions if in your responsibility you decide that they are necessary, as well they may be, to a rapid termination of the war in Vietnam." He then listed actions that amounted to a unilateral cease-fire and withdrawal. . . .
>
> I realized that with this memorandum Mansfield was offering what would be the last chance for me to end "Johnson's and Kennedy's war. . . ." He would even allow me to claim that I was making the best possible end of a bad war my Democratic predecessors had begun. I knew that the opponents of the war would irrevocably become my opponents if my speech took a hard line. But I could not escape the fact that I felt it would be wrong to end the Vietnam war on any terms I believed to be less than honorable.[52]

Nixon's analysis of the "deal" Mansfield offered seemed sound. Mansfield adapted rhetorically to the president, thinking that Nixon might end the war if the majority leader were willing to place the blame for the conflict on Democrats, thus virtually guaranteeing Nixon a second term in office.

Nixon's November 3, 1969 address took a militant stance and became known as the "silent majority" speech. He called this speech "the most effective of my presidency," and "a turning point in the war." Nixon not-so-modestly declared that "very few speeches actually influence history. The November 3 speech was one of them."[53]

Even after Nixon disregarded Mansfield's November advice, though, the majority leader was unwilling to make his public break from the president. Mansfield's strategy mandated that he have a voice at the White House since he continued to believe that the war could be ended only by the executive. Typically, Mansfield tried to stress the positive elements of the speech the day after Nixon clearly rejected his plea. The senator argued that Nixon sincerely wanted peace, but "what is not clear is the how or when." Mansfield complained that the Nixon Doctrine had not yet been applied on the Asian mainland and "the sooner it is applied . . . the better it will be for this Nation and for all concerned."[54]

Mansfield's efforts to support the president provided him with positive political paybacks. After Nixon's silent majority address, one constituent wrote: "although I am a registered Republican in Montana I must congradulate [sic] you on your recent non-partisan statements concerning President Nixon's Viet nam speech." Mrs. Henry [Clare Booth] Luce wrote Mansfield: "as you know (or maybe you don't), I have held you in high esteem and warm affection for many years. By supporting the President's effort to end the war with honour, you have once again demonstrated why so many Americans, like myself, have confidence in your statesmanship." Not everyone saw him as supportive, however. One former Montanan branded Mansfield as a pro-communist who along with his "cohort Senator Fulbright could become unsavory footnotes in history."[55]

The majority leader became involved in several efforts to express Congress's desire for a rapid peace. He tried gently to pressure Nixon by joining Minority Leader Hugh Scott (Pa.) and forty senators, including twenty-six Republicans, in introducing a resolution praising the president's efforts to end the war, but simultaneously calling for free elections in the South, and urging Nixon to call upon North Vietnam for a cease fire. While the White House approved of the resolution, Mansfield admitted that he did not "nourish great expectations" for its success.[56] Mansfield also praised a sense of the Senate resolution introduced by Frank Church (D-Idaho) and Mark Hatfield (R-Ore.) that asked for a more rapid withdrawal of American troops. Yet when Charles Goodell (R-N.Y.) introduced legislation to bring all American military personnel home by December 1, 1970, Mansfield opposed it, claiming that choosing a set date lacked flexibility. Mansfield continued to believe that "the ultimate responsibility [for ending the war] lies with the President and not with the Senate." [57]

MANSFIELD HELPS REPEAL THE GULF OF TONKIN RESOLUTION

Mansfield did not support efforts to repeal the Gulf of Tonkin Resolution during a Democratic administration. In 1966, Mansfield was part of a 92-5 majority voting to table an amendment to repeal it. He argued, "we are in too deep now." Although Mansfield claimed two years later that "had I known what I presently know, the resolution would not have received my vote," he thought that it was a waste of time for the Senate to dwell on the resolution at that point; it was up to historians to decide.[58]

Even though Mansfield had opposed repeal of the resolution during a Democratic administration, he became "interested," "intrigued," and "impressed" by a proposal from Charles Mathias Jr. (R-Md.) to repeal the Gulf of Tonkin, Formosa, Mideast, and similar resolutions with a Republican in the White House. Mansfield had Valeo prepare a memorandum in November of 1969 that Mansfield issued as his own on December 8, when he became a cosponsor of Mathias's proposal. The statement expressed Mansfield's philosophy on presidential power in foreign policy matters and explained the senator's position on public versus private criticism.

> It is my practice to give as much support as I can on matters of foreign policy to an incumbent President. Whether Democrat or Republican. . . . I have tried . . . to present my personal views to the President in private and, in public, to give him the benefit of any doubts which I may have on a particular course of policy.
>
> However, even as the President has his responsibilities, I have mine as a Senator of Montana and the United States. When it is incumbent on me, in my judgment, to express my views on an issue, in public, I must do so in the discharge of the duties which are vested in me by the Constitution.
>
> I . . . [voted for it] because President Johnson asked for the resolution to provide a display of government unity in an effort to prevent the initial U.S. military involvement from widening. When it appeared that the resolution was being interpreted as a blank check, members of the Senate began increasingly to express their opposition to that interpretation.
>
> I would be happy, indeed, to consider repeal of this resolution if President Nixon [here Mansfield inserted "or the Congress, or both together" into Valeo's version] were to request it as a step towards shortening the path to peace.[59]

In 1970 the Mathias proposal passed the Senate and became law when it was passed in the House on January 12, 1971. The Nixon administration did not oppose the repeal, claiming that they were not relying on the resolution for legal justification for conducting the war, although expressing concern that the repeal "may well create the wrong impression abroad about U.S. policy."[60]

Mansfield predicted that the repeal would "receive the gratitude of history." He later argued that the repeal removed "the sole legal foundation for our involvement" in Indochina.[61]

SIHANOUK AND CAMBODIA FALL VICTIM TO THE INDOCHINA WAR

On January 7, 1970, Sihanouk left for France on an extended vacation, leaving Lon Nol and Sihanouk's cousin, Prince Sisowath Sirik Matak, in charge. Sihanouk had called Lon Nol "the only person I could trust because of his faithfulness to the Throne and Nation." In early March, with Lon Nol's encouragement, Cambodian mobs sacked the North Vietnamese and Vietcong legations in Phnom Penh. On March 16, more anti-communist riots unleashed racial hatred and led to the murder of Vietnamese living in Cambodia. Lon Nol demanded that the communists leave their Cambodian sanctuaries, but they refused. On the 17th, Lon Nol authorized the South Vietnamese military to cross the border for a sweep against communist positions. On the 18th, Sihanouk was deposed by a unanimous vote in the Cambodian National Assembly. There is no proof that the U.S. government was involved in the coup, and both Nixon and Kissinger deny complicity. Kissinger spent considerable time in his memoirs disclaiming responsibility, arguing that the administration preferred to keep Sihanouk in power. He linked the administration's lack of knowledge of the coup to Mansfield, because "largely at Senator Mansfield's insistence, no CIA personnel were assigned to Phnom Penh after the restoration of diplomatic relations." Shortly after Sihanouk's fall, Nixon ordered a large CIA contingent to Phnom Penh.

While Nixon and Kissinger did not order the coup, Lon Nol had close ties with the U.S. military. U.S. officials and Lon Nol had been discussing the potential of a coup since 1968. These discussions included the possibility of assassinating Sihanouk. The U.S. military units working in and around Cambodia were anti-Sihanouk. The American military had pressured first Johnson and then Nixon to attack communist positions in Cambodia, which Sihanouk would never have allowed.

After the coup, when Sihanouk pleaded with the United States for help, Nixon took a laissez faire attitude, which was certain to keep Lon Nol at the head of government. The French attempted to organize an international initiative to restore Sihanouk to power, similar to the circumstances under which Souvanna Phouma had been returned to power in 1964, but North and South Vietnam opposed such action. Nixon wanted to send aid immediately to the pro-American government in Cambodia but was dissuaded by Rogers, Laird, and Kissinger, who argued that immediate aid would indicate to the world that the United States was responsible for the coup. The administration did not hesitate long before recognizing the new government, giving that very impression.

Sihanouk believed America was responsible for his ouster and threw his support to the Khmer Rouge communist forces. Kissinger pointed out that once that occurred, the possibility of the prince's return to power had ended because "Sihanouk's return would have meant not a restoration of neutralism but the victory of his new Communist patrons, whom he had lost all capacity to control."[62]

Mansfield was appalled at Cambodian developments and condemned the loss of the last "oasis of peace in Indochina." He praised Nixon on April 2 for not providing aid to the Lon Nol government and argued: "we do know, too, or we should know at this late date—after Viet Nam, after Laos—that each deepening of our involvement in Indochina began with an input of well-meaning aid." Mansfield saw the situation in Cambodia as analogous to Vietnam after the Diem coup and thought it imperative that the United States take the opposite approach. Aid would lead to the commitment of troops. It made no sense to wind down the war in South Vietnam only to increase it in Laos and Cambodia. Cambodia had survived because of Sihanouk and the "void can only be filled by the same kind of fractional infighting that characterized the South Vietnamese political scene."[63]

On April 21, the French Embassy delivered a letter to Mansfield from Sihanouk. The prince wrote from China:

> If your government . . . had listened to the voice of wisdom and human liberalism which was always yours, the peoples of Indochina . . . would have recovered peace in independence a long time ago. Unfortunately, wisdom and good sense have never prevailed . . . and the Vietnamese people first, then the Laotian people, finally the Cambodian people, have . . . fallen into a second war of Indochina.

He blamed the Nixon administration for "the installation in Phnom-Penh of an illegal, dictatorial, bellicist [sic] and racist government, practising [sic] genocide without precedent in modern history, with the exception of the monstrous crimes of the Hitlerian regime." Sihanouk concluded that "we have no other recourse than an armed fight for national liberation and the triumph of justice, even if we have to obtain them at the price of an ideological change in Cambodia."[64]

Shortly after the Sihanouk letter, Mansfield received a cable from the prince's long-time aide, Penn Nouth, also from Beijing. The former prime minister urged Mansfield to "use your great influence to make the great American people understand that they are about to be dangerously drawn by their President into a general war in Indochina." Penn Nouth condemned Lon Nol's "genocide" against ethnic Vietnamese. He praised Congress for its opposition to Nixon's policy, but asked: "what crime did the Khmer people commit against the American people to justify or only to excuse the punishment that President Nixon is inflicting on them?"[65] Mansfield shared both cables with Nixon. After he read Sihanouk's letter to Mansfield, Nixon told Kissinger that the prince "parrots the Communist line in every respect."[66]

Sihanouk not only viewed Mansfield as an ally, but he saw him as a conduit for getting his side of the story to the Congress, the American public, and perhaps even the president. Mansfield continued in the role of go-between for the remainder of the Indochina war, but as Nixon's "parrot" line implies, the senator was never successful in influencing administration policy toward Sihanouk.

Mansfield also received appeals from the Lon Nol government. An April letter from the presidents of the Cambodian Senate and Assembly argued that it was a contradiction for Mansfield to oppose arms for Cambodia when their country's neutrality was threatened by the Viet Cong and North Vietnam. As an independent nation and member of the United Nations, Cambodia had a right to defense from invasion.[67]

Kissinger met informally with the Foreign Relations Committee at Fulbright's home on April 23 to discuss the Cambodian developments. As a result of that meeting, Mansfield sent Nixon a long letter the following day. He wrote that the Lon Nol government was in trouble and Americans were "subjecting ourselves to severe pressures to rescue it from collapse." Typically, Mansfield expressed deference to Nixon's "burdens," said he would respect Nixon's decisions, but had an obligation to express his views. He claimed that even though Vietcong and North Vietnamese forces were leading the Cambodian assault, it also involved Cambodians and was "operating under the symbol of Sihanouk." Mansfield admitted that if Sihanouk's forces won, the new government would "be heavily sustained by North Vietnamese or Viet Cong forces." That, he said, "simply underscores the misfortune of the coup in the first place."

Mansfield argued that U.S. interest still called for an avoidance of the Cambodian conflict. Sending arms would not change the outcome and many would end up in communist hands; U.S. advisors or troops were the only way to have an impact in Cambodia. The senator warned:

> If we begin again on that pattern, I think it is clear where we wind up. We will wind up with another American military commitment and responsibility where none now exists, not under SEATO and certainly not under the Nixon Doctrine. If we assume this responsibility it is likely to be accompanied by another escalation of U.S. military costs and casualties, as the Vietnamese War is converted into a general Indochina war and, perhaps, a general Southeast Asian war. That is a path, Mr. President, which I most respectfully suggest . . . is not likely to be supported either by the Senate or the people of the nation.[68]

Nixon rejected Mansfield's advice, announcing on April 30 his decision to aid the Lon Nol government and attack the sanctuaries in Cambodia. When Nixon speech writer William Safire suggested that invading Cambodia violated Nixon's own doctrine, Kissinger responded: "we wrote the goddamn doctrine, we can change it!"[69] While working on the speech, Nixon expressed concern with "adverse senatorial reaction, especially Mansfield."[70] Before Nixon publicly announced his decision, he met congressional leaders and remembered: "the faces were intent and strained. Some of the strongest doves were there: Fulbright, Mansfield, Aiken, Kennedy. The sincerity of my words must have reached them, even though they remained opposed to the decision I had made. As I left the room, everyone stood and applauded."[71] Mansfield's recollection of the meeting agreed that it was strained, but concurred with little else. The senator related: "When [Nixon] left the room . . . I, of course, stood up with the others as a matter of courtesy and respect for the institution of the Presidency. I do not recall ever, under any circumstances, applauding."[72]

THE END OF MANSFIELD'S "QUIET" CRITICISM

The following day, Mansfield publicly condemned Nixon's decision because it widened the war. He accurately predicted that the invasion would accelerate the divisiveness at home.[73]

The Cambodian escalation had a profound effect on Mansfield. He wrote a memo for his files on May 11, which showed that the invasion changed his assumptions about executive prerogative in the conduct of war. Mansfield was now ready to employ the Senate, a method he admitted was an "awkward way" to terminate a war extended by successive administrations.[74] He argued that "escalation will not rescue bankrupt policy" and explained his radical change in philosophy:

> *for the first time, I am giving the most serious consideration to a termination date after which no more funds will be appropriated for military operations in Indochina. . . .*
>
> The American people feel let down, disappointed, concerned. They have appealed to the White House. They have appealed to the Congress. *Their only hope, I think, is the Senate.*
>
> A withdrawal may bring about disastrous consequences but it will mean no more Americans will die in Indochina. Leave them the weapons and the supplies, the bases and if they have the will they will carry on. If they have not, it is about time that we wrote off this mistaken war.[75] [Emphasis added.]

CHAPTER 13

THE SENATE ASSERTS ITSELF

MANSFIELD JOINS THE FRAY

Mansfield's rhetoric quickly began to reflect his new belief that the Senate would have to take responsibility for ending the war. The Senate was already acting to restrict Nixon's freedom of movement in Southeast Asia, and Mansfield became more involved in those steps. His new thinking freed him to support measures that he was unable to support earlier. Yet Mansfield and other Democrats feared Nixon's ability to effectively use the media, which was now paired with the vicious attacks by Vice President Spiro Agnew on administration critics. The majority leader claimed that "the President charms the TV audiences; the Vice President bombs the TV commentators." J. William Fulbright (D-Ark.) believed that Nixon could always make the public feel that "victory is just around the corner."[1]

Shortly after the Cambodian incursion, Mansfield supported the Cooper-Church Amendment, requiring Nixon to remove all troops from Cambodia by June 30, 1970, thereby holding the president to the date he had announced. Mansfield called it consistent with Nixon's pledge, arguing that the Senate was not attempting to "define the limits of a battlefield in a war," but was making "an effort to confine the war to a country before it spreads to a continent." He claimed that the amendment was not "a rash and reckless step," for had it been on the books in April, it would have saved lives. Nixon considered this measure and others like it unconstitutional, but Mansfield responded that the president's position was "Constitutional distortion." The senator believed that congress must reassert its Constitutional obligations to prevent "expedient decisions by the Executive Branch," like the invasion of Cambodia.[2]

On June 9, 1970, Mansfield spoke against the Byrd-Griffin Amendment that was designed to weaken Cooper-Church. Fulbright called Mansfield's Senate speech "rare and brilliant." Cooper-Church passed the Senate, 58-37, fittingly enough on June 30. For the first time in U.S. history, restrictions were placed on the president's powers to wage a war, although the bill then languished in a

House-Senate conference committee for almost six months. With Mansfield's support, the Senate had begun to assert itself.

In late 1969, the senator had opposed legislation proposing a set date for withdrawal introduced by Charles Goodell (R-N.Y.), saying it lacked flexibility. Now, however, Mansfield was responding to his changed philosophy. Mansfield cosponsored the McGovern-Hatfield Amendment that fixed the date for the withdrawal of troops from Cambodia (June 30), Laos (the end of 1970), and Vietnam (June 30, 1971).

Clearly, Mansfield's May 11 memo demonstrated a change in his oft-stated philosophy that only the president could end the war. Yet Mansfield still acknowledged the executive role, contending that the Senate was actively joining with Nixon to end hostilities. McGovern-Hatfield was defeated 55-39, but the Senate had become a thorn in the president's side. After the defeat, Mansfield wrote a constituent that his "past predictions [about Indochina] had been sound," and the vote on McGovern-Hatfield sent a message that would cause the administration to be "particularly mindful of whatever future action it takes." On the day of its defeat, fourteen senators, including Mansfield and Minority Leader Hugh Scott (Pa.), sent Nixon a letter urging him to propose a cease-fire in South Vietnam.[3]

While the administration ignored Mansfield's pleas to end the war, they continued to use Mansfield's friendship with Sihanouk. In late July, Mansfield, Fulbright, and George Aiken (R-Vt.) met with Secretary of State William Rogers. Rogers asked Mansfield to write a letter to Sihanouk asking for his "assistance in achieving the release of the newsmen held captive in Cambodia," four of whom were American. The administration believed that "Mansfield's past personal acquaintance with Sihanouk provides special basis for appeal from him." While Sihanouk lacked "authority over communist forces in Cambodia," his titular role might prove helpful to the journalists. The State Department offered Mansfield a "suggested letter," but he chose to write his own more personal version.

Sihanouk's response was bitter. He assured Mansfield that his forces would try to help the missing newsmen, but he found it ironic that the western press was so concerned with "the disappearance of 20 or so of its members," when

> tens of thousands of Khmer peasants have died or have been mutilated by the bombs or horribly burned by the napalm which the American planes and those of its satellites in Saigon, Bangkok and Phnom Penh drop each day on the heads of the Khmer nation in the name of American aid to the pro-American Fascists.

Sihanouk called the bombs and napalm "gifts of Mr. Nixon and Lon Nol." He warned Mansfield that Cambodia would be a "hornet's nest and quagmire" for the United States. As was his norm, the prince praised Mansfield as he did in an October article for *Foreign Affairs*.[4]

MANSFIELD'S LAST ELECTION

With midterm elections approaching, Nixon made a five-point peace proposal on October 7: (1)"a cease-fire-in-place"; (2) "an Indochina Peace Conference"; (3) negotiation of a timetable for withdrawal of U.S. forces as part of an overall settlement; (4) a joint "search for a political settlement that truly meets the aspirations of all South Vietnamese"; and (5) the release of all prisoners held by both sides. When the joint leadership was briefed before the speech, everyone endorsed the proposal, as did many influential Americans. It was not surprising that Mansfield supported Nixon's proposal; he had favored "a cease-fire-in-place" since August 1965. The day following Nixon's speech, Mansfield praised the proposal in the Senate as having substance. The president said he appreciated Mansfield's endorsement, calling it "very important in presenting a united front on the peace initiative."[5]

Even with their fundamental break over Cambodia, Nixon and Mansfield remained friendly. In October 1970, President Nixon sent an Air Force plane to Montana to pick up Mansfield so that the senator could join him at the United Nations. Nixon was quoted in the *Great Falls Tribune:* "Mansfield and Scott will return to their seats next January. . . . I'm endorsing them both." A surprised majority leader responded, "I didn't expect that." Nixon later claimed that the endorsement was made "in jest," but it illustrates Mansfield's popularity with national Republicans, a popularity that served him well as majority leader.[6] Even though he often opposed Nixon's policies, his accommodating nature made Mansfield preferable to whoever would replace him as Senate leader.

Mansfield's reelection bid was his most interesting since 1952, but Vietnam was not the major issue. Instead gun control took center stage in the campaign. This was the most troubling issue to Mansfield since the "loss of China" charges in 1952. Mansfield had opposed hand gun legislation until 1968. He was disturbed both by Robert Kennedy's assassination and by the murder of a Montana Marine lieutenant in Washington, D.C.[7]

He later said that the most difficult time for a senator was when he voted against the wishes of his constituents. That happened on the gun control issue when Mansfield received between 25,000 and 30,000 pieces of mail from Montana against the bill, the largest amount of mail he had ever received on any issue.[8] Senator Joseph Tydings (D-Md.), sponsor of the gun bill, sent Mansfield a letter after the legislation's defeat, saying: "your vote for registration and licensing yesterday was an act of the highest political courage."[9]

The senator's opponent in 1970 was Harold "Bud" Wallace, a sporting goods salesman and former swimming coach at the University of Montana. Attacking the gun legislation was Wallace's major issue, but Montana Republicans tried to win Nixon's "silent majority" by calling Mansfield "soft on communism." The senator also was defensive about charges that he was a "Johnny come lately" to the anti-war movement. He was popular enough to withstand the damage from his unpopular stand on gun legislation, and went on to defeat Wallace, 146,593 to 95,133.[10]

At the end of 1970, the Foreign Relations Committee submitted Nixon's funding request to the full Senate on an 8-4 vote; Mansfield joined Fulbright, Albert Gore (D-Tenn.), and Stuart Symington (D-Mo.) in opposition. Mansfield, the committee, and the Senate started to assert themselves in 1970, but still lacked the majority to defeat Nixon's policies. Yet the Senate was quickly approaching that majority. The problem for Senate doves would then be in the House, which still strongly supported the administration. Mansfield summarized his position in a letter to a constituent: "it does not seem that the end of the war in Viet Nam is in sight, but at least the policy of 'putting in' has been replaced by one of withdrawal."[11]

NIXON TAKES THE WAR TO LAOS

Early in 1971, Mansfield appeared on *Face the Nation*. He continued to sound accommodating to the administration, suggesting that Congress and the president were "working in the same direction" to end the war, and that Congress would meet Nixon "more than halfway." Yet he drew a clear line in the sand. While Nixon had met and exceeded his announced troop withdrawals, the situations in Cambodia and Laos would make further withdrawals difficult in 1971. Mansfield opposed the administration's decision to provide air support for Cambodia, a decision that "goes contrary to the intent and the spirit of Cooper-Church." When asked if the tedious process of trying to control the war through appropriations could work, Mansfield replied: "I think it can, and I think one of the good things which the Senate did in the last Congress was to stand up on its hind legs for a change." While admitting difficulties with passing a resolution for a fixed withdrawal date from Indochina, Mansfield said he again would support such legislation.[12]

Nixon and Henry Kissinger expected communist forces to begin moving supplies South for a massive communist drive timed to coincide with the 1972 American presidential elections. In order to disrupt the anticipated built-up, Nixon duplicated the Cambodian incursion by using U.S. air power in support of a South Vietnamese invasion of Laos in early February. Once again, Congress was neither consulted nor informed of these events, and the administration-imposed blackout kept the nation in the dark. Mansfield invited an administration official to his office to express his opposition and complained that "all I've been told is what I read in the newspapers." Despite American assistance, the South Vietnamese army was soundly defeated by General Vo Nguyen Giap's North Vietnamese forces.[13]

Mansfield's opposition to administration policy grew stronger with the escalation in Laos, as seen in his major speech in early 1971 at Olivet College in Michigan. Mansfield praised the Nixon Doctrine as a turning point that "opened the shutters on these musty thought-processes" that were "wedded to the needs of another era." Yet Mansfield posed the rhetorical question: was the administration more interested in "saving lives or saving face?" Both the Cambodian and Laotian incursions broadened the war. Once again, Mansfield defined the doctrine and claimed that the administration had been engaged in "digressions, dodges, and delays" in refusing to carry it out. He warned that "the critical need is an end to the involvement in Indochina: an end, period. In their separate Constitutional authority as necessary and, in cooperation, where possible, the effort must be made by the President and the Congress to meet that need. The Republic deserves no less."[14]

Mansfield wrote a constituent that he was a "tired man." The fact that he had not been successful at ending the war "discourages me but does not stop me."[15]

THE MANSFIELD AMENDMENT—EUROPE

Mansfield shifted to an old strategy to pressure Nixon. The senator had long believed our NATO allies should play a larger role in the defense of Europe, and American forces on foreign soil increased the likelihood the troops would be used. On May 11, 1971, Mansfield reintroduced his amendment and seemed on the verge of gaining passage of a Senate bill calling for the withdrawal of 50 percent of U.S. forces in Europe.

Most doves in Congress planned to fight the administration over the Draft Extension Act, which extended the draft for two years. Nixon expected such hostile actions over Indochina, but he did not expect such action over Europe. The manner in which Mansfield reintroduced his proposal was what caught the administration off guard. Usually, Mansfield introduced such legislation as a "sense of the Senate resolution," not binding on the executive. This time, Mansfield proposed his amendment as binding law. Senators from both parties warned Nixon that Mansfield would probably prevail, since "respect for Mansfield made his colleagues reluctant to vote against him." Kissinger explained why this legislation, emanating from Mansfield, caused the administration difficulties: "he was the Majority Leader, widely respected for his fairness, universally liked for his decency. Mansfield was not a member of a radical fringe but a charter member of the Senate Establishment." Thus the amendment was a formidable challenge.

Nixon assembled his own group of Wise Men to refute the Mansfield proposal. Many of the men who had shaped U.S. policy since World War II convened, including Dean Acheson, Nicholas Katzenbach, George Ball, John

McCloy, Lucius Clay, Henry Cabot Lodge, Cyrus Vance, General Matthew Ridgway, and other former and current military leaders. Acheson called the amendment "asinine" and "sheer nonsense." Averell Harriman was recruited to pressure presidential hopefuls Edmund Muskie (D-Maine) and Hubert Humphrey (D-Minn.) to oppose Mansfield, and both voted against the amendment. Nixon solicited and received support from former presidents Johnson and Harry Truman, and other officials including Dean Rusk, Livingston Merchant, and Douglas Dillon. On May 14, Soviet General Secretary Leonid Brezhnev called for a mutual force reduction, which doomed the amendment. Opponents argued that a unilateral reduction would harm the chances for a mutual one. On May 19, 1971 the legislation was defeated, 61-36.[16]

Reactions to Mansfield's failed effort were mixed. William White condescendingly referred to Mansfield as a "Little American" and called his defeat one of the greatest for a majority leader in memory. Carl Rowan was perplexed by Mansfield, suggesting that historians would go "nuts" trying to assess Mansfield's role in history. Rowan compared Mansfield to a jellyfish who suddenly changed into a shark. The *Norfolk Virginian-Pilot* suggested that Mansfield accomplished something that few thought possible, bringing "together Dean Acheson and Leonid Brezhnev in the cause of Richard M. Nixon."

Others perceived Mansfield as the victor in the squabble. The *Los Angeles Times* concluded that, as someone Nixon had courted and as a "sober, reflective, taciturn man, not a flamethrower," Mansfield was "the least likely man in town to set the White House on its ear." Chalmers Roberts wrote that "Mansfield lost the battle but won the war," because the thirty-six votes Mansfield garnered indicated that the Senate intended to assume its constitutional responsibilities. Fulbright viewed the Mansfield Amendment as a "warning shot across the Administration's bow."[17]

THE MANSFIELD AMENDMENT—INDOCHINA

Europe was but a detour to Mansfield's real purpose, made evident when the senator attached an amendment to the draft extension bill in June 1971. This amendment urged Nixon to withdraw U.S. forces from Vietnam within nine months if American prisoners of war (POWs) were released. The amendment prompted *U.S. News* to ask Mansfield if America was turning isolationist and if it was desirable for the Senate to curb the president's war-making powers. Mansfield replied that it was not a return to isolationism, but rather a "facing up to the reality" of the present, and that the curbing of war-making powers would be positive as long as the president could react "instantly in defense of the country." In contrast to Mansfield's efforts in May, the June amendment was not viewed with horror by the administration because Mansfield offered it as a sense-of-the-Senate resolution. Nixon called it "the least irresponsible of the irresponsible resolutions" introduced to force the United States to withdraw from Indochina. On June 22, that amendment passed the Senate 61-37 but languished in the House before being weakened in a conference committee.[18] One Fulbright biographer viewed Mansfield's June amendment as moving the majority leader into "an active leadership role" over Indochina.[19]

The day after its passage, Mansfield had breakfast with Nixon and the president "rather happily" told his aides that he let Mansfield know that his amendment might wreck delicate negotiations underway. If the negotiations collapsed, Nixon planned to go to the people to tell them Mansfield was to blame. Nixon admitted to H. R. Haldeman and Kissinger that the Mansfield Amendment gave the administration "the excuse for flushing the whole deal" and getting out of Indochina. That is what Mansfield hoped to accomplish with his amendment. However, Nixon indicated to his aides that in order to get out, he would first order a "total bombing of the North to eliminate their capability of attacking."[20] That was not what Mansfield wanted his amendment to accomplish.

The passage of Mansfield's amendment was aided by the publication of the *Pentagon Papers* in the *New York Times*. To Mansfield, the *Pentagon Papers* reiterated that the nation's commitment to Vietnam had been made by the executive branch, "with virtually no participation of the Congress." Mansfield sided with the *New York Times* in its legal battle with the administration, since Congress was often dependent on the media to learn of administration actions.[21]

The *Pentagon Papers* strengthened Mansfield's resolve to use the Senate to end this presidential war. Mansfield believed that the House-Senate conference committee "vitiated" his June amendment. Indeed, the administration actively worked to persuade the House conferees to weaken Mansfield's language.[22] Secretary of State Rogers requested a meeting with Mansfield and came to the senator's office on July 22 to discuss the pending legislation. Mansfield's record of the meeting showed he still tried to accommodate the administration:

> [Rogers] had two suggestions to make: (1) Would I consider withdrawing the Amendment? or (2) Would I consider changes in it? I said the first suggestion was like asking for the moon and he agreed. . . . I said I would be willing to scratch the words "not later than nine months after the date of enactment of this section" and substitute in place the words "at a certain date." He seemed to think that was reasonable.
>
> I also said that I was prepared to introduce a Resolution in support of the President's China Policy; gave it to him to read. He said, "this is great. Can I show it to the President?" I said, certainly.[23]

Mansfield's comment on China was a reaction to Nixon's July 15 announcement that the president was going to visit China. The idea of a Mansfield trip to China also was alive, and Nixon wanted Mansfield to be the first Democrat to visit China, even though Kissinger and Haldeman strongly opposed the idea.[24]

Nixon met with the bipartisan leadership several days after his dramatic July 15 announcement. Kissinger, Nixon, and Rogers stressed the need for secrecy to make the Chinese breakthrough a success. As was his norm, Mansfield spoke last at the bipartisan leadership meeting, promising his caution and support. William Safire wrote that Mansfield's "independent opinion was the most respected of all."[25] As much as Nixon and Mansfield differed on policy in Indochina, they were soul mates where China was concerned. Yet Mansfield made it clear that Nixon's moves in China would not cause the majority leader to back down over the Mansfield Amendment.

The administration attempted to link Mansfield's amendment to China. A memorandum from Clark MacGregor to Nixon recommended that the president emphasize to Mansfield that "adverse action in the Senate on the draft extension Conference Report would be a signal of American weakness on defense preparedness and would damage your efforts for peace." Kissinger urged Nixon to appeal to Mansfield in arguing for the need of quick passage of the draft legislation, because changing to a foreign policy of negotiation from the previous one of confrontation required a "strong defense posture." He also urged an appeal to Mansfield through the China card, arguing that if the U.S. defense posture were weakened, "the effect upon the Peking [Beijing] visit would be great." Kissinger pressed Nixon to hint at a breakthrough with Hanoi and to promise Mansfield, "the political wisdom of passing the bill without delay will become evident within two months." He added:

> the failure of the Congress to provide you with draft authority could seriously jeopardize the progress which you have made in negotiations both under way and pending with the Soviets, the Communist Chinese, and perhaps Hanoi. Our failure to maintain the conventional ground forces capable of reinforcing U.S. diplomacy would be tantamount to an invitation for Soviet mischief-making in that volatile area.[26]

Despite these appeals, Mansfield would not back off his amendment, not even with the promise of his long-desired visit to China. Nixon was discouraged after his long meeting with Mansfield on September 14, believing he "accomplished nothing in the way of getting any cooperation" on draft extension.[27]

Even if his amendment had remained unchanged, Mansfield planned to vote against the draft extension bill because he considered the draft "inadequate and unfair."[28] When Senator Ernest Hollings (D-S.C.) reported to the administration that Mansfield had uncharacteristically told Democrats that this vote "would be a test of party loyalty" and that senators who needed funds for the 1972 election should "take note," William Safire leaked the story for the White House. The story proved false and Safire's leak was exposed.

Characteristically, Mansfield chose to ignore the leak that maligned him. Columnist Mary McGrory believed that if Mansfield had fought back, draft extension might have been defeated. She characterized the senator as "St. Sebastian, forgiving the marksman as the arrows rend his flesh. . . . Everyone else saw it as the inevitable result of a clash between a man who observes the Golden Rule and one who takes his tactics from pro football."

Safire was embarrassed at getting caught up in the situation and thankful for Mansfield's reaction, calling the majority leader "one of the solid islands of integrity in Washington's marshes." The forces of the "island of integrity" nonetheless lost the battle 47-36.[29]

THE SECOND MANSFIELD AMENDMENT ON INDOCHINA

On September 27, 1971, Mansfield reintroduced his Indochina resolution in the Senate. Mansfield perceived that he needed to take the leadership role because "I detect in the Senate, and have for some weeks now, a feeling of apathy, a feeling of 'what's the use?' a feeling of being conditioned to an extension of the war into Laos and Cambodia, an accommodation with the Mylais and other incidents, and a general desire, perhaps, to wish these issues away." He believed that the Senate needed to keep the pressure on to end the war since the House and executive were not going to act.[30]

Mansfield's second Indochina amendment was identical to his first, although it changed the nine-month period for a U.S. withdrawal to six months to reflect the amount of time that had passed. It is not clear why Mansfield did not change the language of the amendment as discussed with Rogers on July 22. Attached to a military procurement bill, the second Mansfield Amendment on Indochina was passed 57-38 on September 30. Mansfield predictably argued, "the purpose of the amendment is not to undermine the President but to help him, to extend a hand of cooperation, and to become involved with him as coequal branches of this Government."[31] Nixon was not grateful for his "half."

Again, the House watered down Mansfield's amendment. The bill emerging from the conference committee kept most of his language, but deleted the six-month deadline. Mansfield wrote a former Montana resident that while disappointed in the House action, "you may rest assured that I do not intend to discontinue my efforts to bring about an end to this tragic war."[32] Unknown to Mansfield, Hanoi had secretly made an offer to the administration to end the war on terms almost identical to Mansfield's. The administration turned Hanoi down. On November 17, when the president signed the procurement bill into law, he indicated that Mansfield's amendment was "without binding force or effect" and "does not represent the policies of the Administration." This led Frank Church (D-Idaho) to respond, "what is he going to do next? Dispatch Henry Kissinger to Capitol Hill and disband the Congress?"[33]

THE THIRD MANSFIELD AMENDMENT ON INDOCHINA

A White House memo warned the administration of what to expect from the majority leader in 1972: Mansfield expected a "contentious atmosphere" with the White House because it was an election year. The senator planned to attach both his NATO troop reduction and total Indochina withdrawal amendments to "the first appropriate bill that hits the Floor." Further, Mansfield would oppose the Defense Appropriation Bill because of the conflict in Indochina.[34] In response to a question on congressional interference with the presidential power to wage war, Mansfield replied: "I think that what we're trying to do in Congress is to restore some of the powers which are ours legally under the Constitution but which we've given in a haphazard manner to Presidents . . . since the time of Franklin D. Roosevelt." Mansfield again warned that Congress had one constitutional power to carry out wars, and that was appropriations.[35]

Mansfield continued to be unhappy with the House for failing to adopt his amendment to end the war, so this time he attached it to the foreign aid bill and introduced it for a third time. The conference committee agreed on all points of the bill except the Mansfield Amendment. Mansfield made it clear that he would not compromise, and he was uncharacteristically harsh on the House Armed Services Committee for refusing to put his amendment up for a vote in the entire House: "a handful of foremen in Congress will stand over the pick-and-shovel representatives of the Nation, and that handful, together with the executive branch will decide on the disposition of the people's intent." He warned the House that he would reintroduce his amendment "until this involvement is cut loose from the life of this Nation." While the House consistently rejected Senate resolutions calling for U.S. withdrawal from Indochina, each vote was getting closer. Kissinger believed that "the day when Congress would legislate a deadline was clearly approaching."[36]

President Nixon scored a major public relations victory with his nationally broadcast speech on January 25, 1972. In the speech, Nixon revealed that Kissinger had secretly been negotiating with North Vietnam since 1969, and that Hanoi had been intransigent in those talks. To break the deadlock, Nixon announced fresh proposals. Within six months of an agreement, the United States would withdraw all forces from Vietnam, all POWs would be exchanged and a ceasefire would be imposed. Internationally supervised presidential elections would be held in South Vietnam, including the National Liberation Front, with President Thieu resigning one month before the election.

Mansfield praised Nixon for new flexibility and for finally "laying the cards on the table" with Congress and the American people. However, Mansfield continued to press his amendment on a fixed date for withdrawal from Indochina.[37]

THE MANSFIELD/SCOTT VISIT TO CHINA

Mansfield had continued to work toward arranging a China trip. He wrote Sihanouk that he wanted to talk to the Chinese about Indochina, but Zhou Enlai turned down Mansfield's requested journey in 1971.[38] After Nixon returned from China, however, he invited Mansfield and Scott to the White House and handed them an invitation from Zhou to visit China.[39] Mansfield's five-year effort had finally paid off.

On March 30, before the party left for China, communist forces in Vietnam launched an offensive designed to improve their position in the Paris talks, influence the U.S. elections, and force China and the Soviet Union to increase aid to North Vietnam. The offensive involved 120,000 North Vietnam regulars with their Vietcong allies. The attack was expected, but the magnitude of the offensive was not. Secretary of Defense Melvin Laird had told members of Congress that such an attack was "not a serious possibility," and Army Chief of Staff William Westmoreland predicted that such a drive would end "in a matter of days" because "the staying power of the enemy is not great." Yet the battles raged until June.

While the Mansfield party was en route to China, Nixon responded to the offensive by resuming bombing near Haiphong and Hanoi. On April 26, Nixon announced a further reduction of U.S. forces to 49,000 and a resumption of public negotiations in Paris. Yet he refused to reduce the bombing that he had ordered to blunt North Vietnam's offensive. The president asserted that the enemy could not win on the battlefield, but only through Congress or through the American people.[40]

When Mansfield returned in early May, he was impressed with China, believing: "the indications are that China is being rebuilt on the basis of a new egalitarianism as exemplified by Chairman Mao's dictum 'serve the people.'" He had long ago shed his fear of Chinese expansionism and predicted: "The new China is preoccupied with peaceful purposes and in particular with the massive problems of feeding, clothing and sheltering and educating 800 million people. Unless provoked, that is likely to remain the preoccupation of the People's Republic for a long time to come."[41] A friendly China removed the original reason for U.S. intervention in Southeast Asia. The Chinese told Mansfield that until U.S. military involvement in Indochina ended, progress could not be made on other issues.[42]

Scott and Mansfield attended a bipartisan leadership meeting on May 8, 1972, immediately after returning to Washington. The president met with the leadership prior to his nationally televised speech. Safire called it as tense a session as he experienced in his four years in the administration. Nixon greeted Mansfield, hoping he was "not too tired—I know how it is. You don't know when to go to the bathroom or when to get up."[43] He then briefed the leaders on the North Vietnamese offensive and Kissinger's frustration at the bargaining table. In order to cut supplies for the communist offensive, Nixon announced his order to bomb the rail lines from China. He also declared his intent to mine Haiphong harbor, a step Johnson always had rejected. Typically, there was no congressional consultation; Nixon merely announced his decision. Nixon ended by requesting: "if you can give me your support, I would appreciate it. If you cannot, I will understand."

As Nixon was leaving the room to address the nation, Mansfield, looking "unusually pale," handed the president his written report on his China trip. Safire recorded that the "usually laconic" Mansfield was visibly incensed. Aiken recalled that Mansfield "was mad and made no bones about it." Mansfield interrupted Admiral Thomas Moorer's opening comments and asked in a trembling voice: "How long ago were these orders issued?"

> MOORER: Today, this afternoon.
>
> MANSFIELD: What it means is that the war is enlarged. It appears to me that we are embarking on a dangerous course. We are courting danger here that could extend the war, increase the number of war prisoners and make peace more difficult to achieve.
>
> LAIRD: As far as extension is concerned, Mike, it was extended by the enemy. It's not fair to charge us with that responsibility.
>
> ROGERS: Compared with bombing Haiphong, this is much more limited wouldn't you say, Admiral?
>
> MOORER: Yes. Mines are a passive weapon.

The debate continued, with Scott and House Minority Leader Gerald Ford (Mich.) defending the administration's decision. Scott stressed that for the first time Nixon agreed to a cease-fire without demanding a withdrawal of North Vietnamese troops from the South—he only demanded the release of POWs.[44] Then, Fulbright moved to the lack of legality for the move:

> FULBRIGHT: I agree with Mike. It seems like an enlargement of the war. There is no longer a Gulf of Tonkin Resolution, and I don't know your justification under the Constitution. You are going to the UN with legal justification of the mining—but what will you tell the American people?
>
> ROGERS: Let's listen to the President.
>
> FULBRIGHT: How about giving us a legal justification?

Rogers was evasive and simply replied: "you know that, Bill. Let's listen to the President now."[45]

Mansfield and Scott had breakfast with the president the next morning to discuss their trip to China. It is not known what was said at the meeting that morning, but later that day, Mansfield condemned both the bombing and mining from the Senate floor, ending his speech: "Mr. President, it does no great nation any harm to admit that a mistake has been made. And sometimes when nations and men will do so, they will be the bigger and better for it."[46]

THE FOURTH MANSFIELD AMENDMENT ON INDOCHINA

One week later, Mansfield reintroduced his amendment to force the president to remove all U.S. forces from Indochina by October 31, 1972. In return, the amendment demanded a release of POWs and recoverable MIAs and a cease-fire enacted between United States and communist forces, South Vietnamese forces were excluded. Mansfield's newest amendment, which cleared the Foreign Relations Committee in June, became the vehicle through which the Senate debated the war that summer. Yet, as Mansfield wrote a citizen, even when the Senate mustered a majority, "the House of Representatives must do likewise."

In July, Mansfield moved the date on his amendment forward to October 1, 1972. The amendment passed on July 24, leading Kissinger to say that the communists only had to wait until "Congress voted us out of the war." Nixon wrote that the Senate was regularly passing measures "to trade a total withdrawal of our troops for the return of our POWs," and the votes in the House were getting closer. The House had "carried the water" for Nixon's foreign policy, but the president believed that he was able to keep a majority in the House only because Vietnamization was reducing American casualties.[47]

A new front in this legislative/executive battle emerged over the Foreign Assistance Authorization bill and Senate amendments attached as riders. Nixon argued in June that such amendments could be "misconstrued by our adversaries to be hostile to my peace proposals." In late July, Nixon sent an additional appeal to the Senate and House leadership, arguing that riders "threaten to delay peace in Vietnam" by removing incentives to negotiate. He claimed the riders threatened the Nixon Doctrine, which he defined as "a new role for the United States, preserving our world interests less by direct involvement and more by supporting the efforts of others." On August 2, the Senate narrowly passed an amendment to a defense procurement bill that authorized funds only for a complete withdrawal of forces from Indochina within four months of its passage, provided that POWs were released. This was the first time the Senate supported binding legislation to end the war. Once again, though, Nixon was insulated from the Senate action because of the results of the House-Senate conference committee.[48]

THE VICE PRESIDENTIAL BID, WATERGATE, AND A FAILED PEACE

With Americans glued to their television sets in 1972 for the president's historic journeys to China and the Soviet Union, the incumbent would prove impossible to defeat. The Democrats' chances of unseating Nixon were weak to begin with, but once long-shot George McGovern wrested the nomination from the Democratic field during the primaries, they were almost non-existent. The McGovern campaign immediately botched the vice presidential selection, assuring a Nixon landslide.

McGovern first asked Edward Kennedy (Mass.), then Gaylord Nelson (Wis.), to be his vice presidential nominee. Both declined. The candidate then turned to Thomas Eagleton (Mo.). Mansfield told McGovern he "couldn't have made a better choice." Then the story of Eagleton's earlier severe depression and electric shock treatment caused him to be dropped from the ticket, and the McGovern campaign never recovered. When asked for his advice, Mansfield cautioned McGovern to keep Eagleton on the ticket. After McGovern decided to drop Eagleton, he asked Mansfield to be his running mate, explaining that "it seemed to me that the Senate Majority Leader would have been a reassuring choice after the divisive chaos of the preceding days." McGovern recalled Mansfield answering that "he would not even consider that. He told me that Lyndon Johnson had tried to persuade him to be his running mate in 1964, but that he had stoutly refused. Mike Mansfield honestly preferred the Senate to the presidency." By the time McGovern selected Sargent Shriver, the damage to his campaign was done.[49]

While doing his part to raise money for his party's candidate, Mansfield typically avoided any stridency. From the Senate, Mansfield cautioned his colleagues to keep the Indochina debate on the issues and not the personalities of the two candidates. In an October draft of a speech, Mansfield included his usual praise and criticism of Nixon, but edited language that he considered too partisan. Such efforts at balance would garner criticism for the Montanan. *Nation* wrote that Mansfield "masquerades as the Democratic leader" and implied that he favored Nixon's reelection, and if that were true, "then he should resign his post as Democratic leader." McGovern thought Mansfield was too easy on Nixon in light of the emerging Watergate scandal.[50]

In the last week of the 1972 presidential campaign, Mansfield made a campaign promise in Missoula that he would ask the Senate to establish a committee to examine the Watergate break-in and other dirty tricks from the campaign, claiming, "it was just plain wrong what happened."[51] Mansfield skillfully avoided giving responsibility for the investigation to James Eastland's (D-Miss.) Judiciary Committee because Eastland was a Nixon partisan. Instead, he created a special committee headed by Sam Ervin (D-N.C.). Nixon feared the Ervin appointment and wrote in his diary: "an indication of the fact that we are going to have a very hard four years is Mansfield's announcement that he wants Ervin's committee to investigate Watergate. Mansfield is going to be deeply and bitterly partisan without question."[52] Ervin turned out to be an effective choice to head the Select Committee.

The year ended badly for Mansfield regarding the war in Vietnam, an issue he cared more about than the presidential election. An October 26 agreement had led Kissinger to declare that "peace is at hand"—just in time for the elections. While Nixon was reelected in a landslide, doves had gained three more Senate seats and the administration faced an increased danger of having funds cut off for the war. Negotiations that started on November 20 to bring that elusive peace reached an impasse on December 14. Mansfield briefly suspended debate, but quickly went on the offensive, threatening "the final conclusion of this war rests either with the President or the Congress." When the administration resumed bombing north of the 20th parallel on December 18, Mansfield exploded, calling the bombing a "Stone Age tactic," and pointing out that bombing had failed for eight years:

> It is long since past time to stop worrying about saving face and concentrate on saving lives and our own sense of decency and humanity. The Senate . . . would be more than willing to give of its advice, counsel, and its full support to the President, to achieve, not through attrition but through negotiation, an end to this tragic war. It is the President's for the asking.[53]

CHAPTER 14

A MISSED OPPORTUNITY
AND THE END OF THE
INDOCHINA WAR

"PEACE WITH HONOR" IN VIETNAM

Congressional Democrats entered the new year in a belligerent mood, threatening to cut off funds if President Richard Nixon failed to quickly end the war in Indochina. Nixon met privately with Majority Leader Mike Mansfield on January 2, 1973, in an effort to lessen the tension with Congress. It is not clear whether Nixon's Christmas bombing was the catalyst, but negotiations with North Vietnam resumed on January 8 and differences were quickly resolved. The peace agreements formally signed in Paris on January 27 were substantially the agreements arrived at in October. Mansfield praised both National Security Advisor Henry Kissinger and President Nixon for the settlement, crediting Nixon's journeys to Beijing and Moscow for laying the foundation for the agreement at Paris. Mansfield argued that the withdrawal of American forces from Vietnam would finally allow for implementation of the Nixon Doctrine. He expanded his interpretation of the doctrine to include the United States "gradually withdraw[ing] militarily from various countries throughout Asia and the world," thus adding troop withdrawals from Europe and Korea to his original interpretation.[1] Mansfield suggested from the Senate: "let us admit our mistakes and learn from the past so that, in remembering, we will never again repeat the mistakes of this tragedy." However, Mansfield was concerned that the peace accords did not apply to Laos or Cambodia.[2]

Made bold by his November landslide, Nixon attacked his congressional opponents. On January 31 Nixon was asked if he had anything "in mind to help heal the wounds in this country." The president's response indicated that he did not: "the least pleasure out of the peace agreement comes from those that were the most outspoken advocates of peace at any price." Barry Goldwater (R-Ariz.) distributed an administration "Vietnam White Paper" in the Senate that claimed: "for four agonizing years Richard Nixon has stood virtually alone in the nation's capital while little, petty men flayed him over American involvement in Indochina. No President has been under more constant and unremitting harassment."[3]

Nixon aides, led by Special Counsel Charles Colson, followed the president's strategy of discrediting war critics. Colson and others referred to the war critics as a "sellout brigade." He told the Public Broadcasting Service, "I think the war would have ended much sooner than it did" had Nixon's critics supported his policy. When pressed for names, Colson included former Secretary of Defense Clark Clifford and Democratic Senators J. William Fulbright (Ark.), George McGovern (S.D.), Frank Church (Idaho), and Edward Kennedy (Mass.).[4] As usual, Mansfield's quiet dissent was viewed as less destructive than that of other war critics.

Typically, Mansfield tried to keep relations harmonious between the Republican executive and Democratic legislative branches. When Hubert Humphrey (D-Minn.) suggested a Democratic response to Nixon's January 20 Inaugural Address, Mansfield responded: "we ought not to attempt a reply to the President at this time. The inauguration is his moment in the spotlight and I see little to be gained in trying to compete with him or by casting the Congress in the role of the opposing gladiator." In late January, Nixon assistant William Timmons thanked Mansfield for his cooperation and promptness in passing an administration-supported resolution to set aside a National Day of Prayer and Thanksgiving for ending the war, and for Mansfield's warm reception of Kissinger when he visited the Senate to discuss the Paris settlement.[5]

Mansfield again helped the administration in early April when South Vietnamese President Nguyen Van Thieu made a controversial visit to the United States. Thieu met with Nixon at the presidential compound in San Clemente, California. Kissinger reported that Thieu was so unpopular in America, however, that only one member of Nixon's cabinet was willing to join Vice President Spiro Agnew for Thieu's arrival ceremony in Washington! Yet Mansfield cohosted a reception with Minority Leader Hugh Scott (Penn.) for the South Vietnamese president, a man for whom Mansfield had little regard.[6]

While Mansfield was preferred to other Senate Democrats, he was not held in high regard by all members of the administration. When Mansfield delivered a speech on China at Johns Hopkins School of Advanced International Study, he sent a copy to Kissinger. Illustrating the administration's contempt for Congress, both J. F. Lehman and Tom Korologos mocked Mansfield for his sharing of his speech. Lehman labeled the speech "trivia," and told Kissinger:

> This is a prime example of the depth of analytic thought obtainable on the Hill. It starts with a simplistic revisionist history of post-war American policy in Asia. It lacks any serious analysis of Sino-Soviet relations omitting in particular any suggestion that Chinese interests in improved relations with the U.S. derives from their concern about Soviet intentions. China is depicted as virtually without a foreign policy. There is no need to reply.

Kissinger did send a brief reply, thanking Mansfield for his thoughtfulness, but he did not comment on the content of the address.[7]

A MISSED OPPORTUNITY IN CAMBODIA

Mansfield quickly shifted his focus from the fragile peace in Vietnam to the continuing conflict in Cambodia. In January 1973, Mansfield again pushed for the return of Prince Norodom Sihanouk, and for Laos to resume independence under King Sri Savang Vatthana. In February a cease-fire was arranged in Laos, but the war continued in Cambodia. Mansfield deplored the administration's bombing of that nation, arguing that Cambodia had been "peripheral" to the Vietnam conflict and that the bombing would lead to more prisoners of war. Moreover, he contended that with the ending of Nixon's need to protect U.S. forces in Vietnam, there was no constitutional justification for bombing. Secretary of State William Rogers claimed to be too busy to appear before the Foreign Relations Committee to explain the legal basis for the administration's bombing. In March, Deputy Assistant Secretary of State William Sullivan callously suggested that "for now, I'd say the justification is the reelection of President Nixon." Rogers finally testified before the committee on April 30 to present the legal justification, one Arthur Schlesinger Jr. concluded was a "feeble argument."[8]

The emerging Watergate scandal was weakening Nixon and providing the impetus for Congress to assert itself. Mansfield became a supporter of legislation to force the end of the Cambodian bombing. On May 2, 1973, the Senate Democratic caucus easily passed a resolution calling for a bombing halt. More important, on May 10 the House, which had always supported Nixon, placed restrictions on the Cambodian bombing. Several days later, Clifford Case (R-N.J.) and Frank Church introduced the Case-Church Amendment to cut off all funding for military involvement in Indochina not authorized by Congress. In late June, an amendment sponsored by Thomas Eagleton (D-Mo.) passed the House, cutting off funds for the Cambodian bombing. Since the Eagleton Amendment was a Senate-passed rider to a supplemental appropriations bill, Nixon could not veto it without cutting off funds to all government agencies. Yet Nixon did veto it, which led Mansfield to say that the amendment would be introduced "again and again and again, until the will of the people prevails."[9]

The White House wanted to avoid a constitutional crisis, so Rogers reached a compromise with Fulbright and the Foreign Relations Committee to end the Cambodian bombing by August 15. Mansfield joined Eagleton, Kennedy, and Edmund Muskie (D-Maine) in opposing the compromise. He argued passionately from the Senate floor:

The warmaking power is that of Congress exclusively, and the war in Cambodia does not have a shred of validity attached to it. It is illegal, it is unconstitutional, it is immoral. Why should we be afraid of a confrontation with the executive branch of this Government? The bombing must stop . . . not on August 15, but now.[10]

The carnage had taken a toll on Mansfield; he had reached the end of his rope. By the summer of 1973, he was more strident than Fulbright and most of his Democratic peers. Although Mansfield was on the losing side of Fulbright's compromise legislation, 64-26, Congress had finally forced an end to America's involvement in the Indochina conflict. Nixon reluctantly signed it into law on July 1. On August 3, 1973, the president wrote Mansfield and Speaker of the House Carl Albert (D-Okla.), comparing the bombing halt to the abandonment of a friend and warning them of dangers to Thailand and other neighboring countries.[11]

Despite his attack on presidential power, Mansfield's friendship with Sihanouk kept him involved in administration discussions about Cambodia. In June 1973, the government in Phnom Penh once again sought Mansfield's support. Prince Sisowath Sirik Matak, Sihanouk's cousin, along with Lon Nol had led the coup to depose Sihanouk; he now wired Mansfield and other members of Congress. Matak claimed genocide was being waged against Cambodians by the Vietcong and North Vietnamese forces who had refused to leave Cambodia despite their agreement to do so in the Paris accords. According to Matak, Vietnam communists wanted to depopulate Cambodia in order to later colonize it. The letter was an appeal to Mansfield for American bombing support in order to preserve the government in Phnom Penh.[12]

The Cambodian ambassador met with Mansfield and Frank Valeo in late June. Mansfield left the meeting early, and Valeo sent Mansfield a memo summarizing what transpired after his departure:

> As for the announced Phnom Penh position to the effect that everything was negotiable "except the return of Sihanouk" that was only a front. Phnom Penh would drop this as soon as there were some indication that Sihanouk was in a position to negotiate and was prepared to negotiate as spokesman for the Resistance.
>
> He acknowledged that the longer negotiations were put off the more difficult it would be for Phnom Penh to stand and the more difficult it would be for Sihanouk or any other non-Khmer-Rouge government to remain in power in Cambodia. He came very close to saying that <u>the sole condition for a settlement, in the last analysis, was some commitment from Sihanouk against reprisals, against persons in Phnom Penh and, secondly, some assurance that Cambodia would not come under the domination of North Vietnam.</u>

Because of his friendship with Sihanouk, the Phnom Penh government wanted Mansfield to serve as an intermediary between Sihanouk and the current government. Valeo told the Cambodian ambassador that Mansfield could not serve in that capacity without the "concurrence of the Executive Branch."[13]

Mansfield wanted to play a role in finding a Cambodian settlement. He immediately wrote Nixon summarizing the meeting with the Cambodian ambassador. The following day, Mansfield sent Kissinger a copy of a Swiss interview with Sihanouk and a film of the prince's visit with the Khmer Rouge forces in Cambodia. Although Mansfield did not ask to be an intermediary, Korologos reported to Kissinger that Mansfield was "dropping broad hints to me that perhaps he would, indeed, like to do something for you, but he is not about to ask." Mansfield made the same point to the *Washington Star-News:* he planned a courtesy call on Sihanouk in Beijing, but "neither Nixon nor Kissinger has approached him about raising substantive issues with the former Cambodian ruler." For his part, Kissinger was negotiating with the Chinese about bringing Sihanouk back to Phnom Penh. Kissinger chose to ignore Mansfield's "broad hints" and continued his own personal diplomacy.[14] In the case of Sihanouk, Kissinger's personal diplomacy could not succeed.

In late July 1973, the Senate Armed Services Committee exposed the 1969-70 secret bombing campaign in Cambodia and the false reports the Pentagon submitted to Congress. The State Department used Mansfield's 1969 conversations with Sihanouk as part of its justification for the bombing, as reported by Oswald Johnston in the *Washington Star-News* on July 25. Sihanouk denied that interpretation to the *New York Times* and Mansfield agreed with Sihanouk, telling Johnston: "I don't recall that in any way, shape or form." On August 8, Joseph Alsop wrote a scathing attack on Mansfield, calling him a "holy idiot" and suggesting that Mansfield could supply the Armed Services Committee with the truth. The truth, as Alsop reported it, was that Sihanouk first told Chester Bowles in 1968 that American bombing would be acceptable and repeated that offer to Mansfield in 1969. President Johnson had not acted on the offer, but Nixon did. Alsop claimed that Nixon gave notice of the secret bombing to the late Richard Russell (D-Ga.) and John Stennis (D-Miss.), the chairman and second-in-command on the Armed Services Committee. According to Alsop, Russell and Stennis agreed with the bombing and saw no need to inform other senators.[15] Thus, Fulbright and the Foreign Relations Committee were ignored and more friendly Democrats advised.

Based partially on the Mansfield/Sihanouk conversations, Rogers had assured several senators and the Foreign Relations Committee that the U.S. bombing of Cambodian sanctuaries "had Sihanouk's tacit support so long as Cambodian lives or property were not in danger." Sihanouk denied Roger's assertion. Mansfield reviewed his notes (recorded by James Lowenstein) and agreed with the prince, recalling Sihanouk as saying: "if the bombs fall where there are no Cambodians how can I know about it, and how can I protest them? But if they fall where there are Cambodians then I know about them and I most certainly protest them." Mansfield recorded:

Insofar as I understood it then and now, there was not in his comment any agreement, actual, tacit or implied, by Sihanouk with the bombing. There was more the complaint that with a pitiful army and difficult terrain what could he do about violations of Cambodian neutrality in remote regions. So I repeat, to the best of my knowledge, there was no concurrence by Sihanouk.

While many claimed Mansfield knew of the secret bombing, the senator denied any knowledge in 1969 of "planned raids," only admitting knowledge of "sorties" mistakenly straying into Cambodia. Moreover, his knowledge of sorties came entirely from media accounts, never from the executive branch. Mansfield claimed: "I have never been told privately or otherwise by anyone in this country, in Cambodia or anywhere else of any planned raids into Cambodia at any time." He added, "the fact that there were over 3,300 planned raids of this nature came as a complete shock to me."[16]

Marshall Wright of the State Department called Mansfield's office to label Alsop's article a "terrible, poisonous piece and we had not a damn thing to do with it and are, in fact, furious about it."[17] Although Alsop could not have uncovered his information without a government source, Wright was probably telling the truth. The White House was the likely source of this anti-Mansfield plant, not the State Department. Once Mansfield denied the administration's Bowles/Mansfield justification for the bombing campaign, the White House needed to get their side of the story out. Alsop was angry with the Democratic Congress for cutting off funds to Cambodia and was "a friend and sometime confidant" of Kissinger. Many of Alsop's peers viewed him "as a high-profile conduit for the government line."[18] In this case, it is likely that Alsop willingly cooperated with Kissinger or someone on his staff.

Mansfield was angry at this administration leak of parts of his private 1969 memorandum to Nixon, believing it to be selective and taken out of context. The leak ignored, for example, his discussion of the need to compensate Cambodians for damage done by these sorties. Mansfield wrote for his files:

> I would suggest, most respectfully, that if we are to quote in part "the content of a cabled report recited by a senior State Department official" classified "secret," it might be well to release to the press and the Senate the full text of the relevant portion of that report which is closer to my recollection of what actually transpired than a paraphrase of a paraphrase.[19]

Apparently Mansfield did not send his complaint to anyone in the administration, nor did he go public with it. In his memoirs Kissinger continued to interpret Sihanouk's 1969 statement to Mansfield as implicit acceptance of U.S. bombing. Yet Kissinger exonerated Mansfield from knowledge of the Menu bombing program, writing that the majority leader "undoubtedly assumed Sihanouk was speaking of accidental bombings."[20] The use of Mansfield's report to justify the bombing continued into the Gerald Ford administration. As late as March 1975, the executive claimed the 1969 bombing was kept secret at Sihanouk's insistence.[21]

After the bombing cut-off, Sihanouk continued to plead his case through Mansfield, rather than directly to the administration. Mansfield might have been able to help Kissinger and Chinese Premier Zhou Enlai persuade Sihanouk to accept the coalition Kissinger claimed he and Zhou favored. Kissinger argued in his memoirs that the coalition government was no longer possible after the bombing cut-off, the Khmer Rouge were destined to win, which caused China to lose interest. William Shawcross believes that Kissinger was the one disinterested in both Sihanouk and negotiation, which is what caused the shift in China's policy.[22]

Nixon, too, blamed the congressional bombing cut-off for the eventual defeat of the Lon Nol government. Yet the settlement Nixon envisioned was not practical. Nixon later argued that the United States could have influenced Lon Nol, that China could "pull the strings" of the Khmer Rouge, and that Sihanouk would listen to Zhou's counsel. The president envisioned Sihanouk accepting a limited role in Lon Nol's government, and argued that the Khmer Rouge would have ceased fighting in return for an end to America's bombing. Once Congress ended the bombing, Nixon's scenario agreed with Kissinger's; the Khmer Rouge had no reason to quit the rebellion.[23] The greatest weakness in Nixon's argument is that it is impossible to imagine Sihanouk serving under Lon Nol, and Nixon was unwilling to force Lon Nol out of government. It is unthinkable to envision the Khmer Rouge ending the rebellion without a capitulation by the government in Phnom Penh. A coalition government without Lon Nol might have equaled that capitulation.

What might have happened had Kissinger taken Mansfield up on his "hints" to negotiate in late July? Sihanouk knew that the Khmer Rouge were using him because of his popularity in the Cambodian rural areas, telling a reporter that the Khmer Rouge "love me. But when they do not need me any more they will simply spit me out." Even knowing his eventual fate with the Khmer Rouge, however, Sihanouk still would not deal with Kissinger. Sihanouk made it clear that he traveled to North Korea in August to avoid meeting Kissinger in Beijing. While in North Korea, Sihanouk cabled his friend Mansfield with a proposal to end the Cambodian civil war. On September 18, Howard K. Smith described Sihanouk as "another opponent of Dr. Kissinger who refuses to meet with him." Sihanouk responded to a question as to why he was so adamant about not seeing Kissinger:

> Kissinger is the number one man responsible for the sufferings of my people. The U.S. invasion in May 1970 was suggested to President Nixon by Kissinger and the bombings, the very heavy bombings, over Cambodia . . . were also suggested to

President Nixon by Mr. Kissinger. So my people and all the fighters of the united front, they consider Kissinger as their number one enemy, and they requested me not to see him.

When asked if he would meet with Mansfield, the prince replied:

> I should be very happy to see him as a personal friend but as a U.S. negotiator, I cannot see him. Why, because he would meet with a failure if he comes to see me. We cannot have a compromise with the traitors in Phnom Penh as the U.S.A. wants us to do.[24]

We will never know whether it was too late for Sihanouk to return to Phnom Penh to perform the "balancing act" he had played so effectively for decades. His hatred of Kissinger and the Nixon administration would not allow him to accept a Chinese/American-created coalition government, even though the government in Phnom Penh seemed willing to accept one. The Nixon/Kissinger loyalty to Lon Nol was one stumbling block, but the Cambodian ambassador made it clear to Mansfield in late June that Lon Nol and his top aides could be replaced. Kissinger's personal diplomacy failed, but it is interesting to speculate on what would have happened if Kissinger had played the Mansfield card.

Mansfield Continues to Seek a Sihanouk Solution

Sihanouk continued to strive to get his case before the American public. The cable he sent Mansfield from North Korea was reported in the *New York Times* several days before Mansfield received it, suggesting that Sihanouk had a larger audience in mind. After reading the report in the *Times*, Mansfield called Kissinger to discuss it and issued a statement urging Nixon to consider Sihanouk's proposals. In the cable, Sihanouk expressed skepticism of Nixon's willingness to cease the bombing. He promised that if the United States suspended the air war and cut off military aid to the Lon Nol government, the Khmer Rouge would forget the past and establish diplomatic relations with America. They would also allow the major "collaborators" in Sihanouk's coup to leave Cambodia, and grant amnesty to those who supported Lon Nol. Since Sihanouk did not believe Nixon would accept these terms, he urged Congress and the American public to force the administration to end its Cambodian interference.[25]

Mansfield discussed Sihanouk with Nixon over breakfast on September 7, 1973. Nixon "was not adversed [sic] to Sihanouk but was concerned about how much power and control he would have."[26] Later in September, Mansfield continued to push his "Sihanouk solution" in a Senate speech on two divergent subjects.

First, he read a translation of his August cable from Sihanouk to the Senate, suggesting that Sihanouk's proposals were "in accord with the realities in Cambodia." Then, Mansfield spoke in favor of Kissinger's nomination to be secretary of state in the wake of Rogers's resignation, calling Kissinger eminently qualified.[27] Mansfield ended his speech with this appeal:

> And I would urge the Secretary of State-designee to consider acting on these proposals of Prince Sihanouk without delay. The war in Cambodia, in my judgment, can be ended promptly via the route of these proposals. In the same stroke . . . we [can] close and bolt the back door to our military reinvolvement in Indochina.[28]

The Mansfield/Sihanouk correspondence continued in late 1973. Mansfield thanked Sihanouk for the North Korean cable and proposals, telling the prince that he "urged a constructive response to them by the Executive Branch." He assured Sihanouk that he was in agreement with the prince about the content of their 1969 conversation concerning U.S. bombing of Cambodia. Sihanouk responded, suggesting a meeting with Mansfield in Beijing. He then launched a tirade against Nixon's policies toward Cambodia. Sihanouk suggested that he would play the role of roving diplomat in a Khmer Rouge government. Penn Nouth, Sihanouk's long-time associate whom Mansfield first met in 1953, would head the proposed government along with several members of the Khmer Rouge.

Mansfield immediately sent copies of Sihanouk's telegram and his own letter to Kissinger, urging the new secretary of state to give the "most immediate and serious consideration" to Sihanouk's proposals. Mansfield responded to Sihanouk in November, telling his friend he shared Sihanouk's cable with Kissinger, praising Penn Nouth, and expressing the hope that Sihanouk's new role in foreign affairs would not deprive the Cambodian people of the inspiration Sihanouk always had provided. Mansfield also sent a copy of this letter to Kissinger.[29] Mansfield worked diligently in 1973 to gain Kissinger's attention and to play a role in a Cambodian solution, but he was ignored.

The French, however, were interested in Mansfield's views. At an October breakfast meeting at French Ambassador Jacques Kosciusko-Morizet's residence, Foreign Minister Michel Jobert asked for Mansfield's views on Sihanouk. Mansfield answered that Sihanouk was

> the only person who could retrieve the situation. Mr. Nixon had begun his Administration with the same view, but then came the aggression in Cambodia in the name of support for our war effort in the Viet Nam war and our too quick move to recognize and come to the aid of the successor government. That government had been overly supported. . . . Now, we were back confronting the reality that Sihanouk offered, possibly, the only way out.

Jobert indicated that Mansfield's views coincided with those of the French, but that they had been unable to determine the position of the Nixon administration. He made it clear that France was "prepared to offer its good offices between Sihanouk and the United States." Indeed, France actively tried to return Sihanouk to Phnom Penh to head a coalition government. Mansfield sent a copy of the notes of this meeting to Kissinger, specifically suggesting that he consider the possibility of taking the French up on their offer.[30] No response was located.

In January 1974, Sihanouk sent two cables to Mansfield. He feared a resumption of U.S. bombing and wanted American aid to the Lon Nol government terminated. Mansfield sent copies of the cables to Nixon and Kissinger, and on January 28, spoke about the cables from the Senate floor:

> There is a deep desire on the part of Prince Sihanouk to once again establish friendly relations with the United States, despite all that has happened, and it would be my strong belief that the best thing this nation could do would be to allow the Cambodian people, themselves, to settle their own differences.[31]

The Cambodian government continued to seek Mansfield's aid, too. Cambodian Ambassador Um Sim met with Valeo in early February. Um Sim was pessimistic about the prospects for the Lon Nol government. Valeo believed that Um Sim recognized "that the only hope—and it is a minimal hope—for himself and others like him—the only hope lies in the return of Sihanouk." Once again, powerful people in Phnom Penh made it clear to Mansfield that Lon Nol could be made to withdraw from government. Um Sim's main concerns were: "what it will take to get Sihanouk to come back (specifically, how deep a purge of the ranks of Phnom Penh's officialdom?)" and "would terms offered by Sihanouk which might be acceptable to Phnom Penh also be approved by the Resistance leaders in Cambodia?" Um Sim wanted Valeo to "solicit Senator Mansfield's intervention in the situation with a view to finding out precisely what Sihanouk would want as a price for Phnom Penh's capitulation." He also wondered if "there was some certainty that Sihanouk could pull off a compromise solution without being disowned by the Resistance leaders?" If Sihanouk could succeed, Um Sim implied that his supporters were "prepared to set the stage for it inside that city." Valeo agreed to share the message with Mansfield and assured Um Sim that Mansfield "would do whatever he could to try to alleviate the suffering of the Cambodian people." Yet Valeo once again made it clear that if Mansfield were to meet Sihanouk in Beijing or contact him in any way, it would be with the knowledge of Kissinger.[32]

It is likely that Mansfield shared this exchange with Kissinger. Since Sihanouk knew that the Khmer Rouge would "spit him out," it seems reasonable that he would have listened to alternatives from his old friend, Mike Mansfield. Yet even though elements in the Cambodian government desired to use Mansfield as an arbitrator, there is no indication that this was ever considered by Nixon or Kissinger. Shawcross believed that successfully returning Sihanouk to Phnom Penh at the head of a coalition government would have been difficult, but possible, had the United States changed its policy of support for Lon Nol.

In 1993 Mansfield indicated that he believed there was a chance at reconciliation between Sihanouk and elements of the Phnom Penh government in early 1974. When asked if he might have succeeded as an intermediary, the senator responded modestly, "who knows?"[33] Kissinger made no serious effort to end the Cambodian war from August 1973 until late 1974, a period in which Mansfield might have proven useful.

After the fall of Phnom Penh, John Gunther Dean, U.S. ambassador to Cambodia, visited Mansfield. Dean, too, had tried to involve Sihanouk in a coalition government. Using the French ambassador to Beijing, Etienne Manac'h, as an intermediary, Ford, Kissinger, and French President d'Estaing made the last effort to bring such a coalition about in December 1974. Such an effort might have borne fruit in 1973 or early 1974, but by the end of 1974, it was too late. Sihanouk had no control over the Khmer Rouge, who knew they would win their revolution.[34]

THE END OF THE NIXON REIGN BRINGS GERALD FORD

Nixon continued to push for military aid for Indochina, appealing to Mansfield in April of 1974 for his support. But Nixon's power was quickly waning, even in the House, which decisively rejected his request to raise the ceiling for military aid to South Vietnam. Mansfield opposed such aid, wanting to see U.S. involvement brought to a complete end.[35]

Watergate replaced Indochina in the headlines throughout 1974. Mansfield viewed the Watergate committee just as he viewed legislation to end the Indochina war: as a necessary reassertion of congressional prerogatives. He believed that the Watergate committee proved that the U.S. system of government worked. Yet Mansfield was appalled by disclosures of illegal activities in the White House.[36]

Valeo suggested that Mansfield developed concern for Nixon's stability as the pressures of Watergate took their toll, and that he tried not to upset Nixon "in any way." Representative Thomas (Tip) O'Neill (D-Mass.) shared Mansfield's concern about Nixon's mental stability. After Nixon behaved strangely at a meeting with House leaders in October 1973, O'Neill called Mansfield and said: "we're coming down the home stretch. The President isn't going to be around too much longer. But I'm worried about him. Is anybody over there watching to make sure he doesn't put his finger on the button?" Mansfield replied: "don't worry about it. We've got [Alexander] Haig [national security council staff], and he's running the show right now." When asked to verify O'Neill's account, Mansfield stated that it was "essentially correct."[37]

There is no evidence of any closeness in the Mansfield/Ford relationship before Ford's elevation to the vice presidency. Most likely due to the damage done by Nixon's taping, the Ford administration did not keep detailed records of meetings. Thus, Mansfield's conversations with Ford largely remain a mystery. As leaders in their respective Houses, Ford and Mansfield certainly had contact over the years, but Ford had not been deeply involved in the issues surrounding Indochina. When he took an interest, he was more hawkish than Mansfield.

Both men were motivated to get the nation back on track after the Watergate derailment and the long involvement in Indochina. That fact, combined with Mansfield's deep respect for the office, led him to bend over backward to cooperate with the new president. For his part, Ford embraced bipartisan consultation as Nixon never had. Shortly after taking office, Ford wrote Mansfield that "your counsel and advice has been welcomed by three Presidents. As the fourth President, I look forward to a working partnership." Valeo believed that Ford and Mansfield became friends. Mansfield described his relationships with both Ford and Kissinger as personally excellent and said that they consulted him frequently on foreign policy issues.[38]

MANSFIELD'S 1974 TRIP TO CHINA

Mansfield had started discussing a second visit to China with the Nixon administration in fall 1972.[39] The Chinese stalled on the visit, and in the summer of 1973 Mansfield speculated: "in consultation with Sihanouk, therefore, the Chinese might very well be waiting for the dust to settle to see what develops in the aftermath of the bombing halt."[40] Shortly thereafter, Tom Korologos wrote Kissinger: "every time I see Mike, he brings up his China visit."[41]

When Ford assumed office, Mansfield shifted his campaign to the new president. In October, Mansfield wrote Ford: "Chinese officials have been amenable to the proposal from the outset, although the problem of timing has presented difficulties until recently." Ford helped Mansfield arrange the visit, urging the majority leader to "emphasize the continuity" of the new administration's China policy.[42]

The Mansfield party entered China on December 9 and departed on the 30th. Mansfield was briefed by Ambassador George Bush, had a one-hour meeting with Premier Zhou Enlai, and had lengthy meetings with other Chinese officials. The end of U.S. fighting in Indochina had eased tensions between China and the United States, but China still found the American presence "messy." This was especially true in Cambodia, where U.S. insistence to include the Lon Nol government in a coalition was viewed as unrealistic. It is not clear why, but Mansfield did not meet with Sihanouk on this visit. Mansfield discussed his visit with Ford and submitted a confidential report to him.[43]

THE FALL OF SAIGON

President Ford inherited a deteriorating military situation in Indochina. His administration spent the first four months of 1975 trying to win congressional acquiescence to release the amount of appropriated military aid for Indochina. Mansfield opposed administration efforts to obtain military aid while supporting humanitarian help.[44]

The Ford administration was willing to gamble that a visit to Indochina would convince members of Congress to increase aid to South Vietnam. Knowing Mansfield's weakness for travel to Asia, the administration dangled a trip to Vietnam before Mansfield and Robert Byrd (D-W.Va.). Kissinger wanted the visit to be sponsored by congressional leadership. As in 1969, Mansfield had no desire to visit Vietnam. Republican and Democratic leaders in the House and Senate refused to sponsor the trip, claiming they had enough information about the situation. Congress was no longer willing to trust administration interpretations of the condition of Indochina. The Foreign Relations Committee had sent Chuck Meisner and Dick Moose to Vietnam[45] and they were horrified by what they found: "the situation had deteriorated greater than anybody in Washington thought." After Fulbright lost his Senate seat in 1974, Meisner and Moose talked directly to Mansfield about their findings. The committee continued to oppose even financial involvement in Indochina.[46]

However, the administration was able to send several members of Congress to Vietnam in late February without the sponsorship of the leadership. Members followed independent programs and were given great latitude to travel. The group met with Ambassador Graham Martin and then with President Thieu on February 27. They asked Thieu tough questions dealing with the treatment of the opposition and of journalists, as well as the need for increased aid.[47] The administration's hope to gain support in Congress through this fact-finding trip failed.

On April 7, Mansfield said he wanted to avoid "pointing the finger" and personally assumed part of the blame for U.S. Indochina policy. He wanted cooperation between branches and parties. His conciliatory tone led to a phone call from Ford to try to gain his support for more aid to save South Vietnam and Cambodia, an appeal the president made to a joint session of Congress on April 10. Ford requested $722 million in military aid and $250 million for humanitarian assistance. Mansfield meant what he said about cooperation, but he was not willing to lengthen the commitment to what he considered a lost cause; he did not support this new request.[48]

The majority leader received appeals from Vietnamese who opposed increased aid and from those who favored it. Two of the former, South Vietnamese Generals Kahn and Ty, visited Valeo on April 18. Both believed that North Vietnam and the National Liberation Front would accept a coalition government in order to obtain American reconstruction aid, but they made it clear that Thieu must be replaced by a "third force." At the same time, South Vietnamese government officials were prodding Mansfield to support military aid to South Vietnam.[49]

With South Vietnam's demise so near, old friends from the "Vietnam Lobby" of the 1950s emerged from the woodwork. Joseph Buttinger wrote Mansfield in 1975, still hoping to salvage a non-communist South Vietnam. Buttinger believed that North Vietnam could be made to live up to the terms of the Paris agreements and would wait several years while "progressive leaders" (not Thieu) in the South could salvage the situation. Of course, American aid was crucial for this scenario to successfully unfold. Buttinger wanted to meet with Mansfield and hoped to testify before the Foreign Relations Committee. Valeo's note on the letter indicated there would be no reply.

Another of the old school, Wesley Fishel, wrote an article for the *Virginia Quarterly Review* in which he claimed a legal justification for two Vietnams. Fishel, too, argued for "strong and respected leadership," which seemed to exclude Thieu. Valeo summarized Fishel's article for Mansfield: "it sounds as though he just arrived in Saigon after a twenty-year lapse, discovered for the first time that the key to the problem lies with the Vietnamese themselves and is ready to start all over again." Earlier, Edward Lansdale had proposed a Vietnam divided in thirds, with the center ruled by a coalition government.[50]

As the situation became more desperate, Mansfield monitored the evacuation efforts in Saigon through the State Department. Initially, he believed the administration was dragging its feet on getting U.S. citizens out of Saigon. Mansfield feared that the evacuation would lead to military reinvolvement in Vietnam, questioning the need for an evacuation bill to provide money for that purpose. On April 29 the White House called him to report the need for a total evacuation of Saigon. Later that day, they telephoned to tell him that the evacuation was complete. The following day, Mansfield spoke in the Senate, praising both Congress and Ford for their cooperation, with veiled criticism of Nixon: "In the end, it took the cooperation of the President and the Congress to bring about a termination. It came, finally, because Congress was unwilling to give the executive branch a blank check in providing the closeout funds. To be sure, it was late."[51]

THE FALL OF PHNOM PENH AND THE *MAYAGUEZ*

The military situation in Cambodia at the start of 1975 was even bleaker than that in South Vietnam. Representative Paul McCloskey Jr. (R-Calif.) made a side trip to Phnom Penh on the congressional visit to South Vietnam and was appalled at the human suffering he found:

> If I could have found the military or State Department leader who has been the architect of this policy, my instinct would be to string him up. Why they are there and what they have done to the country is greater evil than we have done to any country in the world, and wholly without reason, except for our benefit to fight against the Vietnamese.[52]

Shortly after McCloskey's observation, Kissinger wrote Mansfield and other members of Congress with a list of U.S. efforts to negotiate a settlement in Cambodia, in order to justify administration requests for more funding. The State Department's list showed that few efforts were made in 1973 and early 1974, and those listed were vague. For example, one justification read: "throughout the negotiations that led to the Paris Agreement on Viet-Nam in January 1973, the United States repeatedly indicated its desire to see a ceasefire and political settlement in Cambodia." Another listing placed the blame squarely on Congress: "a number of major efforts toward negotiation were made in 1973, efforts which were thwarted by the forced bombing halt in August of that year." Kissinger's list showed more serious efforts were made in late 1974 and early 1975, but the list was disingenuous even then. For example, it stated: "in December 1974 and early January 1975, we concurred in an initiative to open a dialogue with Sihanouk in Beijing. Sihanouk at first agreed to receive an emissary, but later refused." In reality, that proposal was made by France and Kissinger's staff erred, causing Sihanouk to back out.[53]

Um Sim came to see Mansfield on March 11, to report on his recent visit to Cambodia. He reiterated the willingness of Lon Nol and other leaders to step down. Lon Nol, he claimed, "was probably prepared even to go to Peking [Beijing] to ask Sihanouk to return." What the government "needed to know was what would happen if and when they departed." In two instances where the government had tried to contact Sihanouk, "the State Department had discouraged Phnom Penh from proceeding, apparently on the grounds that the contacts would be ineffectual." Um Sim prophetically predicted that if Congress did not pass the aid bill, Cambodia would fall in a month or two. The ambassador pleaded for Mansfield to contact Sihanouk to see what would happen after Lon Nol's government left Cambodia. Again, Mansfield told him he could not do that unless requested to do so by Ford or Kissinger: "a self-generated role of intermediary would be incompatible with [Mansfield's] view of the division of powers in our Government."[54]

Mansfield wanted the opportunity to try to salvage the situation. In an undated memo that was likely spurred by the Um Sim visit, Valeo listed preconditions that Mansfield should get from Ford and Kissinger before accepting a visit to Beijing to talk with Sihanouk: Ford should specifically request the trip; Sihanouk should agree in advance to receive Mansfield and do so on behalf of the Khmer Rouge; the government in Phnom Penh should agree to the trip; and the main objective of the trip should be to end the war and prevent a "bloodbath." If Ford desired, Mansfield would open discussions with China on the joint-preservation of Cambodia's sovereignty and territorial integrity.[55]

Mansfield's final effort to mediate apparently ended with Valeo's memo. But it was too late in March 1975. Kissinger never showed any interest in utilizing Mansfield's credibility with Sihanouk in this cause. Mansfield's contacts with Sihanouk continued, but via cable, which showed why Kissinger's personal diplomacy had not succeeded with Sihanouk. In two undated telegrams to Mansfield, Sihanouk launched scathing, rambling tirades against U.S. policy that decried American involvement in the overthrow of Chilean President Salvador Allende and continued U.S. aid to the Lon Nol government. They also personally attacked Kissinger.

On April 7 Sihanouk warned Mansfield of the dangers of Ford's sending Marines to help with the evacuation of Phnom Penh, and asked him to share the warning with Congress. Mansfield had reached the same conclusion on the Marines when the White House called him on April 3 to announce their use in the evacuation. Mansfield responded that he was a "little bit leery of use of marines. Ought to be plenty of time to get out." He shared Sihanouk's April 7 cable with the White House. There were press rumors that Sihanouk offered peace negotiations in this cable, but the White House correctly concluded that Sihanouk used the telegram to warn the United States about using the evacuation as a pretext for reinvolving American military forces. That did not happen, and Phnom Penh fell to the Khmer Rouge on April 17.[56]

On May 12 Khmer Rouge forces seized the U.S. merchant ship *Mayaguez* in the Gulf of Siam. Ford ordered military operations to rescue the crewmen and met with the leadership to explain his action. Mansfield worried that the bombing raids on Kompong Som and Ream could endanger the *Mayaguez* crew, but also feared new military action in Indochina. Further, Ford had not consulted Congress as called for in the War Powers Act. Thirty-nine seamen were rescued, but thirty-eight Marines died in the effort.[57] The *Mayaguez* incident ended U.S. military involvement in Indochina.

At Mansfield's June 2, 1975 meeting with John Gunther Dean, the former ambassador said "it was a 'poor hand' which he had to play in Cambodia from the beginning." Mansfield responded, "yes, from the moment of Sihanouk's

overthrow and the United States invasion over the border." Valeo's notes indicated no comment from Dean, but the ambassador "felt that Senator Mansfield
had been right in contending all along that Sihanouk was the critical figure."
After Dean left, Valeo commented that perhaps the United States had learned
that it could not become involved in every crisis that occurred in the world.
Mansfield replied, "I wonder if, in fact, it has been learned."[58]

EPILOGUE

THE REMAINDER OF MANSFIELD'S CAREER

M ansfield did not lose interest in Indochina after the end of the second Indochina War. He kept in touch with Sihanouk[1] and attempted to visit Laos and Cambodia during the 1975 congressional recess. Although the Ford administration dissuaded him from doing so in 1975, Mansfield visited Laos when the Senate recessed again in 1976, and once again visited China.[2] Mansfield wrote to Sihanouk before his trip, attempting to gain an invitation to visit Cambodia. No response to Mansfield's letter was located, and the senator did not visit there. When Mansfield heard nothing about Sihanouk for the next year, he tried to find out if Sihanouk was still alive.[3] In 1992, Sihanouk returned to power in an international attempt to restore order to that hapless nation for the first time since 1970.

The Montanan always believed in Sihanouk and never changed his mind, writing in 1990:

> I think that Sihanouk has been one of the shrewdest heads of state in South-east Asia. My friendship / relationship with him was based not only on personal respect for each other, but because he has always placed the interest of Cambodia before anything else and has done so consistently down through the decades.[4]

Before embarking on his 1976 Southeast Asia tour, Mansfield announced that he would not seek a fifth term. Jimmy Carter became president with Mansfield's retirement. Carter was pressured to find a suitable position in his new administration for the popular former majority leader. Carter offered Mansfield the post of ambassador to Mexico, but Mansfield declined. In 1977, Mansfield accepted his eighth and final trip to Indochina under a sixth president.[5] Leonard Woodcock, head of the United Auto Workers, was appointed to lead the group that was sent to Hanoi to seek an accounting of Americans missing in action and to begin to rebuild U.S.-Vietnamese relations. The group also visited Laos, but was turned down in its effort to stop in Cambodia.[6] The trip was not successful.

The normalization of relations with Vietnam that President Carter had hoped to achieve would not begin until 1993 under President Bill Clinton.

One week after the Woodcock mission returned from Indochina, Carter appointed Mansfield ambassador to Japan. In this capacity, Mansfield would twice more meet with Sihanouk, who reemerged in 1978 when the Khmer Rouge found his appeal with the Khmer people useful. With the Cambodian war against Vietnam going badly, Sihanouk was seen as a symbol of unity and national resolve.[7]

When Ronald Reagan defeated Carter in 1980, Mansfield asked Gerald Ford to intervene with Reagan to keep him in Tokyo. Ford did intervene, and Mansfield went on to serve a record twelve years in Japan, retiring at the end of the Reagan presidency. Both Carter and Reagan have stated that having Mike Mansfield serve in Tokyo was the only thing on which they ever agreed.[8] After his tenure in Tokyo, Mansfield returned to the private sector for the first time since his days in Butte.

In 1993, to mark his 90th birthday, the ambassador tolerated separate toasts in his honor by Senate Democrats and Republicans, and acceded to an interview by the *Washington Post*. Characteristically, he disliked the "fuss being made over him." Mansfield said of his birthday, "I'm not going to celebrate it. I'm going to endure it." The *Post* concluded that "Mansfield embodies a career untouched by scandal or deviousness, and remarkably free of personal ambition." Mansfield planned "not to write his memoirs or cooperate in any oral history project on his life and times. 'I think historians will tell the truth 50 years, 100 years from now, when they write. And if you write too soon, you make too many mistakes, writing your own stuff.'"[9] Unlike the other major American players in the Vietnam drama—Eisenhower, Johnson, Rusk, McNamara, Kissinger, Nixon, and Fulbright to name a few—Mansfield never told, and has no intention of telling, his side of the story.

SUMMARY AND CONCLUSIONS

At the time of his Senate retirement, Mansfield said that the war in Southeast Asia was his greatest disappointment, adding: "I did everything I could up here to stop it. More times than I care to remember, I was the only voice to say 'no.' It wasn't easy but I felt I had to do it. The whole war was unnecessary, unwarranted, and uncalled for."[10] Even he must wonder how those historians writing 50 or 100 years from now will view his role. In 1972 Mansfield predicted:

> History may well record that we pursued the correct foreign policies into the early 1960s; that we bought time, through containment and counterforce, to permit the gradual moderation of Communist power, thereby reducing the Marxist

states to the political dimensions of other nations. However that may be, it has been apparent for some time that we persisted in these policies too long. We were blind to changes and to the possibilities of adjusting to mutual interest. In the end, we came to the disaster of Viet Nam. It is part of the price which has been exacted for the obstinate pursuit of the obsolete in foreign policy.[11]

Michael J. Mansfield was one of the first U.S. politicians of the 1950s to recognize the errors caused by the cold war and McCarthyism. Stanley Karnow concluded that Mansfield had "the acuity and courage to change his mind."[12] Mansfield was, above all, adaptable. He came to realize that America's belief in a "*non-existent* monolithic Soviet-Chinese bloc, led directly to the Vietnam war, the worst and most tragic foreign policy failure in American history."[13]

Senator Mansfield has been largely forgotten, which likely has pleased him. Yet no other public official had such a lengthy involvement with America's entanglement in Indochina. For the most part, Mansfield was on the periphery, never in the center of the decision-making loop. Some books about decision-making in the Vietnam era do not even mention him. Yet his views were clearly articulated to five presidents.

Mansfield's reputation as an internationalist served him well in the House during the 1940s. But in 1952 he barely survived the closest and most vicious election campaign of his life to earn a Senate seat. Mansfield was able to adapt to the new conditions of the cold war. After being charged with losing China by Montana Republicans and Senator Joseph R. McCarthy (R-Wis.), the first-term senator resolved not to lose all of Indochina to communist encroachment. The rookie senator became a student of the region, finding little competition for the position of Senate expert on Indochina. He became a protagonist in the Vietnam Lobby, an informal group of prominent Americans who pressured the Eisenhower administration to support Vietnamese nationalist Ngo Dinh Diem. Mansfield's 1954 report after a visit to Vietnam helped to win U.S. support for Diem. When the Eisenhower administration was poised to purge Diem in April 1955, Mansfield successfully fought to retain him.

With the election of his friend, John F. Kennedy, to the presidency, Mansfield adapted to the shift in party leadership and to his new position as majority leader. From that potentially powerful position, Mansfield became a quiet critic, arguing against escalation in private, but supporting Kennedy's policy in his public pronouncements. The Montanan's party position and friendship with Kennedy compromised his independent role as a senator. The compromise was felt most acutely when the administration decided to purge Diem in order to escalate the role of the American military in the conflict. While the Eisenhower administration feared that Mansfield had the power to cut off aid to South Vietnam if Diem were purged, no such concern was expressed by Kennedy's advisors.

With the ascension of his mentor, Lyndon B. Johnson, to the presidency, Mansfield continued his difficult battle of balancing his personal conscience with his responsibility as party leader. He was able to adapt to those competing responsibilities through his rhetorical strategy of private dissent and public support. On three different occasions during 1964 and 1965, when Johnson announced escalation decisions, Mansfield was the only person to speak in opposition. Yet Mansfield refused to break with Johnson. Former Senator Edmund Muskie (D-Maine) explained that a public fight with Johnson "wasn't Mike's way. He tried, in his own quiet way."[14] As Paul Kattenburg put it, Mansfield tried "repeatedly in a highly dignified but firm manner to change the president's mind."[15] After Johnson committed ground troops in July 1965, Mansfield spent the rest of Johnson's tenure trying to find a formula to bring the contestants to the conference table.

Mansfield's ultimate rhetorical adaptation came with the election of Richard M. Nixon. With a Republican in the White House, Mansfield was no longer constrained by his elected Senate position. Yet he still attempted to give President Nixon time to meet his election pledge of bringing the war to a speedy conclusion. By late 1969, however, Mansfield began to break with Nixon. When the president invaded Cambodia in April 1970, the breach was complete. Mansfield adapted to this new escalation by changing his life-long belief in executive supremacy in foreign affairs. The majority leader decided that the war must be ended in the Senate, and he successfully worked to bring an end to the war through congressional action.

It would be easy to fault Mansfield's quiet criticism during the Vietnam conflict. Former Senator Eugene McCarthy argued that the Senate itself "failed pretty badly in taking responsibility for challenging the escalation of the war," adding "I never thought Mike did as much as he should have in challenging involvement in Vietnam."[16] A citizen wrote Mansfield expressing the frustration that the anti-war movement felt with his quiet style:

> When the history of the Great Indochina War is written, I believe your incredibly patient *civility,* your optimistic sanguinity, your politesse about Death and Genocide, will be cited as one major reason why 2 Administrations were able to destroy Southeast Asia and Asians . . . and were so capable of sundering apart our American society.[17] [Emphasis added.]

Kissinger expressed the flip-side of this letter in assessing Mansfield's rhetorical style, calling him

> one of the small band of patriots who have made our maddeningly delicate system of checks and balances actually work. He was a passionate opponent of the war in

Southeast Asia. But his opposition, while fierce, never passed the bounds of *civility* and comity that are so vital to a democracy.[18] [Emphasis added.]

"Civility" is an accurate description of Mansfield that has both positive and negative connotations. In truth, Mansfield's personal philosophy allowed no other approach. Many, including Mansfield, considered his persuasive efforts to have failed. In reality, Congress lacked the power, or at least the will, to change an executive commitment to fight in Vietnam based on what William Conrad Gibbons called the "post World War II consensual pattern of executive-legislative relationships."[19] Time and circumstances returned that will to Congress. Members of Congress who were more vociferous than Mansfield were not more successful in influencing the Johnson or Nixon administrations.

Mansfield's great strength was in his ability to adapt to changed circumstances. He was unique in that he was one of a small handful of officials in Eisenhower's first term who helped to commit the United States to the creation of a non-communist South Vietnam, and yet he consistently opposed the broadening of that commitment to include U.S. forces. Mansfield's crucial decision after Nixon's 1970 Cambodian incursion helped to alter the nation's direction. He concluded that if the executive would not end the war, it must be done by the legislature. While Mansfield would not use his position as leader to pressure colleagues toward that end, he did throw his own considerable credibility into the battle in the Senate, introducing his own amendments and supporting the amendments of others. Mansfield's credibility on this issue was enhanced because of his renowned "civility" and previous restraint. Senate legislation was constantly watered down by the House, but with Watergate weakening the executive branch, the House eventually joined the Senate to reassert congressional prerogatives and force an end to the conflict in Indochina. Mansfield's constant pressure played a vital role in bringing about that end.

Some indicted Mansfield for his slowness in moving to utilize congressional power over the purse, for his quiet criticism, for his initial support for Diem, and for other aspects of his role in the Indochina conflict. Interestingly, the areas in which Mansfield is most vulnerable to criticism deal more with his style than with his positions. What was admirable about Mansfield was the diligence with which he pursued his goals. The drawerful of memos about which Johnson complained illustrated a considerable investment of time, work and thought by Mansfield. He offered each president from Eisenhower through Ford an alternative path in Indochina. It is hardly Mansfield's fault that his advice was usually disregarded. Had Johnson or Nixon taken the path Mansfield offered, the eventual outcome might well have been less destructive.

Even if Mansfield's style could be regarded as a weakness, it was also one of his greatest strengths. It accounted for his being listened to when more vocal war critics had been discounted. Had Mansfield chosen a more bellicose approach, his views would likely have been considered with less attention and respect. Senators who followed other strategies were not more successful. Wayne Morse (D-Ore.) and Ernest Gruening (D-Alaska) may have been right, but their views were never treated seriously. Johnson and Nixon could write off Fulbright, the Chairman of Foreign Relations, but not the majority leader. Mansfield's accommodating style and restrained rhetoric had at least as much to do with his access to power as his position. He *was* listened to at the White House. Both Johnson and Nixon were cognizant of his frequently expressed opinions. Mansfield's disapproval may have helped to moderate some of the decisions Johnson and Nixon made. That cannot be conclusively demonstrated, but Mansfield did help to lead Congress to a reassertion of its constitutional power and an eventual end to an undeclared and mistaken war.

ENDNOTES

INTRODUCTION

1. Stanley Karnow, *Vietnam* (New York: Penguin, 1984), 611-12.
2. Mansfield, "Cambodia and a New China," memorandum for the files, 11 May 1970, MP, XXII, 103, #5.
3. Mansfield, "The Meaning of the Term 'Advice and Consent,'" *The Annals of the American Academy,* September 1953, 132-33.
4. "'A Time to Go,'" *Newsweek,* 15 March 1976, 30.
5. As quoted in Lester Thonssen and A. Craig Baird, *Speech Criticism: The Development of Standards for Rhetorical Appraisal* (New York: Ronald Press, 1948), 58-59.
6. Townsend Hoopes, *The Devil and John Foster Dulles* (Boston: Atlantic, Little, Brown & Co., 1973), 253-57.
7. John Finney, "Retiring Senate Leader," *New York Times,* 5 March 1976, 12.
8. As quoted in Paul Healy, "Mansfield of Montana," *Saturday Evening Post,* October 1974, 89.

CHAPTER 1

1. Mansfield, letter to the author, 14 April 1987. See also Charles Hood, "'China Mike' Mansfield: The Making of a Congressional Authority on the Far East" (Ph.D. diss., Washington State University, 1980), 45-50.
2. Hood, "'China Mike,'" 64-112.
3. As quoted in P. Healy, "Mansfield of Montana," 12. See also Hood, "'China Mike,'" 109-12.
4. Hood, "'China Mike,'" 113-22.
5. As quoted in Hood, "'China Mike,'" 130-36.
6. Ibid., 137-38. See also Mansfield, letter to the author, 28 July 1986; Mansfield, letter to the author, 14 April 1987.

7. Hood, "'China Mike,'" 142-50.
8. As quoted in James Schwartz, "Senator Michael J. Mansfield and United States Military Disengagement from Europe" (Ph.D. diss., University of North Carolina, 1977), 284. See also Hood, "'China Mike,'" 155-64.
9. Mansfield, "American Diplomatic Relations with Korea, 1866-1910" (Master's Thesis, University of Montana, 1934), 13, 29, 57, 81. See also Hood, "'China Mike,'" 169-72.
10. Hood, "'China Mike,'" 179-80, 182, 184, 172-76, 178.
11. As quoted in "When Is a Majority a Majority," *Time*, 20 March 1964, 24.
12. As quoted in Hood, " 181-82, 185, 187.
13. Ibid., 188-89.
14. Ibid., 190-91.
15. Ellis Waldron, *An Atlas of Montana Politics since 1864* (Missoula: University of Montana Press, 1958), 285. See also Donald Spritzer, *Senator James E. Murray and the Limits of Post-War Liberalism* (New York: Garland Publishing, 1985), 36, 41, 57; Elizabeth Wheeler Colman, *Mrs. Wheeler Goes to Washington* (Helena, Montana: Falcon Press, 1989), 170-71; Hood, "'China Mike,'" 195-98.
16. As quoted in Leif Erickson, letter to Mansfield, 27 July 1942, MP, XIV, 3, #1. See also Waldron, *An Atlas of Montana Politics,* 302; Hood, "'China Mike,'" 198-200.
17. As quoted in Hood, "'China Mike,'" 203-6, 298-99.
18. Mansfield, "What Are We Going to Do about the Pacific?" NBC radio address, 30 April 1943, 1, MP, XXI, 36, #12. See also Hood, "'China Mike,'" 209-10, 217-21.
19. Mansfield, "Pacific Danger," CBS radio address, 25 January 1944, 2-3, MP, XXI, 36, #15. See also Hood, "'China Mike,'" 221.
20. Mansfield, "What Are We Going to Do about the Pacific?" NBC radio address, 30 April 1943, 4-5, MP, XXI, 36, #12.
21. As quoted in Hood, "'China Mike,'" 183, 216-17, 300. See also Francis Valeo, interview with the author, Washington, D.C., 17 May 1991.
22. As quoted in P. Healy, "Mansfield of Montana," 11. See also Hood, "'China Mike,'" 213-14, 222-25.
23. *Congressional Record,* 16 January 1945, 277-83. See also Hood, "'China Mike,'" 242, 244-89, 300-1, 328.
24. Medford Evans, "Mr. Mansfield," *American Opinion,* October 1970, 27.
25. *FRUS, 1945, The Far East, China* (Washington, D.C.: GPO, 1969), 7:162-63. See also Hood, "'China Mike,'" 290-91, 331.
26. Maurice McDonough, letter to Mansfield, 7 June 1945 / McDonough, letter to Mansfield, 23 August 1945 / Mansfield, letter to McDonough, 30 August 1945 / Harry Cloke, letter to Mansfield, 13 April 1946 / Mansfield, letter to Cloke, 16 April 1946 / W. G. Dunlap, letter to Mansfield, 20 August 1945 / Mansfield, letter to Dunlap, 28 August 1945, MP, XIV, 5, #8. See also Hood, "'China Mike,'" 230-31, 325.
27. Waldron, *An Atlas of Montana Politics,* 308. See also Schwartz, "Senator Michael J. Mansfield," 304-5; Hood, "'China Mike,'" 222, 227, 241.
28. As quoted in Hood, "'China Mike,'" 12-15, 303, 317.

29. As quoted in Hood, "'China Mike,'" 353.

30. Mansfield, letter to Harry Truman, 17 January 1947, MP, XXII, 113, #10. See also Hood, "'China Mike,'" 349-52.

31. Hood, "'China Mike,'" 349.

32. "Biographical Sketch," *New York Times,* 5 January 1958, IV, 5. See also Eugene J. Kraszewski, "Senator Mike Mansfield and the Origins of American Involvement in the Second Indochina War," Seminar Paper, Cornell University, 1974, 3, MP.

33. Vaughn Davis Bornet, *The Presidency of Lyndon B. Johnson* (Lawrence: University Press of Kansas, 1983), 67.

34. Richard Reeves, *President Kennedy: Profile of Power* (New York: Simon & Schuster, 1993), 442.

35. Schwartz, "Senator Michael J. Mansfield," 319. See also Hood, "'China Mike,'" 16.

36. William Healy, "Montana's Senator Mike," *Sign,* May 1953, 10.

37. See John Forsythe, letter to Mansfield, 9 November 1950 / Mansfield, letter to Forsythe, 15 November 1950, MP, XIV, 23, #13 and MP, XIV, 11, #20 for general information on the 1950 election. See also Waldron, *An Atlas of Montana Politics,* 318, 328, 338; Schwartz, "Senator Michael J. Mansfield," 305-14.

38. As quoted in "Political Advertisement," *Montana Standard* [Butte], 3 November 1952, Mansfield scrapbooks, #10, MP; Colman, *Mrs. Wheeler goes to Washington,* 161-72, 218-25. See also Burton Wheeler with Paul Healy, *Yankee from the West* (Garden City, New York: Doubleday, 1962), 403-9, 413-14; Leif Erickson, interview with Donald Spritzer, 26 August 1976, Mansfield Oral History Project, #7, 9-15, 26-27, MP; Spritzer, *Senator James E. Murray,* 41, 56-57, 76-79, 153; Schwartz, "Senator Michael J. Mansfield," 314-15; T. D., letter to Mansfield, 27 September 1951, MP, XIV, 15, #19.

39. W. Healy, "Montana's Senator Mike," 11. See also Schwartz, "Senator Michael J. Mansfield," 315; "Political Advertisements," 1952 election, Mansfield scrapbooks, #10, MP; Mrs. John Brockus, "Attacks Mike Mansfield on Communist Issue, 1952," Mansfield Oral History Project, 22-196, MP; Mansfield, 1952 campaign speeches, MP, XXI, 36, #64, #66, #67, #69, #70; O. Edmund Clubb, letter to Mansfield, 5 May 1953 / Mansfield, "Memo: 1952 Campaign," MP, XIV, 23, #13.

40. "Senator McCarthy Plugs for Ecton's Election," *Montana Standard* [Butte], 15 October 1952, Mansfield scrapbooks, #10, MP.

41. U.S. Senate, 1st sess., Subcommittee to Investigate the Administration of the Internal Security Act and Other Internal Security Laws, Committee on the Judiciary, *Strategy and Tactics of World Communism: The Significance of the Matusow Case* (Washington, D.C.: GPO, 1955), 1068-69.

42. Harvey Matusow, *False Witness* (New York: Cameron & Kahn, 1981), 166-70. See also Jim Ludwick, "Mansfield: The Senator from Montana" [pamphlet], *Missoulian* [Montana], n.d. [1988], 9; "Matusow Tells of Taking Over $1,000 to Wrongly Denounce Mansfield," *Great Falls Tribune,* 22 February 1955, Mansfield scrapbooks, #13, MP; Schwartz, "Senator Michael J. Mansfield," 316-17.

43. Mansfield, "Campaign Final Speech, 1952," 1, 3, 5, 6 / Mansfield, "Cong. Mansfield, 1952," 1, 5 / Mansfield, "Typed Speech of Cong. Mansfield, 1952," 4, 10, MP, XXI,

36, #64. See also Waldron, *An Atlas of Montana Politics,* 358; Schwartz, "Senator Michael J. Mansfield," 318.

44. As quoted in Grace Lichtenstein, "'Senator Mike' Tours Montana to Say a Political Farewell," *New York Times,* 2 November 1976, 49.

45. Mansfield, "Memo," n.d., MP, XIV, 23, #13.

46. "Matusow Declares He Apologized," *Great Falls Tribune,* 16 February 1955; Mansfield scrapbooks, #13, MP.

CHAPTER 2

1. As quoted in William Conrad Gibbons, *The U.S. Government and the Vietnam War,* Part 1 (Princeton: Princeton University Press, 1986), 52. See also Mansfield, "Lecture notes on Indo-China," n.d., MP, IV, 6; Mansfield, "The Foreign Policy of the United States," 30 June 1951, MP, XXI, 36, #58; Mansfield, "International Policy," 1950-52?, MP, XXI, 36, #67.

2. Robert Scheer, *How the United States Got Involved in Vietnam* (Santa Barbara: Center for the Study of Democratic Institutions, 1965), 33. See also James Arnold, *The First Domino* (New York: William Morrow & Co., 1991), 20; Gibbons, *The U.S. Government and the Vietnam War*, Part 1, 264, 313.

3. John Montgomery, *The Politics of Foreign Aid* (New York: Praeger, 1962), 221.

4. In 1993 Mansfield claimed: "I did not know that Senator Murray was interested in being Majority [Minority] Leader. If I had known, I would have given him my vote" (letter to the author, 2 June 1993).

5. Rowland Evans and Robert Novak, *Lyndon B. Johnson: The Exercise of Power* (New York: The New American Library, 1966), 52-53. See also Mansfield, interview with Seth Tillman, 23 June 1964, 1, JFK Oral History Project, JFK Library; Ross Baker, "Mike Mansfield and the Birth of the Modern Senate," in Richard Baker and Roger Davidson, eds., *First Among Equals: Outstanding Senate Leaders of the Twentieth Century* (Washington, D.C.: Congressional Quarterly, Inc., 1991), 269.

6. Hubert Humphrey, *The Education of a Public Man*, Norman Sherman, ed. (Minneapolis: University of Minnesota Press, 1991), 133.

7. Bobby Baker with Larry King, *Wheeling and Dealing* (New York: W.W. Norton & Co., 1978), 64-65. See also Evans and Novak, *Lyndon B. Johnson*, 63-64.

8. *Congressional Record,* 18 June 1953, 6806; *Congressional Record,* 3 August 1953, 11042.

9. Mansfield, interview with Tillman, 23 June 1964, 45. J. William Fulbright complained to Carl Marcy in the late 1950s: "when [JFK] comes to the [Foreign Relations] Committee meetings, what does he do? He sits down at the front of the table autographing posters of himself." While a member of the House, Kennedy's absenteeism was legendary (Carl Marcy, Oral History Interview, Senate Historical Office, Washington, D.C., 1983, 124-25; Lawrence O'Brien, interview with Michael Gillette, 29 October 1985, 102, LBJ Oral History Project, LBJ Library).

10. See for example William Proxmire, letter to the author, 10 June 1988, 1.

11. *ESSFRC*, 1953 (Washington, D.C.: GPO, 1977), 5:122-37, 298-307.

12. Mansfield, memo, 19 February 1953, MP, XIII, 7, #5.

13. John Cooney, *The American Pope* (New York: Times Books, 1984), 240-41.

14. Ellen Hammer, *A Death in November* (New York: E.P. Dutton, 1987), 49. See also Marvin Gettleman, et al., eds., *Vietnam and America: A Documented History* (New York: Grove Press, 1985), 119; Scheer, *How the United States Got Involved in Vietnam*, 14-15.

15. Gibbons, *The U.S. Government and the Vietnam War*, Part 1, 93, 135. See also Thomas Boettcher, *Vietnam: The Valor and the Sorrow* (Boston: Little, Brown & Co., 1985), 107-9; David Halberstam, *The Best and the Brightest* (New York: Random House, 1972), 147; O'Brien, interview with Gillette, 29 October 1985, 83-84; Denis Warner, *Certain Victory: How Hanoi Won the War* (Kansas City: Sheed Andrews and McMeel, Inc., 1978), 101.

16. William O. Douglas, *North from Malaya* (New York: Doubleday, 1952), 180-81, 185-87. For development of Diem's background see Hammer, *A Death in November*, 47-49; Arnold, *The First Domino*, 222-23; Cecil Currey, *Edward Lansdale: The Unquiet American* (Boston: Houghton Mifflin, 1988), 150; Frederick Nolting Jr., *From Trust to Tragedy* (New York: Praeger, 1988), 2; George McT. Kahin, *Intervention* (New York: Alfred A. Knopf, 1986), 78-80; "The Beleaguered Man," *Time*, 4 April 1955, 22-25; Karnow, *Vietnam* (1984), 144, 213-19; J. Lawton Collins, *Lightning Joe* (Baton Rouge: Louisiana State University Press, 1979), 388; Robert Shaplen, *The Lost Revolution*, rev. (New York: Harper & Row, 1966), 106; David Anderson, *Trapped By Success: The Eisenhower Administration and Vietnam, 1953-1961* (New York: Columbia University Press, 1991), 11-12.

17. William O. Douglas, interview with John Stewart, 9 November 1967, 15, JFK Oral History Project, JFK Library.

18. *FRUS, 1952-1954, Indochina*, Part 1 (Washington, D.C.: GPO, 1982), 13:553-54.

19. John F. Kennedy, letter to John Foster Dulles, 7 May 1953, pre-presidential papers, Box 481, JFK Library.

20. Douglas, *North from Malaya*, 180-81, 185-87.

21. As quoted in Michael Charlton and Anthony Moncrieff, *Many Reasons Why: The American Involvement in Vietnam* (New York: Hill and Wang, 1978), 54.

22. Boettcher, *Vietnam*, 107-9.

23. Nguyen-Thai, letter to Mansfield [plus the article from *The Shield*], 17 March 1954 / Mansfield, letter to Nguyen-Thai, 19 March 1954, MP, XIII, 8, #1.

24. Valeo, interview with the author, Washington, D.C., 17 May 1991. Valeo first met Mansfield in 1947 while working for the Legislative Reference Service in the Library of Congress. Mansfield used the service to learn about Asia, and Valeo was assigned to research Mansfield's requests. By 1953 Valeo was often on loan to the Foreign Relations Committee and he accompanied Mansfield on all three of his 1950s visits to Indochina. After Mansfield's Senate reelection in 1958, Valeo, who was then working for the Foreign Relations Committee, accepted the senator's offer to join his

staff as assistant to the majority whip. Valeo replaced Bobby Baker as secretary to the majority leader in September 1963. He served as secretary to the majority for the next three years, and was then elected secretary to the Senate and served until 1977 (Francis Valeo, letter to the author, 20 February 1990).

25. Transcript of "Meet the Press," 12 July 1953, NBC Television, 2, 8, DDE Library.

26. *Congressional Record,* 30 June 1953, 7644-47; *Congressional Record,* 1 July 1953, 7767-69. See also "The Disenchanted," *Newsweek,* 13 July 1953, 20-21.

27. Mansfield, "Statement of Senator Mike Mansfield," 28 July 1953, MP, XIII, 10, #3.

28. *Congressional Record,* 29 July 1953, 10234-35; *Congressional Record,* 1 July 1953, 7779-89. See also Gibbons, *The U.S. Government and the Vietnam War,* Part 1, 129-35; Memorandum for the Secretary / Memorandum of conversation with the President, 27 July 1953, JFD, White House memoranda, Box #1, DDE Library.

29. William White, "Mansfield to Make Indo-China Inquiry," *New York Times,* 16 September 1953, 1.

30. "Revised Itinerary" for Mansfield and Valeo and locations of various foreign correspondents, MP, XXII, 95, #1.

31. Mansfield, St. Patrick's Day—1965 speech to the Irish Fellowship Club, Chicago, 4, MP, XXII, 75; Mansfield, "The Western Pacific Perspective and Prospective," San Francisco, 25 May 1967, 13, MP, XXII, 76 #1967.

32. Valeo, interview with the author, Washington, D.C., 17 May 1991. See also Mansfield, "Presentation of Laotian Khenes to the Library of Congress," 23 November 1954, MP, XIII, 7, #9.

33. *FRUS, 1952-1954, Indochina,* Part 1, 13:809-10, 824-26. See also Gibbons, *The U.S. Government and the Vietnam War,* Part 1, 143-44 .

34. Mansfield, *Indochina: Report on a Study Mission to the Associated States of Indochina, Vietnam, Cambodia, Laos,* U.S. 83d Cong., 1st sess., S. Rept. (Washington, D.C.: GPO, 1953), iii, 1-8.

35. *ESSFRC,* 1954 (Washington, D.C.: GPO, 1977), 6:46-53. See also Gibbons, *The U.S. Government and the Vietnam War,* Part 1, 145.

36. Douglas MacArthur II, letter to Mansfield, 2 November 1953 / Livingston Merchant, letter to Mansfield, 17 November 1953 / Frederick Nolting Jr., letter to Mansfield, 24 November 1953, MP, XIII, 6, #1.

37. Gibbons, *The U.S. Government and the Vietnam War,* Part 1, 137, 144-45.

38. Volney Hurd, letter to Mansfield, 1 December 1953, MP, XIII, 6.

39. Mansfield, letter to Hurd, 4 December 1953 / Arnaud de Borchgrave, letter to Mansfield, 4 December 1953 / de Borchgrave, letter to Mansfield, 22 December 1953 / de Borchgrave, Copy of 4 December 1953 cable to *Newsweek* / Mansfield, letter to de Borchgrave, 8 December 1953, MP, XIII, 6.

40. As quoted in Warner, *Certain Victory,* 95-96.

41. Mansfield, "Indo-China Crisis," 8 February 1954, MP, XIII, 37, #18. See also "How Deep Into Indochina? Eisenhower, Knowland Answer," *U.S. News & World Report,* 19 February 1954, 62. Democrats, including Mansfield, had been upset by Dulles's January 12 speech in which he announced the administration's doctrine that came to be called "massive retaliation." The doctrine had not been discussed with Congress.

Mansfield was sensitive to Eisenhower's lack of congressional consultation when sending Air Force technicians to Vietnam, because it seemed to indicate an emerging pattern (see John Foster Dulles, "Foreign Policies and National Security," *Vital Speeches of the Day,* 1 February 1954, 232-35; "Dulles Sets Goal of Instant Rebuff to Stop Aggressor," *New York Times,* 13 January 1954, 1).

42. *ESSFRC,* 1954, 6:115, 141-45. A hint at why the administration favored a Catholic leader in Vietnam emerges from the National Security Council meeting of February 4. Allen Dulles, director of the CIA, said what was "disheartening was the evidence that the majority of people in Vietnam supported the Vietminh rebels. There was no dynamism in the leadership of the Franco-Vietnamese forces." Eisenhower interrupted to inquire if it would be possible to take advantage of the religious issue. Understanding that a majority of the population in Vietnam were Buddhists, "the President asked whether it was possible to find a good Buddhist leader to whip up some real fervor. . . . It was pointed out to the President that, unhappily, Buddha was a pacifist rather than a fighter," which led to laughter (*FRUS, 1952-1954, Indochina,* Part 1, 13:1014).

43. *ESSFRC,* 1954, 6:154-84. See also *FRUS, 1952-1954, Indochina,* Part 1, 13:1074-75.

44. Hurd, letter to Mansfield, 21 February 1954 / Hurd, letter to Mansfield, 25 February 1954 / Hurd, letter to Mansfield, 2 March 1954 / Hurd, letter to Mansfield, 29 March 1954 / Mansfield, letter to Hurd, 25 February 1954 / Mansfield, letter to Hurd, 17 March 1954, MP, XIII, 6.

45. Mansfield, memo, Indo-China, 18 March 1954 / Mansfield, "Geneva and Indo-China," 22 March 1954, MP, XIII, 7, #5. See also William vanden Heuvel, letter to Mansfield, 8 March 1954 / Mansfield, letter to vanden Heuvel, 23 March 1954, MP, XIII, 6, #2.

46. Mansfield, letter to vanden Heuvel, 23 March 1954 / Dowling, letter to Mansfield, 1 April 1954, MP, XIII, #6.

47. de Borchgrave, letter to Mansfield, 2 April 1954 / Larry Allen, letter to Mansfield, 23 March 1954 / Allen, letter to Mansfield, 31 March 1954 / Allen, letter to Mansfield, 5 May 1954 / Allen, letter to Mansfield, 26 May 1954 / Mansfield, letter to Allen, 14 May 1954, MP, XIII, #6.

48. *Congressional Record,* 6 April 1954, 4676-77.

49. Catholic politicians in the 1950s were aware that religion could prove limiting, and such a realization undoubtedly helped to form a personal bond between Mansfield and Kennedy. When Mansfield sent Kennedy a letter after his failed 1956 vice presidential bid, for example, Kennedy responded that "'canonical' impediments might have been too much to carry this year" (Mansfield, letter to Kennedy, 24 August 1956 / Kennedy, letter to Mansfield, postmarked 8 September 1956, MP, XVIII, 18, #7).

50. Kennedy, letter to Mansfield, 7 April 1954, MP, XIII, 6, #2; Mansfield, interview with Tillman, 23 June 1964, 1.

51. Mansfield, "Last Chance in Indochina," press release, rough draft, n.d. and unlabeled, MP, XIII, 6, #2; Mansfield notes, n.d. and unlabeled, MP, XIII, 37, #28; Mansfield, "Geneva: Failure of a Policy," 8 July 1954, 23, MP, XIII, 37, #39. See also Gibbons, *The U.S. Government and the Vietnam War,* Part 1, 208-9.

52. Mansfield, letter to de Borchgrave, 14 April 1954 / Mansfield, letter to vanden Heuvel, 15 April 1954 / Mansfield, letter to Hurd, 14 April 1954, MP, XIII, 6. See also Chester Bowles, letter to Mansfield, n.d. / Hurd, letter to Mansfield, 22 April 1954 / vanden Heuvel, letter to Mansfield, 21 April 1954, MP, XIII, 6.

53. Hurd, letter to Mansfield, 18 April 1954, MP, XIII, 6; Hurd, letter to Mansfield, 12 May 1954, MP, XIII, 7. See also Mansfield, letter to Hurd, 23 April 1954, MP, XIII, 6; Mansfield, "Indochina Massacre," 23 April 1954, MP, XIII, 7.

54. *FRUS, 1952-1954, Indochina*, Part 1, 13:1538-40. Valeo disagrees with Sturm's account, remembering the discussion being about sending a group of U.S. military personnel ostensibly to inventory U.S. military equipment, but secretly to train the Vietnamese military (Valeo, interview with the author, Washington, D.C., 17 May 1991). Even Valeo's recollection shows a departure from Mansfield's non-interventionist position.

55. The dates June 25 and July 7 are also listed as Diem's date of arrival in various sources (Currey, *Edward Lansdale*, 149, 376).

56. Wilfred Burchett, *The Furtive War: The United States in Vietnam and Laos* (New York: International Publishers, 1963), 84. See also D. Anderson, *Trapped By Success*, 51-52.

57. As quoted in Charlton and Moncrieff, *Many Reasons Why*, 55; Dulles to J. Lawton Collins, 20 April 1955, JFD Papers, Subject Series, Box 9, Folder 1, Collins Papers, DDE Library. See also Edward Lansdale, *In the Midst of Wars* (New York: Harper & Row, 1972), 155; Joseph Alsop, interview with Richard Challener, 4 March 1966, 10 / G. Frederick Reinhardt, interview with Philip Crowl, 30 October 1965, 10-11, John Foster Dulles Oral History Project, Princeton University Library.

58. vanden Heuvel, letter to Mansfield, 17 June 1954, MP, XIII, 6.

59. Mansfield, "Geneva: Failure of a Policy," 3, 4, 7-8, 10-14, 17-24, 30, 36-37, MP, XIII, 37, #39; Mansfield, unlabeled notes, MP, XIII, 7, #3.

60. Gibbons, *The U.S. Government and the Vietnam War*, Part 1, 245.

61. Dulles to Nixon, 9 July 1954, JFD Papers, Telephone Call Series, Box 2, Folder 5, DDE Library. See also Gibbons, *The U.S. Government and the Vietnam War*, Part 1, 253; Lloyd Gardner, *Approaching Vietnam* (New York: W.W. Norton, 1988), 309. Mansfield regretted his uncharacteristically harsh rhetoric. He prefaced an August speech by discussing "matters of conscience," admitting that "in the heat of debate on the Indochina issue, some of us may have slipped momentarily into partisanship." Mansfield claimed that the Republicans had done the same over the loss of China and he did not want the election of 1954 to resemble the one in 1952. Mansfield reiterated his view of executive dominance in matters of foreign policy, a position he frequently articulated during his career (see Mansfield, "After Geneva: American Policy— Germany and Japan," 1-5, 16, MP, XIII, 37, #41).

62. Karnow, *Vietnam* (1984), 198-99. In his memoirs, Johnson writes that he was surprised to be selected for the Indochina phase of the Geneva Conference since he "knew comparatively little about Indochina." Johnson recalled discovering "when I returned to Washington that this did not automatically disqualify me, since none of my State Department colleagues seemed to have any clear notion of what we could

hope to get out of the conference, and I did not hear of anyone competing for my job" (U. Alexis Johnson, with Jef Olivarius McAllister, *The Right Hand of Power* [Englewood Cliffs: Prentice-Hall, 1984], 202, 204).

63. Statement by the President, 21 July 1954, JFD Papers, Subject Series, Box 9, Folder 3, DDE Library; U. A. Johnson, *The Right Hand of Power*, 215-20, 224-25.

64. Karnow, *Vietnam* (1984), 200-5. See also Kahin, *Intervention*, 52-65; Gibbons, *The U.S. Government and the Vietnam War*, Part 1, 250-56; Marianna Sullivan, *France's Vietnam Policy* (Wesport: Greenwood Press, 1978), 49, 52.

CHAPTER 3

1. See Gregory Olson, "Eisenhower and the Indochina Problem," in *Eisenhower's War of Words: Rhetoric and Leadership,* Martin J. Medhurst, ed. (East Lansing: Michigan State University Press, 1994), 108-9.

2. John Foster Dulles Papers, Telephone Call Series, 13-20 August 1954, Box 2, Folder 1, DDE Library.

3. Anna Kasten Nelson, "John Foster Dulles and the Bipartisan Congress," *Political Science Quarterly* 102 (1987): 49. See also Eleanor Lansing Dulles, *John Foster Dulles: The Last Year* (New York: Harcourt, Brace & World, 1963), 192; Ernest Lindley, "Bipartisan Progress," *Newsweek,* 18 October 1954, 36.

4. See for example Mansfield and Knowland, "The Leading Question," CBS transcript, 2-5, 12, MP, XIII, 7.

5. Valeo, interview with the author, Washington, D.C., 17 May 1991. Mansfield's increased credibility with Dulles was demonstrated when Dulles met with Eisenhower about a mutual security treaty with Nationalist China. Dulles wanted to touch bases with Senate leaders, including Mansfield. Mansfield was the only first-term senator on the list and the Montanan did not hold any leadership post (see Dulles, memorandum of conference with the President, 18 October 1954 / Dulles, memorandum of conversation, 30 October 1954, JFD, White House Memoranda, Box 1, Folder 1, DDE Library).

6. Mansfield, interview with Richard Challener, 10 May 1966, 2, John Foster Dulles Oral History Project, Princeton University Library. See also "Dulles Taking Mansfield as Advisor," *Great Falls Tribune,* 21 August 1954, Mansfield scrapbooks, #12, MP; Gibbons, *The U.S. Government and the Vietnam War*, Part 1, 273; Lindley, "Bipartisan Progress," 36.

7. *ESSFRC,* 1955 (Washington, D.C.: GPO, 1978), 7:5, 15-16, 18, 52. See also Gibbons, *The U.S. Government and the Vietnam War*, Part 1, 272, 275.

8. *ESSFRC,* 1955, 7:12-13. See also *FRUS, 1952-1954, East Asia and the Pacific,* Part 1 (Washington, D.C.: GPO, 1984), 12:847.

9. Dean Rusk as told to Richard Rusk, Daniel Papp, ed., *As I Saw It* (New York: W.W. Norton, 1990), 420, 427, 549; Gibbons, *The U.S. Government and the Vietnam War*, Part 1, 272-73.

10. Mansfield, *Report on Indochina,* U.S. 83rd Cong., 2d sess., S. Rept. (Washington, D.C.: GPO, 15 October 1954), iii, 2. See also Valeo, letter to the author, 20 February 1990.

11. Mansfield, summary of meeting with Guy La Chambre, 27 August 1954 / Mansfield, summary of meeting with C. Douglas Dillon, 28 August 1954, MP, XXII, 95, #2.

12. Mansfield, summary of meeting with Penn Nouth, 1 September 1954 / Mansfield, summary of meeting with Tep Phan, 1 September 1954, MP, XXII, 95, #2. See also Karnow, *Vietnam* (1984), 589.

13. Mansfield, *Report on Indochina,* 12.

14. See for example Mansfield, summary of meeting with Jim Lucas, 30 August 1954 / Mansfield, summary of meeting with Bob Johnson, 31 August 1954 / Mansfield, summary of meeting with Parsons and Ed Sessions, 31 August 1954 / Mansfield, summary of meeting with Donald Heath and John O'Daniel, 10 September 1954, MP, XXII, 95, #2.

15. Bernard Fall, "The Political-Religious Sects of Vietnam," *Pacific Affairs,* September 1955, 235-50. See also Peter Schmid, "Free Indo-China Fights against Time," *Commentary,* January 1955, 23-27; Currey, *Edward Lansdale,* 152; D. Anderson, *Trapped By Success,* 48-49; Lansdale, *In the Midst of Wars,* 171; Arnold, *The First Domino,* 233.

16. *FRUS, 1952-1954, Indochina,* Part 2 (Washington, D.C.: GPO, 1982), 13:1977-80, 1985-91, 1999-2003, 2007-10, 2012-16, 2018-21, 2028-30.

17. Mansfield, summary of meeting with Heath, 2 September 1954 / Mansfield, summary of meeting with M. Bordaz, 2 September 1954 / Mansfield, summary of meeting with Diem, 2 September 1954 / Mansfield, summary of meeting with Tran, 2 September 1954, MP, XXII, 95, #2. See also *FRUS, 1952-1954, Indochina,* Part 2, 13:2001-3.

18. It is not clear who Everett was. Most of his report to Valeo was on the "FOA" (Foreign Operation Administration), and he may have worked for that agency. Fishel was an advisor to Diem and an important figure in U.S. relations with Diem throughout the 1950s. A member of the Michigan State University political science department, Fishel first met Diem in Japan in 1950. He is credited with persuading Diem to come to the United States in 1951. Professor Fishel started the chain that led to Mansfield's meeting Diem by introducing Diem to Cardinal Spellman. Spellman, in turn, introduced Diem to Justice Douglas who hosted the May 1953 luncheon where Mansfield first came to know Diem. Fishel later headed the MSU group that worked for the State Department and CIA from 1956-1962 to improve the efficiency and strength of the Diem government. He became Diem's most trusted non-family advisor. In the late 1950s, one MSU professor described Fishel as a "proconsul" to Diem, and Fishel became the most powerful American in South Vietnam (See Valeo, interview with the author, Washington, D.C., 17 May 1991; Warren Hinkle, Sol Stern, and Robert Scheer, "The University on the Make," *Ramparts,* April 1966, 14-17; Gibbons, *The U.S. Government and the Vietnam War,* Part 1, 90, 264, 313; Currey, *Edward Lansdale,* 150.

19. Summary of meeting with Paul Everett, 4 September 1954 / Summary of meeting with Wesley Fishel, 4 September 1954, MP, XXII, 95, #2.

20. Summary of meeting with La Chambre, 8 September 1954, MP, XXII, 95, #2. See also *FRUS, 1952-1954, Indochina,* Part 2, 13:2009, 2012-13.

21. Both the characters Colonel Hillandale, the hero in the book *The Ugly American,* and Alden Pyle, the villain in Graham Greene's novel *The Quiet American,* were said to be modeled on Lansdale. As late as 1991, Oliver Stone based the character "General Y" in his movie *JFK* on Lansdale. Lansdale arrived in Vietnam shortly before Diem came to power and the French immediately disliked him, giving him the nicknames "Boy Scout" and "Lawrence of Indochina." Mansfield and Lansdale were involved with Indochina for many years and Lansdale's biographer referred to them as "old friends" by 1965. However, this was denied by Mansfield, who suggested that the 1954 meeting was the only one they had in Vietnam, that it lasted only 30-45 minutes and "we did not learn much from each other" (Mansfield, letter to the author, 2 June 1993; Gibbons, *The U.S. Government and the Vietnam War,* Part 1, 141; Currey, *Edward Lansdale,* 291; Richard Corliss, "Who Killed J.F.K.?" *Time,* 23 December 1991, 70).

22. Mansfield, summary of meetings with Lansdale and Meloy, 11 September 1954, MP, XXII, 95, #2.

23. Assistant Secretary of State Robertson, "Rough Draft" of a message to Senator Mansfield, n.d. [1954], MP, XXII, 95, #2.

24. As quoted in Shaplen, *The Lost Revolution,* 118.

25. Mansfield, message sent September 24, 1954, MP, XXII, 95, #2. See also *FRUS, 1952-1954, Indochina,* Part 2, 13:2055-56.

26. Faure-Ely-La Chambre Talks, 26 September 1954, 4, Collins Papers, Box 24, #6, DDE Library. See also *FRUS, 1952-1954, Indochina,* Part 2, 13:2069, 2144; Montgomery, *The Politics of Foreign Aid,* 222.

27. Hammer, *A Death in November,* 58-61.

28. Mansfield, *Report on Indochina,* 11, 14.

29. D. Anderson, *Trapped by Success,* 83.

30. Chester Cooper, *The Lost Crusade* (New York: Dodd, Mead & Co., 1970), 134. When asked if he agreed with Cooper's claim, Mansfield wrote, "I do not know whether Mr. Cooper was correct or not" (letter to the author, 1 February 1990).

31. *FRUS, 1952-1954, Indochina,* Part 2, 13:2159-60. See also "Eisenhower Asks Vietnam Reform," *New York Times,* 25 October 1954, 1; Dulles to embassies, 18 August 1954, Collins Papers, Box 24, Folder 3, DDE Library; Victor Bator, *Vietnam: A Diplomatic Tragedy* (Dobbs Ferry, New York: Oceana, 1965), 183; Hoopes, *The Devil and John Foster Dulles,* 253; Boettcher, *Vietnam,* 107-9; Gibbons, *The U.S. Government and the Vietnam War,* Part 1, 285-87.

32. Valeo, letter to the author, 20 February 1990.

33. Bator, *Vietnam,* 183-84.

34. *FRUS, 1952-1954, Indochina,* Part 2, 13:2142, 2165, 2182, 2214, 2266. See also Mansfield, letter to the author, 11 August 1994.

35. Dulles, letter to Mansfield, 23 August 1954, JFDP, Subject Series, Box 9, DDE Library.

36. Gibbons, *The U.S. Government and the Vietnam War,* Part 1, 285.

37. Mansfield, interview with Challener, 10 May 1966, 1-2, 4-5, 9-11, 15-17.

38. Michael Gravel, ed., *Pentagon Papers* (Boston: Beacon Press, 1971), 1:222-23. See also *FRUS, 1952-1954, Indochina,* Part 2, 13:2145; Gibbons, *The U.S. Government and the Vietnam War,* Part 1, 284.

39. Mansfield, *Report on Indochina,* 4-10.

40. Valeo, letter to the author, 20 February 1990. See also Secret Summary Record of Meeting at American Embassy, Saigon, Viet Nam, 30 November 1962, 38, MP, XXII, 95, #13; Neil Sheehan, *A Bright Shining Lie* (New York: Random House, 1988), 141.

41. Mansfield, "American Foreign Policy in the Far East," Carroll College, Helena, Montana, 22 May 1955, 12-13, MP, XIII, 37, #61. See also Mansfield, summary of meeting with Jacques Compain, 11 September 1954, MP, XXII, 95, #2.

42. Mansfield, letter to James Dudley Jr., 26 November 1954, MP, XIII, 8, #1.

43. As quoted in Scheer, *How the United States Got Involved in Vietnam,* 26-29. See also Cooney, *The American Pope,* 242-43; Thomas A. Dooley Jr., "Delivering the Refugees," in *A Symposium on America's Stake in Vietnam* (New York: American Friends of Vietnam, 1956), 36-41; Thomas A. Dooley Jr., *Deliver Us from Evil: The Story of Viet Nam's Flight to Freedom* (New York: Farrar, Staus & Cudahy, 1956).

44. Ken Post, *Revolution, Socialism and Nationalism in Viet Nam* (Belmont, Calif.: Wadsworth, 1989), 1:224. See also Currey, *Edward Lansdale,* 156-64; Gibbons, *The U.S. Government and the Vietnam War,* Part 1, 257.

45. Kahin, *Intervention,* 75-77, 479. See also Karnow, *Vietnam* (1984), 222; Gibbons, *The U.S. Government and the Vietnam War,* Part 1, 265; Sheehan, *A Bright Shining Lie,* 137; Minutes of Cabinet Meeting, 13 August 1954, Ann Whitman File, Cabinet Series, Box 3, DDE Library; Mansfield, *Report on Indochina,* 9.

46. Lansdale estimates that 400,000 northerners were intimidated not to move south. The Vietminh countered American propaganda, claiming that men traveling south in American ships would be thrown overboard and women sold into prostitution. The Vietminh also encouraged many loyalists to remain in the south for the expected 1956 elections. Estimates on the number of refugees moving from the south to the north range from 90,000-150,000 (Lansdale, *In the Midst of Wars,* 155; Arnold, *The First Domino,* 244; Scheer, *How the United States Got Involved in Vietnam,* 26).

47. Schmid, "Free Indo-China Fights against Time," 24-26. See also Joseph Harnett, "Refugee Resettlement," in *A Symposium on America's Stake in Vietnam,* 42-43; Graham Greene, "Last Act in Indo-China," *New Republic,* 9 May 1955, 10-11; Fall, "The Political-Religious Sects of Vietnam," 235, 243; Karnow, *Vietnam* (1984), 58-59.

48. Sheehan, *A Bright Shining Lie,* 143-144. See also U. A. Johnson, *The Right Hand of Power,* 207; John Mecklin, *Mission in Torment* (Garden City, New York: Doubleday, 1965), 159.

49. Mansfield, "Mike Mansfield Report," October 1954, 5, MP, XIII, 6, #7. See also Secret Summary Record of Meeting at American Embassy, Saigon, Viet Nam, 30 November 1962, 46, MP, XXII, 95, #13.

50. Collins, *Lightning Joe,* 393-94.

51. Dulles to embassies, 6 April 1955, Collins Papers, Box 26, Folder 2, DDE Library.

52. *FRUS, 1952-1954, Indochina,* Part 2, 13:2198-99. See also Collins, *Lightning Joe,* 411; Arnold, *The First Domino,* 249.

53. Briefing Book on Vietnam, 3, Collins Papers, Box 24, #3, DDE Library.

54. As quoted in W. C. Gilbert, trans., *Le Figaro,* 15 October 1954, MP, XIII, 7, #6 and Robert Scigliano, *South Vietnam: Nation Under Stress* (Boston: Houghton Mifflin, 1963), 207. See also Collins, *Lightning Joe,* 385-86; Currey, *Edward Lansdale,* 167.

55. As quoted in Collins, *Lightning Joe,* 383; Collins, telegram to Dulles, 15 November 1954, Collins Papers, Box 25, #2, DDE Library.

56. Collins, *Lightning Joe,* 390-91; Collins, Accomplishments, "Appointment of Dr. Quat as Minister of Defense," n.d., Collins Papers, Box 25, DDE Library.

57. Collins, telegram to Dulles, 6 December 1954, 3-4, Collins Papers, Box 25, #3, DDE Library.

58. *United States-Vietnam Relations, 1945-1967,* Book 10 (Washington, D.C.: GPO, 1971), 806-8.

59. *FRUS, 1952-1954, Indochina,* Part 2, 13:2378-79, 2398. See also D. Anderson, *Trapped By Success,* 83.

60. *FRUS, 1955-1957, Vietnam* (Washington, D.C.: GPO, 1985), 1:2.

61. *FRUS, 1952-1954, Indochina,* Part 2, 13:2393-94. See also Collins, telegram to Paris, 16 December 1954, Collins Papers, Box 25, #3, DDE Library.

62. *FRUS, 1952-1954, Indochina,* Part 2, 13:2400-3.

63. *United States-Vietnam Relations, 1945-1967,* Book 10, 853-55.

CHAPTER 4

1. As quoted in "Struggle Weird in South Vietnam," *New York Times,* 29 April 1955, 3.

2. As quoted in Arnold, *The First Domino,* 260.

3. *United States-Vietnam Relations, 1945-1967,* Book 10, 865-78. See also Collins, *Lightning Joe,* 396-97.

4. *ESSFRC,* 1955, 7:402.

5. Mansfield, letter to Allen, 25 January 1955, MP, XIII, 8, #6.

6. Mansfield, letter to Diem, 13 January 1955, MP, XIII, 8, #1.

7. Unsigned note, Official File series of the WHCF, "OF 181-C Indo-China," DDE Library.

8. Mansfield, letter to the author, postmarked 6 June 1991.

9. Valeo, interview with the author, Washington, D.C., 17 May 1991.

10. Douglas Allen and Ngo Vinh Long consider Fishel, Lansdale, Spellman, Douglas, Joseph Buttinger and such "liberal anti-Communist Democrats" as Mansfield and John Kennedy to have been the influential members of the Vietnam Lobby (Douglas Allen and Ngo Vinh Long, eds., *Coming to Terms: Indochina, the United States and the War* [Boulder: Westview, 1991], 245-46). They could have included Joseph Kennedy, Leo Cherne, Harold Oram, and Congressman Walter Judd (R-Minn.). The

Vietnam Lobby was not a formal group; Mansfield had little contact with any of its members except John Kennedy. Rather, these were powerful men who successfully prodded the Eisenhower administration to support Diem.

11. Robert Scheer and Warren Hinckle, "The 'Vietnam Lobby,'" *Ramparts,* July 1965, 19. See also Gibbons, *The U.S. Government and the Vietnam War,* Part 1, 302-3.

12. Scheer and Hinckle, "The 'Vietnam Lobby,'" 16-21. See also Memo, 1/10/55, signed mjd, MP, XIII, 8, #1; Scheer, *How the United States Got Involved in Vietnam,* 21-25; James Aronson, *The Press and the Cold War* (Indianapolis: Bobbs-Merrill, 1970), 183-85; Cooney, *The American Pope,* 242.

13. Joseph Buttinger, letter to Mansfield, 21 February 1975, MP, XXII, 55, #1.

14. Buttinger, letter to Mansfield, 8 February 1955, MP, XIII, 8, #1; Joseph Buttinger, "Are We Saving South Vietnam?" *New Leader,* 27 June 1955, 54, 57-58; Joseph Buttinger, "Our Policy Toward Vietnam," *New York Times,* 30 January 1955; Joseph Buttinger, "An Eyewitness Report on Vietnam," *Reporter,* 27 January 1955, 19-20; Joseph Buttinger, "Saigon: Intrigue," *New Republic,* 28 February 1955, 9-10; Leo Cherne, "To Win in Indochina We must Win These People," *Look,* 25 January 1955, 61-64; "Hope in Vietnam," *New York Times,* 29 January 1955, 14.

15. See for example "Ovation for Diem," *Time,* 17 January 1955, 37; "Signs of Improvement," *Time,* 31 January 1955, 23-24; "Among the People," *Time,* 7 February 1955, 25; "Diem Besieged," *Time,* 21 March 1955, 31-32; "The Beleaguered Man," *Time,* 22-25 and the cover; "Tremors from Washington," *Time,* 2 May 1955, 34; "The Revolt that Failed," *Time,* 9 May 1955, 24-25; "The Red or the Green," *Time,* 17 October 1955, 40; "The Quarterback," *Time,* 17 October 1955, 40; "A Feudal Fracas in Vietnam," *Life,* 18 April 1955, 46-47; "Night of Lurid Drama," *Life,* 16 May 1955, 48-50; Scheer, *How the United States Got Involved in Vietnam,* 24; Buttinger, "Are We Saving South Vietnam?" 54-57.

16. "Too Much Vietnam Gloom," *America,* 29 January 1955, 442; "Fractional Struggle in Vietnam," *America,* 26 March 1955, 663; "Diem's Critics-Graham Greene," *America,* 28 May 1955, 225.

17. Gibbons, *The U.S. Government and the Vietnam War,* Part 1, 301-5. See also Scheer and Hinckle, "The 'Vietnam Lobby,'" 20; Cooney, *The American Pope,* 244-45; Daily Activities Book, Collins Papers, Box 24, #10, DDE Library; *FRUS, 1955-1957, Vietnam,* 1:146; Post, *Revolution,* 224; D. Anderson, *Trapped By Success,* 158-59; Boettcher, *Vietnam,* 109; Aronson, *The Press and the Cold War,* 182-87; Cooper, *The Lost Crusade,* 133; Collins, *Lightning Joe,* 389; Scheer, *How the United States Got Involved in Vietnam,* 25; "Douglas Arrives in Saigon," *New York Times,* 1 July 1955, 4.

18. *ESSFRC,* 1955, 7:399-401, 413.

19. Arnold writes that Diem replaced the cabinet members with family members and northern Catholics and never again achieved a cross-section of the nation in his cabinet, but rather, a "Catholic-based president's sect" (*The First Domino,* 280).

20. This account of Diem's struggle with the sects draws from the following sources: Collins Papers, Box 25, Folder 1, 3, Box 26, Folder 1-6, May (1)-(2), DDE Library; Fall, "The Political-Religious Sects of Vietnam," 235-53; Collins, *Lightning Joe,* 397-407; Lansdale, *In the Midst of Wars,* 244-312; Gibbons, *The U.S. Government*

and the Vietnam War, Part 1, 293-99; D. Anderson, *Trapped By Success*, 97-119; Arnold, *The First Domino*, 264-81; Hammer, *A Death in November*, 71-74; Joseph Buttinger, *Vietnam: A Dragon Embattled* (New York: Praeger, 1967), 2:865-85; Cooper, *The Lost Crusade*, 139-43; Shaplen, *The Lost Revolution*, 119-28; Karnow, *Vietnam* (1984), 222-23; George Herring, *America's Longest War* (New York: John Wiley & Sons, 1979), 51-54.

21. Ely told Collins that while the American "saw the sects as anarchic groups in a normal society," Ely saw them "as highly organized bodies in an anarchic society." The sects were the strongest anti-Vietminh force in the South and if elections were held in their area, Ely predicted that the government would gain 100 percent of the vote (*FRUS, 1955-1957, Vietnam*, 1:155).

22. Papers of John Foster Dulles: Telephone Calls Series, Box 3, Telephone Conv-General, 7 March 1955-29 April 1955 (3), DDE Library; Papers of John Foster Dulles: Telephone Calls Series, Box 10, Telephone Conv-White House, 7 March 1955 to August 29, 1955 (3), DDE Library; *FRUS, 1955-1957, Vietnam*, 1:175-76.

23. Mansfield, 1 April 1955 memo, MP, XXII, 107, #11; *FRUS, 1955-1957, Vietnam*, 1:176-77.

24. *FRUS, 1955-1957, Vietnam*, 1:196-97. See also Collins to Dulles, 31 March 1955, Box 25, DDE Library; Dulles to Collins, 8 April 1955, Collins Papers, Box 26, DDE Library.

25. "The Beleaguered Man," 22-25; "A Feudal Fracas in Vietnam," 46-47.

26. *FRUS, 1955-1957, Vietnam*, 1:219, 221-22.

27. Ibid., 1:230, 234-35. See also *United States-Vietnam Relations 1945-1967*, Book 10, 894-906.

28. *FRUS, 1955-1957, Vietnam*, 1:236-41, 271.

29. Dulles to Collins, 20 April 1955, JFD Papers, Subject Series, Box 9, Folder 1, Collins Papers, DDE Library. See also Gibbons, *The U.S. Government and the Vietnam War*, Part 1, 295; *FRUS, 1955-1957, Vietnam*, 1:271.

30. *FRUS, 1955-1957, Vietnam*, 1:260-70. See also *United States-Vietnam Relations, 1945-1967*, Book 10, 915-22.

31. Mansfield, memo, 21 April 1955, MP, XXII, 107, #11; *FRUS, 1955-1957, Vietnam*, 1:277.

32. As quoted in Shaplen, *The Lost Revolution*, 122.

33. Gibbons, *The U.S. Government and the Vietnam War*, Part 1, 295-96; D. Anderson, *Trapped By Success*, 109; *FRUS, 1955-1957, Vietnam*, 1:280-87.

34. Shaplen, *The Lost Revolution*, 122. See also Gibbons, *The U.S. Government and the Vietnam War*, Part 1, 295-96; D. Anderson, *Trapped By Success*, 109-10; *FRUS, 1955-1957, Vietnam*, 1:294-98; Currey, *Edward Lansdale*, 175-77; Gravel, *Pentagon Papers*, 1:233-34.

35. Mansfield, letter to the author, 2 June 1993.

36. Buttinger, letter to Mansfield, 12 March 1958, MP, XIII, 8, #1. See also Buttinger, letter to Mansfield, 21 February 1975, MP, XXII, 55, #1. Hilaire du Berrier claims to have been a translator for an aide to Ngo Dinh Luyen in Washington at this time. Du Berrier's book is a right-wing diatribe but it offers interesting insights about Fishel

and others arriving in Washington to influence the government decision on Diem (Hilaire du Berrier, *Background to Betrayal* [Boston: Western Islands, 1965], 91-108).

37. Francis Valeo, memo to Mansfield, memorandum on conversation with Wesley Fishel, 25 April 1955, MP, XXII, 107, #11; *FRUS, 1955-1957, Vietnam,* 1:288-89.

38. Mansfield, summary of remarks of General Lawton Collins, 27 April 1955, MP, XXII, 107, #11; *FRUS, 1955-1957, Vietnam,* 1:292-93.

39. Valeo, interview with the author, Washington, D.C., 17 May 1991.

40. *FRUS, 1955-1957, Vietnam,* 1:299-301, 307-11.

41. D. Anderson, *Trapped By Success,* 76, 112. See also Currey, *Edward Lansdale,* 177; Shaplen, *The Lost Revolution,* 124.

42. Mansfield, untitled speech, 29 April 1955, MP, XIII, 37, #56; *Congressional Record,* 2 May 1955, 5288-91.

43. *FRUS, 1955-1957, Vietnam,* 1:337-38.

44. Alsop, interview with Challener, 4 March 1966, 10-11; Arnold, *The First Domino,* 278.

45. Collins, *Lightning Joe,* 405-6; *FRUS, 1955-1957, Vietnam,* 1:340, 344-45.

46. Hilaire du Berrier, "Report from Saigon," *American Mercury,* September 1958, 49; Bernard B. Fall, *Viet-Nam Witness* (New York: Frederick A. Praeger, 1960), 286.

47. *FRUS, 1955-1957, Vietnam,* 1:343. See also Tillman Durdin, "Vietnam Ponders New Government," *New York Times,* 8 May 1955, 3; Collins, *Lightning Joe,* 407; Lansdale, *In the Midst of Wars,* 319.

48. Nguyen Ton Hoan, letter to Mansfield, 14 September 1955, MP, XIII, 8, #1.

49. Diem, letter to Mansfield, 4 May 1955 / Mansfield, letter to Diem, 17 May 1955, MP, XXII, 95, #5. See also Mansfield, "American Foreign Policy in the Far East," Carroll College, Helena, Montana, 22 May 1955, 12-13, MP, XIII, 37, #61.

50. Hoopes, *The Devil and John Foster Dulles,* 253-57.

51. Wesley Fishel, *Vietnam: Anatomy of a Conflict* (Itasca, Illinois: F.E. Peacock, 1968), 125.

52. Boettcher, *Vietnam,* 107.

53. Mansfield, letter to Heath, 20 May 1955, MP, XIII, 37, #61.

54. Mansfield, interview with Challener, 10 May 1966, 8.

55. Mansfield, letter to the author, 1 February 1990, 1.

56. Hinh entered the country anyway and tried to rally Hoa Hao troops still fighting Diem's army. On 18 June, the national army routed Tran Van Soai's army and Hinh fled to Cambodia. By 30 June, Diem's troops defeated Hoa Hao leader Ba Cut and organized sect resistance came to an end. The Cao Dai sect largely avoided involvement in the "battle of the sects" (see Fall, "The Political-Religious Sects of Vietnam," 253; Durdin, "Vietnam Ponders New Government," 3; C. L. Sulzberger, "Diem Opposes Allied Policy in South Vietnam," *New York Times,* 8 June 1955, 28).

57. "The Red or the Green," 40. See also Gibbons, *The U.S. Government and the Vietnam War,* Part 1, 299-300; Collins, *Lightning Joe,* 406; Currey, *Edward Lansdale,* 180; Kidder to Dulles, 29 April 1955, Collins Papers, Box 26, Folder 5, DDE Library; Herring, *America's Longest War,* 54-55; Arnold, *The First Domino,* 300.

58. Mansfield, Statement of Senator Mike Mansfield, 25 July 1955, 2, MP, XIII, 37, #70. See also "The Quarterback," 40; Francis Spellman, "Text of Cardinal's Speech . . ." *New York Times,* 31 August 1954, 12.

59. Mansfield and Valeo, conversation with Tillman and Peggy Durdin, 12 August 1955, MP, XXII, 95, #3.

60. Mansfield and Valeo, conversation with Diem, 18 August 1955 / Mansfield and Valeo, conversation with Ambassador and Frank Meloy, 18 August 1955, MP, XXII, 95, #3.

61. Mansfield and Valeo, conversation with Col. William Tudor, 25 August 1955, MP, XXII, 95, #3.

62. Ben Kiernan, *How Pol Pot Came to Power* (London: Verso, 1985), 42, 158-64. See also *ESSFRC,* 1955, 7:397-98.

63. Valeo, letter to the author, 20 February 1990.

64. Graham Greene, "'To Hope till Hope Creates,'" *New Republic,* 12 April 1954, 12. See also Francis Valeo, "Sihanouk of Cambodia," *Baltimore Sun,* 11 January 1979, A15.

65. Mansfield, *Vietnam, Cambodia, and Laos,* U.S. 84th Cong., 1st sess., S. Rept. (Washington, D.C.: GPO, 6 October 1955), 7, 12, 13, 15. See also Gibbons, *The U.S. Government and the Vietnam War,* Part 1, 301.

66. Gibbons, *The U.S. Government and the Vietnam War,* Part 1, 301-2. See also John O'Daniel, letter to Mansfield, 24 March 1958, MP, XIII, 8, #1; Scheer and Hinckle, "The 'Vietnam Lobby,'" 20-21; Frances Fitzgerald, *Fire in the Lake* (Boston: Little, Brown & Co., 1972), 83-84; Reeves, *President Kennedy,* 115; Boettcher, *Vietnam,* 408-9; *A Symposium on America's Stake in Vietnam* (New York: American Friends of Vietnam, 1956), 109 and inside of front cover; D. Anderson, *Trapped By Success,* 158-59.

67. Mansfield, letter to the author, 19 April 1988. See also O'Daniel, letter to Mansfield, 24 March 1958, MP, XIII, 8, #1; Wesley Fishel, ed., *Problems of Freedom* (New York: The Free Press, 1961), ix-xiv.

68. Huynh Sanh Thong, letter to Mansfield, 1 February 1957, MP, XIII, 8, #1. See also Scheer, *How the United States Got Involved in Vietnam,* 31-33, 59-60.

69. O'Daniel, letter to Mansfield, 24 March 1958, MP, XIII, 8, #1. See also Bosley Crowther, "Mankiewicz Version of Novel by Greene," *New York Times,* 6 February 1958, 24; "Loser on Points," *Newsweek,* 10 February 1958, 107; Graham Greene, *The Quiet American* (London: William Heinemann, 1955).

70. Heath, letter to Mansfield, 2 May 1955, MP, XIII, 8, #1; Mansfield, letter to Heath, 20 May 1955, MP, XIII, 37, #61. See also Joseph Alsop, "A Reporter At Large," *New Yorker,* 25 June 1955, 35; Aronson, *The Press and the Cold War,* 184-86; Hinckle, Stern, and Scheer, "The University on the Make," 11-22; Scheer, *How the United States Got Involved in Vietnam,* 34-37.

71. *A Symposium on America's Stake in Vietnam,* 8-14. See also John F. Kennedy, *The Strategy of Peace,* Allan Nevins, ed. (New York: Harper & Row, 1960), 64-65; Gibbons, *The U.S. Government and the Vietnam War,* Part 1, 303-5, 338.

72. As quoted in Buttinger, letter to Mansfield, 21 February 1975, MP, XXII, 55, #1. See also William Conrad Gibbons, *The U.S. Government and the Vietnam War*, Part 3 (Princeton: Princeton University Press, 1989), 82-83, 265-67, 397; Cooper, *The Lost Crusade*, 133.

73. Montgomery, *The Politics of Foreign Aid*, 223.

74. See for example Arnold, *The First Domino*, 383.

75. Heath, letter to Mansfield, 2 May 1955, MP, XIII, 8, #1; Mansfield, letter to Heath, 20 May 1955, MP, XIII, 37, #61.

76. Valeo, letter to the author, 20 February 1990.

77. As quoted in Pierre Melandri, "The Repercussions of the Geneva Conference: South Vietnam under a New Protector," Mark Rubin trans., in *Dien Bien Phu and the Crisis of Franco-American Relations, 1954-1955,* Lawrence Kaplan, Denise Artaud, and Mark Rubin, eds. (Wilmington, Delaware: SR Books, 1990), 200; Arnold, *The First Domino*, 82.

78. As quoted in Moya Ball, "A Case Study of the Kennedy Administration's Decision-making Concerning the Diem Coup of November, 1963," *Western Journal of Speech Communication* 54 (1990): 561; John Newman, *JFK and Vietnam* (New York: Warner Books, 1992), 375; U. A. Johnson, *The Right Hand of Power*, 412. See also Eldridge Durbrow, interview with Ted Gittinger, 3 June 1981, 52 / William Trueheart, interview with Ted Gittinger, 2 March 1982, 40-41, LBJ Oral History Project, LBJ Library.

79. As quoted in Buttinger, letter to Mansfield, 21 February 1975, MP, XXII, 55, #1; U. A. Johnson, *The Right Hand of Power*, 227. See also D. Anderson, *Trapped By Success*, 117-18; Shaplen, *The Lost Revolution*, 127; Lansdale, *In the Midst of Wars*, 244.

80. Shaplen, "A Reporter in Vietnam," *New Yorker,* 22 September 1962, 128; *ESSFRC,* 1965 (Washington, D.C.: GPO, 1990), 17:123.

81. As quoted in Schmid, "Free Indo-China Fights against Time," 23; D. Anderson, *Trapped By Success*, 106, 207.

CHAPTER 5

1. Mansfield, letter to Diem, 12 January 1956, MP, XXII, 95, #5.

2. "Personal and Otherwise," *Harper's Magazine,* January 1956, 24.

3. In a February speech, Mansfield admitted shortcomings in the elections in South Vietnam and Cambodia, but praised the beginnings of democracy in that part of the world (Mansfield, "United States Foreign Policy and Southeast Asia," 16 February 1956, 14, MP, XXI, 38, #12).

4. Mansfield, "Reprieve in Viet Nam," *Harper's Magazine,* January 1956, 46-51.

5. "Z," "The War in Vietnam: We Have Not Been Told the Whole Truth," *New Republic,* 12 March 1962, 22-23.

6. Bowles, letter to Mansfield, 6 January 1956, MP, XIII, 8, #1.

7. Mansfield, letter to Bowles, 17 January 1956, MP, XIII, 8, #1.

8. Kahin, *Intervention*, 53, 61.

9. Mansfield, letter to Armand Girard, 24 February 1967, MP, XIII, 75, #2. See also Mansfield, interview with Challener, 10 May 1966, 7.

10. William Langer, letter to Mansfield, 8 March 1956, MP, XIII, 6, #2. See also Hilaire du Berrier, "How We Helped Ho Chi Minh," *The Freeman,* 19 April 1954, 516-18; du Berrier, "Report from Saigon," 43; du Berrier, *Background to Betrayal.*

11. Hilaire du Berrier, letter to Mansfield, 3 July 1956, MP, XIII, 6, #2.

12. du Berrier, letter to Humphrey, 4 May 1956 / Humphrey, letter to Mansfield, 6 July 1956, MP, XIII, 6, #2.

13. Mansfield, letter to du Berrier, 6 July 1956, MP, XIII, 6, #2.

14. "Diem's Shaky Foundations," *Economist,* 23 June 1956; Merry Bromberger, "The Mistaken Solitude of Mr. Diem," *Constellation,* August 1956, 67-72; Nguyen Thai Binh, letter to Mansfield, 6 March 1956 / Tran Van Tung, letter to Mansfield, 12 April 1956, MP, XIII, 8, #1.

15. Mansfield/Dooley correspondence, MP, XIII, 7, #11. See also Mansfield, letter to the author, 19 April 1988.

16. *ESSFRC,* 1956 (Washington, D.C.: GPO, 1978), 8:160-61.

17. Mansfield, letter to Diem, 26 February 1957 / Diem, letter to Mansfield, 14 March 1957, MP, XXII, 95, #5.

18. Diem, letter to Mansfield, 14 March 1957, MP, XXII, 95, #5. See also Mansfield, letter to the author, 2 June 1993; *FRUS, 1955-1957, Vietnam,* 1:773-76.

19. Ann Whitman, International Meeting File, Box 2, DDE Library. See also D. Anderson, *Trapped By Success,* 160-65; Aronson, *The Press and the Cold War,* 38-41; Gibbons, *The U.S. Government and the Vietnam War,* Part 1, 332-33.

20. *FRUS, 1955-1957, Vietnam,* 1:794-99, 807-11.

21. *Congressional Record,* 13 May 1957, 6759-64. See also "The Tough Miracle Man of Vietnam," *Life,* 13 May 1957, 164.

22. *Congressional Record,* 13 May 1957, 6759.

23. Huynh Sanh Thong, letter to Mansfield and attached note, 1 February 1957, MP, XIII, 8, #1. See also "Z," "The War in Vietnam," 22-23.

24. Norman Thomas, letter to Mansfield, 13 May 1957 / John O'Daniel, letter to Mansfield, 24 March 1958, MP, XIII, 8, #1. See also *A Symposium on America's Stake in Vietnam,* 110 and inside back cover.

25. Montana Republicans tried to get Burton Wheeler out of retirement to challenge Mansfield for his Senate seat in 1958, but Wheeler declined (see Wheeler, *Yankee from the West,* 413-14; Colman, *Mrs. Wheeler goes to Washington,* 225).

26. Mansfield, letter to Dulles, 9 August 1956 / Dulles, letter to Mansfield, 9 August 1956 / Eisenhower, letter to Mansfield, 9 August 1956, JFD, General Correspondence, Box 3, Folder 1, DDE Library. See also Schwartz, "Senator Michael J. Mansfield," 360-61.

27. du Berrier, "Report from Saigon," 43-44, 48-49, 51. See also Mansfield, letter to du Berrier, 6 July 1956, MP, XIII, 6, #2; du Berrier, letter to R. J. Scanian, 27 August

1958 / Mansfield, letter to Sam Guilluly, 1 April 1958 / note initialed mjd, 30 June 1958, MP, XIV, 40, #16; Schwartz, "Senator Michael J. Mansfield," 361.

28. As quoted in Wolf Ladejinsky, "Vietnam: The First Five Years," *Reporter,* 24 December 1959, 20-23.

29. As quoted in Aronson, *The Press and the Cold War,* 187-88; Hammer, *A Death in November,* 45.

30. As quoted in Adrian Jaffe and Milton Taylor, "A Crumbling Bastion," *New Republic,* 19 June 1961, 19.

31. Gibbons called the Manifesto a "frank and compelling statement of the problems facing Vietnam, and an urgent appeal to Diem to take corrective action" (*The U.S. Government and the Vietnam War,* Part 1, 339). For the full text of the Manifesto, see Bernard B. Fall, *The Two Viet-Nams,* rev. ed. (New York: Praeger, 1967), 442-46 or Gravel, *Pentagon Papers,* 1:316-21.

32. Fishel did request that Mansfield keep the information "confidential." See Wesley Fishel, letter to Mansfield, 12 November 1960, MP, XIII, 47, #11.

33. See for example *FRUS, 1958-1960, Vietnam* (Washington, D.C.: GPO, 1986), 1:227-33.

34. Buttinger, *Vietnam,* 2:930-81. See also Gibbons, *The U.S. Government and the Vietnam War,* Part 1, 331-34, 339-42; Kahin, *Intervention,* 93-121; D. Anderson, *Trapped By Success,* 132, 182; Arnold, *The First Domino,* 346.

35. Kahin, *Intervention,* 97-121. See also Hammer, *A Death in November,* 100; Buttinger, *Vietnam,* 2:965, 974, 979-83; Karnow, *Vietnam* (1984), 227-35; Gibbons, *The U.S. Government and the Vietnam War,* Part 1, 333-39; Sheehan, *A Bright Shining Lie,* 184-96; D. Anderson, *Trapped By Success,* 176; Arnold, *The First Domino,* 331, 351.

36. Mansfield, letter to Herbert Hoover Jr., 20 September 1955, MP, XXII, 107, #11.

37. Mansfield, "United States Foreign Policy and Southeast Asia," 16 February 1956, 21-31, MP, XXI, 38, #6; Mansfield, "The United States and the Far East," 22 May 1955, 13-14, MP, XXI, 38, #29. See also Sheehan, *A Bright Shining Lie,* 67, 116, 207-8, 308-9; D. Anderson, *Trapped By Success,* 176; *ESSFRC, 1956,* 8:276-77, 412-14.

38. As quoted in *FRUS, 1955-1957, Vietnam,* 1:585-86. See also Mansfield, letter to John Hollister, 2 March 1956 / Herbert Hoover Jr., letter to Mansfield, 22 September 1955 / Hoover Jr., letter to Mansfield, 17 November 1955 / Hollister, letter to Mansfield, 28 September 1955 / Hollister, letter to Mansfield, 16 November 1955 / Hollister, letter to Mansfield, 25 February 1956, MP, XXII, 107, #11.

39. Gibbons, *The U.S. Government and the Vietnam War,* Part 1, 321-22. See also D. Anderson, *Trapped By Success,* 169, 180.

40. D. Anderson, *Trapped By Success,* 167-69, 178. See also Currey, *Edward Lansdale,* 199-206; *FRUS, 1958-1960, Foreign Economic Policy* (Washington, D.C.: GPO, 1992), 4:431.

41. As quoted in Arnold, *The First Domino,* 347-49. See also D. Anderson, *Trapped By Success,* 179.

42. After reading a report that Mansfield would investigate the charges in Scripps-Howard, du Berrier wrote Mansfield a letter begging to get in on the Vietnam aid

investigation, suggesting that "an Austrian left-wing socialist leader [Buttinger] and his personal clique, aided by a smart public relations man [Oram], have succeeded until now in maintaining a complete blackout on all such reports" (du Berrier, letter to Mansfield, 29 July 1959, MP, XIV, 40, #16).

43. As quoted in Gibbons, *The U.S. Government and the Vietnam War*, Part 1, 322-26; *FRUS, 1958-1960, Vietnam,* 1:225-27. See also D. Anderson, *Trapped By Success,* 181.

44. "Z," "The War in Vietnam," 23. See also Gibbons, *The U.S. Government and the Vietnam War*, Part 1, 325-26.

45. When asked about memos of this nature, Valeo said: "in most of these cases he asked me for a memo. I very rarely volunteered memos on my own initiative. He used a lot of [Valeo's material]. The initiative is important; I don't think I initiated an awful lot, I didn't pick subjects for him to work on, it was the other way around, he picked the subjects and then I elaborated or developed them basically, and then that resulted in a memorandum. That was the usual procedure between us." Valeo did much of Mansfield's speech drafting and considers that he had influence on Mansfield over twenty-five years, but says Mansfield "was his own man" and a "deep thinker in his own right. I had a fluency with words that he didn't have" (Valeo, interview with the author, Washington, D.C., 17 May 1991).

46. Valeo, "Draft report on Vietnamese inquiry," 10 September 1959, MP, XXII, 103, #3. See also Gibbons, *The U.S. Government and the Vietnam War*, Part 1, 324.

47. Valeo, interview with the author, Washington, D.C., 17 May 1991. See also Marcy, Oral History Interview, Senate Historical Office, Washington, D.C., 1983, 136-37; D. Anderson, *Trapped By Success,* 182; Montgomery, *The Politics of Foreign Aid*, 233-34. Marcy and Valeo took the restored railway from Hue to Saigon that was a showcase of the Diem regime. The railroad was shut down by Vietcong action shortly after their trip.

48. Marcy to J. William Fulbright, 8 December 1959, Carl Marcy Papers, National Archives, Box 3 (1959-1961).

49. Gibbons, *The U.S. Government and the Vietnam War*, Part 1, 324-25.

50. Valeo, interview with the author, Washington, D.C., 17 May 1991.

51. As quoted in *FRUS, 1958-1960, Vietnam,* 1:382. See also Gibbons, *The U.S. Government and the Vietnam War*, Part 1, 326; Mansfield, *United States Aid Program in Vietnam,* U.S. 86th Cong., 2d sess., S. Rept. (Washington, D.C.: GPO, 26 February 1960), iii.

52. As quoted in Gibbons, *The U.S. Government and the Vietnam War*, Part 1, 326-27.

53. Mansfield, letter to the author, 1 February 1990.

54. Mansfield, telegram to Diem, 12 November 1960, MP, XIII, 48, #2. See also Stanley Karnow, "Diem Defeats His Own Best Troops," *Reporter,* 19 January 1961, 24-29. The U.S. had contact with the rebels, but the degree of U.S. involvement is unclear. Diem believed that Durbrow favored the coup, damaging U.S. relations with the Vietnamese leader (see Gibbons, *The U.S. Government and the Vietnam War*, Part 1, 342; Fishel, letter to Mansfield, 12 November 1960, MP, XIII, 47, #11; D. Anderson, *Trapped By Success,* 192-93; Newman, *JFK and Vietnam,* 6, 26-29).

55. Fishel, letter to Mansfield, 12 November 1960, MP, XIII, 47, #11. See also *FRUS, 1958-1960, Vietnam,* 1:426-31.

56. Gibbons, *The U.S. Government and the Vietnam War,* Part 1, 334.

57. *ESSFRC,* 1960 (Washington, D.C.: GPO, 1983), 12:680. See also Gibbons, *The U.S. Government and the Vietnam War,* Part 1, 307, 328.

58. "Mansfield Criticizes Policies," *New York Times,* 29 December 1960, 2. See also *FRUS, 1958-1960, Vietnam,* 1:273-74; *Congressional Record,* 7 September 1959, 18306-7; Cooper, *The Lost Crusade,* 164; U. A. Johnson, *The Right Hand of Power,* 295-303.

59. *FRUS, 1958-1960, East Asia-Pacific Region, Cambodia, Laos* (Washington, D.C.: GPO, 1992), 16:1021-22.

CHAPTER 6

1. As quoted in Alfred Steinberg, *Sam Johnson's Boy* (New York: Macmillan Co., 1968), 450. See also Evans and Novak, *Lyndon B. Johnson,* 98.

2. Evans and Novak, *Lyndon B. Johnson,* 99, 116. See also "Field Commander," *Time,* 26 November 1956, 23.

3. George Reedy, interview with the author, Milwaukee, 15 September 1987.

4. Valeo, interview with the author, Washington, D.C., 17 May 1991.

5. Lyndon Johnson, letter to Mansfield, 24 August 1958 / Johnson, letter to Mansfield, 15 September 1959 / Johnson, letter to Mansfield, 29 January 1959, MP, XVIII, 18, #1.

6. Lyndon Johnson, letter to Mansfield, 30 June 1960, MP, XVIII, 18, #1. See also Evans and Novak, *Lyndon B. Johnson,* 254; Walter Spolar, interview with Ronalt Grele, 9 June 1966, 5-6, JFK Oral History Project, JFK Library.

7. Mansfield, confidential recollections of a phone call from President-elect John Kennedy, 11 November 1960, MP, XXII, 103, #1.

8. Mansfield, transcript of a phone conversations with Lyndon Johnson, 11 November 1960, MP, XXII, 103, #1.

9. Mansfield, letter to the author, 18 August 1987.

10. As quoted in B. Baker, *Wheeling and Dealing,* 132-35.

11. Evans and Novak, *Lyndon B. Johnson,* 306-8. See also, Harry McPherson, *A Political Education* (Boston: Little, Brown, and Co., 1972), 183; Robert Byrd, *The Senate, 1789-1989* (Washington, D.C.: GPO, 1988), 1:679; Doris Kearns, *Lyndon Johnson and the American Dream* (New York: Harper and Row, 1976), 164-65.

12. Evans and Novak, *Lyndon B. Johnson,* 306-8.

13. As quoted in Steinberg, *Sam Johnson's Boy,* 547-48, 624. See also Schwartz, "Senator Michael J. Mansfield," 371; B. Baker, *Wheeling and Dealing,* 135.

14. As quoted in Schwartz, "Senator Michael J. Mansfield," 375-76, and *Congressional Record,* 6 November 1963, 21246-47. See also *Congressional Record,* 26 July 1962, 14858-69; *Congressional Record,* 27 July 1962, 14873-903; *Congressional Record,* 7

November 1963, 21302, 21277-79, 21282-84, 21371-72; "A Victory for Kennedy That May Bring Him Trouble," *U.S. News & World Report,* 27 August 1962, 44-45; Douglas Cater, "The Contentious Lords of the Senate," *Reporter,* 16 August 1962, 27-29; "The Senate: A Crisis in Leadership," *Newsweek,* 18 November 1963, 29-30; Mary McGrory, "Chaos in the Senate—Days Without End," *America,* 23 November 1963, 653.

15. Mansfield, "The Senate and Its Leadership," 25 November 1963, 25-26, MP, XXII, 78, #33.

16. Steinberg, *Sam Johnson's Boy,* 548.

17. For further development of this argument, see Gregory Olson, "Mike Mansfield's Ethos in the Evolution of United States Policy in Indochina" (Ph.D. diss., University of Minnesota, 1988), 151-92.

18. The most thorough study of Mansfield's effectiveness as leader in his early years concluded that his record was "impressive" (John Stewart, "Independence and Control: The Challenge of Senatorial Party Leadership," Ph.D. diss., University of Chicago, 1968, 53, 72, 75, 77).

19. Marcy, Oral History Interview, Senate Historical Office, Washington, D.C., 1983, 52.

20. As quoted in Clark Clifford with Richard Holbrooke, *Counsel to the President* (New York: Random House, 1991), 342-44. See also Karnow, *Vietnam* (1984), 247; Thomas Schoenbaum, *Waging Peace and War* (New York: Simon and Schuster, 1988), 384-85; Rusk, *As I Saw It,* 428; Kahin, *Intervention,* 127.

21. William Conrad Gibbons, *The U.S. Government and the Vietnam War,* Part 2 (Princeton: Princeton University Press, 1986) 10-11; Jane Hamilton-Merritt, *Tragic Mountains* (Bloomington: Indiana University Press, 1993), 95, 97, 104.

22. As quoted in Moya Ball, *Vietnam-on-the-Potomac* (New York: Praeger, 1992), 19.

23. Mansfield, Phone conversation with Kennedy, 2 January 1961, MP, XXII, 103, #9.

24. Mansfield, memo to President-Elect, "Observations on the Laotian Situation," n.d. [January 1961], 1-2, MP, XXII, 103, #9. See also Rusk, *As I Saw It,* 429; Schoenbaum, *Waging Peace and War,* 389; Gibbons, *The U.S. Government and the Vietnam War,* Part 2, 10-11.

25. Souvanna Phouma, letter to Mansfield, 7 January 1961, 1-2, MP, XXII, 103, #16.

26. Mansfield, "The Laotian Situation" [memo to Kennedy], 21 January 1961, MP, XXII, 103, #16.

27. Mansfield, "Supplemental memo on the proposal for a neutral commission in Laos composed of India, Pakistan, and Afghanistan" [memo to Kennedy], 23 January 1961, MP, XXII, 103, #16.

28. Mansfield, "The Laotian Question" [confidential memo to Rusk], 22 March 1961, 1-3 / Mansfield, confidential memo to Kennedy, 22 March 1961, MP, XXII, 103, #16.

29. Montague Kern, Patricia Levering, and Ralph Levering, *The Kennedy Crises* (Chapel Hill: University of North Carolina Press, 1983), 47. See also *Congressional Record,* 24 March 1961, 4706-7; *Congressional Record,* 29 March 1961, 5114-15.

30. As quoted in U. A. Johnson, *The Right Hand of Power,* 322-25. See also *FRUS, 1961-1963, Laos Crisis* (Washington, D.C.: GPO, 1994), 24:146-47.

31. Gibbons, *The U.S. Government and the Vietnam War*, Part 2, 29. See also Kahin, *Intervention*, 128. While many pressured Kennedy to "get even" for the Bay of Pigs, Mansfield sent a long letter arguing that "the courageous thing to do and the sensible thing to do" would be to not yield to "the temptation to give vent to our anger at our own failure" (Herbert Parmet, *J.F.K.* [New York: Dial Press, 1983], 217).

32. Mansfield, "The Laotian Situation" [memo to Kennedy], 1 May 1961, 1-6 and attached note, MP, XXII, 103, #16. See also Newman, *JFK and Vietnam*, 49-54.

33. Gibbons, *The U.S. Government and the Vietnam War*, Part 2, 32.

34. Newman, *JFK and Vietnam*, 52-56, 62.

35. As quoted in Gibbons, *The U.S. Government and the Vietnam War*, Part 2, 26.

36. As quoted in Rusk, *As I Saw It*, 430.

37. As quoted in Gibbons, *The U.S. Government and the Vietnam War*, Part 2, 30-31. See also Kahin, *Intervention*, 128-29, 132; Karnow, *Vietnam* (1984), 248; Schoenbaum, *Waging Peace and War*, 390; Moya Ball, "A Descriptive and Interpretive Analysis of the Small Group Communication of Presidents Kennedy, Johnson, and Their Key Advisers Concerning the Decisions from January 1961 to July 1965 to Expand the Vietnam War" (Ph.D. diss., University of Minnesota, 1988), 98-99, 173, 182, 185.

38. Mansfield, "Luncheon with Ambassador Mikhail Menshikov" [confidential memo to Kennedy], 10 May 1961, MP, XXII, 103, #8.

39. Mansfield, "Observations on the Forthcoming Talks in Vienna" [confidential memo to Kennedy], 26 May 1961, MP, XXII, 103, #8.

40. As quoted in M. Ball, *Vietnam-on-the-Potomac*, 33. See also Mansfield, interview with Tillman, 23 June 1964, 7.

41. Mansfield, interview with Tillman, 23 June 1964, 25. See also *FRUS, 1961-1963, Laos Crisis,* 24:625-33; Gibbons, *The U.S. Government and the Vietnam War*, Part 2, 113.

42. *ESSFRC*, 1962 (Washington, D.C.: GPO, 1986), 14:31, 637. See also Rusk, *As I Saw It*, 434; Schoenbaum, *Waging Peace and War*, 390-91; Newman, *JFK and Vietnam*, 90, 119, 147, 268, 276-77, 293.

43. Mansfield, memo to Kennedy, 19 July, 1962, MP, XXII, 103, #15.

44. As quoted in Arnold, *The First Domino*, 376.

45. *FRUS, 1961-1963, Vietnam* (Washington, D.C.: GPO, 1990), 1:1-23. See also D. Anderson, *Trapped By Success*, 175, 196; Gibbons, *The U.S. Government and the Vietnam War*, Part 2, 33; M. Ball, *Vietnam-on-the-Potomac*, 52.

46. Mansfield, "Laos and Vietnam" [confidential memo to Kennedy], 20 September 1961, 2-3, MP, XXII, 103, #16. See also Mansfield, interview with Tillman, 23 June 1964, 37, 39-40.

47. Gibbons, *The U.S. Government and the Vietnam War*, Part 2, 85-86.

48. Arnold, *The First Domino*, picture between 224-225. See also Nolting, *From Trust to Tragedy*, 20.

49. Mansfield, "Laos and Vietnam" [confidential memo to Kennedy], 20 September 1961, 3-4, MP, XXII, 103, #16.

50. Mansfield, confidential memo to Kennedy, 2 November 1961, 1-4, MP, XXII, 103, #16. See also Reeves, *President Kennedy*, 255; Newman, *JFK and Vietnam*, 126-36.

51. As quoted in William Berman, *William Fulbright and the Vietnam War* (Kent, Ohio: Kent University Press, 1988), 10. See also *ESSFRC*, 1962, 14:57; Gibbons, *The U.S. Government and the Vietnam War*, Part 2, 119.

52. Wesley Fishel, letter to Mansfield, 5 December 1962, MP, XXII, 53, #6.

53. Mansfield, "Interests and Policies in Southeast Asia," East Lansing, Michigan, 10 June 1962, 1, MP, XXII, 78, #29.

54. When asked in 1987, Mansfield remembered little about this address. (Mansfield, letter to the author, 18 August 1987).

55. Mansfield, "Interests and Policies in Southeast Asia," East Lansing, Michigan, 10 June 1962, 2 including insert, MP, XXII, 78, #29. See also Gibbons, *The U.S. Government and the Vietnam War*, Part 2, 127.

56. Mansfield, "Interests and Policies in Southeast Asia," East Lansing, Michigan, 10 June 1962, 6-12, MP, XXII, 78, #29.

57. As quoted in *FRUS, Vietnam, 1961-1963* (Washington, D.C.: GPO, 1990), 2:448; Harold Chase and Allen Lerman, eds., *Kennedy and the Press: The News Conferences* (New York: Thomas Crowell Co., 1965), 269. See also Gibbons, *The U.S. Government and the Vietnam War*, Part 2, 119, 127. On 9 September 1963, when asked if he still believed in the domino theory, Kennedy responded, "I believe it" (David Burner and Thomas West, *The Torch is Passed: The Kennedy Brothers and American Liberalism* [New York: Antheneum, 1984], 141).

58. Mansfield, letter to Marcia Melton, 23 January 1964, MP, XIII, 48, #2.

59. The address was not mentioned in either *Time* or *Newsweek*. The *New York Times* summarized the speech, concluding that Mansfield criticized U.S. policy in Southeast Asia ("Mansfield Urges New Asian Policy," *New York Times,* 11 June 1962, 2).

60. Mecklin, *Mission in Torment*, 130-31.

61. Madame Tran Van Chuong, letter to Mansfield, 14 June 1962, MP, XXII, 105, #19.

62. Mansfield, letter to Madame Tran Van Chuong, 15 June 1962, MP, XXII, 105, #19.

63. Valeo, notes for Mansfield on a meeting with the Vietnamese Ambassador, 16 June 1962, MP, XXII, 105, #19.

64. Valeo, notes for Mansfield on a meeting with the Ambassador of Viet Nam and Madame Tran Van Chuong, 30 October 1962, 1-4, MP, XXII, 105, #19. In truth, the ambassador and his wife talked to other American officials in 1962, including Lansdale. In August 1963 Ambassador Tran resigned in protest over Diem's policies, and Hammer and others suggest that the couple was involved in planning the eventual Diem coup. Valeo kept in contact with the Tran Van Chuongs until their death in 1987 and says that in frequent conversations about Vietnam, "they never discussed an involvement in the coup," but "given their attitude at that time it is certainly a possibility" (Valeo, letter to the author, 12 September 1990; Hammer, *A Death in November,* 150-51, 171, 173, 194-95, 267, 302-3; Gibbons, *The U.S. Government and the Vietnam War*, Part 2, 155).

65. Dr. Pham Huy Co, letter to Mansfield, 13 March 1963, MP, XIII, 48, #1.

Chapter 7

1. Mansfield, "Southeast Asia—Viet Nam" [secret memo to Kennedy], 18 December 1962, MP, XXII, 103, #15. See also Mansfield, J. Caleb Boggs, Claiborne Pell and Benjamin Smith, *Viet Nam and Southeast Asia,* U.S. 88th Cong., 1st sess., S. Rept. (Washington, D.C.: GPO, 1963); Mansfield, *Two Reports on Vietnam and Southeast Asia to the President of the United States,* U.S. 93d Cong., 1st sess., S. Rept. (Washington, D.C.: GPO, 1973).

2. Mansfield, conversation with Herbert Spivack, 28 November 1962, MP, XXII, 95, #10.

3. Valeo, "Sihanouk of Cambodia."

4. Mansfield, Boggs, Pell, and Smith, *Vietnam and Southeast Asia,* 13; Mansfield, "Southeast Asia—Viet Nam" [secret memo to Kennedy], 18 December 1962, 11-12, MP, XXII, 103, #15.

5. Philip Sprouse, telegram to Secretary of State, 27 March 1963 / Sprouse, letter to Mansfield, 30 November 1962 / Penn Nouth, letter to Sprouse, 29 November 1962 / Spivack, letter to Frank Meloy, 19 December 1962, MP, XXII, 53, #9; Sprouse, letter to Mansfield, 11 December 1962 / Cocsal Chhum, letter to Sprouse, 1 December 1962, MP, XXII, 53, #8.

6. Nolting, *From Trust to Tragedy,* 85-86; Valeo, letter to the author, 12 September 1990. See also Secret Summary Record of Meeting at American Embassy, Saigon, Viet Nam, 30 November 1962, 30, 52, MP, XXII, 95, #13.

7. Where not cited otherwise, the following material comes from Secret Summary Record of Meeting at American Embassy, Saigon, Viet Nam, 30 November 1962, 2-3, 6, 22-23, 28-30, 38, 49, 52, MP, XXII, 95, #13.

8. As quoted in *FRUS, 1961-1963, Vietnam,* 2:798. Harkins was unduly optimistic from the moment he arrived in Vietnam, often distorting the battlefield situation. Years later, Harkins described himself as more optimistic than the people who had been in Vietnam longer than he. However, Harkins claims that he knew that the situation would collapse if Diem were deposed. Harkins's reports to the administration were similar to the one he gave Mansfield; he had used the same one year prediction with McNamara in July and Diem in September. The one year estimate caused John Newman to wonder: "how could [Harkins] possibly think that victory could be achieved in just twelve months? We do not know what motivated Harkins, but whatever it was, it surely defies a sound military explanation." Nolting was usually in agreement with Harkins. Harkins described Nolting as "absolutely perfect" and "just my type of man." When Henry Cabot Lodge replaced Nolting as ambassador, the optimistic agreement between the top representatives of the State and Defense Departments ceased (Sheehan, *A Bright Shining Lie,* 323-26; Paul Harkins, interview with Ted Gittinger, 10 November 1981, 8, 20-22, LBJ Oral History Project, LBJ Library; Newman, *JFK and Vietnam,* 191-95, 199, 225, 232, 244-55, 270, 281-82, 286-92, 297, 304-9, 314-19; *FRUS, 1961-1963, Vietnam* [Washington, D.C.: GPO, 1991], 4:209).

9. French General Henri Navarre used that same light at the end of the tunnel claim in 1953, and it was first repeated by U.S. officials in that same year! Nolting started pushing the light at the end of tunnel metaphor in August, injecting it into Diem's speeches (Stanley Karnow "Giap Remembers," *New York Times Magazine,* 24 June 1990, 59; Gibbons, *The U.S. Government and the Vietnam War,* Part 1, 141; Newman, *JFK and Vietnam,* 290).

10. Trueheart, interview with Gittinger, 2 March 1982, 27-28, LBJ Oral History Project, LBJ Library.

11. Mecklin, *Mission in Torment,* 103, 129.

12. As quoted in Hammer, *A Death in November,* 82. See also Halberstam, *The Best and the Brightest,* 208.

13. Mansfield, unnamed memorandum, n.d. [1962], 1-2, MP, XXII, 95, #10.

14. *FRUS, 1961-1963, Vietnam,* 4:797. See also Memorandum of conversation between Diem and Mansfield party, 30 November 1962, MP, XXII, 95, #10; Valeo, letter to the author, 20 February 1990. Trueheart also stated that Diem's monologues on the history of Vietnam often lasted over four hours with no one else getting a word in. Journalist Robert Shaplen interviewed Diem in 1962 and reported: "a simple question, I soon found, was likely to send him off on a dissertation of an hour or more. As he talked, recalling his past life and intertwining it with that of his country, his gaze seemed to be focused on something beyond me and beyond the walls of the palace; the result was an eerie feeling that I was listening to a monologue delivered at some other time and in some other place—perhaps by a character in an allegorical play." Other journalists in the early 1960s reported similar experiences. Diem's lengthy discourse was nothing new; Edward Lansdale reported that Diem lectured him for five hours in 1955. However, Mansfield's perception of a changed Diem was shared by many who knew him from the 1950s. On Lansdale's trip to Vietnam in late 1960, Diem insisted that Nhu be present, and Nhu answered questions posed to his brother. More than once Lansdale said, "I am talking to your brother, not to you. I asked Diem what *he* thought." Even so, Nhu kept supplying answers and Diem merely nodded in agreement. Lansdale considered this an "evil portent" and that pattern continued on Lansdale's 1961 meeting with Diem. After Mansfield's visit, Chester Bowles met with Diem and found him "to be living in an unreal world of his own;" Alsop had a similar experience (Trueheart, interview with Gittinger, 2 March 1982, 23; Shaplen, "A Reporter in Vietnam," 104; Denis Warner, "The Many-Fronted War In South Vietnam," *Reporter,* 13 September 1962, 33; Denis Warner, "Agony in Saigon: The Lady & the Cadaver," *Reporter,* 10 October 1963, 41; "South Viet Nam," *Time,* 4 August 1961, 27; Lansdale, *In the Midst of Wars,* 328; Currey, *Edward Lansdale,* 221, 237-38; Chester Bowles, *Promises to Keep* [New York: Harper & Row, 1971], 415-16; Joseph Alsop, with Adam Platt, *"I've Seen the Best of It"* [New York: W.W. Norton, 1992], 461-62).

15. Mansfield, unnamed memorandum, n.d. [1962], 1-2, MP, XXII, 95, #10. See also Mansfield, conversation with Nhu, 30 November 1962, 1-2 / Memorandum of conversation, Nhu and Mansfield party, 1 December 1962, 3-4, 6-8 / Takashi Oka, interview with Nhu, 2 November 1962, MP, XXII, 95, #10.

16. Mansfield, conversation with Joseph Brent, 1 December 1962 / Mansfield, conversation with Lord Selkirk, 3 December 1962, MP, XXII, 95, #10. See also Harkins, interview with Gittinger, 10 November 1981, 10, 14, LBJ Oral History Project, LBJ Library.

17. Lodge described Nhu as "a striking figure. He has a handsome, cruel face and is obviously very intelligent. His talk last night was like a phonograph record and, in spite of his obvious ruthlessness and cruelty, one feels sorry for him. He is wound up as tight as a wire. He appears to be a lost soul, a haunted man who is caught in a vicious circle. The Furies are after him" (Newman, *JFK and Vietnam*, 389).

18. Mansfield, conversation with Nhu, 30 November 1962, 1-2 / Memorandum of conversation, Nhu and Mansfield party, 1 December 1962, 3-4, 6-8, MP, XXII, 95, #10. See also Kahin, *Intervention*, 140-41; Gibbons, *The U.S. Government and the Vietnam War*, Part 1, 92; Newman, *JFK and Vietnam*, 181, 198, 286-87, 328-31, 394-95; Sheehan, *A Bright Shining Lie*, 308-11.

19. Nolting, *From Trust to Tragedy*, 21, 86. Nolting's version does not account for the actual statement prepared by the embassy being found in Mansfield's papers.

20. Embassy in Saigon, Proposed Statement for Press on Departure, Saigon, December 2, 1962 (Senator Mansfield and Colleagues), MP, XXII, 53, #6.

21. David Halberstam, "Mansfield Is Cool on Vietnam War," *New York Times,* 3 December 1962, 12. See also Gibbons, *The U.S. Government and the Vietnam War*, Part 2, 131-32; Buttinger, *Vietnam*, 2:1180; Mecklin, *Mission in Torment*, 117-18.

22. Trueheart, interview with Gittinger, 2 March 1982.

23. Nolting, *From Trust to Tragedy*, 86, 98, 140. See also Harkins, interview with Gittinger, 10 November 1981, 57; Hammer, *A Death in November*, 83, 314; Halberstam, *The Best and the Brightest*, 208.

24. Nolting, *From Trust to Tragedy*, 85-86. See also Mecklin, *Mission in Torment*, 100; Kahin, *Intervention*, 142; Newman, *JFK and Vietnam*, 205-7, 212-15, 217-19, 226, 294, 303, 309-10, 315; *FRUS, 1961-1963, Vietnam* (Washington, D.C.: GPO, 1991), 3:67-69.

25. Trueheart, interview with Gittinger, 2 March 1982, 29, 39.

26. Valeo, letter to the author, 12 September 1990.

27. As quoted in Gibbons, *The U.S. Government and the Vietnam War*, Part 2, 131.

28. Oka, letter to Mansfield, 9 December 1962 / Mansfield, "Meeting with Newsmen in Hong Kong," 9 December 1962, MP, XXII, 95, #10.

29. Fishel, letter to Mansfield, 5 December 1962, MP, XXII, 53, #6.

30. Mansfield, interview with Tillman, 23 June 1964, 24.

31. As quoted in Karnow, *Vietnam* (1984), 268.

32. Kahin, *Intervention*, 146. Kahin cited the public report released in February 1963 and not the private report, even though the December meeting was clearly based on the private report. Newman erroneously concluded that the two reports represented two different trips to Vietnam (Kahin, *Intervention*, 146, 479; Newman, *JFK and Vietnam*, 327).

33. As quoted in Karnow, *Vietnam* (1984), 268.

34. As quoted in Kahin, *Intervention*, 146-47. See also Kenneth O'Donnell, David Powers and Joe McCarthy, *"Johnny, We Hardly Knew Ye"* (Boston: Little, Brown and Co., 1972), 15-16.

35. Mansfield, letter to Esther McGuire, 28 September 1970, MP, XIII, 86, #2. See also Mansfield, letter to Neil Paine, 31 May 1973 / Mansfield, letter to John Nicolella, 13 June 1973, MP, XIII, 108, #2.

36. Halberstam, *The Best and the Brightest*, 208.

37. Mansfield, *Two Reports on Vietnam and Southeast Asia*, 5, 7-10, 14; Mansfield, "Southeast Asia—Viet Nam," [secret memo to Kennedy] 18 December 1962, 9, 16, MP, XXII, 103, #15; Mansfield, Boggs, Pell and Smith, *Viet Nam and Southeast Asia*, 1-5, 7-9, 19-20.

38. "Senators Warn of Growing Risks in Vietnam War," *New York Times*, 25 February 1963, 1; "War Without End," *New Republic*, 9 March 1963, 1.

39. See for example M. Ball, *Vietnam-on-the-Potomac*, 54, 70.

40. Gibbons, *The U.S. Government and the Vietnam War*, Part 2, 134-36. See also Mecklin, *Mission in Torment*, 149-50; Sheehan, *A Bright Shining Lie*, 292-305.

41. Andrew Glass, "Mike Mansfield, Majority Leader," in Norman Ornstein, ed., *Congress in Change* (New York: Praeger, 1975), 154. See also P. Healy, "Mansfield of Montana," 10.

42. *Congressional Record*, 21 February 1963, 2786. See also Mansfield, letter to Rusk, 1 October 1963, MP, XXII, 114 or 115.

43. *Newsweek* deviated from the administration view of the war before *Time*. Under the guidance of Henry Luce, *Time* continued its lack of objectivity about Diem and the war. Karnow sarcastically concluded that "true to their tradition, *Time* and *Life* stood up for America," or at least the Time-Life view of America. As a result, Halberstam claims that the military establishment in Saigon favored *Time*. As *Time's* correspondent in Vietnam, Charles Mohr found that his stories were rewritten to reflect the administration view of the war. Mohr was told that he was too close to the scene to see the big picture. As late as August 1963, *Time's* editors rewrote a Mohr story that had suggested the war was being lost and replaced it with an optimistic piece. Mohr resigned in protest. *Newsweek*, too, was vulnerable to administration pressure. After Sully's expulsion, he was replaced by Kenneth Crawford whose reporting was more sympathetic to the administration (Karnow, *Vietnam* [1984], 488-89; Aronson, *The Press and the Cold War*, 197, 200-2; Malcolm Browne, *Muddy Boots and Red Socks* [New York: Time Books, 1993], 189; George Goodman, "Our Man in Saigon," *Esquire*, January 1964, 60; Halberstam, *The Best and the Brightest*, 205).

44. Telephone conversation between Mansfield and Bradlee, 31 August 1962, MP, XXII, 103, #1. See also "Vietnam: The Unpleasant Truth," *Newsweek*, 20 August 1962, 40-41; Kahin, *Intervention*, 142; Browne, *Muddy Boots and Red Socks*, 190; Mecklin, *Mission in Torment*, 129-36, 177.

45. Mansfield, letter to McNamara, 17 June 1963 / Sheehan, et al., telegram to Mansfield, 12 July 1963 / Trueheart, telegram to Secretary of State, 7 July 1963, MP, XXII, 114 or 115. See also Browne, *Muddy Boots and Red Socks*, 229.

46. Hood, "'China Mike,'" 34. See also *Congressional Record,* 10 June 1965, 13098-100.

47. Rusk, *As I Saw It,* 438-40; Kahin, *Intervention,* 149-50; Karnow, *Vietnam* (1984), 285; Schoenbaum, *Waging Peace and War,* 397.

48. Mansfield, "Observations on Viet Nam" [memorandum to Kennedy], 19 August 1963, MP, XXII, 102, #11. One scholar suggests that Kennedy lacked patience with long memoranda like those Mansfield wrote and the norm for members of his administration was to write only short ones (M. Ball, "A Descriptive and Interpretive Analysis," 135).

49. *Congressional Record,* 20 September 1963, 17595-96.

50. Several communication scholars have recently agreed with Mansfield's 1963 position that the administration painted itself into a corner with its Vietnam rhetoric, which would have made it difficult to change course (see M. Ball, "A Descriptive and Interpretive Analysis," 508; Denise Bostdorff and Steven Goldzwig, "Idealism and Pragmatism in American Foreign Policy Rhetoric: The Case of John F. Kennedy and Vietnam," *Presidential Studies Quarterly* 24 [1994]: 515-30).

51. Mansfield, "Observations on Viet Nam" [memorandum to Kennedy], 19 August 1963, 1-8, MP, XXII, 102, #11. By August 1963 the administration had been discussing a coup for at least two and one-half years and Kennedy found Diem inept. In September, Kennedy would not answer a question about Diem's ability to succeed if Nhu were retained (see M. Ball, "A Descriptive and Interpretive Analysis," 245-46, 252; Bostdorff and Goldzwig, "Idealism and Pragmatism in American Foreign Policy Rhetoric," 522-23).

52. See for example Lichtenstein, "'Senator Mike,'" 49; Hood, "'China Mike,'" 344-47.

53. "Johnny, We Hardly Knew Ye, and Now You'd Be 70 Already," *Denver Post,* 29 May 1987, 2A. See also Arthur Schlesinger Jr., "What Would He Have Done," *New York Times,* 29 March 1992, 3; Jack Anderson, "The Roots of Our Vietnam Involvement," *Washington Post,* 4 May 1975, C7; Schoenbaum, *Waging Peace and War,* 401; Newman, *JFK and Vietnam,* 423-27; George McGovern, *Grassroots* (New York: Random House, 1977), 102; Tip O'Neill with William Novak, *Man of the House* (New York: Random House, 1987), 176.

54. Ludwick, "Mansfield," 13, 19, 23.

55. As quoted in Charlton and Moncrieff, *Many Reasons Why,* 81. See also J. Anderson, "The Roots of Our Vietnam Involvement," C7.

56. Rusk, *As I Saw It,* 197, 293, 296, 323, 441-42. See also Edwin Guthman and Jeffrey Shulman, eds., *Robert Kennedy: In His Own Words* (Toronto: Bantam Books, 1988), 394-95; Robert Kennedy, interview with John Bartlow Martin, 30 April 1964, 254-55, Robert Kennedy, interview with John Bartlow Martin, 14 May 1964, 338-39, JFK Oral History Project, JFK Library; Kahin, *Intervention,* 146-47, 479.

57. Robert Kennedy, interview with John Bartlow Martin, 29 February 1964, 20-21, JFK Oral History Project, JFK Library.

58. O'Brien, interview with Gillette, 29 October 1985, 77. See also Ball, *Vietnam-on-the-Potomac,* 14-16.

59. As quoted in Reeves, *President Kennedy,* 484-85.

60. J. Anderson, "The Roots of Our Vietnam Involvement," C7. See also Karnow, *Vietnam* (1984), 268-69; Kahin, *Intervention*, 147.

61. Ellen Hammer, *Vietnam* (New York: Holt, Rinehart, and Winston, 1966), 177-78. See also M. Ball, "A Descriptive and Interpretive Analysis," 261; Sullivan, *France's Vietnam Policy*, 67-68; Gibbons, *The U.S. Government and the Vietnam War*, Part 2, 200-8.

62. As quoted in "Diem's Death a Shock to Mansfield," *Inter Lake* [Kalispell, Montana], n.d. [1963], Mansfield scrapbooks, #89. See also Gibbons, *The U.S. Government and the Vietnam War*, Part 2, 206; *Congressional Record*, 5 November 1963, 21061.

63. The Foreign Relations Committee concluded that "ultimate responsibility for the coup that was to remove Diem comes to rest with the U.S. Government" (*U.S. Involvement in the Overthrow of Diem, 1963*, U.S. 92d Cong., 2d sess., S. Rept. [Washington D. C.: GPO, 1972], 15). For development of Kennedy administration involvement in the coup, see Hammer, *A Death in November*, 169-311 and M. Ball, *Vietnam-on-the-Potomac*, 70-83.

64. *ESSFRC*, 1963 (Washington, D.C.: GPO, 1986), 15:879-97. Kennedy helped plan the coup but took Diem's murder hard, Alsop said he was "shaken to his very marrow" by Diem's death. Robert Kennedy, Richard Nixon, Lodge, Taylor and others came to view the coup as a mistake (Hammer, *A Death in November*, 32, 296, 300-1; Nolting, *From Trust to Tragedy*, 136; Rusk, *As I Saw It*, 440; Alsop, *"I've Seen the Best of It,"* 463).

65. Mansfield, interview, "A Size-Up of President Nixon," *U.S. News & World Report*, 6 December 1971, 57. See also Charlton and Moncrieff, *Many Reasons Why*, 83.

66. Lansdale, U.S. Mission Council Briefing for Codel Mansfield, 2 December 1965, 32, MP, XXII, 99, #4. See also Currey, *Edward Lansdale*, 278; Sheehan, *A Bright Shining Lie*, 371-73; Sullivan, *France's Vietnam Policy*, 71; Trueheart, interview with Gittinger, 2 March 1982, 56-59.

67. As quoted in "True or False? JFK was a secret dove who would have pulled military forces out of Vietnam upon re-election," *Vietnam*, June 1992, 6. See also Nolting, *From Trust to Tragedy*, 137-38.

68. E. H. Oliver, trans., "The Greatest Homage," *Realities Cambodgiennes*, 6 December 1963, 4 / E. H. Oliver, trans., "Thank You, Senator," *Realities Cambodgiennes*, 6 December 1963, 6, MP, XXII, 52, #6. See also Hammer, *A Death in November*, 308-9.

69. Hammer, *A Death in November*, 309. See also Rusk, *As I Saw It*, 322, 440-41, 443; Schoenbaum, *Waging Peace and War*, 409, 416.

CHAPTER 8

1. As quoted in M. Ball, "A Descriptive and Interpretive Analysis," 429-30.

2. Gibbons, *The U.S. Government and the Vietnam War*, Part 2, 42. See also Lyndon Johnson, *The Vantage Point* (New York: Holt, Rinehart and Winston, 1971), 53.

3. Valeo, letter to the author, 12 September 1990.

4. Hammer, *A Death in November*, 34-35. See also Nolting, *From Trust to Tragedy*, 19-22; Kahin, *Intervention*, 133, 165.

5. As quoted in Bill Moyers, "Flashbacks," *Newsweek*, 10 February 1975, 76; Stanley Karnow, *Vietnam* (New York: Viking, 1991), 338-39. See also Schoenbaum, *Waging Peace and War*, 422.

6. George Ball, *The Past Has Another Pattern* (New York: W.W. Norton & Co., 1982), 374-75; Alsop, *"I've Seen the Best of It,"* 465, 475-76. See also M. Ball, "A Descriptive and Interpretive Analysis," 314.

7. As quoted in Mansfield, "Luncheon Meeting Dem. National Committee," 11 January 1964, Mansfield Oral History Project, 22-49.

8. Kahin, *Intervention*, 190-91.

9. Bornet, *The Presidency of Lyndon B. Johnson*, 67. See also Kathleen J. Turner, *Lyndon Johnson's Dual War* (Chicago: University of Chicago Press, 1985), 56, 263.

10. Mansfield, "Southeast Asia and Viet Nam," [memo to Lyndon Johnson], 7 December 1963, 1-2, MP, XXII, 103, #13.

11. Columnist Jack Anderson wrote that Republican claims in the 1950s that Democrats had "lost China" had left a deep impression on Johnson. In the three or four times Anderson discussed Vietnam with the president, Johnson repeated two themes: "They're not going to say Lyndon Johnson lost Vietnam" and "Lyndon Johnson isn't going to be the first American president to lose a war" (J. Anderson, "The Roots of Our Vietnam Involvement," C7).

12. As quoted in Karnow, *Vietnam* (1984), 326.

13. Mansfield, "Viet Namese Situation" [memo to the President], 6 January 1964, 1, MP, XXII, 103, #13.

14. Kahin, *Intervention*, 191.

15. As quoted in *FRUS, 1964-1968, Vietnam* (Washington, D.C.: GPO, 1992), 1:8-15. See also Gibbons, *The U.S. Government and the Vietnam War*, Part 2, 215-18; Kahin, *Intervention*, 191-92.

16. Robert S. McNamara, with Brian VanDeMark, *In Retrospect: The Tragedy and Lessons of Vietnam* (New York: Times Books, 1995), 106-7. See also Robert S. McNamara, "We Were Wrong, Terribly Wrong," *Newsweek*, 17 April 1995, 48.

17. *FRUS, 1964-1968, Vietnam*, 1:15-16; Kahin, *Intervention*, 192; Gibbons, *The U.S. Government and the Vietnam War*, Part 2, 218.

18. Kahin, *Intervention*, 194-202. See also Gibbons, *The U.S. Government and the Vietnam War*, Part 2, 219.

19. Mansfield, "The Vietnamese Situation" [memo to the President], 1 February 1964, 1-3, MP, XXII, 103, #13.

20. Mansfield, letter to Marcia Melton, 23 January 1964, MP, XIII, 48, #2.

21. Mansfield, "Luncheon Meeting Dem. National Committee," 11 January 1964, 22-49, Mansfield Oral History Project.

22. *FRUS, 1964-1968, Vietnam*, 1:67.

23. *Congressional Record*, 19 February 1964, 3114-15; *Congressional Record*, 20 February 1964, 3277-81. See also Gibbons, *The U.S. Government and the Vietnam*

War, Part 2, 220-21. Mansfield and Javits resumed this colloquy on March 2 (see *Congressional Record*, 2 March 1964, 4086-87).

24. Gareth Porter, ed., *Vietnam: The Definitive Documentation of Human Decisions* (Stanfordville, New York: Earl Coleman Enterprises, Inc., 1979), 2:261; Gibbons, *The U.S. Government and the Vietnam War*, Part 2, 219-20, 222.

25. As quoted in Steinberg, *Sam Johnson's Boy*, 621 and O'Donnell, Powers, and McCarthy, *"Johnny, We Hardly Knew Ye,"* 399. See also Schwartz, "Senator Michael J. Mansfield," 372; Gibbons, *The U.S. Government and the Vietnam War*, Part 2, 219-20; Clifford, *Counsel to the President*, 607.

26. William White, "Sees Mansfield Hurting Viet-Nam," *Cleveland Press*, 26 February 1964, MP, XIII, 48 #5.

27. Mansfield, letter to John Higley, 4 March 1964, MP, XIII, 49, #1.

28. *ESSFRC*, 1964 (Washington, D.C.: GPO, 1987), 16:152.

29. *PPP, Johnson, 1963-64* (Washington, D.C.: GPO, 1965), 1:370, 475.

30. Summary Record of NSC Meeting No. 526, 3 April 1964, 2:00 P.M., vol. 1, Box 1, NSC Meeting File, NSF, 3-4, 6, LBJ Library.

31. *Congressional Record*, 20 April 1964, 8414-15; *Congressional Record*, 21 May 1964, 11552. See also Gibbons, *The U.S. Government and the Vietnam War*, Part 2, 252.

32. Mansfield, letter to President Johnson and attached note, 25 and 26 May 1964, 1-2, MP, XXII, 102, #12.

33. Mansfield, memo to Lyndon Johnson, 9 June 1964, 1, MP, XXII, 102, #12. See also Gibbons, *The U.S. Government and the Vietnam War*, Part 2, 272.

34. *ESSFRC*, 1955, 7:65, 101, 126, 170-75, 281; *ESSFRC*, 1957 (Washington, D.C.: GPO, 1979), 9:1, 25-26, 251-60, 358-59, 363-76, 385-94, 407. See also Gibbons, *The U.S. Government and the Vietnam War*, Part 1, 276-81, 343-49.

35. Gibbons, *The U.S. Government and the Vietnam War*, Part 2, 129-30. See also *PPP, Kennedy, 1962* (Washington, D.C.: GPO, 1963), 679.

36. Mark Stoler, "Aiken, Mansfield and the Tonkin Gulf Crisis: Notes from the Congressional Leadership Meeting at the White House, August 4, 1964," *Vermont History*, Spring 1982, 82. See also Gibbons, *The U.S. Government and the Vietnam War*, Part 2, 294; Rusk, *As I Saw It*, 445; Karnow, *Vietnam* (1991), 360, 373-77; W. Berman, *William Fulbright and the Vietnam War*, 19-24.

37. Mansfield, statement, 4 August 1964, MP, XXII, 103, #13. See also Stoler, "Aiken, Mansfield and the Tonkin Gulf Crisis," 82, 86.

38. Notes taken at Leadership Meeting and summary of meeting, 4 August 1964, Leadership Breakfast Meeting Minutes File, DSDUF, Box 2, LBJ Library. See also Stoler, "Aiken, Mansfield and the Tonkin Gulf Crisis," 86-94.

39. Johnson intentionally had Mansfield speak last at these leadership meetings, after "the more hawkish ones" had been persuaded to come on board. Fulbright suggested that Johnson always asked Speaker of the House John McCormack (D-Mass.) to speak first, using him as a "stalking horse." McCormack would always agree with Johnson. Johnson would then ask others and when he got to Mansfield, the majority leader would usually have a prepared statement. House Majority Leader Carl Albert

(D-Okla.) said that Johnson always asked for opinions at these meetings, "but sometimes [the opportunity to disagree] came pretty late. We were always after the fact in giving advice." George Reedy, a long-time Johnson aide, may have said it best when he asserted that Johnson "could script a meeting like nobody else I ever heard of" (J. William Fulbright with Seth Tillman, *The Price of Empire* [New York: Pantheon, 1989], 108-9; George Reedy, conversation with the author, Milwaukee, 2 July 1993; Halberstam, *The Best and the Brightest*, 600; Melvin Small, *Johnson, Nixon, and the Doves* [New Brunswick: Rutgers University Press, 1988], 58).

40. Mansfield, letter to the author, 19 April 1988. See also Mansfield, letter to John Patterson Jr., 12 August 1964, MP, XIII, 68, #5; Mansfield, "Speech at Montana Democratic Convention 1964," Mansfield Oral History Project, 22-47.

41. Pat Holt, Oral History Interview, Senate Historical Office, Washington, D.C., 1980, 178, 197.

42. Marcy, Oral History Interview, Senate Historical Office, Washington, D.C., 1983, 152-53. See also Gibbons, *The U.S. Government and the Vietnam War*, Part 2, 301-13, 316, 329, 334-35; Fulbright, *The Price of Empire*, 104-6; *Congressional Record,* 6 August 1964, 18399.

43. Reedy, interview with the author, Milwaukee, 15 September 1987.

44. McGovern, *Grassroots*, 103-4.

45. Evans and Novak, *Lyndon B. Johnson*, 458-59. See also "'Democrats' Change of Pace," *Time,* 20 July 1964, 30.

46. Mansfield, "Speech at Montana Democratic Convention 1964," Mansfield Oral History Project, 22-47; Mansfield, letter to Marvin Morrow, 2 September 1964, MP, XIV, 32, #16. See also O'Donnell, Powers, and McCarthy, *"Johnny, We Hardly Knew Ye,"* 398-400; Hubert Humphrey, *The Education of a Public Man*, Norman Sherman, ed. (Garden City, New York: Doubleday, 1976), 221.

47. The Republican meant either mountain goats or bighorn sheep.

48. "When Is a Majority a Majority," 24. See also *PPP, Johnson, 1963-64* (Washington, D.C.: GPO, 1965), 2:1310; Clifford, *Counsel to the President*, 398; Schwartz, "Senator Michael J. Mansfield," 384-85.

49. Kahin, *Intervention*, 236-59. See also *ESSFRC,* 1964, 16:351; Gibbons, *The U.S. Government and the Vietnam War*, Part 2, 363-77; W. Berman, *William Fulbright and the Vietnam War*, 33.

50. Mansfield, "Developments in Viet Nam" [memo to the President], 9 December 1964, 1-2, MP, XXII, 103, #13.

51. Lyndon Johnson, letter to Mansfield, 17 December 1964 / Bundy, "Senator Mansfield's memorandum of December 9" [memo for the President], 16 December 1964, 1-3, MP, XXII, 103, #13. See also Gibbons, *The U.S. Government and the Vietnam War*, Part 2, 379; Brian VanDeMark, *Into the Quagmire* (New York: Oxford University Press, 1991), 40-42.

CHAPTER 9

1. As quoted in John Bartlow Martin, *Adlai Stevenson and the World* (Garden City, New York: Doubleday, 1977), 824.

2. Humphrey, *The Education of a Public Man* (1991), 324.

3. Evans and Novak, *Lyndon B. Johnson*, 498-99. See also Lawrence O'Brien, *No Final Victories* (New York: Ballantine, 1974), 173; *PPP, Johnson, 1965* (Washington, D.C.: GPO, 1966), 1:59.

4. Valeo, interview with the author, Washington, D.C., 17 May 1991.

5. Kearns, *Lyndon Johnson and the American Dream*, 262.

6. G. Ball, *The Past Has Another Pattern,* 377-78, 383-84, 396. See also Mansfield, letter to the author, 25 April 1990; Rusk, *As I Saw It*, 451, 473; M. Ball, "A Descriptive and Interpretive Analysis," 504-5; Schoenbaum, *Waging Peace and War*, 431-32, 440; Karnow, *Vietnam* (1991), 420-21.

7. As quoted in Schoenbaum, *Waging Peace and War*, 413-15.

8. G. Ball, *The Past Has Another Pattern*, 390.

9. John Burke and Fred Greenstein, *How Presidents Test Reality* (New York: Russell Sage Foundation, 1989), 173, 238.

10. Valeo, interview with the author, Washington, D.C., 17 May 1991.

11. Jack Valenti, interview IV with Joe B. Frantz, 3 March 1971, 26, LBJ Oral History Project, LBJ Library.

12. Mansfield, letter to the author, 25 April 1991. See also Schoenbaum, *Waging Peace and War*, 432-33, 440-41, 451, 455, 457-58, 466, 467, 469-70, 471, 498; Kahin, *Intervention*, 245-54; M. Ball, "A Descriptive and Interpretive Analysis," 35, 503-4; Rusk, *As I Saw It*, 417-19, 454, 458, 472-73, 497-98; Clifford, *Counsel to the President,* 538, 552, 569, 603; David Humphrey, "Tuesday Lunch at the Johnson White House: A Preliminary Assessment," *Diplomatic History* 8 (1984): 81-87; Henry Graff, *The Tuesday Cabinet* (Englewood Cliffs: Prentice-Hall, 1970), 3-6.

13. *Congressional Record,* 29 July 1965, 18743.

14. Mansfield, "Major Steps in Escalation since August 2, 1964," 24 March 1965, MP, XXII, 102, #13; G. Ball, *The Past Has Another Pattern*, 390.

15. As quoted in L. Johnson, *The Vantage Point*, 124-25; NSF, Meeting Notes File, "2/6/65 7:45 p.m. NSC Meeting," Box 1, 2-3, LBJ Library. See also McNamara, *In Retrospect*, 171.

16. As quoted in Gibbons, *The U.S. Government and the Vietnam War*, Part 3, 61-64. See also Kahin, *Intervention*, 277.

17. NSF, Meeting Notes File "2/7/65 8 a.m. NSC Meeting," Box 1 and Name File, "Vietnam, Mansfield memo and reply," Box 6, LBJ Library.

18. As quoted in Graff, *The Tuesday Cabinet*, 46.

19. Burke and Greenstein, *How Presidents Test Reality*, 169.

20. NSF, NSC Meetings, "Vol. 3, Tab 30, 2/10/65 Vietnam," Meeting Notes File, "2/10/65 2:10 p.m. NSC Meeting," Box 1, LBJ Library. See also Burke and Greenstein, *How Presidents Test Reality*, 166-68; Karnow, *Vietnam* (1984), 413;

G. Ball, *The Past Has Another Pattern*, 390; Gibbons, *The U.S. Government and the Vietnam War*, Part 3, 77-80.

21. Mansfield, "Further observations on Viet Nam" [memo to the President], 10 February 1965, 1-2, MP, XXII, 102, #13. See also Burke and Greenstein, *How Presidents Test Reality*, 169; Gibbons, *The U.S. Government and the Vietnam War*, Part 3, 80-81.

22. NSF, Name File, "Vietnam, Mansfield memo and reply," Box 6, LBJ Library.

23. Mansfield, letter to Corporal R. H. M. Smith, 27 February 1965, MP, XIII, 69, #1. See also *Congressional Record,* 11 February 1965, 2619; Mansfield, Exact Quotes, MP, XIII, 113 or 114, 17; Peter Poole, *The United States and Indochina* (Hinsdale, Illinios: Dryden Press, 1973), 139-40.

24. *Congressional Record,* 1 March 1965, 3775-76. See also Cooper, *The Lost Crusade,* 263-65; Gibbons, *The U.S. Government and the Vietnam War*, Part 3, 138-39.

25. Mansfield, notes from a telephone conversation with McNamara, 6 March 1965, MP, XXII, 103, #1. See also Mansfield, "Major Steps in Escalation since August 2, 1964," 24 March 1965, MP, XXII, 102, #13; Karnow, *Vietnam* (1991), 431-32.

26. As quoted in Gibbons, *The U.S. Government and the Vietnam War*, Part 3, viii.

27. As quoted in Gibbons, *The U.S. Government and the Vietnam War*, Part 3, 125-26. See also Clifford, *Counsel to the President*, 406; VanDeMark, *Into the Quagmire*, 99.

28. Mansfield, letter to the President, 24 March 1965, 1-4, MP, XXII, 103, #1.

29. Lyndon Johnson, letter to Mansfield, 12 April 1965, McGeorge Bundy Files, vols. 9, 10, and 11, Box 3, LBJ Library. See also Gibbons, *The U.S. Government and the Vietnam War*, Part 3, 205-8; VanDeMark, *Into the Quagmire*, 104-5.

30. McGovern, *Grassroots*, 104-5. Like Kennedy, Johnson preferred short memos and the "drawerful" of Mansfield epistles were probably more reading than Johnson wanted. See Valenti, interview IV with Frantz, 3 March 1971, 26.

31. Mansfield, "Memorandum from Mansfield," 28 April 1965, MP, XXII, 102, #13.

32. As quoted in Gibbons, *The U.S. Government and the Vietnam War*, Part 3, 242, 255-56, 272; VanDeMark, *Into the Quagmire*, 140-41 and Burke and Greenstein, *How Presidents Test Reality*, 137.

33. W. Berman, *William Fulbright and the Vietnam War*, 16-18. See also "Are Our Policies Turning Obsolete?" *Business Week,* 4 April 1964, 28; Lester Thonssen, ed., *Representative American Speeches: 1963-1964* (New York: H.W. Wilson Co., 1964), 91-114.

34. Fulbright, *The Price of Empire*, 107-9.

35. Marcy added: "I've often thought that . . . Fulbright probably knew more about the history and the background characteristics of Indochina than Rusk, or certainly than . . . McNamara, or Johnson. The policy makers were so busy making policy that they had no time to read or to think. Fulbright took time to read and think, but he was not able at that time to determine policy" (Marcy, Oral History Interview, Senate Historical Office, Washington, D.C., 1983, 139-40. See also Holt, Oral History Interview, Senate Historical Office, Washington, D.C., 1980, 202).

36. Fulbright, *The Price of Empire*, 110-11. See also K. Turner, *Lyndon Johnson's Dual War,* 126, 130; Kahin, *Intervention*, 324-25; W. Berman, *William Fulbright and the*

Vietnam War, 37-38; Gibbons, *The U.S. Government and the Vietnam War*, Part 2, 222-23, Part 3, 70, 211-38; Karnow, *Vietnam* (1991), 434; *Congressional Record*, 8 April 1965, 7492-94.

37. As quoted in J. William Fulbright, *The Arrogance of Power* (New York: Random House, 1966), 58 and W. Berman, *William Fulbright and the Vietnam War*, 39. Mansfield's rhetorical strategy was also consciously chosen. See letter to the author, 18 August 1987.

38. Fulbright, *The Price of Empire*, 109. In his memoirs, Rusk said little about the dissent of either Fulbright or Mansfield. Rusk called Fulbright an "instinctive maverick." He admitted that there is room for mavericks in the Senate, but suggested that mavericks should not head important committees. Rusk told Marcy: "you know, Fulbright would make a wonderful president of a university, but it's terrible to have him as chairman of a committee." He called Mansfield a "fascinating character" and mentions the many memos Mansfield sent to Johnson expressing his reasons for opposing Vietnam policy, but Rusk did not comment on their content (see Rusk, *As I Saw It*, 546, 549; Marcy, Oral History Interview, Senate Historical Office, Washington, D.C., 1983, 165).

39. Most who write of Kennedy's decision not to select Fulbright as secretary of state suggest that Kennedy rejected Fulbright because of his record on civil rights (see for example Robert Kennedy, interview with Bartlow Martin, 29 February 1964, 5-6 and Clifford, *Counsel to the President*, 339). Both Marcy and Holt believe that Johnson had the appointment of Fulbright "set up." Fulbright did not want to leave the Senate and had Richard Russell go to Kennedy to prevent the offer from being made (see Marcy, Oral History Interview, Senate Historical Office, Washington, D.C., 1983, 128 and Holt, Oral History Interview, Senate Historical Office, Washington, D.C., 1980, 149-50). The history of America's involvement in Vietnam would have been very different had Fulbright become secretary of state instead of Rusk. While Kennedy acted as his own secretary of state, Johnson became dependent on Rusk. Fulbright's advice might have led Johnson away from escalation in Vietnam.

40. Holt, Oral History Interview, Senate Historical Office, Washington, D.C., 1980, 131-34, 199. See also Fulbright, *The Price of Empire*, 115; Marcy, Oral History Interview, Senate Historical Office, Washington, D.C., 1983, preface, 98-101; W. Berman, *William Fulbright and the Vietnam War*, 1-50; Rusk, *As I Saw It*, 202.

41. Tristram Coffin, *Senator Fulbright: Portrait of a Public Philosopher* (New York: E.P. Dutton & Co., 1966), 252-53. See also Holt, Oral History Interview, Senate Historical Office, Washington, D.C., 1980, 207; Gibbons, *The U.S. Government and the Vietnam War*, Part 3, 303-4; Fulbright, *The Arrogance of Power*, 59.

42. Marcy, Oral History Interview, Senate Historical Office, Washington, D.C., 1983, 163-64. See also Holt, Oral History Interview, Senate Historical Office, Washington, D.C., 1980, 177, 199; *Congressional Record*, 15 June 1965, 13656-57; W. Berman, *William Fulbright and the Vietnam War*, 41-50; G. Ball, *The Past Has Another Pattern*, 403; Fulbright, *The Price of Empire*, 112-20; Fulbright, *The Arrogance of Power*, 59-61; Gibbons, *The U.S. Government and the Vietnam War*, Part 3, 304-5.

43. As quoted in R. Baker, "Mike Mansfield and the Birth of the Modern Senate," in Baker and Davidson, *First Among Equals*, 288.
44. As quoted in Karnow, *Vietnam* (1991), 420.
45. Kahin, *Intervention*, 321-50.
46. Burke and Greenstein, *How Presidents Test Reality*, 257.
47. Harry McPherson, interview with T. H. Baker, 24 March 1969, 19-20, LBJ Oral History Project, LBJ Library.
48. Mansfield may have held the 5 June memorandum and sent it with the 9 June one. See VanDeMark, *Into the Quagmire*, 157-58.
49. Confidential memo of Mansfield, 3 June 1965; Mansfield, memorandum to the President, "Viet Nam," 5 June 1965, 1-4, Mansfield, "Viet Nam," 9 June 1965, 1, MP, XXII, Box 102, #13. See also Kahin, *Intervention*, 345, 349-50; Gibbons, *The U.S. Government and the Vietnam War*, Part 3, 281-83, 294-96. McNamara concluded that Mansfield's advice against a Gulf of Tonkin-type resolution was exactly what Johnson wanted to hear, but it was the "wrong" answer because at some point, Johnson needed a popular mandate to pursue the war (see McNamara, *In Retrospect*, 191-92).
50. As quoted in Gibbons, *The U.S. Government and the Vietnam War*, Part 3, 288.
51. Telephone call between Ball and the President, 6/14/65, Papers of G. Ball, Box 7, LBJ Library.
52. Mansfield, letter to the President, 22 June 1965 / Mansfield, "Suggestions on the Vietnamese Situation," 14 June 1965, MP, XXII, 102, #13. See also Gibbons, *The U.S. Government and the Vietnam War*, Part 3, 319.
53. McGeorge Bundy, memo to Mansfield, 29 June 1965, NSF Subject File: Vietnam Mansfield, LBJ Library; Lyndon Johnson, letter to Mansfield, n.d., NSF Name File, Box 6, LBJ Library.
54. As quoted in Gibbons, *The U.S. Government and the Vietnam War*, Part 3, 350-51.
55. *Congressional Record*, 21 July 1965, 17797-99. See also G. Ball, *The Past Has Another Pattern*, 403.
56. Meeting on Vietnam, 7/21/65 / Meeting on Vietnam, 7/22/65, 12:00 P.M. / Meeting on Vietnam, 7/22/65, 3:00 P.M., LBJ Library. See also Clifford, *Counsel to the President*, 413-14; Kahin, *Intervention*, 366-87; Gibbons, *The U.S. Government and the Vietnam War*, Part 3, ix-x, 390, 412; Karnow, *Vietnam* (1991), 440.
57. Mansfield, memo to the President, 23 July 1965, 1-3, MP, XXII, 102, #13. See also Ball, memo to Lyndon Johnson, 24 July 1965, NSF Name File, Box 6, LBJ Library. After his "day in court" on July 21, Ball became a team player and supported the administration's position.
58. Meetings on Vietnam, 7/25/65, LBJ Library. See also Clifford, *Counsel to the President*, 418-21; Kahin, *Intervention*, 387, 390, 529.
59. The meeting grew out of a 22 July memorandum from Marcy to Fulbright, in which Marcy argued: "we seem to be on the verge of another important decision regarding Viet Nam—one on which the views of the Senate will not be sought until after the decision." Marcy suggested a meeting of senators to seek common ground and "call

privately on the President" (Marcy to Fulbright, 22 July 1965, Marcy Papers, National Archives, Washington, D.C.).

60. Kahin, *Intervention*, 391, 529.

61. Mansfield, et. al., memo to the President, "Meeting on Viet Nam," 27 July 1965, 1-3, MP, XXII, 102, #13.

62. Gibbons, *The U.S. Government and the Vietnam War*, Part 3, 435.

63. Lyndon Johnson, letter to Mansfield, 28 July 1965 / Robert McNamara, memo for the President, 28 July 1965, 1-6, MP, XXII, 102, #13. See also Kahin, *Intervention*, 529; Gibbons, *The U.S. Government and the Vietnam War*, Part 3, 435-36. Gibbons writes that Johnson added a handwritten note to Mansfield by McNamara's response on point six [public support]: "could you organize a group of our Dem. Senators to help in this respect?" That note is not on Mansfield's copy of McNamara's memo, raising the possibility that Mansfield received the wrong copy of McNamara's memo.

64. The president did not admit that his decision was made before his meeting with congressional leaders; Johnson ended the NSC meeting by saying, "but this is something we will decide with the leadership." Bundy wrote in his notes from the NSC meeting that the president's "unspoken object was to protect his legislative program" (see NSF, Meeting Notes, "7/21-27/65 Meetings on Vietnam," Box 1 and "7/27/65 NSC Meeting; Joint Leadership Meeting," Box 1, LBJ Library).

65. Those present from the administration were Johnson, Rusk, McNamara, Valenti, O'Brien, McGeorge Bundy, General Earle Wheeler, Admiral William Raborn, Henry Cabot Lodge, Bill Moyers, Horace Busby, Douglas Cater, Joseph Califano Jr., and Richard Goodwin. Other senators in attendance were Dirksen, Long, Bourke Hickenlooper (R-Iowa), George Smathers (D-Fla.) and Thomas Kuchel (R-Calif.). From the House, McCormack, Gerald Ford (R-Mich.), Carl Albert (D-Okla.), Hale Boggs (D-La.) and Leslie Arends (R-Ill.) were present. See Jack Valenti, *A Very Human President* (New York: W.W. Norton & Co., 1975), 354.

66. Mansfield, letter to the author, 25 April 1990.

67. The account of this meeting before Mansfield spoke comes from the LBJ Library, NSF, Meeting Notes, "7/21-27/65 Meetings on Vietnam," and "7/27/65 NSC Meeting; Joint Leadership Meeting." The two accounts of this meeting come from notes taken at the meeting by McGeorge Bundy and Jack Valenti. This account comes largely from Valenti's notes. Mansfield's remarks come from the statement he prepared in advance of the meeting, located in his papers (Mansfield, "Notes on Viet Nam," 26 July 1965, 1, MP, XXII, 102, #13). Mansfield may not have had the time to read his complete statement. He wrote on his typed text, "when the time has come that I can't express my opinion, in confidence" (which apparently was not said at the meeting) and "as the Minority Leader has said, there is apathy among the people & I would add disquiet & concern as well & it applies to the Senate also" (which apparently was said at the meeting). Everyone writing of Mansfield's comments bases it on the notes taken at that meeting and no one seems to have had access to the actual statement located in Mansfield's papers. Bundy's account makes Mansfield's role less dramatic than portrayed by Valenti. Bundy reinterpreted his notes of this meeting

in 1969 and recorded Mansfield's part of the meeting in this way: "Senator Mansfield asked the President's indulgence and read a statement in which there appeared remarks about apathy, disquiet, and apprehension. He thought that nothing should be put out from the meeting except by the President. He said he would support the President's position as a Senator and as Majority Leader." Bundy recorded Hickenlooper, Kuchel, Boggs, Arends, and McCormack speaking after Mansfield. Valenti's notes show Mansfield's words of caution coming at the end of the meeting and recorded them in this way: "I agree with Dirksen in (sic) [on] apathy in the country. I would not be true to myself if I didn't speak. This position has certain inevitability. Whatever pledge we had was to assist [South Vietnam] in its own defense. Since then there has been no government of legitimacy. We ought to make that decision every day. We owe this government nothing—no pledge of any kind. We are going deeper into war. Even total victory would be vastly costly. Best hope for salvation is quick stalemate and negotiations. We cannot expect our people to support a war for 3-5 years. What we are about is an anti-Communist crusade, on — Escalation begets escalation." Johnson's recollection had McCormack closing the meeting after Mansfield's dissent (L. Johnson, *The Vantage Point*, 151; Kahin, *Intervention*, 386-97; Gibbons, *The U.S. Government and the Vietnam War*, Part 3, 427).

68. Valenti, *A Very Human President*, 354-56.

CHAPTER 10

1. *Congressional Record,* 29 July, 1965, 18815-16, 18823, 18861-65; *Congressional Record,* 30 July 1965, 18938-41; *Congressional Record,* 6 August 1965, 19674-75. See also Gibbons, *The U.S. Government and the Vietnam War*, Part 3, 443-45, 452-58.

2. *Congressional Record,* 13 August 1965, 20430; *Congressional Record,* 29 August 1965, 21058-59. Others agreeing with Fulbright about Johnson administration hostility toward negotiation include Kahin (*Intervention*, 245-54, 324-25, 400) and Moya Ball ("A Descriptive and Interpretive Analysis," 501).

3. Mansfield, letter to Lyndon Johnson, 30 August 1965, MP, XXII, 102, #13.

4. Mansfield, memo to the President, 30 August 1965, 1-2 / Mansfield, Statement of Mansfield, n.d., 1-8, MP, XXII, 102, #13.

5. Mansfield, "Viet Nam: Narrowing the Issues," 1 September 1965, 5, MP, XIII, 67, # 4.

6. Jean LaCouture, Konrad Kellen and Joel Carmichael, trans., *Vietnam: Between Two Truces* (New York: Random House, 1966), 282. See also "How to End the War— Mansfield's Five Points," *U.S. News & World Report,* 13 September 1965, 19.

7. "A Small Something for Hanoi," *Time,* 10 September 1965, 19.

8. Max Ascoli, "Charity Begins Abroad," *Reporter,* 7 October 1965, 24; Max Ascoli, "The Freedom to End Freedom," *Reporter,* 5 May 1966, 10.

9. As quoted in M. Ball, *Vietnam-on-the-Potomac*, 163. See also Clifford, *Counsel to the President*, 426.

10. Daniel Inouye, interview with Dorothy Pierce McSweeny, 2 May 1969, 25-26, LBJ Oral History Project, LBJ Library. One advantage of a Johnson-sponsored trip was that Mansfield's party was given the use of an air force jet. At the same time, Fulbright and Wayne Morse (D-Ore.) were attending a meeting in New Zealand. Carl Marcy recalled that Fulbright and Morse had to struggle to find an old prop plane for their trip; the president could be vindictive! (see Marcy, Oral History Interview, Senate Historical Office, Washington, D.C., 1983, 193).

11. Mansfield, *Two Reports on Vietnam and Southeast Asia*, 17; Mansfield, Edmond Muskie, Daniel Inouye, George Aiken, and J. Caleb Boggs, *The Vietnam Conflict: The Substance and the Shadow*, U.S 89th Cong., 2nd sess., S. Rept. (Washington, D.C.: GPO, 1966). See also Mansfield, press release, 10 November 1965 and group itinerary, n.d., MP, XXII, 94.

12. Mansfield, memoranda of conversation with Sri Savang Vatthana / Mansfield, memoranda of conversation with Souvanna Phouma / Mansfield, briefing with Ambassador Sullivan, 28 November 1965, MP, XXII, 99, #7.

13. Mansfield, telegram to President and Secretary, 1 December 1965, MP, XXII, 99, #1; Sihanouk, letter to Mansfield, January 1966, MP, XXII, 114 or 115. See also Valeo, interview with the author, Washington, D.C., 17 May 1991; Meloy to Rusk, 11/17/65 and Emory Swank to Department of State, 11/28/65, International Meetings and Travel: Mansfield: S.E. Asia, LBJ Library; Huot Sambath, letter to Mansfield, 20 June 1966 / unnamed, n.d., note in files, MP, XXII, 52, #6.

14. Mansfield, *Two Reports on Vietnam and Southeast Asia,* 31; Mansfield, *The Vietnam Conflict,* 8-9.

15. Mission Briefing for Codel Mansfield, 2 December 1965, 1-13, MP, XXII, 99, #4.

16. As quoted in Halberstam, *The Best and the Brightest*, 615.

17. One writer contrasted Mansfield's report of 14,000 North Vietnamese troops to the 170,000 U.S. troops there. Even South Korea's 21,000 troops outnumbered those from the North (Howard Zinn, *The Logic of Withdrawal* [Boston: Beacon Press, 1967], 78).

18. Mission Briefing for Codel Mansfield, 2 December 1965, 13-50, MP, XXII, 99, #4.

19. Mansfield, memoranda of conversation with Tran Van Do / Mansfield, memoranda of conversation with Nguyen Cao Ky / Mansfield, memoranda of conversation with Nguyen Van Thieu, 3 December 1965, MP, XXII, 99, #4.

20. Lodge to Rusk, 12/3/65, International Meetings and Travel: Mansfield: S.E. Asia, LBJ Library.

21. Mansfield, memo to Lyndon Johnson, 18 December 1965, NSF, Internatl. Meetings and Travel, Box 30, LBJ Library.

22. Mansfield, *Two Reports on Vietnam and Southeast Asia,* 18, 20, 26-33.

23. Mansfield, letter to the author, 25 April 1990. See also Kahin, *Intervention*, 400.

24. George Aiken, interview with Paige Mulhollan, 10 October 1968, 16, LBJ Oral History Project, LBJ Library. See also Inouye, interview with Dorothy Pierce

McSweeny, 2 May 1969, 26, LBJ Oral History Project, LBJ Library; Eugene McCarthy, *Up 'Til Now* (New York: Harcourt Brace Jovanovich, 1987), 171.

25. Mansfield, *The Vietnam Conflict,* 2-5, 7, 11-13.

26. Ibid., 12; Mansfield, *Two Reports on Vietnam and Southeast Asia,* 29, 31.

27. "A Fretful Congress Confronts Vietnam," *Newsweek,* 17 January 1966, 17.

28. "Mansfield Report: Real Danger of Bigger War," *U.S. News & World Report,* 17 January 1966, 11; "A Fretful Congress Confronts Vietnam," 17.

29. One historian suggests that the private report said "far more concretely" than the public one "that the conflict in Vietnam was teetering on the brink of disaster; that is, it was quickly becoming 'open-ended' and had the potential for spilling over all of Southeast Asia, perhaps touching China as well" (W. Berman, *William Fulbright and the Vietnam War,* 51).

30. E. W. Kenworthy, "Mansfield Report Seen as Urging U.S. to Get Peace Pact Quickly," *New York Times,* 9 January 1966, 1-2.

31. McGeorge Bundy to Lyndon Johnson, 12/10/65, International Meetings and Travel File, Mansfield: S.E. Asia, LBJ Library.

32. Telephone call between Ball and the President, 30 December 1965 / Telephone call between Ball and Mansfield, 30 December 1965, Papers of G. Ball, Box 7, LBJ Library.

CHAPTER 11

1. James Rowe, interview with Michael Gillette, 10 November 1982, 3-4 / James Rowe, interview with Joe Frantz, 16 September 1969, 43-44, LBJ Oral History Project, LBJ Library.

2. Mansfield, letter to the author, 19 April 1988. See also *Congressional Record,* 23 January 1973, 1846.

3. Reedy, conversation with the author, Milwaukee, 17 March 1988. See also Valeo, interview with the author, Washington, D.C., 17 May 1991; Halberstam, *The Best and the Brightest,* 535; Evans and Novak, *Lyndon B. Johnson,* 563.

4. As quoted in R. Baker, "Mike Mansfield and the Birth of the Modern Senate," in Baker and Davidson, *First Among Equals,* 288. See also Schwartz, "Senator Michael J. Mansfield," 394.

5. Mansfield, interview with Challener, 10 May 1966, 15-16.

6. Mansfield, interview with Tillman, 23 June 1964, 36-37; "Why Kennedy's Program is in Trouble with Congress," *U.S. News & World Report,* 17 September 1962, 63-64.

7. Mansfield, letter to the author, 18 August 1987.

8. Evans and Novak, *Lyndon B. Johnson,* 563. See also Mansfield, letter to Tom Rounsley, 4 April 1966, MP, XIII, 72, #4; Hartke, et al., letter to Lyndon Johnson, 27 January 1966, NSC Country File, Vietnam, Box 102, #1, LBJ Library; W. Berman, *William Fulbright and the Vietnam War,* 52-53; McCarthy, *Up 'Til Now,* 172.

9. As quoted in Gibbons, *The U.S. Government and the Vietnam War,* Part 3, 129.

10. Walt Rostow, *The Diffusion of Power* (New York: Macmillan, 1972), 396. See also Evans and Novak, *Lyndon B. Johnson,* 564; Schwartz, "Senator Michael J. Mansfield," 394; H. Humphrey, *The Education of a Public Man* (1991), 221; George McGovern, interview with Paige Mulhollan, 30 April 1969, LBJ Oral History Project, LBJ Library.

11. McCarthy, *Up 'Til Now*, 184. See also *Congressional Record,* 1 March 1966, 4376-77. For further evidence of Mansfield and others working with the White House to thwart Morse in March, see Telephone conversations of G. Ball, February and March 1966, Papers of G. Ball, Box 7, LBJ Library.

12. Tom Wicker, "Mansfield Bids Japan or Burma Lead Peace Movement," *New York Times,* 19 April 1966, 1; "Text of Mansfield's Vietnam Statement," *New York Times,* 19 April 1966, 8. See also *Congressional Record,* 18 April 1966, 8223-24; Graff, *The Tuesday Cabinet*, 192; L. Johnson, *The Vantage Point*, 583; Telephone Conversation between Ball and Sisco, 4/20/66, Papers of G. Ball, Box 7, LBJ Library.

13. Mansfield, memo to Lyndon Johnson, 6/13/66, Name File, Mansfield, NSF, LBJ Library.

14. Rostow, memo to Lyndon Johnson, 6/15/66 / Johnson. memo to Mansfield, 6/22/66, Name File, Mansfield, NSF, LBJ Library.

15. Mansfield, letter to Lyndon Johnson, 25 June 1966, NSF Name File, Box 6, LBJ Library.

16. Rostow, memo to Lyndon Johnson, 26 June 1966 / Lyndon Johnson memo to Mansfield, 26 June 1966, NSF Name File, Box 6, LBJ Library.

17. W. Berman, *William Fulbright and the Vietnam War*, 72. See also Rostow, *The Diffusion of Power,* 396.

18. Mansfield, letter to Lyndon Johnson, 13 October 1966 / Johnson, letter to Mansfield, 19 November 1966, NSF Name File, Box 6, LBJ Library.

19. Mansfield, telephone conversation between Ambassador Arthur Goldberg and Senator Mansfield, 4 October 1966, MP, XXII, 103, #1; Mansfield, "Exact Quotes," 2, 4, 10, 12, MP, XXII, 113 or 114. See also Larry Berman, *Lyndon Johnson's War* (W.W. Norton & Co., 1989), 187-88.

20. Mansfield, "Viet Nam and the United Nations," Johns Hopkins University, 10 November 1966, 2, 4, 7-14, MP, XXII, 75, #1966. See also Mansfield, memo to Arthur Goldberg, 11 November 1966, NSF Name File, Box 6, LBJ Library.

21. Memo of meeting with U Thant, 18 November 1966 / Memo on the Baltimore Sun Story, 12 November 1966, NSF Name File, Box 6, LBJ Library. See also Paul Ward, "Thant Reaffirms Statement that U.N. Has No Viet Role," *Baltimore Sun,* 12 November 1966, 1A; *Congressional Record,* 16 March 1967, 7064; *Congressional Record,* 15 May 1967, S 6878; Mansfield, "Central Concerns of American Foreign Policy," Chapel Hill, 13 March 1967, 19, MP, XXII, 76, 1967; Mansfield, Memorandum of Senator Mike Mansfield, 1 May 1967, 3, MP, XXII, 105, #16; Schoenbaum, *Waging Peace and War*, 455.

22. Mansfield, Press Release, 13 December 1966, MP, XXI, 43, #53; Max Frankel, "Mansfield Urges Wider Cease-Fire," *New York Times,* 14 December 1966, 1.

23. Mansfield, "Statement of Senator Mike Mansfield," 19 December 1966, MP, XXII, 105, #17.

24. Rusk, *As I Saw It*, 466.

25. Mansfield, "Possible 'Signals' from North Viet Nam" [memo to the President], 6 January 1967, 1-4, MP, XXII, 103, #12.

26. Lyndon Johnson, letter to Mansfield, 9 January 1967, 1-2, MP, XXII, 103, #12.

27. Mansfield, letter to Orville Gray, 13 March 1967, MP, XIII, 75, #3.

28. Mansfield, "Central Concerns of American Foreign Policy," Chapel Hill, 13 March 1967, 16-18, MP, XXII, Box 76, 1967.

29. Mansfield, "Central Concerns of American Foreign Policy," Chapel Hill, 13 March 1967, 21, MP, XXII, Box 76, 1967. Mansfield first proposed "face-to-face discussion between China and the United States at the highest practicable level" in June 1966, five years before President Richard Nixon would achieve that breakthrough (Mansfield, "Viet Nam and China: The Shadow of War—The Substance of Peace," New York, 16 June 1966, 1-13, MP, XXI, 43, #40).

30. Mansfield, "Central Concerns of American Foreign Policy," Chapel Hill, 13 March 1967, 16, 21-22 / Mansfield, "Brotherhood and World Peace," Newark N.J., 16 February 1967, 7, MP, XXII, 76, 1967. See also *Congressional Record*, 6 February 1967, 2667-68.

31. *Congressional Record*, 28 February 1967, 4764-66; *Congressional Record*, 1 March 1967, 4938-39, 4944-49. See also David Turner, "Mike Mansfield and Vietnam" (Ph.D. diss., University of Kentucky, 1984), 208-9.

32. Mansfield, written comments on copy of Senator Robert Kennedy's 2 March 1967 Senate speech, MP. See also *Congressional Record*, 2 March 1967, 5285; Ross Baker, *Friend and Foe in the U.S. Senate* (New York: Free Press, 1980), 162.

33. As quoted in Steinberg, *Sam Johnson's Boy*, 804.

34. Mansfield, letter to Lyndon Johnson, 17 March 1967 / Lyndon Johnson, letter to Mansfield, 18 March 1967, MP, XXII, 103, #12.

35. Mansfield, "Vietnam" [memo to the President], 29 April 1967, 1-3 / Mansfield, "Memo of Senator Mike Mansfield," 1 May 1967, 1-2, MP, XXII, 103, #12. See also *Congressional Record*, 12 April 1967, 9268-71; *Congressional Record*, 17 April 1967, 9796-97; Currey, *Edward Lansdale*, 237; Gibbons, *The U.S. Government and the Vietnam War*, Part 3, 455; L. Berman, *Lyndon Johnson's War*, 15; Schoenbaum, *Waging Peace and War*, 451.

36. Mansfield, "Vietnam" [memo to the President] 29 April 1967, 4-5, MP, XXII, 103, #12.

37. Rostow, memo to Lyndon Johnson, 4/30/67, NSF: Mansfield, LBJ Library. See also Mansfield, "Memo of Senator Mike Mansfield," 1 May 1967, 1-2, MP, XXII, 103, #12.

38. Rostow, memo to Lyndon Johnson, 30 April 1967, NSF Name File, Box 6, LBJ Library.

39. Mansfield, "Memo of Senator Mike Mansfield," 1 May 1967, 1-2, MP, XXII, 103, #12.

40. Mansfield, memo to Lyndon Johnson, 3 May 1967, NSF Name File, Box 6, LBJ Library.
41. President's Appointment File [Diary Backup], "May 3, 1967," LBJ Library.
42. Rostow, memo to Lyndon Johnson, 2 May 1967 / Rostow, "Possible Recourse to United Nations on Vietnam," n.d., NSF Name File, Box 6, LBJ Library. See also Mansfield, memo to Lyndon Johnson, 3 May 1967, 2 NSF Name File, Box 6, LBJ Library.
43. *Congressional Record,* 15 May 1967, S 6861-63, 6875, 6878.
44. John Herbers, "6 Senators Warn President on War," *New York Times,* 16 May 1967, 1, 6.
45. E. W. Kenworthy, "Mansfield Fears a New World War 'Incubates' in Asia," *New York Times,* 12 July 1967, 1-2; *Congressional Record,* 11 July 1967, 18369-70.
46. Mansfield, note attached to unnamed Mansfield memo and Mansfield, unnamed memo, 13 July 1967, 1-2, MP, XXII, 103, #12. No copy of this memo was located in the LBJ Library. See also Mansfield, "Memo of Senator Mike Mansfield," 1 May 1967, 1-2, MP, XXII, 103, #12.
47. Manatos, memo to the President, 12 August 1967, Office Files of Mike Manatos, Box 73, LBJ Library.
48. McGovern, interview with Paige Mulhollan, 30 April 1969, LBJ Oral History Project, LBJ Library, 11-12.
49. Rowe, letter to Lyndon Johnson, August 1967 / James Jones, memo to W. Marvin Watson, 24 August 1967, Office Files of Mike Manatos, Box 73, LBJ Library; Rowe, interview with Gillette, 10 November 1982, 4. Lady Bird Johnson ended up attending the Washington dinner for Mansfield.
50. Arthur Goldberg, interview with Ted Gittlinger, 23 March 1983, 19-20, LBJ Oral History Project, LBJ Library.
51. John Sherman Cooper, letter to Mansfield, 29 August 1967, MP, XXII, 103, #12. Cooper's 1967 response to Mansfield's end-of-the-session letter said, "you have given due regard to the requests of the Administration and at the same time you have insisted upon the independence of the Senate. You hold the confidence of every member of the Senate and that is the best test of your leadership and our regard for you" (Cooper, letter to Mansfield, 18 December 1967, MP, XVIII, 32, #7 or 8).
52. Mansfield, letter to Lyndon Johnson, 30 August 1967, MP, XXII, 103, #12. See also Mansfield, letter to the author, 25 April 1990.
53. "Mansfield Proposes Session on Pacific Security," *New York Times,* 16 September 1967, 4. See also Mansfield, *The Rim of Asia,* U.S. 90th Cong., 1st sess., S. Rept. (Washington, D.C.: GPO, 1967), iii-iv, 2, 13-15; Lyndon Johnson, letter to Mansfield, 2 September 1967, Office Files of Mike Manatos, Box 73, LBJ Library.
54. L. Berman, *Lyndon Johnson's War,* 83-84. See also, Schoenbaum, *Waging Peace and War,* 459.
55. 10/23/67 5:36 p.m. Democratic Leadership, Tom Johnson's notes of meetings, Boxes 1 and 2, LBJ Library. See also L. Berman, *Lyndon Johnson's War,* 89-90; Hamilton-Merritt, *Tragic Mountains,* 173.

56. Robert McNamara, "On the Mistakes of War" [interview with Carl Bernstein], *Time,* 11 February 1991, 70-72. See also Karnow, *Vietnam* (1991), 24-25, 521-25; Clifford, *Counsel to the President,* 434, 456-59; Sheehan, *A Bright Shining Lie,* 290, 681-93. Because of his change of heart, McNamara was forced out of Defense in early 1968 and was appointed president of the World Bank.

57. Mansfield, letter to senators, 9 October 1967, MP, XXII, 103, #1. See also Mondale, letter to Mansfield, 27 October 1967 / Moss, letter to Mansfield, 12 October 1967 / Clark, letter to Mansfield, 13 October 1967 / Dominick, letter to Mansfield, 12 October 1967, MP, XXII, 103, #1.

58. Rostow, memo to Lyndon Johnson, 27 October 1967, 1:00 p.m., NSC Country File, Vietnam, LBJ Library.

59. One copy of this transcript in Mansfield's papers has the "do not" added and another does not, but the context makes it likely that Mansfield said "do not."

60. Mansfield, conversation between Arthur Goldberg and Mansfield, 30 October 1967, MP, XXII, 103, #1.

61. Mansfield, phone conversation with Lyndon Johnson, 1 November 1967, MP, XXII, 103, #1.

62. *PPP, Johnson, 1967* (Washington, D.C.: GPO, 1968), 2:972. See also Graff, *The Tuesday Cabinet,* 168.

63. *Submission of the Vietnam Conflict to the United Nations,* Hearings before the Committee on Foreign Relations, United States Senate on S. Con. Res. 44 & 180, U.S. 90th Cong., 1st Sess., S. Rept. (Washington, D.C.: GPO, 1967), 1, 150, 162, 170, 173. See also *Congressional Record,* 12 October 1967, 28856-59; *Congressional Record,* 25 October 1967, 30024-29; *Congressional Record,* 30 November 1967, 34350-59.

64. Mansfield, "Two Faces of Violence," Bal Harbour, Florida, 22 January 1968, 17, MP, XXII, 76, 1968.

65. *Congressional Record,* 20 November 1967, S 16755; John Finney, "Mansfield Calls for Direct Talks Between Saigon and the Liberation Front," *New York Times,* 21 November 1967, 6.

66. As quoted in L. Berman, *Lyndon Johnson's War,* 99.

67. Marcy, Oral History Interview, Senate Historical Office, Washington, D.C., 1983, 167.

68. Schoenbaum, *Waging Peace and War,* 437-38, 442-44. On Rusk's relations with the committee see Holt, Oral History Interview, Senate Historical Office, Washington, D.C., 1980, 162.

69. Mansfield, memo to the President, 21 November 1967, 1-2, MP, XXII, 103, #12. See also W. Berman, *William Fulbright and the Vietnam War,* 90-91.

70. McPherson, memo to Lyndon Johnson, 7 December 1967, Office Files of Mike Manatos, Box 73, LBJ Library.

71. W. Berman, *William Fulbright and the Vietnam War,* 79-80.

72. Valeo, interview with the author, Washington, D.C., 17 May 1991. See also Mansfield, letter to the author, 6 June 1991.

73. Glass, "Mike Mansfield, Majority Leader," in Ornstein, *Congress in Change,* 154.

74. McPherson, *A Political Education*, 74-75.

75. Manatos, memo to LBJ, 7 February 1968 / Manatos, memo to LBJ, 15 February 1968, Office Files of Mike Manatos, Box 73, LBJ Library. See also, Mansfield, memo to Lyndon Johnson, 19 February 1968 / Lou Schwartz, memo to Rostow, 13 March 1968, NSF Country File, Vietnam, Box 102, #2 and #1, Folder 5, LBJ Library.

76. Manatos, memo to Lyndon Johnson, 26 January 1968, Office Files of Mike Manatos, Box 73, LBJ Library.

77. *Congressional Record,* 7 March 1968, 5660.

78. 2/6/68, 8:30 a.m. Democratic Congressional Leadership Breakfast, Tom Johnson's notes of meetings, Boxes 1 and 2, LBJ Library. See also L. Berman, *Lyndon Johnson's War*, 145-54; Clifford, *Counsel to the President*, 474-75.

79. *Congressional Record,* 26 February 1968, 4088-91; *Congressional Record,* 7 March 1968, 5659-61. See also Karnow, *Vietnam* (1984), 556; L. Berman, *Lyndon Johnson's War*, 178-80.

80. *Congressional Record,* 23 January 1968, S 271. See also McCarthy, letter to Mansfield, n.d. [1968], MP, XVIII, 19, #1.

81. As quoted in Clifford, *Counsel to the President*, 497-99.

82. L. Berman, *Lyndon Johnson's War*, 101-4, 194-99. See also Sheehan, *A Bright Shining Lie*, 691, 721.

83. L. Johnson, *The Vantage Point*, 419.

84. This account is a compilation of two separate interviews found in P. Healy, "Mansfield of Montana," 89 and Herbert Schandler, *The Unmaking of a President* (Princeton: Princeton University Press, 1977), 271-72. See also Mansfield, letter to the author, 19 April 1988.

85. L. Berman, *Lyndon Johnson's War*, 235-36. See also Clifford, *Counsel to the President*, 522, 524; Rusk, *As I Saw It*, 417, 480-83; Schoenbaum, *Waging Peace and War*, 473-79; Karnow, *Vietnam* (1984), 562-65.

86. Clifford, *Counsel to the President*, 530.

87. *Congressional Record,* 2 April 1968, 8569-77. See also L. Johnson, *The Vantage Point*, 493-95.

88. Mansfield, letter to Charles Forsberg, 17 April 1968 / Mansfield, letter to S. N. Tideman, 17 April 1968, MP, XIII, 81, #1. See also *Congressional Record,* 19 April 1968, 10016-17; *Congressional Record,* 23 April 1968, 10270-71.

89. Mansfield, letter to Lyndon Johnson, 16 May 1968, Office Files of Mike Manatos, Box 73, LBJ Library.

90. Mansfield, statement, August 1968, MP, XXII, 76, #44.

91. Mansfield, "Toward a Discerning Internationalism," New York, 26 November 1968, 19, 21, MP, XXII, 76, #1968.

92. As quoted in Burke and Greenstein, *How Presidents Test Reality*, 43.

93. Mansfield, letter to the author, 18 August 1987. See also Fulbright, *The Price of Empire*, 123.

94. See for example W. Berman, *William Fulbright and the Vietnam War*, 198.

95. See for example McNamara, "On the Mistakes of War," 71; Valeo, interview with the author, Washington, D.C., 17 May 1991.

96. William Proxmire, letter to the author, 10 June 1988. See also Reedy, interview with the author, Milwaukee, 15 September 1987; Valeo, letter to the author, 20 February 1990.

97. Nixon, *No More Vietnams* (New York: Arbor House, 1985), 96.

Chapter 12

1. As quoted in Richard Nixon, *RN* (New York: Grosset & Dunlap, 1978), 122-26.

2. Stephen Ambrose, *Nixon* (New York: Simon & Schuster, 1987), 1:342-44.

3. As quoted in Gettleman, et al., *Vietnam and America*, 53. See also H. Bruce Franklin, *M.I.A. or Mythmaking in America* (Brooklyn: Lawrence Hill, 1992), 194.

4. Ambrose, *Nixon* 1:343-44, 617.

5. Ambrose, *Nixon* 1:401-2.

6. Stephen Ambrose, *Nixon* (New York: Simon & Schuster, 1989), 2:28, 30-31, 34.

7. As quoted in Ambrose, *Nixon,* 2:42-45, 48.

8. Ambrose, *Nixon*, 2:54-55, 61-62, 64, 68-79, 81, 85-86, 88, 102-4.

9. Ambrose, *Nixon*, 1:494; Ambrose, *Nixon*, 2:109, 129, 141-44, 146-51. See also Schoenbaum, *Waging Peace and War*, 476. Only one piece of correspondence from Vice President Nixon to Mansfield was located in the senator's papers (Nixon, note to Mansfield, 25 April 1959, MP, Leadership file, Cuba).

10. As quoted in Nixon, *RN,* 366 and Herring, *America's Longest War*, 219. See also Jonathan Schell, *The Time of Illusion* (New York: Alfred A. Knopf, 1976), 23; Townsend Hoopes, "Legacy of the Cold War in Indochina," *Foreign Affairs* 48 (1970): 611-12; Ambrose, *Nixon*, 2: 230.

11. Marvin Kalb and Bernard Kalb, *Kissinger* (Boston: Little, Brown, and Co., 1974), 221.

12. Bryce Harlow, memo to Nixon, 23 June 1969, Ex Fo 8; Sihanouk, telegram to Mansfield, 8 July 1969, Ex Co 26, Nixon Project, National Archives. See also Henry Kissinger, *White House Years* (Boston: Little, Brown and Co., 1979), 179.

13. Rowland Evans Jr., and Robert Novak, *Nixon in the White House* (New York: Random House, 1971), 106-7. See also D. Turner, "Mike Mansfield and Vietnam," 224.

14. Nixon made every effort to keep records from his administration unavailable to the public and the Nixon Project is not even allowed to say whether or not these breakfast meetings were taped! If they were recorded, some future scholar will be better able to assess Mansfield's role during the Nixon years (Byron Parham, Nixon archivist, conversation with the author, Washington, D.C., 16 May 1991).

15. As quoted in R. Baker, "Mike Mansfield and the Birth of the Modern Senate," in Baker and Davidson, *First Among Equals*, 289. See also P. Healy, "Mansfield of Montana," 89.

16. Mansfield, letter to Mr. and Mrs. Joe Petrich, 9 July 1969, MP, XIII, 82, #3.

17. Nixon, letter to Mansfield, 7 March 1976, Mansfield scrapbooks, #280, MP.

18. Valeo, interview with the author, Washington, D.C., 17 May 1991. See also Mansfield, interview, "A Critical Look at Congress," *U.S. News & World Report,* 1 December 1969, 26.

19. Mansfield, letter to David Dunn, 29 January 1969, MP, XIII, 82, #3.

20. W. Berman, *William Fulbright and the Vietnam War,* 106.

21. Karnow, *Vietnam* (1984), 594; Robert Semple Jr., "Mansfield Urges Dialogue on War," *New York Times,* 30 May 1969, 31; *Congressional Record,* 26 May 1969, S 5631.

22. William Safire, *Before the Fall* (New York: Belmont Tower Books, 1975), 136-42. See also *PPP, Nixon, 1969* (Washington, D.C.: GPO, 1971), 369-75; *Congressional Record,* 16 May 1969, 12882.

23. Mansfield, statement to the Annual Democratic Congressional Dinner, Washington, D.C., 26 June 1969, 2, MP, XXII, 1969.

24. *PPP, Nixon, 1969,* 548. See also *Congressional Record,* 28 July 1969, 20958; *Congressional Record,* 8 October 1969, 29114; *Congressional Record,* 4 November 1969, 32782; Kalb and Kalb, *Kissinger,* 224.

25. As quoted in Karnow, *Vietnam* (1984), 590.

26. See for example Mansfield, notes on meetings with Rusk and Rostow, 21 December 1966, MP, XXII, 115, #2.

27. Bowles, letter to Mansfield, 16 January 1968, MP, XXII, 114 or 115. See also *Congressional Record,* 23 January 1968, S 270-71.

28. Karnow, *Vietnam* (1984), 590.

29. Bowles, letter to Mansfield, 16 January 1968, MP, XXII, 114 or 115..

30. Mansfield, letter Sihanouk, 24 January 1968 / Sihanouk, letter to Mansfield, 20 February 1968, MP, XXII, 114 or 115.

31. Valeo, interview with the author, Washington, D.C., 17 May 1991.

32. *Congressional Record,* 26 March 1969, 7634; *Congressional Record,* 26 May 1969, S 5630.

33. Mansfield, letter to Nixon, 2 May 1969, Ex Co 26, Nixon Project.

34. Valeo, interview with the author, Washington, D.C., 17 May 1991. See also Statement of Mansfield, 29 August 1969, MP, XXII, 113, #7.

35. Valeo, interview with the author, Washington, D.C., 17 May 1991. See also Mansfield, letter to the author, 2 June 1993; Hearings Before the Subcommittee on United States Security Agreements and Commitments Abroad, Kingdom of Laos, Committee on Foreign Relations, U.S. Senate, 91st Cong., 1st sess, part 2 (Washington, D.C., GPO, 1970), 382-83; "Laos: The Unseen Presence," *Time,* 17 October 1969, 39; "Mansfield in Vientiane, Meets Laotian Premier," *New York Times,* 24 August 1969, 9; Hamilton-Merritt, *Tragic Mountains,* 176-77; "Democratic Majority Leader of the American Senate Visits Laos," *Lao Press Bulletin,* 23 August 1969; "U.S. Senator Mansfield Visits Laos," *Xat Lao,* 25 August 1969, MP, XXII, 113, #7.

36. Sihanouk, telegram to Nixon, 18 August 1969, Ex Fo, Nixon Project. See also Valeo, interview with the author, Washington, D.C., 17 May 1991; Phnom Penh Embassy, 1st telegram to Secretary of State, 26 August 1969, MP, XXII, 114 or 115;

"Mansfield in Cambodia," *New York Times,* 22 August 1969, 5; Mansfield, *Perspective on Asia: The New U.S. Doctrine and Southeast Asia* (Washington, D.C.: GPO, 1969), iii-iv.

37. Sihanouk's words seem to have influenced Kissinger. Seymour Hersh reported that "shortly after Mansfield's trip, Kissinger became even more obsessed with personally picking targets for the secret bombings, to avoid civilian casualties at all costs" (Seymour Hersh, *The Price of Power: Kissinger in the Nixon White House* [New York: Summit, 1983], 177).

38. Lowenstein's account of this meeting was shared with the State Department who interpreted it very differently than Mansfield. Both Mansfield and Sihanouk denied that the prince intended to approve American bombing.

39. James Lowenstein, Sihanouk and Mansfield, memorandum of conversation, 22 August 1969, MP, XXII, 114 or 115.

40. Phnom Penh Embassy, telegrams to Secretary of State, 26 August 1969 / Richard Nethercut letter to Department of State, 5 September 1969, MP, XXII, 113, #7.

41. Mansfield, letter to Sihanouk, 24 September 1969 / Sihanouk, letter to Mansfield, 12 September 1969, MP, XXII, 112, #7.

42. Statement of Mansfield, 29 August 1969, MP, XXII, 113, #7. See also E. W. Kenworthy, "Mansfield Plans Asia Policy Study," *New York Times,* 30 August 1969, 3. Mansfield's private report was not located. The Senator was impressed with the questions Kissinger asked in San Clemente.

43. Mansfield, *Perspective on Asia,* 1-5, 11-15. See also Valeo, interview with the author, Washington, D.C., 17 May 1991; Kenworthy, "Mansfield Plans Asia Policy Study," 3.

44. Nixon, letter to Mansfield, 11 September 1969 FO 8, Nixon Project.

45. Nixon, *RN,* 394-95.

46. "Mansfield Urges Cutback in U.S. Presence in Asia," *New York Times,* 22 September 1969, 10.

47. "Study of U.S. Combat Role in Laotian War is Demanded by Senator Cooper," *New York Times,* 19 September 1969, 12; Richard Halloran, "Nixon Reassures Premier of Laos on U.S. Stand," *New York Times,* 8 October 1969, 18; Richard Halloran, "Laotian Chief Says He Is Confident U.S. Will Aid in Defense," *New York Times,* 9 October 1969, 1, 5.

48. "Mansfield: A Leader with a New Look," *U.S. News & World Report,* 11 August 1969, 16.

49. Mansfield, Statement, 6 September 1969, MP, XXII, 55, #1.

50. "Vietnam: The Lull Hits Home," *Newsweek,* 3 November 1969, 23.

51. Nixon, *No More Vietnams,* 113.

52. As quoted in Nixon, *RN,* 408-9. The memo was not located in Mansfield's or Nixon's papers.

53. Nixon, *RN,* 409; Nixon, *No More Vietnams,* 113-16; *PPP, Nixon, 1969,* 901-9.

54. *Congressional Record,* 4 November 1969, 32781-82.

55. Gordon Henneford, letter to Mansfield, 15 November 1969 / Harold McCracken, letter to Mansfield, 7 November 1969, MP, XIII, 83, #3; Luce, letter to Mansfield, 12 November 1969, MP, XIII, 84, #1.

56. "Senators Back Cease-Fire Plea," *New York Times,* 8 November 1969, 10. See also Scott, note to Mansfield, n.d. / Statement of Mansfield, 7 November 1969, MP, XXII, 55, #7.

57. Church and Hatfield, letter to Mansfield, 7 October 1969, MP, XIII, 83, #2; Mansfield, letter to Mr. and Mrs. Michael Servoss, 28 October 1969, MP, XIII, 83, #2; Mansfield, letter to Mr. and Mrs. Franklin Kohl, 5 November 1969, MP, XIII, 84, #2.

58. Gibbons, *The U.S. Government and the Vietnam War*, Part 2, 335-42. See also Karnow, *Vietnam* (1984), 491; Mansfield, letter to Mrs. Nordahl Johnson, 28 March 1968, MP, XIII, 80, #3; *Congressional Record,* 1 March 1968, 4377; *Congressional Record,* 7 March 1968, S 2376.

59. Valeo, memo to Mansfield, 20 November 1969, MP, XXII, 55, #1; Mansfield, statement of Mansfield, 8 December, 1969, MP, XXII, 55, #8. See also *Congressional Record,* 8 December 1969, 37564.

60. Marcy, memo for Mansfield, 12 March 1970 / H. G. Torbert Jr., letter to Fulbright, 12 March 1970, MP, XXII, 55, #8. See also W. Berman, *William Fulbright and the Vietnam War*, 132.

61. *Congressional Record,* 10 July 1970, 23746-47; *Congressional Record,* 27 September 1971, 33458-59.

62. Hersh, *The Price of Power*, 175-83. See also Kissinger, *White House Years*, 457-83; Nixon, *RN,* 446-47; Nixon, *No More Vietnams,* 116-19; Karnow, *Vietnam* (1984), 604-7; Alexander Haig with Charles McCarry, *Inner Circles: How America Changed the World* (New York: Warner, 1992), 233-34; Walter Isaacson, *Kissinger* (New York: Simon & Schuster, 1992), 256-58.

63. Mansfield, "A View from the Senate," New York, 29 April 1970, 21, MP, XXII, #1970. See also *Congressional Record,* 2 April 1970, 10053.

64. Sihanouk, letter to Mansfield, 21 April 1970, MP, XXII, 114 or 115.

65. Penn Nouth, telegram to Mansfield, 7 May 1970, MP, XXII, 114 or 115.

66. As quoted in Kissinger, *White House Years*, 489.

67. Presidents of Cambodian Senate and Assembly, letter to Mansfield, 21 April 1970, MP, XXII, 114 or 115.

68. Mansfield, letter to Nixon, 24 April 1970 / Mansfield, letter to Nixon, 8 May 1970, MP, XXII, 114 or 115. See also Kissinger, *White House Years*, 495.

69. As quoted in Karnow, *Vietnam* (1968), 609.

70. H. R. Haldeman, *The Haldeman Diaries* (New York: G.P. Putnam's Sons, 1994), 157.

71. Nixon, *RN,* 451. See also Haldeman, *The Haldeman Diaries,* 158; *PPP, Nixon, 1970* (Washington, D.C.: GPO, 1971), 405-10.

72. Mansfield, letter to the author, 11 August 1994.

73. "Excerpts from Mansfield Speech on War," *New York Times,* 2 May 1970, 5.

74. Mansfield, letter to Michael Lopach, 28 May 1970, MP, XIII, 85, #4.

75. Mansfield, "Cambodia and a New China," memorandum for the files, 11 May 1970, MP, XXII, 103, #5.

CHAPTER 13

1. Mansfield, Remarks at the Annual Convention Luncheon of the American Paper Industry, New York, 17 March 1970, 2, MP, XXII, 1970; W. Berman, *William Fulbright and the Vietnam War*, 129, 135.
2. Mansfield, statement, 20 May 1970, MP, XXII, 55, #1.
3. *Congressional Record,* 9 June 1970, 18905-11. See also W. Berman, *William Fulbright and the Vietnam War*, 134; Mansfield, letter to Lenore Merel, 2 September 1970 / Mansfield, letter to John Coyne, 14 October 1970, MP, XIII, 86, #2; Ambrose, *Nixon*, 2:358, 367.
4. Mansfield, memorandum for the files, 11 August 1970, MP, XXII, 103, #5; Mansfield, letter to Rogers, 11 August 1970 / Rogers, letter to Mansfield, 12 August 1970 / Mansfield, letter to Sihanouk, 11 August 1970 / Mansfield, letter to Charles Lucet, 11 August 1970 / Sihanouk, letter to Mansfield, 25 August 1970 / Frank Sieverts, memorandum to David Abshire, 10 August 1970 / Mansfield, draft letter to Sihanouk, n.d., MP, XXII, 114 or 115. See also Norodom Sihanouk, "The Future of Cambodia," *Foreign Affairs,* 49 (1970): 1, 6.
5. *Congressional Record,* 8 October 1970, 35592; *PPP, Nixon, 1970*, 825-30. See also Kissinger, *White House Years*, 971-81; Ambrose, *Nixon*, 2:389.
6. As quoted in Schwartz, "Senator Michael J. Mansfield," 401-3.
7. Mansfield, letter to Rex Dougherty, 2 July 1968 / Mansfield, letter to Anna Mae Rill, 12 July 1968 / Mansfield, letter to H. Jelkon, 3 July 1968 / Mansfield, letter to Joseph Twitchell, 20 June 1968, MP, XIII, 81, #3. See also Schwartz, "Senator Michael J. Mansfield," 399-401.
8. Mansfield, letter to Mr. and Mrs. Palmer Scott, 3 April 1970, MP, XIII, 85, #4. See also Mansfield, interview, "Why Kennedy's Program Is In Trouble With Congress," *U.S. News & World Report,* 17 September 1962, 67; Glass, "Mike Mansfield, Majority Leader," in Ornstein, *Congress in Change,* 153.
9. Joseph Tydings, letter to Mansfield, 19 September 1968, MP, XVIII, 21, #1.
10. Schwartz, "Senator Michael J. Mansfield," 401-3. See also David Broder and Don Oberdorfer, "Mike Mansfield, without Fuss," *Washington Post,* 16 March 1993, E4; Mansfield, letter to Mel Ruder, 15 September 1970, MP, XIV, 86, #9. Even with a hotly contested race, Mansfield raised only $87,000, spending a mere $20,000 of that amount.
11. Mansfield, letter to Mrs. C. D. Meyer, 11 December 1970, MP, XIII, 86, #2. See also W. Berman, *William Fulbright and the Vietnam War*, 137-38.
12. *Congressional Record,* 27 January 1971, 755-58.
13. Ken Belieu, memorandum to the President, 4 February 1971, Ex ND 18/165, Nixon Project. See also W. Berman, *William Fulbright and the Vietnam War*, 140; Herring, *America's Longest War*, 235.
14. Mansfield, "The Nixon Doctrine," *Vital Speeches,* 1 May 1971, 418-21.
15. Mansfield, letter to Peggy Glantz, 20 March 1971, MP, XIII, 104, #3.

16. Kissinger, *White House Years* 938-49. See also Schwartz, "Senator Michael J. Mansfield," 50, 76-122; G. Ball, *The Past Has Another Pattern*, 450; *PPP, Nixon, 1971* (Washington, D.C.: GPO, 1972), 636.

17. *Congressional Record,* 9 June 1971, 18848-861. See also "Mansfield's Rebellion," *Newsweek,* 24 May 1971, 18-19; Mary McGrory, "Who Would Ever Have Thought It?" *America,* 5 June 1971, 585.

18. "Is America Going Isolationist? Size-Up by Key Senators," *U.S. News & World Report,* 28 June 1971, 24. See also *Congressional Record,* 21 June 1971, 20971; *Congressional Record,* 24 June 1971, 21945; *Congressional Record,* 28 June 1971, 22271-72; *Congressional Record,* 12 July 1971, 24439; *Congressional Record,* 5 August 1971, 30101, 30103; Safire, *Before the Fall,* 677-78.

19. W. Berman, *William Fulbright and the Vietnam War,* 146.

20. As quoted in Haldeman, *The Haldeman Diaries,* 305.

21. W. Berman, *William Fulbright and the Vietnam War,* 144-45. See also Valeo, interview with the author, Washington, D.C., 17 May 1991.

22. Dick Cook, memorandum to General Haig, 16 July 1971, CF ND 21, Nixon Project.

23. Memorandum of Senator Mike Mansfield, 22 July 1971, MP, XXII, 103, #5.

24. Haldeman, *The Haldeman Diaries,* 307. The China trip was discussed at breakfast with Nixon in August 1970 and in April 1971. See Mansfield, memo to file, 13 August 1970, MP, XXII, 103, #5; Mansfield, memo to file, 26 April 1971, MP, XXII, 114 or 115; Dwight Chapin, memorandum to Haldeman, 16 April 1971, Ex FO 8, Nixon Project.

25. Safire, *Before the Fall,* 373-77.

26. MacGregor, White House memorandum, 11 September 1971 / MacGregor to Nixon, 13 September 1971 / Kissinger to Nixon, 13 September 1971, CF ND 21, Nixon Project.

27. As quoted in Haldeman, *The Haldeman Diaries,* 354.

28. *Congressional Record,* 15 September 1971, 31942.

29. Safire, *Before the Fall,* 486-91. See also *Congressional Record,* 17 September 1971, 32361; Haldeman, *The Haldeman Diaries,* 354.

30. *Congressional Record,* 27 September 1971, 33458-61; *Congressional Record,* 30 September 1971, 34224-25.

31. *Congressional Record,* 30 September 1971, 34225-44; *Congressional Record,* 28 October 1971, 37993.

32. Mansfield, letter to Cecelia Steveley, 21 October 1971, MP, XIII, 105, #5.

33. *PPP, Nixon, 1971,* 1114. See also Hersh, *The Price of Power,* 423-43, 482; W. Berman, *William Fulbright and the Vietnam War,* 147-48; Franklin, *M.I.A.,* 62.

34. Tom Korologos, memorandum to Clark MacGregor through Bill Timmons, 18 January 1972, LE Box 5, Nixon Project.

35. Mansfield, interview, "A Size-Up of President Nixon," 56-58.

36. *Congressional Record,* 15 December 1971, 47118-120; Kissinger, *White House Years,* 1042; John Finney, "Mansfield's Message—It's Time For a Change," *New York Times,* 7 November 1971, Sect. IV, 1-2; Mansfield, "New Approaches to

Foreign Relations," Chapel Hill, 26 October 1971, 13 / Mansfield, "The United States and the Soviet Union: Power in Transition," Baltimore, 18 November 1971, 2-3, MP, XXII, 1971.

37. *PPP, Nixon, 1972* (Washington, D.C.: GPO, 1974), 100-5. See also *Congressional Record,* 26 January 1972, 1316; *Congressional Record,* 7 February 1972, 2831-32; W. Berman, *William Fulbright and the Vietnam War*, 151.

38. Mansfield, memo of Senator Mike Mansfield, 26 April 1971 / Mansfield, letter to Sihanouk, 2 June 1971 / Cyrus Eaton, letter to Mansfield, 23 November 1971 / Sihanouk, cable to Eaton, 16 November 1971, MP, XXII, 114 or 115; Kissinger, letter to Mansfield, 13 December 1971, MP, XXII, 113, #9.

39. Dick Cook, memorandum for Nixon through MacGregor and Timmons, 29 February 1972, FO 8, Box 71, Nixon Project.

40. *PPP, Nixon, 1972,* 550-54. See also Karnow, *Vietnam* (1991), 654-56; W. Berman, *William Fulbright and the Vietnam War*, 151.

41. Mansfield, "U.S. Foreign Policy in a Changing Pacific and Asia," 21 March 1974, 9, MP, XXII, 49, #103.

42. Mansfield and Hugh Scott [interview], "Inside Red China Today," *U.S. News and World Report,* 29 May 1972, 44-49. See also Mansfield and Hugh Scott, *Journey to the New China,* U.S. 92d Cong., 2d sess., S. Rept. (Washington, D.C.: GPO, 1972), 5-7.

43. As quoted in Safire, *Before the Fall,* 422.

44. It is not clear if the Democrats would have known of Nixon's new conditions; he announced them in his speech to the nation that he delivered as this meeting continued.

45. As quoted in Safire, *Before the Fall,* 422-28. See also George Aiken, *Senate Diary* (Brattleboro, Vermont.: Stephen Greene Press, 1976), 55-56; *PPP, Nixon, 1972,* 583-87, B-8; W. Berman, *William Fulbright and the Vietnam War*, 153-54.

46. *Congressional Record,* 9 May 1972, 16355.

47. *Congressional Record,* 16 May 1972, 17579-80; *Congressional Record,* 12 June 1972, 20516; *Congressional Record,* 14 June 1972, 20763-64; *Congressional Record,* 18 July 1972, 24231-33; *Congressional Record,* 19 July 1972, 24318, 24385-87; *Congressional Record,* 24 July 1972, 2507-71, 25078-81; *Congressional Record,* 17 August 1972, 28621-22; *Congressional Record,* 26 September 1972, 32192; *Congressional Record,* 2 October 1972, 33138; *Congressional Record,* 9 October 1972, 34387-88. See also Mansfield, letter to Jeanne Keller, 17 May 1972, MP, XIII, 106, #6; Nixon, *No More Vietnams* 142; Karnow, *Vietnam* (1991), 661; Richard Cook, memorandum for Nixon through MacGregor and Timmons, 29 February 1972, FO 8, Box 71, Nixon Project.

48. *PPP, Nixon, 1972,* 669-70. See also Nixon, letters to Mansfield, Scott, Ford, Boggs, and Albert, 27 July 1972, FO 3-2, Box 36, Nixon Project; W. Berman, *William Fulbright and the Vietnam War*, 159.

49. McGovern, *Grassroots,* 198-99, 212-13, 222. See also O'Neill, *Man of the House,* 208. Eagleton sent Mansfield a bitter hand-written note after hearing that the majority leader declined the offer: "Congratulations! Joe Robinson ran for Veep with Al Smith. Sen. Jim Reed of Missouri declined the Veep nomination in 1928 saying: 'I

refuse to take a back seat on a hearse!'" (Thomas Eagleton, note to Mansfield, 14 August 1974, MP, XXII, 65, #25).

50. "The Mansfield Touch," *Nation,* 24 April 1972, 517. See also Ludwick, "Mansfield," 26; O'Neill, *Man of the House*, 208; *Congressional Record,* 17 August 1972, 28622; Mansfield, "China Revisited: A New Era in Asia," Phoenix, 26 October 1972, 15, MP, XXII, 1972.

51. Mansfield, interview, "Why Congress Is in the Doghouse," *U.S. News & World Report,* 16 August 1976, 30. See also Schwartz, "Senator Michael J. Mansfield," 403-7; Theodore White, *Breach of Faith* (New York: Atheneum, 1975), 229-31.

52. Nixon, *RN,* 772-73. See also T. White, *Breach of Faith*, 230.

53. Mansfield, Statement of 20 December 1972, MP, XXII, 48, #49. See also W. Berman, *William Fulbright and the Vietnam War*, 165; Kissinger, *White House Years*, 1453; Stephen Ambrose, *Nixon* (New York: Simon & Schuster, 1991), 3:17, 45, 46.

Chapter 14

1. In 1973 Mansfield merged his original Mansfield Amendment to withdraw troops from Europe with his interpretation of the Nixon Doctrine, which would lead to troop withdrawals from Asia. Mansfield wanted 50 percent of land-based military personnel on foreign soil sent home over a three-year period, but the president would decide where the withdrawals would be made. In June, Mansfield's proposal lost 46-44 (see Mansfield, statement, 21 September 1973, MP, XXI, 49, #60; Mansfield, statement before the Subcommittee on Arms Control, International Law and Organizations, 25 July 1973, MP, XXI, 49, #52. See also Aiken, *Senate Diary*, 298-99).

2. James Naughton, "Congress Critics of War Threaten to Fight Funding," *New York Times,* 3 January 1973, 1. See also *Congressional Record,* 26 January 1973, 2202; *Congressional Record,* 29 January 1973, 2376-77; *Congressional Record,* 27 February 1973, 5538; W. Berman, *William Fulbright and the Vietnam War*, 166-68; Herring, *America's Longest War*, 248-51; Karnow, *Vietnam* (1984), 654; Ambrose, *Nixon*, 3:46.

3. *PPP, Nixon, 1973* (Washington, D.C.: GPO, 1975), 54-55. See also John Herbers, "Nixon Aides Move against War Foes," *New York Times,* 4 February 1973, 29.

4. Herbers, "Nixon Aides Move against War Foes," *New York Times,* 4 February 1973, 29.

5. Humphrey, letter to Mansfield, 11 January 1973 / Mansfield, letter to Humphrey, 18 January 1973, MP, XXII, 66, #16; Timmons, letter to Mansfield, 26 January 1973, MP, XXII, 113, #9.

6. Henry Kissinger, *Years of Upheaval* (Boston: Little, Brown, and Co., 1982), 309-11; Spiro Agnew, letter to Mansfield, 13 April 1973, MP, XXII, 74, #7.

7. Korologos, note to Kissinger, n.d. / J. F. Lehman, memorandum to Kissinger, 18 May 1973 / Kissinger, letter to Mansfield, 4 June 1973 / Mansfield, "China and the United States," 15 March 1973, CO 34-2, Box 20, Nixon Project.

8. Arthur Schlesinger Jr., *The Imperial Presidency* (Boston: Houghton Mifflin, 1973), 197. See also *Congressional Record,* 18 January 1973, 1321; *Congressional Record,* 5 April 1973, 11146; W. Berman, *William Fulbright and the Vietnam War,* 170-71; John Finney, "Nixon Criticized over Bombings," *New York Times,* 12 April 1973, 6; Bernard Gwertzman, "Rogers Defends Cambodia Raids," *New York Times,* 1 May 1973, 1.

9. As quoted in William Shawcross, *Sideshow* (New York: Simon & Schuster, 1979), 284. See also *Congressional Record,* 14 May 1973, 15436-37; *Congressional Record,* 31 May 1973, 17686; Nguyen Tien Hung and Jerrold Schecter, *The Palace File* (New York: Harper & Row, 1986), 203, 508; W. Berman, *William Fulbright and the Vietnam War,* 174-77; Kissinger, *Years of Upheaval,* 355-59.

10. *Congressional Record,* 29 June 1973, 22307-8. See also W. Berman, *William Fulbright and the Vietnam War,* 176-78.

11. *PPP, Nixon, 1973,* 686.

12. Cambodian government representatives approached Mansfield through Valeo as early as May 1970, tacitly admitting they had miscalculated in purging Sihanouk (see Valeo, memorandum for the Files, 12 May 1970, MP, XXII, 103, #5).

13. Matak, letter to Mansfield, 25 June 1973 / Valeo, memo to Mansfield, 28 June 1973, MP, XXII, 114 or 115. Valeo did not use the ambassador's name. Either Sonn Voeunsai represented Cambodia in Washington or Um Sim had recently assumed the position.

14. Mansfield, letter to Nixon, 29 June 1973, MP, XXII, 114 or 115; Korologos, memo to Kissinger, 31 July 1973 / Mansfield, letter to Kissinger, 30 June 1973 / William Stearman, memo to Kissinger, 27 July 1973 / Kissinger, letter to Mansfield, 31 July 1973, CO 26, Box 14, Nixon Project; George Sherman, "Diplomacy on Cambodia Awaits Bombing Cutoff," *Washington Star-News,* 29 July 1973, 1; Kissinger, *Years of Upheaval,* 343-55.

15. Mansfield, memorandum, 26 July 1973 / Mansfield, memorandum, 8 August 1973, MP, XXII, 114 or 115; Oswald Johnston, "U.S. Says Sihanouk OKd Bombing," *Washington Star-News,* 25 July 1973, A5; Joseph Alsop, "The Cambodian 'Cover-Up,'" *Washington Post,* 8 August 1973; Shawcross, *Sideshow,* 93, 288-89, 330; W. Berman, *William Fulbright and the Vietnam War,* 181. Nixon verifies Alsop's account that Russell and Stennis were consulted, but offers no explanation for how he could justify ignoring the Foreign Relations Committee (Nixon, *No More Vietnams,* 108-11).

16. Mansfield, memorandum, 8 August 1973, MP, XXII, 114 or 115.

17. Note concerning telephone call from Marshall Wright and signed "dls," 8 August 1973, MP, XXII, 114 or 115.

18. Alsop, *"I've Seen the Best of It,"* 475, 478.

19. Mansfield, memorandum, 8 August 1973, MP, XXII, 114 or 115.

20. Kissinger, *White House Years,* 251.

21. Cambodia Perspective, March 1975, Robert Wolthius File, Box 1, Ford Library.

22. Kissinger, *Years of Upheaval,* 343-55, 360-61; Shawcross, *Sideshow,* 335-43. See also Sherman, "Diplomacy on Cambodia Awaits Bombing Cutoff," *Washington Star-News,* 29 July 1973, 1.

23. Nixon, *No More Vietnams*, 176-81.
24. Lloyd Rives, letter to Valeo with enclosed transcripts of interviews, 20 September 1973, MP, XXII, 114 or 115.
25. Mansfield, Statement, 13 August 1973, MP, XXII, 49, #55; Mansfield, memo for the files, 17 August 1973 / Sihanouk, telegram to Mansfield, 10 August 1973, MP, XXII, 103, #5.
26. Mansfield, memorandum for the files, "Breakfast with the President," 7 September 1973, MP, XXII, 103, #5.
27. Kissinger met with Mansfield and Fulbright on 27 August to discuss Senate confirmation. Both senators favored the nominee and believed that Kissinger was necessary to protect the foreign policy gains of an administration weakened by Watergate. In the Foreign Relations Committee only McGovern opposed Kissinger's nomination, and Kissinger was confirmed 78-7 in the Senate (W. Berman, *William Fulbright and the Vietnam War*, 184-85; Ambrose, *Nixon* 3:214).
28. Mansfield, "Nomination of Dr. Kissinger and the Cambodian Situation," 20 September 1973, MP, XXII, 49, #59.
29. Mansfield, letter to Sihanouk, 6 September 1973 / Sihanouk, cable to Mansfield, 15 October 1973 / Mansfield, letter to Kissinger, 15 October 1973 / Mansfield, letter to Sihanouk, 8 November 1973 / Mansfield, letter to Kissinger, 14 November 1973, MP, XXII, 114 or 115.
30. Valeo, notes of a meeting with Mansfield, Jobert, and Kosciusko-Morizet, 11 October 1973 / Mansfield, letter to Kissinger, 15 October 1973, MP, XXII, 114 or 115. See also Shawcross, *Sideshow*, 335-43.
31. Mansfield, press release, 17 January 1974, and Sihanouk cables to Mansfield and J. William Fulbright, 11 December 1993 and n.d. [December 1993] / Marshall Wright, letter to Mansfield, 25 January 1974 / Mansfield, statement, 28 January 1974, MP, XXII, 114 or 115. See also Korologos, letter to Salpee Sahagian, 18 January 1974 / George Springsteen Jr., memo for Brent Scowcroft, 6 March 1974 / Mansfield, letter to Nixon, 28 January 1974 / Mansfield, statement of Senator Mike Mansfield, 28 January 1974, CO 26, Box 14, Nixon Project.
32. Valeo, memo to Mansfield, 8 February 1974, MP, XXII, 114 or 115.
33. Mansfield, letter to the author, 2 June 1993.
34. Shawcross, *Sideshow*, 325-28, 335-43; Valeo, memo to Mansfield, 2 June 1975, MP, XXII, 114 or 115.
35. Nixon, letter to Mansfield, 30 April 1974, Gen FO 3-2, Box 37, Nixon Project. See also Mansfield, "U.S. Foreign Policy in a Changing Pacific and Asia," 21 March 1974, 14, MP, XXII, 49, #103; *Congressional Record,* 27 March 1974, 8393-94; *Congressional Record,* 6 May 1974, 13245-55; *Congressional Record,* 21 June 1974, 20431.
36. Ludwick, "Mansfield," 26. See also Mansfield, "Democrats' Reply to State of Union," *U.S. News & World Report,* 11 February 1974, 91; Mansfield, "Remarks at the Annual Convention of the Arkansas Bankers Association," Hot Springs, Arkansas, 7 May 1974, 1-8, MP, XXII, #1974.

37. Valeo, interview with the author, Washington, D.C., 17 May 1991; O'Neill, *Man of the House*, 253-55; Mansfield, letter to the author, 2 June 1993.

38. Ford, letter to Mansfield, 17 December 1974 / Max Friedersdorf, memo to Ford, 22 December 1975 / Mansfield, letter to Ford, 19 December 1975 / Dorothy, note to Marge, n.d. / Mansfield, letter to Ford, 28 December 1976 / Ford, letter to the Mansfields, 2 January 1976 / Mansfield, letter to Ford, 23 January 1975 / Timmons, memo, 20 August 1974 / Timmons, letter to Mansfield, 25 September 1974 / Ford, letter to Mansfield, 15 August 1974 / Mansfield, letter to Ford, 12 September 1974, WHCF, Name File, Ford Library. See also *PPP, Ford, 1974* (Washington, D.C.: GPO, 1975), 31-32, 281-82; *Congressional Record,* 1 May 1975, 12661; Valeo, interview with the author, Washington, D.C., 17 May 1991; Mansfield, response to questions from Leo Michel, 16 May 1975, MP, XXI, 50, #19; Gerald Ford, *A Time to Heal* (New York: Harper & Row, 1979), 134, 153-54.

39. Mansfield, letter to Nixon and supporting material, n.d. [early 1973], FO 8, Nixon Project.

40. Mansfield, memorandum for the Files, 30 July 1973 / Mansfield, memorandum, "Possible explanation for the delay in the visit," 30 July 1973, MP, XXII, 112, #18.

41. Korologos, memo to Kissinger, 31 July 1973, CO 26, Box 14, Nixon Project; Mansfield, memorandum for the files, "Breakfast with the President," 7 September 1973, MP, XXII, 103, #5.

42. Mansfield, letter to Ford, 17 October 1974 / Ford, letter to Mansfield, 23 October 1974, WHCF, FO 8, Box 35, Ford Library. See also Korologos, memo to William Timmons, 5 December 1974, WHCF, Name File, Ford Library.

43. Mansfield, *China: A Quarter Century after the Founding of the People's Republic,* U.S. 94th Cong, 1st sess., S. Rept. (Washington, D.C.: GPO, January 1975), v-vii, 30-32. See also Richard Solomon, memo to Kissinger, 7 January 1975, WHCF, PR 7-1, Ford Library.

44. Mansfield, letter to Margaret Hileman, 3 February 1975 / Mansfield, letter to Kermit Midthun, 24 February 1975, MP, XIII, 118, #1; Mansfield, letter to Carroll O'Connor, 25 March 1975, MP, XIII, 118, #2; Mansfield, letter to Jim Flaherty, 15 April 1975, MP, XIII, 118, #3; Mansfield, letter to Harold Birkland, 2 April 1975 / Mansfield, letter to Joseph Engel III, 10 April 1975 / Engel, letter to Mansfield, 19 March 1975 / Josie, note to Mansfield, 2 March 1975, MP, XIII, 118, #4. See also *Congressional Record,* 21 January 1975, 846.

45. Moose had traveled to Indochina with James Lowenstein in earlier years and Kissinger wrote that their "annual visits to Southeast Asia had been the terror of our officials because the two opposed the war and were adept at turning up bureaucratic bungling." In 1973 they visited Cambodia and discovered that the U.S. Embassy staff was directing the bombing campaign, which was "being employed against the more densely populated areas of Cambodia" (Kissinger, *White House Years*, 519; W. Berman, *William Fulbright and the Vietnam War*, 173).

46. Linwood Holton, memo to Kissinger, 21 January 1975 / Friedersdorf, memo to Ford, 13 February 1975, Wolthius File, Box 5, Ford Library. See also Marcy, Oral History

Interview, Senate Historical Office, Washington, D.C., 1983, 220; Holt, Oral History Interview, Senate Historical Office, Washington, D.C., 1980, 222.

47. Cabled summary of Congressional visit, March 1975 / Codel Meeting with President Thieu, 27 February 1975, Wolthius File, Box 5, Ford Library.

48. Comments on Vietnam Situation, 2 April 1975, Wolthius File, Box 5, Ford Library. See also *Congressional Record*, 7 April 1975, S 5271-72; Friedersdorf, Recommended Telephone Call for Ford, 11 April 1975 / note from Ford?, 11 April 1975 / Friedersdorf, Recommended Telephone Call to Mansfield, 10 April 1975 / WHCF, PR 7-2, Ford Library; *PPP, Ford, 1975* (Washington, D.C.: GPO, 1977) 1:459-73; Ford, *A Time to Heal*, 253-54.

49. Nguen Huu Chau, letter to Mansfield, 11 January 1975 / David Truong, letter to Mansfield, 25 March 1975 / Valeo, note to Mansfield, 25 March 1975 / Valeo, memo to Mansfield, 18 April 1975 / Valeo, note to Mansfield, 24 April 1975 / Tran Kim Phuong, letter to Mansfield, 17 April 1975, MP, XXII, 114, #5. See also *Congressional Record*, 21 April 1975, 10952-53.

50. Buttinger, letter to Mansfield, 21 February 1975, MP, XXII, 55, #1; Valeo, note to Salpee, n.d. / Valeo, note to Mansfield, 15 August 1974, MP, XXII, 114, #5. See also Wesley Fishel, "One Vietnam or Two?" *Virginia Quarterly Review* 50 (1974): 348-67; Edward Lansdale, "Viet Nam: Still the Search for Goals," *Foreign Affairs* 47 (1968): 95; Currey, *Edward Lansdale*, 273.

51. Dean Brown, letter to Mansfield, 25 April 1975, WHCF, Name File, Ford Library; William Kendall, memorandums to Friedersdorf, 29 April 1975 [two memos], Wolthius Files, Box 5, Ford Library. See also Frank Snepp, *Decent Interval* (New York: Vintage Books, 1977), 359; *Congressional Record*, 23 April 1975, 11357; *Congressional Record*, 30 April 1975, 12482.

52. As quoted in Shawcross, *Sideshow*, 352.

53. Kissinger, letter to Mansfield, 4 March 1975 / Summary of Negotiating Efforts on Cambodia, n.d., MP, XXII, 102, #3. See also Shawcross, *Sideshow*, 335-43.

54. Valeo, Note for the Files, 11 March 1975, MP, XXII, 114 or 115.

55. Valeo, "Suggested Preconditions for an Intercession with Prince Sihanouk in Peking," n.d., MP, XXII, 114 or 115.

56. Sihanouk, telegram to Mansfield, 7 April 1975 /Sihanouk, two undated telegrams to Mansfield and other senators [spring 1975] / Mansfield, cablegram to Sihanouk, 29 April 1975, MP, XXII, 114 or 115. See also Congressional Reaction to Events in South Viet Nam and Cambodia, Wolthius File, Box 5; Scowcroft, memo to Friedersdorf, n.d. / Kendall, memo for Friedersdorf, 7 April 1975, WHCF, Nd 18/CO 26, Box 32, Ford Library.

57. Ron Nessen, *It Sure Looks Different from the Inside* (New York: Playboy Press, 1978), 123-24. See also Ford, *A Time to Heal*, 281-83; Christopher Jon Lamb, *Belief Systems and Decision Making in the Mayaguez Crisis* (Gainesville: University of Florida Press, 1989), 92; Thomas Franck and Edward Weisband, *Foreign Policy by Congress* (New York: Oxford University Press, 1979), 73; Karnow, *Vietnam* (1991), 701.

58. Valeo, memo to Mansfield, 2 June 1975, MP, XXII, 114 and 115.

EPILOGUE

1. See for example Sihanouk, telegram to Mansfield, 9 October 1975, MP, XXII, 104, #115.
2. Mansfield, letter to Ford, 16 July 1975, MP, XXII, 112, #14. See also Ford, letter to Mansfield, 30 July 1976, MP, XXII, 112, #17. America continued to have diplomatic relations with Laos, but not with Vietnam or Cambodia.
3. Mansfield, letter to Sihanouk, 14 April 1976, MP, XXII, 114 or 115. See also Mansfield, letter to Ford, 25 August 1976, MP, XXII, 112, #16; Scowcroft, Schedule Proposal via William Nicholson, 7 September 1976, Ford Library; Shawcross, *Sideshow*, 380; Mansfield, letter to the author, 17 October 1991.
4. Mansfield, letter to the author, 24 September 1990.
5. Mansfield, letter to Carter, 10 March 1977, WHCF, FO 46, Jimmy Carter Library. See also Carter, letter to Mansfield, 10 March 1977, WHCF, CO 42, Jimmy Carter Library; Mansfield, letter to the author, 17 October 1991.
6. "Carter Is Said to Ask Mansfield to Head Mission to North Vietnam," *New York Times,* 18 February 1977, A4; "President Sending a Mission to Hanoi," *New York Times,* 26 February 1977, 1, 4; "Carter Meets Inquiry Commission Going to Hanoi and Laos, and Looks to Normal Relations with Vietnam," *New York Times,* 13 March 1977, 8; "U.S. Inquiry Group Leaves for Vietnam and Laos," *New York Times,* 14 March 1977, 4; "Vietnam's Friendly Reception of U.S. Mission Is Seen as Reflecting Need for Aid to Spur Economy," *New York Times,* March 1977, A14. See also "Presidential Commission on Americans Missing and Unaccounted for in Southeast Asia: Report on Trip to Vietnam and Laos March 16-20, 1977," 1-4, 12, 16, CO 172, Carter Library.
7. When asked what was discussed at those meetings, Mansfield remembered: "he discussed his proposal to create a four party coalition including the Khmer Rouge. This was achieved through agreement and is in effect the proposal which has recently been put to a vote by the Cambodian people" (Mansfield, letter to the author, 2 June 1993).
8. Ludwick, "Mansfield," 28-29.
9. As quoted in Broder and Oberdorfer, "Mike Mansfield," E1, E4.
10. Doug Lowenstein, "'The system works,' says Mansfield," *Great Falls Tribune,* 12 March 1976, Mansfield scrapbooks, #280, MP.
11. Mansfield, "Towards a Foreign Policy of Mutuality," Bozeman, Montana, 10 June 1972, 16, MP, XXII, #1972.
12. Karnow, *Vietnam* (1984), 284-85.
13. Mansfield, "The Best of Times—The Worst of Times," *Vital Speeches of the Day,* 15 December 1976, 135.
14. As quoted in Ludwick, "Mansfield," 23.
15. Paul Kattenburg, *The Vietnam Trauma in American Foreign Policy* (New Brunswick: Transaction Books, 1982), 235.
16. As quoted in R. Baker, "Mike Mansfield and the Birth of the Modern Senate," in Baker and Davidson, *First Among Equals,* 287.

17. Joan Cazden, letter to Mansfield, 27 August 1970, MP, XIII, 86, #2.

18. Kissinger, *White House Years*, 939.

19. Gibbons, *The U.S. Government and the Vietnam War*, Part 2, 127.

BIBLIOGRAPHY

BOOKS

Aiken, George. *Senate Diary*. Brattleboro, Vermont: Stephen Greene Press, 1976.

Allen, Douglas, and Ngo Vinh Long, eds. *Coming to Terms: Indochina, the United States and the War*. Boulder: Westview, 1991.

Alsop, Joseph, with Adam Platt. *"I've Seen the Best of It."* New York: W.W. Norton, 1992.

Ambrose, Stephen. *Nixon*. Vol. 1. New York: Simon & Schuster, 1987.

———. *Nixon*. Vol. 2. New York: Simon & Schuster, 1989.

———. *Nixon*. Vol. 3. New York: Simon & Schuster, 1991.

Anderson, David. *Trapped By Success: The Eisenhower Administration and Vietnam, 1953-1961*. New York: Columbia University Press, 1991.

Arnold, James. *The First Domino*. New York: William Morrow & Co., 1991.

Aronson, James. *The Press and the Cold War*. Indianapolis: Bobbs-Merrill, 1970.

Baker, Bobby, with Larry King. *Wheeling and Dealing*. New York: W.W. Norton & Co., 1978.

Baker, Ross. *Friend and Foe in the U.S. Senate*. New York: Free Press, 1980.

Ball, George. *The Past Has Another Pattern*. New York: W.W. Norton & Co., 1982.

Ball, Moya. *Vietnam-on-the-Potomac*. New York: Praeger, 1992.

Bator, Victor. *Vietnam: A Diplomatic Tragedy*. Dobbs Ferry, New York: Oceana, 1965.

Berman, William. *William Fulbright and the Vietnam War*. Kent, Ohio: Kent University Press, 1988.

Berman, Larry. *Lyndon Johnson's War*. W.W. Norton & Co., 1989.

Boettcher, Thomas. *Vietnam: The Valor and the Sorrow*. Boston: Little, Brown & Co., 1985.

Bornet, Vaughn Davis. *The Presidency of Lyndon B. Johnson*. Lawrence: University Press of Kansas, 1983.

Bowles, Chester. *Promises to Keep.* New York: Harper & Row, 1971.

Browne, Malcolm. *Muddy Boots and Red Socks.* New York: Time Books, 1993.

Burchett, Wilfred. *The Furtive War: The United States in Vietnam and Laos.* New York: International Publishers, 1963.

Burke, John, and Fred Greenstein. *How Presidents Test Reality.* New York: Russell Sage Foundation, 1989.

Burner, David, and Thomas West. *The Torch is Passed: The Kennedy Brothers and American Liberalism.* New York: Antheneum, 1984.

Buttinger, Joseph. *Vietnam: A Dragon Embattled.* New York: Praeger, 1967.

Byrd, Robert. *The Senate, 1789-1989.* Washington, D.C.: GPO, 1988.

Charlton, Michael, and Anthony Moncrieff. *Many Reasons Why: The American Involvement in Vietnam.* New York: Hill and Wang, 1978.

Chase, Harold, and Allen Lerman, eds. *Kennedy and the Press: The News Conferences.* New York: Thomas Crowell Co., 1965.

Clifford, Clark, with Richard Holbrooke. *Counsel to the President.* New York: Random House, 1991.

Coffin, Tristram. *Senator Fulbright: Portrait of a Public Philosopher.* New York: E.P. Dutton & Co., 1966.

Collins, J. Lawton. *Lightning Joe.* Baton Rouge: Louisiana State University Press, 1979.

Colman, Elizabeth Wheeler. *Mrs. Wheeler Goes to Washington.* Helena, Montana: Falcon Press, 1989.

Cooney, John. *The American Pope.* New York: Times Books, 1984.

Cooper, Chester. *The Lost Crusade.* New York: Dodd, Mead & Co., 1970.

Currey, Cecil. *Edward Lansdale: The Unquiet American.* Boston: Houghton Mifflin, 1988.

Dooley, Thomas A., Jr. *Deliver Us from Evil: The Story of Viet Nam's Flight to Freedom.* New York: Farrar, Staus & Cudahy, 1956.

Douglas, Allen, and Ngo Vinh Long, eds. *Coming to Terms: Indochina, the United States and the War.* Boulder: Westview, 1991.

Douglas, William O. *North from Malaya.* New York: Doubleday, 1952.

du Berrier, Hilaire. *Background to Betrayal.* Boston: Western Islands, 1965.

Dulles, Eleanor Lansing. *John Foster Dulles: The Last Year.* New York: Harcourt, Brace & World, 1963.

Evans, Rowland, Jr., and Robert Novak. *Lyndon B. Johnson: The Exercise of Power.* New York: The New American Library, 1966.

Evans, Rowland, Jr., and Robert Novak, *Nixon in the White House.* New York: Random House, 1971.

Fall, Bernard B. *The Two Viet-Nams.* Rev. ed. New York: Praeger, 1967.

———. *Viet-Nam Witness.* New York: Frederick A. Praeger, 1960.

Fishel, Wesley. *Vietnam: Anatomy of a Conflict.* Itasca, Illinois: F.E. Peacock, 1968.

————, ed. *Problems of Freedom.* New York: The Free Press, 1961.

Fitzgerald, Frances. *Fire in the Lake.* Boston: Little, Brown & Co., 1972.

Ford, Gerald. *A Time to Heal.* New York: Harper & Row, 1979.

Franck, Thomas, and Edward Weisband. *Foreign Policy by Congress.* New York: Oxford University Press, 1979.

Franklin, H. Bruce. *M.I.A. or Mythmaking in America.* Brooklyn: Lawrence Hill, 1992.

Fulbright, J. William. *The Arrogance of Power.* New York: Random House, 1966.

Fulbright, J. William, with Seth Tillman. *The Price of Empire.* New York: Pantheon, 1989.

Gardner, Lloyd. *Approaching Vietnam.* New York: W.W. Norton, 1988.

Gettleman, Marvin E., et al. *Vietnam and America: A Documented History.* New York: Grove Press, 1985.

Gibbons, William Conrad. *The U.S. Government and the Vietnam War.* Part 1. Princeton: Princeton University Press, 1986.

————. *The U.S. Government and the Vietnam War.* Part 2. Princeton: Princeton University Press, 1986.

————. *The U.S. Government and the Vietnam War.* Part 3. Princeton: Princeton University Press, 1989.

Graff, Henry. *The Tuesday Cabinet.* Englewood Cliffs: Prentice-Hall, 1970.

Gravel, Michael, ed. *Pentagon Papers.* Vol. 1. Boston: Beacon Press, 1971.

Greene, Graham. *The Quiet American.* London: William Heinemann, 1955.

Guthman, Edwin, and Jeffrey Shulman, eds. *Robert Kennedy: In His Own Words.* Toronto: Bantam Books, 1988.

Haig, Alexander, with Charles McCarry. *Inner Circles: How America Changed the World.* New York: Warner, 1992.

Halberstam, David. *The Best and the Brightest.* New York: Random House, 1972.

Haldeman, H. R. *The Haldeman Diaries.* New York: G.P. Putnam's Sons, 1994.

Hamilton-Merritt, Jane. *Tragic Mountains.* Bloomington: Indiana University Press, 1993.

Hammer, Ellen. *A Death in November.* New York: E.P. Dutton, 1987.

————. *Vietnam.* New York: Holt, Rinehart, and Winston, 1966.

Herring, George. *America's Longest War.* New York: John Wiley & Sons, 1979.

Hersh, Seymour. *The Price of Power: Kissinger in the Nixon White House.* New York: Summit, 1983.

Hoopes, Townsend. *The Devil and John Foster Dulles.* Boston: Atlantic, Little, Brown & Co., 1973.

Humphrey, Hubert. *The Education of a Public Man.* Edited by Norman Sherman. Minneapolis: University of Minnesota Press, 1991.

————. *The Education of a Public Man.* Edited by Norman Sherman. Garden City, New York: Doubleday, 1976.

Isaacson, Walter. *Kissinger.* New York: Simon & Schuster, 1992.

Johnson, Lyndon. *The Vantage Point.* New York: Holt, Rinehart and Winston, 1971.

Johnson, U. Alexis, with Jef Olivarius McAllister. *The Right Hand of Power.* Englewood Cliffs: Prentice-Hall, 1984.

Kahin, George McT. *Intervention.* New York: Alfred A. Knopf, 1986.

Kalb, Marvin, and Bernard Kalb. *Kissinger.* Boston: Little, Brown, and Co., 1974.

Karnow, Stanley. *Vietnam.* Rev. ed. New York: Viking, 1991.

———. *Vietnam.* New York: Penguin, 1984.

Kattenburg, Paul. *The Vietnam Trauma in American Foreign Policy.* New Brunswick: Transaction Books, 1982.

Kearns, Doris. *Lyndon Johnson and the American Dream.* New York: Harper and Row, 1976.

Kennedy, John F. *The Strategy of Peace.* Edited by Allan Nevins. New York: Harper & Row, 1960.

Kern, Montague, Patricia Levering, and Ralph Levering. *The Kennedy Crises.* Chapel Hill: University of North Carolina Press, 1983.

Kiernan, Ben. *How Pol Pot Came to Power.* London: Verso, 1985.

Kissinger, Henry. *White House Years.* Boston: Little, Brown and Co., 1979.

———. *Years of Upheaval.* Boston: Little, Brown, and Co., 1982.

LaCouture, Jean, Konrad Kellen and Joel Carmichael, trans. *Vietnam: Between Two Truces.* New York: Random House, 1966.

Lamb, Christopher Jon. *Belief Systems and Decision Making in the Mayaguez Crisis.* Gainesville: University of Florida Press, 1989.

Lansdale, Edward. *In the Midst of Wars.* New York: Harper & Row, 1972.

Martin, John Bartlow. *Adlai Stevenson and the World.* Garden City, New York: Doubleday, 1977.

Matusow, Harvey. *False Witness.* New York: Cameron & Kahn, 1981.

McCarthy, Eugene. *Up 'Til Now.* New York: Harcourt Brace Jovanovich, 1987.

McGovern, George. *Grassroots.* New York: Random House, 1977.

McNamara, Robert S., with Brian VanDeMark. *In Retrospect: The Tragedy and Lessons of Vietnam.* New York: Times Books, 1995.

McPherson, Harry. *A Political Education.* Boston: Little, Brown, and Co., 1972.

Mecklin, John. *Mission in Torment.* Garden City, New York: Doubleday, 1965.

Montgomery, John. *The Politics of Foreign Aid.* New York: Praeger, 1962.

Nessen, Ron. *It Sure Looks Different from the Inside.* New York: Playboy Press, 1978.

Newman, John. *JFK and Vietnam.* New York: Warner Books, 1992.

Nguyen Tien Hung and Jerrold Schecter. *The Palace File.* New York: Harper & Row, 1986.

Nixon, Richard. *No More Vietnams.* New York: Arbor House, 1985.

———. *RN.* New York: Grosset & Dunlap, 1978.

Nolting, Frederick, Jr. *From Trust to Tragedy.* New York: Praeger, 1988.

O'Brien, Lawrence. *No Final Victories.* New York: Ballantine, 1974.

O'Donnell, Kenneth, David Powers, and Joe McCarthy. *"Johnny, We Hardly Knew Ye."* Boston: Little, Brown and Co., 1972.

O'Neill, Tip, with William Novak. *Man of the House.* New York: Random House, 1987.

Parmet, Herbert. *J.F.K.* New York: Dial Press, 1983.

Poole, Peter. *The United States and Indochina.* Hinsdale, Illinios: Dryden Press, 1973.

Porter, Gareth, ed. *Vietnam: The Definitive Documentation of Human Decisions.* Vol. 2. Stanfordville, New York: Earl Coleman Enterprises, Inc., 1979.

Post, Ken. *Revolution, Socialism and Nationalism in Viet Nam.* Belmont, California: Wadsworth, 1989.

Reeves, Richard. *President Kennedy: Profile of Power.* New York: Simon & Schuster, 1993.

Rostow, Walt. *The Diffusion of Power.* New York: Macmillan, 1972.

Rusk, Dean, as told to Richard Rusk, Daniel Papp, ed. *As I Saw It.* New York: W.W. Norton, 1990.

Safire, William. *Before the Fall.* New York: Belmont Tower Books, 1975.

Schandler, Herbert. *The Unmaking of a President.* Princeton: Princeton University Press, 1977.

Scheer, Robert. *How the United States Got Involved in Vietnam.* Santa Barbara: Center for the Study of Democratic Institutions, 1965.

Schell, Jonathan. *The Time of Illusion.* New York: Alfred A. Knopf, 1976.

Schlesinger, Arthur, Jr. *The Imperial Presidency.* Boston: Houghton Mifflin, 1973.

Schoenbaum, Thomas. *Waging Peace and War.* New York: Simon and Schuster, 1988.

Scigliano, Robert. *South Vietnam: Nation Under Stress.* Boston: Houghton Mifflin, 1963.

Shaplen, Robert. *The Lost Revolution.* Rev. ed. New York: Harper & Row, 1966.

Shawcross, William. *Sideshow.* New York: Simon & Schuster, 1979.

Sheehan, Neil. *A Bright Shining Lie.* New York: Random House, 1988.

Small, Melvin. *Johnson, Nixon, and the Doves.* New Brunswick: Rutgers University Press, 1988.

Snepp, Frank. *Decent Interval.* New York: Vintage Books, 1977.

Spritzer, Donald. *Senator James E. Murray and the Limits of Post-War Liberalism.* New York: Garland Publishing, 1985.

Steinberg, Alfred. *Sam Johnson's Boy.* New York: Macmillan Co., 1968.

Sullivan, Marianna. *France's Vietnam Policy.* Wesport: Greenwood Press, 1978.

A Symposium on America's Stake in Vietnam. New York: American Friends of Vietnam, 1956.

Thonssen, Lester, ed. *Representative American Speeches: 1963-1964.* New York: H.W. Wilson Co., 1964.

Thonssen, Lester, and A. Craig Baird. *Speech Criticism: The Development of Standards for Rhetorical Appraisal.* New York: Ronald Press, 1948.

Turner, Kathleen J. *Lyndon Johnson's Dual War.* Chicago: University of Chicago Press, 1985.

Valenti, Jack. *A Very Human President.* New York: W.W. Norton & Co., 1975.

VanDeMark, Brian. *Into the Quagmire.* New York: Oxford University Press, 1991.

Waldron, Ellis. *An Atlas of Montana Politics since 1864.* Missoula: University of Montana Press, 1958.

Warner, Denis. *Certain Victory: How Hanoi Won the War.* Kansas City: Sheed Andrews and McMeel, Inc., 1978.

Wheeler, Burton, with Paul Healy. *Yankee from the West.* Garden City, New York: Doubleday, 1962.

White, Theodore. *Breach of Faith.* New York: Atheneum, 1975.

Zinn, Howard. *The Logic of Withdrawal.* Boston: Beacon Press, 1967.

SCHOLARLY ARTICLES AND PARTS OF BOOKS

Baker, Ross. "Mike Mansfield and the Birth of the Modern Senate." In *First Among Equals: Outstanding Senate Leaders of the Twentieth Century.* Edited by Richard Baker and Roger Davidson. Washington, D.C.: Congressional Quarterly, Inc., 1991.

Ball, Moya. "A Case Study of the Kennedy Administration's Decision-making Concerning the Diem Coup of November, 1963." *Western Journal of Speech Communication* 54 (1990).

Bostdorff, Denise, and Steven Goldzwig. "Idealism and Pragmatism in American Foreign Policy Rhetoric: The Case of John F. Kennedy and Vietnam." *Presidential Studies Quarterly* 24 (1994).

Dooley, Thomas A., Jr. "Delivering the Refugees." In *A Symposium on America's Stake in Vietnam.* New York: American Friends of Vietnam, 1956.

Fall, Bernard."The Political-Religious Sects of Vietnam." *Pacific Affairs,* September 1955.

Fishel, Wesley. "One Vietnam or Two?" *Virginia Quarterly Review* 50 (1974).

Glass, Andrew. "Mike Mansfield, Majority Leader." In *Congress in Change.* Edited by Norman Ornstein. New York: Praeger, 1975.

Harnett, Joseph. "Refugee Resettlement." In *A Symposium on America's Stake in Vietnam.* New York: American Friends of Vietnam, 1956.

Hoopes, Townsend. "Legacy of the Cold War in Indochina." *Foreign Affairs* 48 (1970).

Humphrey, David. "Tuesday Lunch at the Johnson White House: A Preliminary Assessment." *Diplomatic History* 8 (1984).

Lansdale, Edward. "Viet Nam: Still the Search for Goals." *Foreign Affairs* 47 (1968).

Mansfield, Michael. "The Meaning of the Term 'Advice and Consent,'" *The Annals of the American Academy,* September 1953.

Melandri, Pierre. "The Repercussions of the Geneva Conference: South Vietnam under a New Protector." Mark Rubin trans. In *Dien Bien Phu and the Crisis of Franco-American Relations, 1954-1955.* Edited by Lawrence Kaplan, Denise Artaud, and Mark Rubin. Wilmington, Delaware: SR Books, 1990.

Nelson, Anna Kasten. "John Foster Dulles and the Bipartisan Congress." *Political Science Quarterly* 102 (1987).

Olson, Gregory A. "Eisenhower and the Indochina Problem." In *Eisenhower's War of Words: Rhetoric and Leadership.* Edited by Martin Medhurst. East Lansing: Michigan State University Press, 1994.

Sihanouk, Norodom. "The Future of Cambodia." *Foreign Affairs,* 49 (1970).

Stoler, Mark. "Aiken, Mansfield and the Tonkin Gulf Crisis: Notes from the Congressional Leadership Meeting at the White House, August 4, 1964." *Vermont History,* Spring 1982.

MAGAZINE AND NEWSPAPER ARTICLES

Alsop, Joseph. "A Reporter At Large." *New Yorker,* 25 June 1955.

———. "The Cambodian 'Cover-Up.'" *Washington Post,* 8 August 1973.

"Among the People." *Time,* 7 February 1955.

Anderson, Jack. "The Roots of Our Vietnam Involvement." *Washington Post,* 4 May 1975.

"Are Our Policies Turning Obsolete?" *Business Week,* 4 April 1964.

Ascoli, Max. "Charity Begins Abroad." *Reporter,* 7 October 1965.

———. "The Freedom to End Freedom." *Reporter,* 5 May 1966.

"The Beleaguered Man." *Time,* 4 April 1955.

"Biographical Sketch." *New York Times,* 5 January 1958.

Broder, David, and Don Oberdorfer. "Mike Mansfield, without Fuss." *Washington Post,* 16 March 1993.

Bromberger, Merry. "The Mistaken Solitude of Mr. Diem." *Constellation,* August 1956.

Buttinger, Joseph. "An Eyewitness Report on Vietnam." *Reporter,* 27 January 1955.

———. "Our Policy Toward Vietnam." *New York Times,* 30 January 1955.

———. "Saigon: Intrigue." *New Republic,* 28 February 1955.

———. "Are We Saving South Vietnam?" *New Leader,* 27 June 1955.

"Carter Is Said to Ask Mansfield to Head Mission to North Vietnam." *New York Times*, 18 February 1977.

"Carter Meets Inquiry Commission Going to Hanoi and Laos, and Looks to Normal Relations with Vietnam." *New York Times*, 13 March 1977.

Cater, Douglas. "The Contentious Lords of the Senate." *Reporter*, 16 August 1962.

Cherne, Leo. "To Win in Indochina We must Win These People." *Look*, 25 January 1955.

Corliss, Richard. "Who Killed J.F.K.?" *Time*, 23 December 1991.

Crowther, Bosley. "Mankiewicz Version of Novel by Greene." *New York Times*, 6 February 1958.

"Democratic Majority Leader of the American Senate Visits Laos." *Lao Press Bulletin*, 23 August 1969.

"'Democrats' Change of Pace." *Time*, 20 July 1964.

"Democrats' Reply to State of Union." *U.S. News & World Report*, 11 February 1974.

"Diem Besieged." *Time*, 21 March 1955.

"Diem's Critics-Graham Greene." *America*, 28 May 1955.

"Diem's Death a Shock to Mansfield." *Inter Lake* [Kalispell, Montana], n.d. [1963].

"Diem's Shaky Foundations." *Economist*, 23 June 1956.

"The Disenchanted." *Newsweek*, 13 July 1953.

"Douglas Arrives in Saigon." *New York Times*, 1 July 1955.

du Berrier, Hilaire. "How We Helped Ho Chi Minh." *The Freeman*, 19 April 1954.

———. "Report from Saigon." *American Mercury*, September 1958.

Dulles, John Foster. "Foreign Policies and National Security." *Vital Speeches of the Day*, 1 February 1954.

"Dulles Sets Goal of Instant Rebuff to Stop Aggressor." *New York Times*, 13 January 1954.

"Dulles Taking Mansfield as Advisor." *Great Falls Tribune*, 21 August 1954.

Durdin, Tillman. "Vietnam Ponders New Government." *New York Times*, 8 May 1955.

"Eisenhower Asks Vietnam Reform." *New York Times*, 25 October 1954.

Evans, Medford. "Mr. Mansfield." *American Opinion*, October 1970.

"Excerpts from Mansfield Speech on War." *New York Times*, 2 May 1970.

"A Feudal Fracas in Vietnam." *Life*, 18 April 1955.

"Field Commander." *Time*, 26 November 1956.

Finney, John. "Mansfield Calls for Direct Talks Between Saigon and the Liberation Front." *New York Times*, 21 November 1967.

———. "Mansfield's Message—It's Time For a Change." *New York Times*, 7 November 1971.

————. "Nixon Criticized over Bombings." *New York Times,* 12 April 1973.

————. "Retiring Senate Leader." *New York Times,* 5 March 1976.

"Fractional Struggle in Vietnam." *America,* 26 March 1955.

Frankel, Max. "Mansfield Urges Wider Cease-Fire." *New York Times,* 14 December 1966.

"A Fretful Congress Confronts Vietnam." *Newsweek,* 17 January 1966.

Goodman, George. "Our Man in Saigon." *Esquire,* January 1964.

"The Greatest Homage." E. H. Oliver, trans. *Realities Cambodgiennes,* 6 December 1963.

Greene, Graham. "Last Act in Indo-China." *New Republic,* 9 May 1955.

————. "'To Hope till Hope Creates.'" *New Republic,* 12 April 1954.

Gwertzman, Bernard. "Rogers Defends Cambodia Raids." *New York Times,* 1 May 1973.

Halberstam, David. "Mansfield Is Cool on Vietnam War." *New York Times,* 3 December 1962.

Halloran, Richard. "Laotian Chief Says He Is Confident U.S. Will Aid in Defense." *New York Times,* 9 October 1969.

————. "Nixon Reassures Premier of Laos on U.S. Stand." *New York Times,* 8 October 1969.

Healy, Paul. "Mansfield of Montana." *Saturday Evening Post,* October 1974.

Healy, William. "Montana's Senator Mike." *Sign,* May 1953.

Herbers, John. "Nixon Aides Move against War Foes." *New York Times,* 4 February 1973.

————. "6 Senators Warn President on War." *New York Times,* 16 May 1967.

Hinkle, Warren, Sol Stern, and Robert Scheer. "The University on the Make." *Ramparts,* April 1966.

"Hope in Vietnam." *New York Times,* 29 January 1955.

"How Deep Into Indochina? Eisenhower, Knowland Answer." *U.S. News & World Report,* 19 February 1954.

"How to End the War—Mansfield's Five Points." *U.S. News & World Report,* 13 September 1965.

"Is America Going Isolationist? Size-Up by Key Senators." *U.S. News & World Report,* 28 June 1971.

Jaffe, Adrian, and Milton Taylor. "A Crumbling Bastion." *New Republic,* 19 June 1961.

"Johnny, We Hardly Knew Ye, and Now You'd Be 70 Already." *Denver Post,* 29 May 1987.

Johnston, Oswald. "U.S. Says Sihanouk OKd Bombing." *Washington Star-News,* 25 July 1973.

Karnow, Stanley. "Diem Defeats His Own Best Troops." *Reporter,* 19 January 1961.

————. "Giap Remembers." *New York Times Magazine,* 24 June 1990.

————. "Mansfield Fears a New World War 'Incubates' in Asia." *New York Times,* 12 July 1967.

————. "Mansfield Plans Asia Policy Study." *New York Times,* 30 August 1969.

Kenworthy, E. W. "Mansfield Report Seen as Urging U.S. to Get Peace Pact Quickly." *New York Times,* 9 January 1966.

Ladejinsky, Wolf. "Vietnam: The First Five Years." *Reporter,* 24 December 1959.

"Laos: The Unseen Presence." *Time,* 17 October 1969.

Lichtenstein, Grace. "'Senator Mike' Tours Montana to Say a Political Farewell." *New York Times,* 2 November 1976.

Lindley, Ernest. "Bipartisan Progress." *Newsweek,* 18 October 1954.

"Loser on Points." *Newsweek,* 10 February 1958.

Lowenstein, Doug. "'The system works,' says Mansfield." *Great Falls Tribune,* 12 March 1976.

Ludwick, Jim. "Mansfield: The Senator from Montana" [pamphlet]. *Missoulian* [Montana], n.d. [1988].

Mansfield, Michael. "The Best of Times—The Worst of Times." *Vital Speeches of the Day,* 15 December 1976.

————. "A Critical Look at Congress." *U.S. News & World Report,* 1 December 1969.

————. "Democrats' Reply to State of Union." *U.S. News & World Report,* 11 February 1974.

————. "The Nixon Doctrine." *Vital Speeches,* 1 May 1971.

————. "Reprieve in Viet Nam." *Harper's Magazine,* January 1956.

————. "A Size-Up of President Nixon." *U.S. News & World Report,* 6 December 1971.

————. "Why Congress Is in the Doghouse." *U.S. News & World Report,* 16 August 1976.

————. "Why Kennedy's Program Is In Trouble With Congress." *U.S. News & World Report,* 17 September 1962.

Mansfield, Michael, and Hugh Scott. "Inside Red China Today." *U.S. News and World Report,* 29 May 1972.

"Mansfield Criticizes Policies." *New York Times,* 29 December 1960.

"Mansfield in Cambodia." *New York Times,* 22 August 1969.

"Mansfield in Vientiane, Meets Laotian Premier." *New York Times,* 24 August 1969.

"Mansfield: A Leader with a New Look." *U.S. News & World Report,* 11 August 1969.

"Mansfield Proposes Session on Pacific Security." *New York Times,* 16 September 1967.

"Mansfield Report: Real Danger of Bigger War." *U.S. News & World Report,* 17 January 1966.

"The Mansfield Touch." *Nation*, 24 April 1972.

"Mansfield Urges Cutback in U.S. Presence in Asia." *New York Times*, 22 September 1969.

"Mansfield Urges New Asian Policy." *New York Times*, 11 June 1962.

"Mansfield's Rebellion." *Newsweek*, 24 May 1971.

"Matusow Declares He Apologized." *Great Falls Tribune*, 16 February 1955.

"Matusow Tells of Taking Over $1,000 to Wrongly Denounce Mansfield." *Great Falls Tribune*, 22 February 1955.

McGrory, Mary. "Chaos in the Senate—Days Without End." *America*, 23 November 1963.

———. "Who Would Ever Have Thought It?" *America*, 5 June 1971.

McNamara, Robert S. "On the Mistakes of War." *Time*, 11 February 1991.

———. "We Were Wrong, Terribly Wrong." *Newsweek*, 17 April 1995.

Moyers, Bill. "Flashbacks." *Newsweek*, 10 February 1975.

Naughton, James. "Congress Critics of War Threaten to Fight Funding." *New York Times*, 3 January 1973.

"Night of Lurid Drama." *Life*, 16 May 1955.

"Ovation for Diem." *Time*, 17 January 1955.

"Personal and Otherwise." *Harper's Magazine*, January 1956.

"President Sending a Mission to Hanoi." *New York Times*, 26 February 1977.

"The Quarterback." *Time*, 17 October 1955.

"The Red or the Green." *Time*, 17 October 1955.

"The Revolt that Failed." *Time*, 9 May 1955.

Scheer, Robert, and Warren Hinckle. "The 'Vietnam Lobby.'" *Ramparts*, July 1965.

Schlesinger, Arthur, Jr. "What Would He Have Done." *New York Times*, 29 March 1992.

Schmid, Peter. "Free Indo-China Fights against Time." *Commentary*, January 1955.

Semple, Robert, Jr. "Mansfield Urges Dialogue on War." *New York Times*, 30 May 1969.

"The Senate: A Crisis in Leadership." *Newsweek*, 18 November 1963.

"Senator McCarthy Plugs for Ecton's Election." *Montana Standard* [Butte], 15 October 1952.

"Senators Back Cease-Fire Plea." *New York Times*, 8 November 1969.

"Senators Warn of Growing Risks in Vietnam War." *New York Times*, 25 February 1963.

Shaplen, Robert. "A Reporter in Vietnam." *New Yorker*, 22 September 1962.

Sherman, George. "Diplomacy on Cambodia Awaits Bombing Cutoff." *Washington Star-News*, 29 July 1973.

"Signs of Improvement." *Time*, 31 January 1955.

"A Small Something for Hanoi." *Time*, 10 September 1965.

"South Viet Nam." *Time*, 4 August 1961.

Spellman, Francis. "Text of Cardinal's Speech . . ." *New York Times,* 31 August 1954.

"Struggle Weird in South Vietnam." *New York Times,* 29 April 1955.

"Study of U.S. Combat Role in Laotian War is Demanded by Senator Cooper." *New York Times,* 19 September 1969.

Sulzberger, C. L. "Diem Opposes Allied Policy in South Vietnam." *New York Times,* 8 June 1955.

"Text of Mansfield's Vietnam Statement." *New York Times,* 19 April 1966.

"Thank You, Senator." E. H. Oliver, trans. *Realities Cambodgiennes,* 6 December 1963.

"'A Time to Go.'" *Newsweek,* 15 March 1976.

"Too Much Vietnam Gloom." *America,* 29 January 1955.

"The Tough Miracle Man of Vietnam." *Life,* 13 May 1957.

"Tremors from Washington." *Time,* 2 May 1955.

"True or False? JFK Was a Secret Dove Who Would Have Pulled Military Forces Out of Vietnam upon Re-election." *Vietnam,* June 1992.

"U.S. Inquiry Group Leaves for Vietnam and Laos." *New York Times,* 14 March 1977.

"U.S. Senator Mansfield Visits Laos." *Xat Lao,* 25 August 1969.

Valeo, Francis. "Sihanouk of Cambodia." *Baltimore Sun,* 11 January 1979.

"A Victory for Kennedy That May Bring Him Trouble." *U.S. News & World Report,* 27 August 1962.

"Vietnam's Friendly Reception of U.S. Mission Is Seen as Reflecting Need for Aid to Spur Economy." *New York Times,* March 1977.

"Vietnam: The Lull Hits Home." *Newsweek,* 3 November 1969.

"Vietnam: The Unpleasant Truth." *Newsweek,* 20 August 1962.

"War Without End." *New Republic,* 9 March 1963.

Ward, Paul. "Thant Reaffirms Statement that U.N. Has No Viet Role." *Baltimore Sun,* 12 November 1966.

Warner, Denis. "Agony in Saigon: The Lady & the Cadaver." *Reporter,* 10 October 1963.

———. "The Many-Fronted War In South Vietnam." *Reporter,* 13 September 1962.

"When Is a Majority a Majority." *Time,* 20 March 1964.

White, William. "Mansfield to Make Indo-China Inquiry." *New York Times,* 16 September 1953.

———. "Sees Mansfield Hurting Viet-Nam." *Cleveland Press,* 26 February 1964.

Wicker, Tom. "Mansfield Bids Japan or Burma Lead Peace Movement." *New York Times,* 19 April 1966.

"Z." "The War in Vietnam: We Have Not Been Told the Whole Truth." *New Republic,* 12 March 1962.

Government Documents

Congressional Record, 16 January 1945-1 May 1975.

Executive Sessions of the Senate Foreign Relations Committee, 1953. Vol. 5. Washington, D.C.: GPO, 1977.

Executive Sessions of the Senate Foreign Relations Committee, 1954. Vol. 6. Washington, D.C.: GPO, 1977.

Executive Sessions of the Senate Foreign Relations Committee, 1955. Vol. 7. Washington, D.C.: GPO, 1978.

Executive Sessions of the Senate Foreign Relations Committee, 1956. Vol. 8. Washington, D.C.: GPO, 1978.

Executive Sessions of the Senate Foreign Relations Committee, 1957. Vol. 9. Washington, D.C.: GPO, 1979.

Executive Sessions of the Senate Foreign Relations Committee, 1960. Vol. 12. Washington, D.C.: GPO, 1983.

Executive Sessions of the Senate Foreign Relations Committee, 1962. Vol. 14. Washington, D.C.: GPO, 1986.

Executive Sessions of the Senate Foreign Relations Committee, 1963. Vol. 15. Washington, D.C.: GPO, 1986.

Executive Sessions of the Senate Foreign Relations Committee, 1964. Vol. 16. Washington, D.C.: GPO, 1987.

Executive Sessions of the Senate Foreign Relations Committee, 1965. Vol. 17. Washington, D.C.: GPO, 1990.

Foreign Relations of the United States, 1945, The Far East, China. Vol. 7. Washington, D.C.: GPO, 1969.

Foreign Relations of the United States, 1952-1954, East Asia and the Pacific. Vol. 12. Part 1. Washington, D.C.: GPO, 1984.

Foreign Relations of the United States, 1952-1954, Indochina. Vol. 13. Part 1. Washington, D.C.: GPO, 1982.

Foreign Relations of the United States, 1952-1954, Indochina. Vol. 13. Part 2. Washington, D.C.: GPO, 1982.

Foreign Relations of the United States, 1955-1957, Vietnam. Vol. 1. Washington, D.C.: GPO, 1985.

Foreign Relations of the United States, 1958-1960, Vietnam. Vol. 1. Washington, D.C.: GPO, 1986.

Foreign Relations of the United States, 1958-1960, Foreign Economic Policy. Vol. 4. Washington, D.C.: GPO, 1992.

Foreign Relations of the United States, 1958-1960, East Asia-Pacific Region, Cambodia, Laos. Vol. 16. Washington, D.C.: GPO, 1992.

Foreign Relations of the United States, 1961-1963, Vietnam. Vol. 1. Washington, D.C.: GPO, 1990.

Foreign Relations of the United States, 1961-1963, Vietnam. Vol. 2. Washington, D.C.: GPO, 1990.

Foreign Relations of the United States, 1961-1963, Vietnam. Vol. 3. Washington, D.C.: GPO, 1991.

Foreign Relations of the United States, 1961-1963, Vietnam. Vol. 4. Washington, D.C.: GPO, 1991.

Foreign Relations of the United States, 1961-1963, Laos Crisis. Vol. 24. Washington, D.C.: GPO, 1994.

Foreign Relations of the United States, 1964-1968, Vietnam. Vol. 1. Washington, D.C.: GPO, 1992.

Hearings Before the Subcommittee on United States Security Agreements and Commitments Abroad, Kingdom of Laos, Committee on Foreign Relations. U.S. Senate, 91st Cong., 1st sess., part 2. Washington, D.C., GPO, 1970.

Mansfield, Michael. *China: A Quarter Century after the Founding of the People's Republic.* U.S. 94th Cong, 1st sess., S. Rept. Washington, D.C.: GPO, January 1975.

———. *Indochina: Report on a Study Mission to the Associated States of Indochina, Vietnam, Cambodia, Laos.* U.S. 83d Cong., 1st sess., S. Rept. Washington, D.C.: GPO, 1953.

———. *Perspective on Asia: The New U.S. Doctrine and Southeast Asia.* Washington, D.C.: GPO, 1969.

———. *Report on Indochina.* U.S. 83rd Cong., 2d sess., S. Rept. Washington, D.C.: GPO, 15 October 1954.

———. *The Rim of Asia.* U.S. 90th Cong., 1st sess., S. Rept. Washington, D.C.: GPO, 1967.

———. *Two Reports on Vietnam and Southeast Asia to the President of the United States,* U.S. 93d Cong., 1st sess., S. Rept. Washington, D.C.: GPO, 1973.

———. *United States Aid Program in Vietnam,* U.S. 86th Cong., 2d sess., S. Rept. Washington, D.C.: GPO, 26 February 1960.

———. *Vietnam, Cambodia, and Laos,* U.S. 84th Cong., 1st sess., S. Rept. Washington, D.C.: GPO, 6 October 1955.

Mansfield, Michael, J. Caleb Boggs, Claiborne Pell, and Benjamin Smith. *Viet Nam and Southeast Asia,* U.S. 88th Cong., 1st sess., S. Rept. Washington, D.C.: GPO, 1963.

Mansfield, Michael, Edmond Muskie, Daniel Inouye, George Aiken, and J. Caleb Boggs. *The Vietnam Conflict: The Substance and the Shadow.* U.S 89th Cong., 2nd sess., S. Rept. Washington, D.C.: GPO, 1966.

Mansfield, Michael, and Hugh Scott. *Journey to the New China,* U.S. 92d Cong., 2d sess., S. Rept. Washington, D.C.: GPO, 1972.

Public Papers of the Presidents of the United States, Kennedy, 1962. Washington, D.C.: GPO, 1963.

Public Papers of the Presidents of the United States, Johnson, 1963-64. Vol. 1. Washington, D.C.: GPO, 1965.

Public Papers of the Presidents of the United States, Johnson, 1963-64. Vol. 2. Washington, D.C.: GPO, 1965.

Public Papers of the Presidents of the United States, Johnson, 1965. Vol. 1. Washington, D.C.: GPO, 1966.

Public Papers of the Presidents of the United States, Johnson, 1967. Vol. 2. Washington, D.C.: GPO, 1968.

Public Papers of the Presidents of the United States, Nixon, 1969. Washington, D.C.: GPO, 1971.

Public Papers of the Presidents of the United States, Nixon, 1970. Washington, D.C.: GPO, 1971.

Public Papers of the Presidents of the United States, Nixon, 1971. Washington, D.C.: GPO, 1972.

Public Papers of the Presidents of the United States, Nixon, 1972. Washington, D.C.: GPO, 1974.

Public Papers of the Presidents of the United States, Nixon, 1973. Washington, D.C.: GPO, 1975.

Public Papers of the Presidents of the United States, Ford, 1974. Washington, D.C.: GPO, 1975.

Public Papers of the Presidents of the United States, Ford, 1975. Vol. 1. Washington, D.C.: GPO, 1977.

Submission of the Vietnam Conflict to the United Nations, Hearings before the Committee on Foreign Relations, United States Senate on S. Con. Res. 44 & 180, U.S. 90th Cong., 1st Sess., S. Rept. Washington, D.C.: GPO, 1967.

U.S. Involvement in the Overthrow of Diem, 1963, U.S. 92d Cong., 2d sess., S. Rept. Washington D. C.: GPO, 1972.

U.S. Senate, 1st sess., Subcommittee to Investigate the Administration of the Internal Security Act and Other Internal Security Laws, Committee on the Judiciary, *Strategy and Tactics of World Communism: The Significance of the Matusow Case.* Washington, D.C.: GPO, 1955.

United States-Vietnam Relations, 1945-1967. Book 10. Washington, D.C.: GPO, 1971.

UNPUBLISHED MATERIAL

Ball, Moya. "A Descriptive and Interpretive Analysis of the Small Group Communication of Presidents Kennedy, Johnson, and Their Key Advisers Concerning the Decisions from January 1961 to July 1965 to Expand the Vietnam War." Ph.D. diss., University of Minnesota, 1988.

Hood, Charles. "'China Mike' Mansfield: The Making of a Congressional Authority on the Far East." Ph.D. diss., Washington State University, 1980.

Kraszewski, Eugene J. "Senator Mike Mansfield and the Origins of American Involvement in the Second Indochina War." Seminar Paper, Cornell University, 1974, Mansfield Papers.

Mansfield, Michael. "American Diplomatic Relations with Korea, 1866-1910." Master's Thesis, University of Montana, 1934.

Olson, Gregory A. "Mike Mansfield's Ethos in the Evolution of United States Policy in Indochina." Ph.D. diss., University of Minnesota, 1988.

Schwartz, James. "Senator Michael J. Mansfield and United States Military Disengagement from Europe." Ph.D. diss., University of North Carolina, 1977.

Stewart, John. "Independence and Control: The Challenge of Senatorial Party Leadership." Ph.D. diss., University of Chicago, 1968.

Turner, David. "Mike Mansfield and Vietnam." Ph.D. diss., University of Kentucky, 1984.

INTERVIEWS AND CORRESPONDENCE

Aiken, George. Interview with Paige Mulhollan, 10 October 1968. LBJ Oral History Project, LBJ Library.

Alsop, Joseph. Interview with Richard Challener, 4 March 1966. John Foster Dulles Oral History Project, Princeton University Library.

Douglas, William O. Interview with John Stewart, 9 November 1967. JFK Oral History Project, JFK Library.

Durbrow, Eldridge. Interview with Ted Gittinger, 3 June 1981. LBJ Oral History Project, LBJ Library.

Erickson, Leif. Interview with Donald Spritzer, 26 August 1976. Mansfield Oral History Project, Mansfield Library.

Goldberg, Arthur. Interview with Ted Gittlinger, 23 March 1983. LBJ Oral History Project, LBJ Library.

Harkins, Paul. Interview with Ted Gittinger, 10 November 1981. LBJ Oral History Project, LBJ Library.

Holt, Pat. Oral History Interview. Senate Historical Office, Washington, D.C., 1980.

Inouye, Daniel. Interview with Dorothy Pierce McSweeny, 2 May 1969. LBJ Oral History Project, LBJ Library.

Kennedy, Robert. Interview with John Bartlow Martin, 29 February 1964. JFK Oral History Project, JFK Library.

———. Interview with John Bartlow Martin, 30 April 1964. JFK Oral History Project, JFK Library.

———. Interview with John Bartlow Martin, 14 May 1964. JFK Oral History Project, JFK Library.

Mansfield, Michael. Correspondence with the author, 28 July 1986-11 August 1994.

————. Interview with Seth Tillman, 23 June 1964. JFK Oral History Project, JFK Library.

————. Interview with Richard Challener, 10 May 1966. John Foster Dulles Oral History Project, Princeton University Library.

Marcy, Carl. Oral History Interview. Senate Historical Office, Washington, D.C., 1983.

McGovern, George. Interview with Paige Mulhollan, 30 April 1969. LBJ Oral History Project, LBJ Library.

McPherson, Harry. Interview with T. H. Baker, 24 March 1969. LBJ Oral History Project, LBJ Library.

O'Brien, Lawrence. Interview with Michael Gillette, 29 October 1985. LBJ Oral History Project, LBJ Library.

Parham, Byron [Nixon archivist]. Conversation with the author, Washington, D.C., 16 May 1991.

Proxmire, William. Letter to the author, 10 July 1988.

Reedy, George. Conversation with the author, Milwaukee, 2 July 1993.

————. Conversation with the author, Milwaukee, 17 March 1988.

————. Interview with the author, Milwaukee, 15 September 1987.

Reinhardt, G. Frederick. Interview with Philip Crowl, 30 October 1965. John Foster Dulles Oral History Project, Princeton University Library.

Rowe, James. Interview with Joe Frantz, 16 September 1969. LBJ Oral History Project, LBJ Library.

————. Interview with Michael Gillette, 10 November 1982. LBJ Oral History Project, LBJ Library.

Spolar, Walter. Interview with Ronalt Grele, 9 June 1966. JFK Oral History Project, JFK Library.

Trueheart, William. Interview with Ted Gittinger, 2 March 1982. LBJ Oral History Project, LBJ Library.

Valenti, Jack. Interview IV with Joe B. Frantz, 3 March 1971. LBJ Oral History Project, LBJ Library.

Valeo, Francis. Interview with the author, Washington, D.C., 17 May 1991.

————. Letters to the author, 20 February 1990 and 12 September 1990.

INDEX

A

Acheson, Dean, 67, 189, 192, 223, 224
Agnew, Spiro, 219, 236
Aiken, George: and the Gulf of Tonkin
    Resolution, 135; and Michael J.
    Mansfield, 170; and overthrow of Ngo
    Dinh Diem, 119; and Richard Nixon,
    212; and the Senate Foreign Relations
    Committee, 189, 191; trip to Indochina,
    165, 169; and Vietnam policy, 158
Albert, Carl, 238, 291-92n. 39
Allen, Larry, 28, 49
Allott, Gordon, 194
Alsop, Joseph, 66, 211, 239, 240, 285n. 14
America First Committee, 10
American Friends of Vietnam (AFV), 52,
    64-67, 75, 76, 77, 78, 81, 115
Annenberg, Walter, 66
Arends, Leslie, 297n. 65, 298n. 67
Army of South Vietnamese (ARVN), 168
Arnett, Peter, 115
Aronson, James, 78
"Awesome foursome," 141

B

Ba Cut, 274n. 56
Baker, Bobby, 18, 88, 264n. 24
Ball, George: and the Mansfield European
    Amendment, 223; rhetorical strategy of,
    152; and Robert McNamara, 141; and
    Vietnam policy, 140, 142, 144, 152,

155-56, 193, 296n. 57; and the Wise
    Men, 192, 193
Bao Dai, 20, 21, 24, 36, 37, 45, 62, 71
Bartlett, Charles, 118
Bates, William, 186
Bayh, Birch, 174
Bigart, Homer, 114-15
Binh Xuyen sect, 36, 53, 55, 58, 59, 61, 62
Boggs, Hale, 297n. 65, 298n. 67
Boggs, J. Caleb, 105, 112, 165
Boun Oum, 96
Bowles, Chester: and the American
    Friends of Vietnam, 66; and Michael J.
    Mansfield, 29; and Ngo Dinh Diem,
    72, 73, 285n. 14; and Norodom
    Sihanouk, 204; and Vietnam policy,
    94, 101
Bradlee, Ben, 115
Bradley, Omar, 192
Brezhnev, Leonid, 224
Bridges, Styles, 93
Browne, Malcolm, 115
Buddhist community: and the Catholic
    Church, 43, 44, 78
Bundy, McGeorge: and the Gulf of Tonkin
    Resolution, 134; and Lyndon Johnson,
    152, 155; and Michael J. Mansfield,
    129, 138, 141, 143-44, 145, 149, 152,
    154, 155, 156; and the Tuesday lunch
    group, 140; and the United Nations,
    144; and Vietnam policy, 128, 129, 138,

Y

`Z